South Asian Migrations in Global History

South Asian Migrations in Global History

Labour, Law and Wayward Lives

Edited by Neilesh Bose

BLOOMSBURY ACADEMIC
LONDON • NEW YORK • OXFORD • NEW DELHI • SYDNEY

BLOOMSBURY ACADEMIC
Bloomsbury Publishing Plc
50 Bedford Square, London, WC1B 3DP, UK
1385 Broadway, New York, NY 10018, USA
29 Earlsfort Terrace, Dublin 2, Ireland

BLOOMSBURY, BLOOMSBURY ACADEMIC and the Diana logo
are trademarks of Bloomsbury Publishing Plc

First published in Great Britain 2021
This paperback edition published in 2022

Copyright © Neilesh Bose, 2021

Neilesh Bose has asserted his right under the Copyright, Designs
and Patents Act, 1988, to be identified as Author of this work.

Cover design: Terry Woodley
Cover image: detail from *Ghadar di Gunj* (Echoes of Mutiny), a compilation
of nationalist and socialist poetry, Urdu edition, 1914. Courtesy of SAADA
South Asian American Digital Archive.
(© awaiting confirmation from design)

All rights reserved. No part of this publication may be reproduced or transmitted
in any form or by any means, electronic or mechanical, including photocopying,
recording, or any information storage or retrieval system, without prior
permission in writing from the publishers.

Bloomsbury Publishing Plc does not have any control over, or responsibility for,
any third-party websites referred to or in this book. All internet addresses given in
this book were correct at the time of going to press. The author and publisher
regret any inconvenience caused if addresses have changed or sites have
ceased to exist, but can accept no responsibility for any such changes.

Every effort has been made to trace copyright holders and to obtain their
permissions for the use of copyright material. The publisher apologizes for any errors
or omissions and would be grateful if notified of any corrections that
should be incorporated in future reprints or editions of this book.

A catalogue record for this book is available from the British Library.

Library of Congress Cataloging-in-Publication Data
Names: Bose, Neilesh, editor.
Title: South Asian migrations in global history : labor, law, and wayward lives /
edited Neilesh Bose.
Description: London ; New York : Bloomsbury Academic, 2020. | Includes bibliographical
references and index.
Identifiers: LCCN 2020032057 (print) | LCCN 2020032058 (ebook) | ISBN 9781350124677
(hardback) | ISBN 9781350197343 (paperback) | ISBN 9781350124684 (ebook) |
ISBN 9781350124691 (epub)
Subjects: LCSH: South Asians–Migrations. | Foreign workers, South Asian–History. |
South Asians–Foreign countries. | South Asian diaspora. | South Asia–Emigration and
immigration–Historiography. | Globalization.
Classification: LCC DS339.4 .S668 2020 (print) | LCC DS339.4 (ebook) | DDC 304.80954–dc23
LC record available at https://lccn.loc.gov/2020032057
LC ebook record available at https://lccn.loc.gov/2020032058

ISBN:	HB:	978-1-3501-2467-7
	PB:	978-1-3501-9734-3
	ePDF:	978-1-3501-2468-4
	eBook:	978-1-3501-2469-1

Typeset by Integra Software Services Pvt. Ltd.

To find out more about our authors and books visit www.bloomsbury.com
and sign up for our newsletters.

Contents

List of illustrations	vii
Notes on contributors	viii
Foreword *Victor V. Ramraj*	xii
Acknowledgements	xv
List of abbreviations	xviii

Prologue: Archives, paper regimes and mobility
Uma Dhupelia-Mesthrie — 1

Introduction *Neilesh Bose* — 7

Part I Impacts of Indentured Labour

1 Gokhale, Polak and the end of Indian indenture in South Africa, 1909–1911 *Goolam Vahed* — 37

2 Imperial labour: Labour, security and the depoliticization of oil production in the Arabian Peninsula *Andrea Wright* — 63

3 Legal discourse on 'coolies' migration from India to the sugar colonies, 1837–1922 *Ashutosh Kumar* — 85

Part II Law in Migration Histories

4 Slavery, abolitionism, indentured labour: The problem of exit and the border between land and sea in colonial India *Riyad Sadiq Koya* — 113

5 Who is Asiatic? Drawing the boundary in the legal and political framing of Indian South Africans, 1860–1960 *Marina Martin* — 139

Part III Historical Biography

6 Taraknath Das: A global biography *Neilesh Bose* — 157

7 From British colonial subject to Mexican 'Naturalizado': Pandurang Khankhoje's life beyond the reach of imperial power (1924–1954) *Daniel Kent-Carrasco* — 179

8 A woman of peace and calm: The story of Senthamani Govender *Devarakshanam Betty Govinden*	201
Epilogue: Ocean currents and wayward crossings *Renisa Mawani*	225
Select bibliography	231
Index	249

Illustrations

3.1	Original Copy of Terms of Service in Tamil for Trinidad	90
3.2	Original Copy of Terms of Service in Tamil language for Fiji	91
3.3	Original Copy of Terms of Service in Telugu language	91
3.4	A picture of an old immigrant's ticket, PA-16, NAM	92
3.5 a)	Original Copy of Terms of Service for Natal	93
3.5 b)	Emigration Pass for Men for Fiji	94
3.5 c)	Men's Emigration Pass for Fiji	95
8.1	Birth certificate	202
8.2	Kandasami Sami Gounden	203
8.3	General view, Clifton Tea Estate	205
8.4	The factory with Indian barracks	205
8.5	Indians picking tea leaves	206
8.6	The factory – Clifton Tea Estate	206
8.7	Managing Director's house	207
8.8	Information on Nallathambi's father	211
8.9	Granny's wedding day	212
8.10	The family – Granny with husband and children, Asothie, Savy, Vigie and Devan	213
8.11	Granny at the centre of the family	218
8.12	Granny with Asothie, her daughter, Mags, her grand-daughter and Verushka and Rishane, her great-granddaughter and great-grandson	219

Contributors

Neilesh Bose is Associate Professor of History and Canada Research Chair of Global and Comparative History at the University of Victoria in British Columbia, Canada. With interests in cultural and intellectual histories, globalization, religion, secularism and migration, he is the author of *Recasting the Region: Language, Culture, and Islam in Colonial Bengal* (Oxford University Press, 2014) and the editor of *Beyond Bollywood and Broadway: Plays from the South Asian Diaspora* (Indiana University Press, 2009). Other writings include articles in *BC Studies*, *Modern Asian Studies* and *South Asia Research* and review essays in *Modern Intellectual History*, the *Journal of Colonialism and Colonial History* and *South Asian Review*. He has edited special sections in *South Asia: Journal of South Asian Studies* (2018, with Kris Manjapra and Iftekhar Iqbal), *History and Theory* (2017), *Performing Islam* (2016, with Fawzia Afzal-Khan and Jamil Khoury) and *South Asian History and Culture* (2014).

Uma Dhupelia-Mesthrie is Senior Professor of History at the University of the Western Cape. She is author of *From Cane Fields to Freedom: A Chronicle of Indian South Africans* (Kwela Books, 2000) and *Gandhi's Prisoner? The Life of Gandhi's Son, Manilal* (Kwela Books, 2004). Additionally, she is the editor of *Sita: Memoirs of Sita Gandhi* (Durban Local History Museum, 2003) and the special issue 'Paper Regimes', published in *Kronos: A Journal of Southern African History* (2014). She has written extensively on immigration and surveillance histories, land dispossession and restitution, and India-South Africa connected histories. Currently, she is writing a manuscript titled *Letters from Phoenix Settlement: Maintaining Gandhi's Heritage in South Africa, 1915 to 1976*.

Devarakshanam Govinden is the author of the award-winning book, *Sister Outsiders: Representation of Identity and Difference in Selected Writings by South African Indian Women* (Pretoria and Leiden: UNISA Press and Koninklijke Brill NV, 2008). She is a member of the Academic Advisory Board of the *Journal for the Study of Indentureship and its Legacies*.

Daniel Kent-Carrasco is Research Professor in the History Division of CIDE (Centro de Estudios y Docencia Económicas), in Mexico City. He is a Mexican historian interested in the past and present of the Third World. His work looks at the contemporary intellectual, cultural and political history of India, South Asia, Mexico and Latin America. He obtained his PhD from King's College of the University of London.

Riyad Sadiq Koya is a writer based in Santa Rosa, CA, USA His article 'The Campaign for Islamic Law in Fiji: Comparison, Codification, Application', in *Law and History Review* (2014) explores debates on the application of religious personal laws for Indian indentured labourers in the nineteenth and twentieth centuries. His research interests include labour and empire, plantation economies, religion and law, citizenship and Pacific and Indian Ocean histories.

Ashutosh Kumar is a historian of the Global South and a fellow at New Delhi's Nehru Memorial Museum and Library. He has held fellowships at the University of Leeds, the New Delhi Centre for the Study of Developing Societies (CSDS), the Centre for the Study of Slavery, Resistance and Abolition at Yale University and the Indian Institute of Advanced Studies in Shimla, India. He is the author of *Coolies of the Empire: Indentured Indians in the Sugar Colonies, 1830–1920* (Cambridge University Press, 2017) and with Crispin Bates and Marina Carter, *The Indian Labour Diaspora: A Resource Text for Students* (Edinburgh University Press, 2017). With Claude Markovitz, he is the co-editor of the forthcoming edited volume titled *Re-visiting the First World War: Indian Soldiers in the Global Conflict*.

Marina Martin is Researcher and Departmental Coordinator in South Asian Legal History at the Max Planck Institute for European Legal History. She is interested in the colonial histories and legacies of exchanges and encounters between Britain, India and South Africa, with a focus on citizenship, immigration and membership. Her current book project explores the legal, political and economic conditions that gave rise to the so-called 'Indian Question' in South Africa during the British colonial period and beyond. Marina is also a specialist in the modern economic, institutional and legal history of money and credit, specifically the system and instrument known as 'hundi' or 'hawala'. She received her PhD in Economic History from the London School of Economics. She has held fellowships with the Collaborative Research Institute at Goethe University, Frankfurt, the University of Pretoria in South Africa and LSE's Asia Research Centre, as well as Yale University's MacMillan Centre for International and Area Studies

Renisa Mawani is Professor of Sociology and Chair of the Law and Society program at the University of British Columbia. She is the author of *Colonial Proximities* (University of British Columbia Press, 2009) and *Across Oceans of Law* (Duke University Press, 2018), a finalist for the UK Socio-Legal Studies Association Theory and History Book Prize and the winner of the Association of Asian American Studies Book Prize for Outstanding Contribution to History. With Iza Hussin, she is co-editor of 'The Travels of Law: Indian Ocean Itineraries' published in *Law and History Review* (2014). Alongside Sheila Giffen and Christopher Lee, she is co-editor of 'Worlds at Home: On Cosmopolitan Futures' published in *Journal of Intercultural Studies* (2019). With Rita Dhamoon, Davina Bhandar and Satwinder Bains, she is co-editor of *Unmooring the Komagata Maru* (University of British Columbia Press, 2019). With Antoinette Burton, she is co-editor of *Animalia: An Anti-Imperial Bestiary of Our Times* (Duke University Press, 2020). She has served on the editorial boards of *Law and Society Review* and *Law and Social Inquiry* and has been elected to the Board of Trustees for the Law and Society Association (2019–2022).

Victor V. Ramraj is Professor of Law and Chair in Asia-Pacific Legal Relations at the University of Victoria in British Columbia, Canada. Since 2017, he has served as the Director of the Centre for Asia-Pacific Initiatives. He spent sixteen years at the National University of Singapore and was twice seconded from there to the Center for Transnational Legal Studies in London. His research spans comparative constitutional law, transnational regulation, emergency powers, and the state–company relationship. He has edited or co-edited several collections published by Cambridge University Press, including *Emergencies and the Limits of Legality* (2008) and *Emergency Powers in Asia: Exploring the Limits of Legality* (2010, with Arun K. Thiruvengadam). He is also the editor of the forthcoming *Covid-19 in Asia: Law and Policy Contexts* (Oxford University Press). His research has appeared as chapters in multiple edited collections and as articles in leading journals in Asia, Africa, Europe and North America.

Goolam Vahed is Professor of History at the University of Kwa-Zulu Natal. His research interests include identity formation, citizenship, ethnicity, migration and transnationalism among Indian South Africans and the role of sport and culture in South African society. He has published widely in peer-reviewed journals and edited volumes as well as written several single-authored books along with three co-authored books. With Thembisa Waetjen, he is the co-author of *Schooling Muslims in Natal: Identity, State and the Orient Islamic Educational*

Institute (University of KwaZulu-Natal Press, 2015). With Ashwin Desai, he has co-authored two books: *The South African Gandhi: Stretcher-bearer of empire* (Stanford University Press, 2016) and *A History of the Present. A Biography of Indian South Africans, 1994–2019* (Oxford University Press, 2019).

Andrea Wright is Assistant Professor in the Department of Anthropology and the Program in Asian & Middle Eastern Studies at William & Mary. Her research explores the oil industry in the Arabian Sea from the 1940s to the present, in order to understand connections between energy, governance and rights. She is currently working on two book projects grounded in the historical anthropology of the oil industry. *From Slavery to Contract: An Anthropological History of Labor and Oil in the Arabian Sea* looks at the history of transnational labour at British oil projects in the Gulf and Arabian Peninsula. *Between Dreams and Ghosts: Indian Migration and Middle Eastern Oil* examines labour migration as a social process that draws upon and influences not only migrants' own communities but also contemporary governance and capitalism.

Foreword

Victor V. Ramraj

Paradoxically, the modern state seems to be at its strongest and weakest point since the rise of the state system in the nineteenth century. On the one hand, people, goods, services, information and ideas move more freely around the world than ever – and yet we are, in the third decade of the twenty-first century, in the midst of a period of rising nationalism, protectionism and xenophobia as nations erect barriers, figurative and literal, to impede free movement. At the same time, many academic disciplines are caught up in their own methodological struggles concerning the significance of the modern state and the role that it plays or ought to play in scholarly research. In particular, these disciplines struggle with the centrality to their research agendas of *methodological nationalism* – neatly summarized by Andreas Wimmer and Nina Glick Schiller as 'the assumption that the nation/state/society is the natural social and political form of the modern world'.[1] They bemoan how the social sciences 'have become obsessed with describing processes within nation-state boundaries as contrasted with those outside, and have correspondingly lost sight of the connections between such nationally-defined territories'.[2] This preoccupation with the nation-state is not, of course, unique to the social sciences. Until recently, mainstream legal education and practice have been dominated by the assumption that law is the exclusive domain of the state or derived from the formal consent of states.[3] And history too has taken a local or national turn, often at the expense of a full appreciation of the connections between the nation and its wider context, constructing the past 'through an optic of a world divided into national communities'.[4]

More recently, however, scholars in a range of disciplines have stressed the importance of looking beyond statist structures, adopting methodologies that challenge state-centrism – approaching law, history, economics or other disciplines in ways that acknowledge the importance of the global or the trans-local to a fuller understanding of the world. Such an approach does not require a rejection of the local or the modern state but suggests the importance of multiple levels of analysis. Neil Coe, Philip Kelly and Henry Yueng, in their recent work on economic geography, speak helpfully of the importance of using different *scales* to understand the economic world: the body, the home or the workplace, and the local, urban, regional, national, macro-regional and global.[5] This kind of approach is important, they explain, because 'economic processes work at *multiple scales simultaneously*'. It echoes appeals by historians to recognize the importance of the local and national as 'crucial contexts of all peoples' historical experiences' while bringing historical focus 'also to large-scale, trans-regional, and global processes that have touched many peoples and profoundly influenced the development of individual societies as well as the world as a whole'.[6] Law too has sought to transcend the strictures of the modern state though transnational non-state forms of regulation, even as state actors, from courts to domestic regulatory agencies, are compelled to rethink their accustomed response.[7]

Taken together, the essays in this volume bring together many of these approaches and themes – the relationship between local and global histories; the multiple scales of the economic and social worlds; and the complex relationships between state and non-state configurations of law. Not only do they offer a stunning array of narratives – through the eyes of northern Indian immigrants aboard a colonial era ship, indentured and contract labourers in colonial South Africa and the contemporary Persian Gulf, politically activist émigrés in British Columbia and post-revolutionary Mexico, and an Indian South African woman facing the vicissitudes of an unsettled life – they do so while layering onto them the complexities of place and territory, movement and agency. The essays reveal how place is both increasingly fixed, legally defined and territorially bounded, as successive structures of empire and state seek to define, redefine and exclude categories of persons – British colonial subject, slave, indentured labourer, skilled and unskilled labourer. At the same time, they show the inevitability of movement and connection – voluntary and imposed – of peoples and ideas around the globe, in service of or resistance to powerful political and economic forces. In so doing, they adopt contrasting perspectives of increasingly bounded space, in which territory defines those within it and excludes many who come from outside, but also a perspective of agency, pushing place and territory into the background. Agency is claimed in defiance of place and even in transit through it.

A global and comparative history that seeks to bring place and movement into a single volume is an ambitious undertaking and an invitation to us to hold together and strive to reconcile not only the multiple perspectives of postmodern historical inquiry, but to do so while embracing the tensions and contradictions of place and movement, and the complicated and often gendered social, political and legal categories they construct. All the more so because the essays in this volume offer a rich and textured account of slaves and indentured labourers, men and women in their daily lives, and political activists who grappled with ideas, themselves arising from place but untethered to it. This collection therefore offers a fresh set of perspectives on the past – confronting place and movement through a multitude of perspectives. And while we must be mindful of presentism, some of the essays offer a direct insight into the contemporary – illuminating the past, while reflecting on its contemporary significance. Whether the past – or our engagement with it – provides insight into the present is perhaps the defining philosophical question of historical inquiry; this collection invites reflection on contemporary challenges of globalization – of migrant and precarious labour, of global supply chains, of gender and ideology, of power and resistance, of place, identity and belonging. These are challenges and themes that are very much alive in this collection. They speak to the significance of the framing questions and the energy that Neilesh Bose brought to the workshop at the Centre for Asia-Pacific Initiatives (CAPI) at the University of Victoria in the fall of 2017 where many of the authors in this volume first gathered. It was a privilege for CAPI to host that workshop and it gives me great pleasure to invite you to settle into a comfortable place, turn the page and join the authors on this intellectual journey.

Notes

1 A. Wimmer & N.G. Schiller, 'Methodological Nationalism and Beyond: Nation-State Building, Migration and the Social Sciences' *Global Networks* 2, No. 4 (2002): 302.
2 Wimmer and Schiller, 307.
3 For example, see Hans Kelsen, 'Law, State and Justice in the Pure Theory of Law' *Yale Law Journal* 57 (1948): 377 and Joost Pauwelyn, 'Is It International Law or Not, and Does It Even Matter?' in *Informal International Lawmaking*, eds. Joost Pauwelyn, Ramses A. Wessel, and Jan Wouters (Oxford: Oxford University Press, 2012), 125–61.
4 Jerry H. Bentley, 'The Task of World History' in *The Oxford Handbook of World History*, ed. Jerry H. Bentley (Oxford: Oxford University Press, 2011), 9.
5 'Geography: How do we think spatially?' in *Economic Geography: A Contemporary Introduction*, 3rd ed. (Hoboken, NJ: Wiley-Blackwell Publishing, 2020), 29.
6 Bentley, 13.
7 Nicole Roughan, *Authorities* (Oxford: Oxford University Press, 2013), Victor V. Ramraj, 'Transnational Non-State Regulation and Domestic Administrative Law' in *Comparative Administrative Law*, eds. S. Rose-Ackerman et al., 2nd ed. (Cheltenham, UK: Edward Elgar, 2017), 582–97.

Acknowledgements

As I write these acknowledgments, the world is facing a pandemic that has touched nearly every facet of social, political and economic life. Like migrants in any other part of the world, both migrants inside South Asia as well as those from South Asia historically linked to the Persian Gulf, Southeast Asia, Africa and various other regions are experiencing the extremes associated with crises. Many find that socially and politically constructed barriers to mobility, regulation and surveillance of their movements, and consequent access to their homes and families as well as access to healthcare and medicine resembles much of what occurred in times of indenture as well as times of chaos at the end of indenture or the end of formal empire.

In an era of hyper-documentation and extensive yet fleeting digital commentary, the lives of migrants and their histories are frequently tracked and documented in ways unimaginable in earlier historical periods. Though many such efforts are certainly sincere, many emerge only fleetingly for political talking points or abstract critiques of larger systems of power. When the crisis subsides, some migrants and their histories will likely return to an invisible background far from the official record, whereas some others may become hyper-visible in new and unexpected ways.

This book is an attempt to systematically explore the history of South Asian migrations in a global historical framework in a manner that would address that condition. The book is inspired by papers delivered at the *Between Indigenous and Immigrant* workshop held at the University of Victoria, situated on the traditional and unceded lands of the Lekwongen peoples and home to the Songhees, Esquimalt, and W̱SÁNEĆ peoples. Held 26–28 October 2017, this workshop built on the foundation of numerous conversations and public-facing engagements that emerged within, but are not limited to, the Canadian nation-space about indigeneity, immigration and the global nature of historical frameworks that encompass both processes. Many of the chapters in this book first appeared at that workshop. Others have emerged out of the many conversations inspired by those that took part there as well as drawing on longer conversations in many places throughout the world.

Generous support provided by numerous units at the University of Victoria, including the Law School, the Centre for Asia-Pacific Initiatives, the

Centre for Global Studies, the Faculty of Humanities, the Asian Canadians on Vancouver Island Project, the Department of English and the Department of History made this conference possible. The Simon Fraser University Institute for Trans-Pacific Cultural Research, the University of the Fraser Valley South Asian Studies Institute, the UBC Centre for India and South Asia Research and the UBC Asian Canadian and Asian Migration Studies programmes also provided crucial sources of support. Finally, the entire event fell within the domain of the Tier II Canada Research Chair in global and comparative history, a chair I currently hold at the University of Victoria. The numerous threads of insight yielded by original research conducted by the authors included in this book honours the many investments in scholarship and public engagement represented by the Canada Research Chair programme funded by the government of Canada.

The gathering included scholars from a variety of institutions across North America and this book features scholars based in Germany, South Africa, Canada, the United States of America, Mexico and India. I thank all those who attended the workshop and presented their research, including Victor V. Ramraj, Sana Aiyar, Sara Shneidermann, Anneeth Kaur Hundle, Seema Sohi, Gajendra Singh, Joanna Ogden, Samip Mallick, Vivek Bald, Nilanjana Bhattacharjya, Davina Bhandar, Renisa Mawani, Marina Martin, Andrea Wright, Neha Vora and Bikrum Singh-Gill. Those who were unable to attend but who contributed to this volume include Ashutosh Kumar, Riyad Koya, Daniel Kent-Carrasco, Devaraskshanam Betty Govinden, Goolam Vahed and Uma Dhupelia-Mesthrie. I acknowledge and greatly appreciate the assistance provided by graduate students Matthew Huijsmans and Mark Alexander Hill. Without their commitment, labour and attention to detail, the workshop simply would not have been possible. Many thanks to Varsha Venkatasubramanian for preparing the index.

This book has been in the making for many years. Without the many generative conversations over these years with friends, interlocutors and mentors throughout the world, I doubt the book would have come into existence. Some on this list may be surprised to be included in the context of South Asian migration in global history but all have influenced my own thinking that has resulted in the making of this book. These interlocutors include Fawzia Afzal-Khan, Sana Aiyar, Sunil Amrith, Anubha Anushree, Gaiutra Bahadur, Vivek Bald, Sandeep Banerjee, Arnab Banerji, Sara Beam, Davina Bhandar, Nilanjana Bhattacharjya, Subho Basu, Greg Blue, Shane Book, Martin Bunton, Sukanya Chakrabarti, Uday Chandra, David Chang, Chris Chekuri, Rajendra Chetty, Hardeep Dhillon, J. Daniel Elam, Harald Fischer-Tine, Navyug Gill, Rajesh

Gopie, Gayatri Gopinath, Leonard Gordon, Ronnie Govender, Devarakshanam Govinden, Thomas Hansen, Yoshina Hargobin, Moon Ho-Jung, Mark Alexander Hill, Matthew Huijsmans, Anneeth Kaur Hundle, Daniel Kent-Carrasco, Samia Khatun, Riyad Koya, Ashutosh Kumar, David Ludden, Kama Maclean, Samip Mallick, Kris Manjapra, Auritro Majumdar, Patrick Manning, Renisa Mawani, Dilip Menon, Shayoni Mitra, Dann Naseemulllah, Joanna Ogden, Shruti Patel, Kriben Pillay, John Pincince, John Price, Sourav Ray, Priya Satia, Dwaipayan Sen, J. Barton Scott, Dina Siddiqi, Amritjit Singh, Bikrum Singh-Gill, Nico Slate, Seema Sohi, Pon Sounnavaseng, Arun Thiruvengadam, Aladdin Ullah, Goolam Vahed, Elizabeth Vibert and Henry Yu.

At the University of Victoria, the Department of History, the Centre for Asia-Pacific Initiatives, and the Centre for Global Studies all provided active hubs of support and collegiality. In particular, I thank John Lutz, Jordan Stanger-Ross, Jason Colby, Penny Bryden, Rob Alexander, Simon Devereaux, Andrew Mackenzie, Victor V. Ramraj, Helen Lansdowne, Oliver Schmidtke, Paul Bramadat, Matthew Koch, Beatriz de Alba-Koch, Rachel Cleves, Supriya Routh, Sikata Banerjee, Pooja Parmar, Reeta Tremblay, Sudhir Nair, Rishi Gupta, Aditi Gupta, Raveendra Chittoor, Sada Niang, Rita Dhamoon and Reeta Tremblay. Respondents for relevant presentations I delivered at New York University, George Washington University, University of the Witswatersrand (Wits), the University of Lisbon, the ETH Zurich.

The 2017 gathering began with Gaiutra Bahadur's reflections in print and in person on indentured women and the recoveries of such histories in multiple frameworks. Following Bahadur, Saidiya Hartman and generations of historians from many fields who commit their energies to exploring the lives of the unlettered, the dispossessed and the otherwise under-documented, any historical investigation, as an act of commemoration, is necessarily incomplete. This book represents one chapter in the longer arc of historical labours that explore how the textured lives of many people, who are marginal to some yet central to others, feature within larger frameworks of thinking about the past.

This book is not the first, and surely will not be the last, to explore histories of South Asian migrants throughout the world. Enabled by the advances of historians of earlier generations, as well as enlivened by those whose work falls outside the remit of traditional scholarship, this book is not only a testament to the lives explored within its pages, but a love letter embracing the lives of migrants who fall off the historical record, wherever they may be found.

Abbreviations

ADMA	Abu Dhabi Marine Areas
ADNOC	Abu Dhabi National Oil Company
ADPC	Abu Dhabi Petroleum Company
AIOC	Anglo-Iranian Oil Company
ANC	African National Congress
APOC	Anglo-Persian Oil Company
BA	Bachelor of Arts
BAPCO	Bahrain Petroleum Company
CA	California
CAPI	Centre for Asia-Pacific Initiatives
CLEC	Colonial Land and Emigration Commission
COSATU	Congress of SA Trade Unions
EIC	East India Company
FEDSAW	Federation of South African Women
FH	Free Hindusthan
GoB	Government of Britain
GoI	Government of India
INC	Indian National Congress
IPC	Iraq Petroleum Company
IWW	International Workers of the World
LCA	Labour Catchment Area

NAI	National Archives of India
NAP	National Archives of South Africa, Pretoria
NIC	Natal Indian Congress
NSA	National School of Agriculture (Mexico)
NYU	New York University
PLM	Partido Liberal Mexicano
PMB	Pietermaritzburg Archives Repository
POE	Protector of Emigrants
SA	South Africa
SAADA	South Asian American Digital Archive
SAIC	South African Indian Congress
TOS	Trucial Oman Scouts
UBC	University of British Columbia
UNSW	University of New South Wales

Prologue: Archives, paper regimes and mobility

Uma Dhupelia-Mesthrie

The biography of Latchimin commences in 1832 in Rae Bareilly near Lucknow and ends in 1911 in Yamba, on the Clarence River in the northern part of New South Wales. The in-between years of her life patched together from ship records and archives reveal her passage as an indentured woman. Widowed at age twenty-eight, and with three sons between the ages of eight and four, she travelled to St Vincent's in the West Indies in 1871 and returned to India on expiry of her contract followed by another indentured contract to Fiji in 1884, accompanied by a husband and ten children. Her final passage took her to Sydney in 1890 as a widow and free immigrant with eight children where, in subsequent years, she created a new identity for herself as Elizabeth Philips. Stories like this and that of other families in Australia with indentured backgrounds in both the British and French empires, as Margaret Allen argues, 'demonstrate the global mobility and agency of Indians within the indentured labour scheme and after they left indenture'.[1] These biographies of migration and remigration are revealed through the arduous searches of family members – supplemented by the historian – in multiple archives across the globe. An important element in Latchimin's biography is her ability to enter Australia as a free immigrant before the passage of the Immigration Restriction Act of 1898 by New South Wales, which imposed a written test in a European language on all would-be immigrants. This act was superseded in 1901 when the newly established Federation of Australia in 1901 effectively excluded fresh Indian immigration by the imposition of a dictation test on would-be immigrants.[2]

Hyslop has observed that the period from the late nineteenth century through the first decades of the twentieth century was a time of considerable human movement across the globe but mobility was 'not everywhere, and not for everyone'.[3] White settler colonies drew on the precedent of the colony of Natal, which in 1897 imposed a literacy test in a European language to end immigration from India. *The Free Hindusthan*, founded by Taraknath Das, was not slow to link these growing restrictions with the increase of anti-Indian sentiments in Vancouver, where Canadians pioneered their own system of exclusion with the introduction of the 'continuous voyage order' effectively prohibiting Indian arrivals since there was no direct passage between India and Canada.[4] The story of these exclusions transcends local and national histories; they are at once transnational histories, histories of imperial networks and global histories of restrictions on 'people of colour'. These stories appear in the histories produced in recent times.[5]

Many of us begin our journeys with local, regional or national histories. Such was my encounter with an archival collection initiated by the Chief Immigration Officer of the Cape Colony to document passenger arrivals in the colony and to regulate movement of Indians between India and the Cape Colony.[6] The series was motivated by the Immigration Act of 1902 which, following Natal and Australia, introduced a literacy test for entry. Additionally, the Immigration Act of 1906 initiated a permit system to allow Indians already resident in the colony to travel to India and return. The numbered files ending with an 'a' to signify Asian are mainly an archive of Indian mobility since the Chinese, who were governed by separate legislation, are constituted in a series of their own. The variety of domicile and permit applications provides extensive biographical information about individuals, their first entry into the colony, their place of origin in India, their occupations, the location of their families and the extent of movement between India and South Africa. As with most officially generated archives, the delights for the social historian include the voices of ordinary persons engaging with the bureaucracy, detailing activities in India as permits expired or desperate letters from wives abandoned in India searching for husbands. The archives provided an opportunity to write a social history of Indians in Cape Town, to pay attention to the neglected histories of women and children and workers such as early stonebreakers, factory workers, cleaners and gardeners – the little known stories of Indian immigration and settlement.[7]

However, it soon became clear how this archive, though locally created by legislation by one British colony, linked to a bigger history of immigration exclusions. Furthermore, I found the need to venture beyond this racially segregated archive and to consider the separate Chinese series and the separate series of white arrivals, which pointed to the literacy test as an exclusionary device for white undesirables, including those from eastern and southern Europe, Latin America and those with criminal records or mental illnesses. Bringing down the archival walls set up by colonial systems bent on segregating people and leading to segregated histories led to a more nuanced understanding of immigration exclusions. This also led me to the role of the immigration officer at the port who encountered arrivals from every spectrum of life. How did the personal subjectivities of the officer frame the immigration encounter? How different was an immigration officer in the Cape from those in, for instance, Natal, or Ellis Island?[8] What were the 'ceremonies' and 'rituals' of entries at the Cape port for Indian arrivals and how did these compare with McKeown's elaborations of Chinese admissions in America?[9]

The documents in the Cape Archives contained photographs and thumbprints of permit applicants and this led one into histories of anthropometry, photography and dactylography that went beyond the little Cape Colony and pointed to the flow of information about technologies in the empire, from India to the metropole to the colonies, and from out of Europe. As the title of Breckenridge's book suggests, questions about identity and surveillance in South Africa were a crucial part of a global context.[10] The Cape permits spoke to other documents of mobility developed across the world and the evolution of practices of identifying individuals. How, for instance, did the permit compare with the documents that 'gypsies' were compelled to carry in Europe?[11] As a project of surveillance, how did intentions behind the permit system tie in with James Scott's analysis of the modern state and its need to render people legible?[12] Breckenridge's and Szreter's volume on registration systems across the world also provoked thinking about the passenger arrival forms of the Cape Colony as a form of registration and about birth certificates and their lack in India and their requirement at the Cape ports for the admission of minor children.[13]

The paper systems of surveillance developed in the Cape Colony were not just a local aberration but could be found in global practice. There are remarkable similarities between the Indian permit of the Cape, its successor the certificate of identity in South Africa, and the re-entry certificates issued to Indians under the Immigration Restriction Amendment Act of 1920 in New Zealand.[14] Margaret Allen's work on the certificate of exemption from the dictation test in Australia led to a collaborative effort in which we attempted a comparative history of documents produced by Australia and South Africa to regulate the movement of both Indians and Chinese.[15] This brought us into conversation with other surveillance histories in the world and an appreciation of the work of Simone Browne and the concept of *racializing surveillance*, 'those moments when enactments of surveillance reify boundaries and borders along racial lines, and where the outcome is often discriminatory treatment'.[16] Our immigration histories had something in common with systems to monitor African Americans both falling under the rubric of 'racializing surveillance'. As with all comparative histories, there were differences too between the Australian and South African contexts in terms of bureaucracy, efficiency, cases of corruption and resistance to these documents.

Edited volumes do much to bring together scholars across the world working on similar themes such as the mobility of slaves, indentured labour, free passenger immigration, exclusions, identification practices and surveillance systems. The historian's challenge is to retain that balance between local histories and national histories – for they bring with it a special spectrum of readers.[17] Endeavours such as the analysis of South Asian migration in global historical frameworks as seen in this volume integrate multiple archives across geographical spaces, bridging the narrow concerns with the particularities of the local and national. Latchimin's biography peeks out from archives in multiple locations as far spread as the West Indies, India, Fiji and Australia. She was not confined and neither should we be.

Notes

1. Margaret Allen, 'Circuitous Routes: Journeys from India to Australia by Way of the Sugar Colonies' in *Indians and the Antipodes: Networks, Boundaries, and Circulation*, eds. Sekhar Bandyopadhyay and Jane Buckingham (New Delhi: Oxford University Press, 2018), 67.
2. Jeremy C. Martens, *Empire and Asian Migration: Sovereignty, Immigration Restriction and Protest in the British Settler Colonies, 1888–1907* (Crawley: UWA Publishing, 2018), 128–41.
3. Jonathan Hyslop, 'Oceanic Mobility and Settler-Colonial Power: Policing the Global Maritime Force in Durban Harbour c. 1890–1910' *The Journal of Transport History* 36, no. 2 (2015): 264.
4. Marilyn Lake and Henry Reynolds, *Drawing the Global Colour Line: White Men's Countries and the International Challenge of Racial Equality* (Cambridge; Cambridge University Press, 2008), 187, Adam M. McKeown, *Melancholy Order: Asian Migration and the Globalization of Borders* (New York: Columbia University Press, 2008), 206–207.
5. Martens, *Empire and Asian Migration*; Lake and Reynolds, *Drawing the Global Colour Line*; McKeown, *Melancholy Order*.
6. See Uma Dhupelia-Mesthrie, 'The Form, the Permit and the Photograph: An Archive of Mobility between South Africa and India' *Journal of Asian and African Studies* 46, no. 6 (2011): 650–662.

7   See Uma Dhupelia-Mesthrie, 'The Passenger Indian as Worker: Indian Immigrants in Cape Town in the Early Twentieth Century' *African Studies* 68, no. 1 (2009): 111–134 as well as Uma Dhupelia-Mesthrie, 'Split-Households: Indian Wives, Cape Town Husbands and Immigration Laws, 1900s to 1940s' *South African Historical Journal* 66, no. 4 (2014): 635–655.

8   Uma Dhupelia-Mesthrie, 'Betwixt the Oceans: The Chief Immigration Officer in Cape Town, Clarence Wilfred Cousins (1905–1915)' *Journal of Southern African Studies* 42, no. 3 (2016): 463–481 and Uma Dhupelia-Mesthrie, 'The Desirable and Undesirable in the Life of the Chief immigration Officer in Cape Town, Clarence Wilfred Cousins, 1905–1915' *Itinerario* 42, no. 1 (2018): 50–66.

9   Uma Dhupelia-Mesthrie, 'False Fathers and False Sons: Immigration Officials in Cape Town, Documents and Verifying Minor Sons from India in the First Half of the Twentieth Century,' *Kronos* 40 (2014): 99–132, McKeown, *Melancholy Order*, 269, 277–278.

10 Keith Breckenridge, *Biometric State: The Global Politics of Identification and Surveillance in South Africa, 1850 to the Present* (Cambridge: Cambridge University Press, 2014). See also Martine Kaluszynski, 'Republican Identity: Bertillonage as Government Technique' in *Documenting Individual Identity: The Development of State Practices in the Modern World*, eds. Jane Caplan and John Torpey (Princeton and Oxford: Princeton University Press, 2001). See also Christopher Pinney, *Camera Indica: The Social Life of Indian Photographs* (Chicago: University of Chicago Press, 1997) and Alan Sekula, 'The Body and the Archive' in *The Contest of Meaning: Critical Histories of Photography*, ed. Richard Bolton (Cambridge: MIT Press, 1992), 343ff.

11 Kaluszynski, 'Republican Identity', 133ff; see also *Identification and Registration Practices in Transnational Perspective: People, Papers and Practices*, eds. I. About, J. Brown, and G. Lonergan (Basingstoke: Palgrave Macmillan, 2013).

12 James C. Scott, *Seeing Like a State: How Certain Schemes to Improve the Human Condition Have Failed* (New Haven: Yale University Press, 1998).

13 Keith Breckenridge and Simon Szreter, *Registration and Recognition: Documenting the Person in World History* (Oxford: Oxford University Press, 2012), Dhupelia-Mesthrie, 'False Fathers and False Sons'.

14 Michael Roche and Sita Venkateswar, 'Indian Migration to New Zealand in the 1920s: Deciphering the Immigration Restriction Amendment Act, 1920' in *Indians and the Antipodes*, eds. Bandyopadhyay and Buckingham (Delhi: Oxford University Press, 2018). 129–161.

15 Uma Dhupelia-Mesthrie and Margar et Allen, 'Controlling Transnational Asian Mobilities: a Comparison of Documentary Systems in Australia and South Africa, 1890s to 1940s' in *Making Surveillance States: Transnational Histories*, eds. Robert Heynen and Emily van der Meulen (Toronto: University of Toronto Press, 2019), 133–162.

16 Simone Browne, 'Race and Surveillance' in *Routledge Handbook of Surveillance Studies*, eds. Kirstie Ball, Kevin D. Haggerty, and David Lyon (Oxford: Routledge, 2012), 72.
17 See Ann Curthoys and Marilyn Lake, 'Introduction' in *Connected Worlds: History in Transnational Perspective*, eds. Ann Curthoys and Marilyn Lake (Canberra: ANU E Press, 2005), 13.

Introduction

Neilesh Bose

In the twenty-first century, linking the history of globalization with the history of migrations and mobility needs no explanation. Migrations and mobility in most histories of globalization fixate on trans-Atlantic slavery and the historical trajectories set into motion by such a process, including the development of capitalism, abolition and free labour, all staple elements of the modern world. Moving outside the Atlantic world, the question of how South Asian migrants relate to border regimes, surveillance systems, labour recruitment strategies, law and legal activism, land settlement and collusion or confrontation with settler colonies appears clear to specialists of various regions but rarely emerges within one shared framework of inquiry. Whether in western Canada, Singapore, South Africa, East Africa, the Middle East or Great Britain, the long-term presence, politics and life-worlds of South Asian migrants compels an investigation in line with the history of globalization. Such a twenty-first century landscape follows a detailed system of indentured labour from colonial India that spread to various corners of the Indian Ocean, Pacific Islands and parts of the Caribbean from the early nineteenth century through to the end of World War I. Furthermore, significant Indian mercantile capital and maritime expansion into Western Asia, Eastern Africa, Southern Africa and Burma, linked to rice cultivation, imperial expansion, legal employment and land settlement, grew in parallel with the rise of indentured labourer communities in various parts of the world. Finally, as recent historians of North America have shown, South Asian migration intersects with North American issues of citizenship, surveillance and the politics of racial assimilation in the twentieth century.[1] It is further commonplace amongst

---

This introduction has benefited greatly from comments by anonymous referees as well as countless conversations and commentary on several drafts by Riyad Koya.

historians to note that South Asian mobility and migration is not merely a modern occurrence, but a process that includes sturdy roots in pre-modern South Asian pasts as well as evinces patterns inside territorial South Asia.[2]

Though cognizant of these histories, this collection places such work directly into conversation with the formal history of modern globalization. As two heralded scholars recently claim, global history 'seems to be everywhere. Wherever you look – the course offerings of history departments, the catalogues of publishers, the programmes of history conferences – the words "global history" appear'.[3] In one of the most recent reflections of the history of globalization,[4] space and migration appear as key touchstones for thinking about globalization anew, outside only modernization or the free-flow of capital. For Dilip Menon, global histories in the twenty-first century uncover 'geographies of affinity', or ways of belonging outside the nation or the state system, 'generated through migration, marriage, and commerce as also parallel networks of religion and religious practices exceed the affiliations with contemporary nation-states as much as colonial cartographies'.[5] Migration appears, therefore, as a central element in any contemporary understanding of the history of globalization. A focus on the significance of modern migrations from Asia emerged clearly from the late Adam McKeown,[6] whose research on Asian migrations in the context of a history of globalization has been fine-tuned through recent research into aspects of South Asian migration in global contexts by scholars such as Sunil Amrith, Renisa Mawani and Radhika Mongia, among others.[7] Such important interventions point to the need for further exploration of the particular role of South Asian migrations and their relationships to the modern world system, within legal, economic and microhistorical perspectives, in line with global historical frameworks.

How shall historians capture, and explore, the historical significance of South Asian migrants within a modern global migration history?[8] Migration history in this context refers to the impact that large-scale migration patterns, as well as individual migrant actors, has posed for changes in global history since the early nineteenth century CE. Building on the work of global migration historians Adam McKeown, Patrick Manning and Tiffany Trimmer, Dirk Hoerder and Amit Mishra,[9] this book places South Asian migrations in the modern world into macro, micro and meso scales of analysis.[10] Such an emplacement asks how the modern world system – defined primarily but not only by modern state formation, border controls, legal regimes and microhistorical subjectivities – looks from the vantage point of modern South Asian migrations. Such a play with scales of history[11] emerges as eminently possible through the study of migrations at the level of institutional change, legal change and individual microhistory. Aspects of the world system relevant here feature the emergence of legal systems regulating the flow of labour across nation-states,[12] struggles for citizenship in states across the 'global colour line',[13] and changes in the modern state form after the abolition of trans-Atlantic slavery and the rise of indentured labour.[14] All of these facets of globalization require a detailed study of South Asian migrations in the world system.[15]

South Asian migrations in modern global history

Within existing approaches to the history of migrations within a framework of global transformation,[16] trans-Atlantic models – preceding and including slavery and abolition – and subsequent nineteenth- and twentieth-century migration into the Global North, remain a relatively undisturbed framework for the histories of migrations within modern globalization. Even though the periodization of 'modern' remains a point of ongoing contention, and likely will long elude any easy resolution,[17] the broad convergence of liberal republican revolutions, the transformation of overseas companies into conquest states and the emergence of liberal ideals from the 1770s to the 1830s marks the opening of the modern world.[18] The impact of migration on the making of this world after the 1830s has overwhelmingly focused on Atlantic empirical trajectories – of European or African migrations westward into the Americas – or models of assimilation into a liberal modern state. However, scholars such as Wang Gungwu,[19] the team of Joya Chatterji, Claire Alexander and Annu Jalais,[20] Sunil Amrith,[21] Sanjay Subrahmanyam,[22] and G. Balachandran,[23] as well as the late world historian Adam McKeown[24] have pioneered numerous types of historical studies of migration outside Atlantic conceptual or empirical models.[25] Other endeavours to situate Asian migration outside an Atlantic world model have placed mobility and migration within broadly conceived intra-Asia networks. Published in three volumes from 2015 to 2019, *Asia Inside Out* features a multidisciplinary and multilingual team of scholars that maps connections and mobilities within Asia, inclusive of layers of South, East and Southeast Asian peoples, goods, objects and ideas from antiquity to the present.[26] Most relevant for a consideration of modern South Asian migrations is Volume 3, 'Itinerant People', which contains empirically dense studies of a range of movements inside a broader Asian history, from the trafficking of prisoners and convicts throughout Asia to the movements of exiled Thai princes in the Indian Ocean.

This book follows such interventions by focusing specifically on South Asian migrants in the era of modern empire, from the 1830s onwards, 'reinforcing older connections across time and space and by forging new connections'.[27]

The historiography of South Asian migration

Identifying connections across time and space in South Asian migrations evinces multiple strands of historical inquiry. The early days of modern South Asian migration history began with histories of the process of approximately 1.3 million indentured labourers transported to various points in the British Empire from the 1830s to the 1920s, as well as migrants to Southeast Asia and Britain.[28] Key texts in this genre feature Hugh Tinker's 1974 classic, *A New System of Slavery: The Export of Indian Labour Overseas, 1830–1920*,[29] placing indentured labour in a continuum from the slavery it replaced, providing a model for Brij V. Lal's 1983 *Girmitiya: The Origins of the Fiji Indians*.[30] Ashutosh Kumar's *Coolies of the Empire: Indentured Indians in the Sugar Colonies, 1830–1920* is the most recent book to tackle Indian indentured labour within a broadly British imperial and global historical framework deploying methods used in labour history and cultural history. Inclusive of detailed analysis of major components of the system such as labour recruitment, passages of migrants and petitions, this book offers a comprehensive account of the rise and fall of the indentured labour system attentive to points of origin in India as well as points of destination in the Caribbean, the Pacific and portions of Africa.[31] Outside social and labour history, scholars have produced textured research into seamen and sailors,[32] merchants[33] and travellers of various types into Britain.[34]

Cultural histories, encompassing new directions in history at large, enveloped the study of South Asian migrations in historical frameworks from the 1990s onwards. These works feature explorations of gender and sexuality,[35] family histories,[36] historical anthropology[37] and circulation within colonial spaces.[38] A movement from within cultural history has seen a focus on literature, poetics and historical memory, as embodied by the work of Gaiutra Bahadur, Khal Torabully and Rajiv Mohabir.[39] Building on early labour histories as well as cultural histories, another strand of the field integrates convicts and prisoners into broader histories of migration.[40] Recently, works of synthesis and multimedia exhibitions have appeared,[41] marking a visibility of the topic of indentured labour for public and specialist audiences, and strengthening its base within global history.

It would be impossible to survey the field of South Asian migrations history without a consideration of Indian Ocean history. Ever since K.N. Panikkar's 1945 *India and the Indian Ocean: An Essay on the Influence of Sea Power on Indian History*, historians in South Asia have worked on aspects of macro-regional Indian Ocean history.[42] Anticipating the work of Fernand Braudel, encompassing studies of the environment, geography and disease as well as anthropocentric approaches to change, Indian Ocean historians have enlarged fields of economic history, labour history, merchant networks and studies of maritime trade.[43] The staggering contributions of Sanjay Subrahmanyam, inclusive of numerous languages and archives, began in Indian Ocean history, which provided the raw material for bigger picture insights into 'connected histories' of portions of South Asia, Western Asia and Iberian regions into a vision of an early modern 'Eurasia'.[44] Another important intervention relevant to migration histories, Sugata Bose's *A Hundred Horizons: The Indian Ocean in an Age of Global Empire* integrates economic, cultural and political history into a narrative about India in Indian Ocean historical contexts. Bose's intervention compels readers to consider the nineteenth and twentieth centuries inside a broader historical narrative about modern history and empire, as earlier works avoided a focus on modern Indian Ocean histories.

Current iterations draw from older strands of Indian Ocean studies and durable subjects of history – merchants, long-distance slavery, family networks – infused with a consciousness of environmental history, debt and commercialization, histories of religion and legal history.[45] In the twenty-first century, a richly interdisciplinary approach, replete with literary criticism and cultural studies, has renewed older emphases on circulation in newly framed 'South–South' lanes in different parts of the Indian Ocean.[46] If the direction of the field moved away from social histories of labourers framed within Indian nationalist terms to Indian Ocean inter-regional arenas in the early twenty-first century, recent attempts in the last decade have crossed into Atlantic and Pacific arenas.[47] These endeavours scatter in two particular historical directions. One subset configures the study of South Asian migrations into broader processes of empire, state formation, surveillance and the history of racial assimilation in the Americas.[48] Another strand focuses primarily on post-World War II politics of migration and culture in the era of nation-states.[49] Both registers currently add the now visible North American layer to the many vectors of research into South Asian migrations history.

One thematic angle into the history of South Asian migrants in global historical frameworks prompted by North American and Australian historiography is that of settler colonialism as a lens into the history of South Asian migrations in global histories. Explorations of South Asian migration histories in North America[50] as well as Australia[51] engage explicitly with the role of South Asian migrants within the contexts of dispossession of indigenous peoples, frontier violence and settler state formation. Such themes are well-known sites of inquiry in recent imperial histories[52] as historians have recently begun to consider the role of South Asian migrants within histories of settler colonies of the British Empire, such as Canada, South Africa and Australia.

Another thematic angle into the history of migrations features detailed engagement with areas previously relegated to the study of internal regional and national or proto-national dynamics into frameworks of movement, mobility and immobility, such as the regional space of Bengal as the canvas for a study of migration. This is evident in Alexander, Chatterji and Jalais' *The Bengal Diaspora: Rethinking Muslim Migration*,[53] an interdisciplinary study of Bengali Muslim migration through historical, sociological and anthropological frameworks. Based primarily on 227 oral histories of individual migrants, this work probes mobility and immobility in the twentieth century from the perspective of Bengali Muslim migrants. Challenging the common focus on migration from locations in the colonial and post-colonial world only to destinations in the Global North, this book centres on Bengal as a source and a destination, 'acknowledging the fact that there is a Bengal diaspora within Bengal as well as outside it'.[54] Such an approach underscores the important fact often overlooked in studies of migration and globalization that although 'South–South' migrations remain the largest in the world, they are under-conceptualized within historical frameworks. Offering a historically detailed critique of the popular separation of refugees from 'economic' migrants, this work dents any hazy valorization of 'networks' or 'diasporic spaces', by historicizing and situating the rise and fall of networks and their possibilities in concrete space and time. Producing a wide variety of critical responses from various humanist and social science disciplines, this most recent iteration of South Asian migration history provides a fine-grained understanding of the trans-regionally dynamic processes of nationalism, nostalgia and social memory construction armed with rigorous empirical and ethnographic work.[55]

A focus on specifically Muslim migration offers important correctives to the relative absence of Bengali Muslim voices in many works on the partition of Bengal in the global context of Islamophobia, though a range of scholars have begun to address this absence from new angles.[56] A focus on Bengali Muslims helps fill out aspects of history previously out of reach as well as highlight the symbolic power in Islam, which 'can inspire more amorphous, liminal supralocal, utopian or absolute imaginings that temporarily transcend everyday lived space', an aspect of the history of religion not usually analysed within histories of South Asian migrations.[57] Nonetheless, slippages between 'Bengal', 'Bengali' and 'Muslim' in such a context show how the particular links between religion, language and literary culture, and migration point to questions for further research. Such questions feature the importance of new forms of religion as well as the importance of religion, religious reformist organizations and religious life as shaping and sustaining both literal and metaphorical migrations in and from South Asia in modern history. The most recent exploration of Islam in the Indian Ocean shifts the focus away from heavily documented port cities to inter-regional arenas such as the river basins of the Indus and the Ganga, in the northwest and eastern zones of South Asia, respectively. These areas include historically rich and variegated populations of Muslims as well as expressions of Islam in South Asia. Sugata Bose and Ayesha Jalal's *Oceanic Islam: Muslim Universalism and European Imperialism* advances such an approach in order to 'to map new directions in comparative, connective and border-crossing historical scholarship'.[58] Inclusive of original research within western and eastern Indian Ocean zones as well as new analyses of figures such as Sayyid Ahmad Khan and Muhammad Iqbal, this book introduces a framework of oscillation between strands of Muslim universalism and European imperialism in the Indian Ocean.

The recent work of Wilson Jacob Chacko explores the contours of God and empire in a Muslim Indian Ocean framework through a detailed biography of Sayyid Fadl bin 'Alawi –known in India as Pookaya Thangal (1824–1900).[59] Born in Mamapuram in southwest India, educated in traditional Muslim subjects and fluent in Arabic and Malayalam, Sayyid Fadl appeared on the radar of the East India Company due to repeated activism on behalf of Mapilla (Muslim) as well as lower caste peoples. The Company exiled him in 1852 to his 'home country' of Arabia, never allowed to return to India. Though buried in Istanbul, his spirit remains alive in Malayalam hagiographies of Mamapuram saints, which emphasize both aspects of religious devotion and miracle work along with social reform.[60] A comprehensive assessment of the significance of such individuals in a migrations history requires a sensitivity to religion and ethics as well as a focus on the historical conditions underpinning migration in a global framework.[61]

These developments in both the study of migration and the historical study of religion necessitate further research into the history of religious reform in the nineteenth century, a trans-regional process that encompassed Indian migration along routes of indenture as well as pathways of *hajjis*, entrepreneurs, lawyers and political activists among others, during this time period. Forays into these topics have yielded insight into Islam within spaces of indentured labourers in South Africa, as well as the creation of a sacred geography through the efforts of migrants.[62] A multi-sited history of religious reformist organizations such as the *Brahmo Samaj* and the *Arya Samaj* in regions far from their points of origin, whether in southern Africa, the Caribbean or Fiji for the latter, or Assam for the former, emerges as a focal point for future research.[63] Further investigation exploring the relationships between the different manifestations of 'reformist' activity in territorial India compared to the 'reform' occurring in spaces of Indian migrants, promises to uncover these nuances of religion's role in migration histories.

A constant starting point running through each iteration of South Asian migration history, however enlivened by shifting thematic and methodological turns, remains the decade of the 1830s as an important pivot for the creation of a global modern system. Identifying a clear periodization for substantial decline in migration patterns remains the subject of ongoing research. During the 1830s, the world-historical markers of the abolition of trans-Atlantic slavery and the imposition of an indenture system linking South Asia to the late company state and a plantation complex throughout the world took shape in a recognizable form, across portions of the Caribbean, Pacific Islands, southern Africa and various points in the Indian Ocean. As McKeown notes, historical discussions of globalizations past and present remain steeped in familiar markers of the 1820–1913 period of intensifying migration, a de-globalizing period of borders, regulations and reductions in migrations from 1914 to 1950, and a re-globalizing period from 1950 to the present. Such approaches tend to conform to Atlantic evidence and Anglo-Atlantic models of historical change, as trends and patterns in South Asian migrations histories don't follow such a timeline. As opposed to trends in the Atlantic world, migrations in the Indian Ocean increased in the twentieth century, especially after World War I in the Bay of Bengal, as shown by Sunil Amrith.[64]

Yet maintaining South Asian exceptionalism in migration histories encounters the problem of structural and institutional facets of South Asian migrations that cry out for contextualization in broader historical frameworks, such as the legal restrictions on labourers in international law, struggles for citizenship, interactions across lines of racial and cultural difference in migrant settings and historical memories of migration. When approaching histories of South Asian migrations in global frames, guidelines for empirically situating the easily understood conclusion that 'no one globalization is the true globalization',[65] remain out of sight for many historians. Though this cliché holds true for the prospect of linking any region to a history of globalization, historians in this volume aim to configure not necessarily 'true' globalization but patterns of globalization that do not relegate South Asian migrations to experiences left out of the broader global story pursued primarily by those working in Atlantic and Eurocentric histories. Such a push, represented by the chapters in this book, proceeds with the realization that any impulse toward a global history carries with it the dangers of a modern imperialism cloaked in the fuzziness of an undifferentiated world. An undifferentiated world history potentially hides relationships of power and different historical trajectories shaped by modern colonialism.[66] Additionally, the overwhelming presence of British imperial history – important as that presence is – potentially hides or minimizes the importance of historical developments outside the domain of British imperial power. It is precisely because the current approaches to the history of globalization only hazily appreciate the significance of South Asian migrations that a continual and rigorous revision of former narratives must proceed with full force, lest the study of globalization yield only to cues taken from the Euro-Atlantic-African West.

Plan of the book

Situating South Asian migrations within global historical frameworks builds upon a recent shift in orientation that has begun to confront Indian exceptionalism in migration history within wider frameworks of connected imperial and global histories.[67] Though regionally bounded histories – whether of labourers, merchants, convicts, seamen, long-distance nationalists or family networks, to name some major thriving themes alive in the field– remain doubtlessly crucial for textured understandings of places previously relegated only to appendages of imperial histories, this volume aims to synthesize the spirit of these strands into a broader history of globalization. How do South Asian migrations configure aspects of global history outside only particular local histories? This edited volume addresses this question by outlining and probing three sites relevant to global historical research, including indenture and its afterlives, law and its effects and historical biography. These three areas of consideration provide avenues for reflection on the history of South Asian migrations outward across time and space, between frames of company, empire and nation. A focus on these three thematic areas not only activates longer continuities of indentured histories but places oceanic histories alongside modern and contemporary globalized contexts in North America and the Middle East, providing material for future comparative and connected historical research and reflection.

The first section, 'Indenture of Indentured Labour', inclusive of three essays by Goolam Vahed, Andrea Wright and Ashutosh Kumar, explores the most current research on indentured labour from colonial India in a global and comparative context. This section explores how the important field of indentured histories has been reoriented towards global historical frameworks. Given the rise of indentured labour at the onset of the abolition of slavery and the rise of a 'global plantation complex'[68] in the 1830s, indenture provides a basis from which to consider questions about the broader history of South Asian migrations in global historical frameworks. In a 2017 review of indentured labour studies, Crispin Bates stresses the 'creative practice of the subaltern that conflicted with the structure, expectations, and agenda of the imperial labour regime'[69] following Allen's emphasis both on long-term continuities in indentured labour as well as worker agency.[70] There was, as Allen states, a structural link between slave and indentured labour trades in South Asia and the Indian Ocean. Such a link mandates the need to 'examine the indentured labour system's origins in a broader imperial context, a context that reached from the Caribbean to the South Atlantic, India, and Southeast Asia, and moreover involved the British East India Company corporate state as well as imperial policy makers in London'.[71] Though the indenture system itself was not the engine of the largest volume of migration from South Asia in sheer numbers, the indenture historiography helps position the broader history of South Asian migrations inside one of the forms of globalization. Given its links to the Atlantic world, the presence of a global plantation complex as well as its links to slavery, abolition and the global regulation of labour,[72] the broader symbolic impact and historical trace of indenture throughout the modern world integrates the various strands of South Asia-oriented migration histories into a global history framework.

Advancing the study of indentured labour into the context of broader global transformation, Ashutosh Kumar's 'Legal Discourses on "Coolies" Migration from India to the Sugar Colonies, 1837–1922' brings together a detailed study of regulations around food provisions, demonstrating a measure of freedom and possibility – however limited – for indentured labourers in the context of emergent legal changes in the nineteenth century. Goolam Vahed's 'Gokhale,

Polak and the end of Indian indenture in South Africa, 1909–1911' offers a history of the end of indenture by triangulating the worlds of Mohandas Gandhi, G.K. Gohkale and Henry Polak, creating a connected global history of the end of indenture in South Asia. Moving away from local social history, Vahed places South African indenture into a larger global story of the transition from empire to nation-state. Andrea Wright's pioneering research on contract and freedom shows continuities from the era of indenture to the present-day landscape of Indian labourers in Bahrain through a historical anthropology of the precarious condition of labourers in the present. Wright's incorporation of historical frameworks into a study of Indian labourers in Bahrain complements a broader history of modern migrations into the Persian Gulf, building upon the many advances in Indian Ocean labour histories of slavery and indenture, from the work of Gwyn Campbell, Indrani Chatterjee, Richard Allen, Clare Anderson and others.[73] These works focus primarily on the eighteenth- and nineteenth-century transitions related to trans-Atlantic abolition and imperial conquest, focusing on how convicts, incarceration and forms of labour and reciprocity created something new in the Indian Ocean, distinguished from the Atlantic world. The chapters by Kumar, Wright and Vahed extend the historical line of vision to the present, cross lines of formal decolonization and integrate thematic studies of indenture into broader global narratives of empire, liberalism and nation-state.

The second section, 'Law in Migration Histories', features chapters by Marina Martin and Riyad Koya, exploring how legal history interacts with new histories of South Asian migrants in a context of globalization. Legal history has received a revival and reorientation within South Asian historiography as well as global history. Marina Martin's 'Who is Asiatic? Drawing the Boundary in the Legal and Political Framing of Indian South Africans, 1860–1960' analyses the term 'Asiatic', revealing how the category was used for Indians while other conceivable 'Asiatic' groups were excluded from the classification for political and economic reasons. The discussion provides a critical appraisal of the way in which identity was politicized and how law cemented boundaries between groups. It also shows how the language of exclusion and legitimacy in particular contexts hinged not only on colour lines but also on the prevailing economic and political status quo. Following the recent work of Radhika Mongia, Riyad Koya's contribution argues that the Westphalian model cited by European border theorists as an antecedent to contemporary national borders does not apply fully to the context of nineteenth and twentieth-century India vis-à-vis the Indian Ocean world. In his chapter, Koya argues that slave trafficking and the problem of 'exit', rather than entry, comprised central elements of this system relevant to India and the Indian Ocean world of the nineteenth and twentieth centuries. This section builds on scholarship in settler colonialism, legal history and the social histories of Indian indentured labourers by emphasizing how laws enacted to specifically curtail or regulate the movement of Indian bodies in imperial contexts produced globally resonant consequences.

The final section on historical biography includes an analysis of figures on the margins of multiple historical terrains but whose 'global biographies' shed light on how migration contributed to larger forces of historical change. With essays by Neilesh Bose on Taraknath Das (1884–1958), Daniel Kent-Carrasco on Pandurang Khankhojé (1884–1967) and Devarakshanam Govinden on Senthamani Govender (born 1923), this section follows cues in Sugata Bose's evocative formulation of 'expatriate patriots'[74] and the long-distance nationalism of Gandhi, Bose and Tagore. Moving beyond such well-known figures, this section considers individuals whose movements led to unexpected transformations far from territorial India. Das spent most of his adult life in the US and Canada before and after Asian exclusion acts and Khankhoje spent nearly thirty years in Mexico just after the Mexican Revolution only to return to India after independence. Govinden's life spans colonial, apartheid and democratic South Africa. Govinden's essay about a living figure offers additional insights from literary and cultural studies with regard to blending the limits of history, memory and biography. Inspired by the work of Gaiutra Bahadur and Saidiya Hartman,[75] this section aims to uncover how figures at the margins of archives figure specifically in migrant histories.

The portion of this book's title, 'Wayward Lives', invokes Hartman's *Wayward Lives, Beautiful Experiments: Intimate Histories of Social Upheaval*,[76] a work of history about African-American women in early twentieth-century US locales, which discusses the familiar challenge of writing histories against multiple grains. Khankhoje, Das and Govinden definitively lived 'wayward lives', if not also beautiful experiments, as this book ponders how individual lives that escape easy inclusion into nationalist or local histories fit into broader historical changes. Histories of these figures do not easily resonate with a straightforward life nor do they fit into a cohort with one singular politics. Familiar models of nationalism via exile do not fully explain these figures. Rather, they lived 'one, long strange trip', to paraphrase historian Benjamin Zachariah's phrase used to describe the life of Har Dayal. Instead of reading these figures as a component of the makings of standard issue Indian nationalism,[77] they rather show a concerted effort to embody dominant aspirations of the late imperial period: science and agriculture; citizenship in powerful states; and living through and beyond apartheid; all connected at some level to Indian origins and politics.

This section also draws on the spirit of biography from earlier times, such as Omar Ali's history of Malik Ambar, the many lives explored by Sanjay Subrahmanyam or the sixteenth-century Ethiopian slave by Ananya Chakravarti.[78] In each case, the limits of biographical writing pose important cues for reflection on broader world-historical transformation. For the three figures studied in depth in this book, the edges of empires, such as those of the US-Canada border in the early twentieth century, or Mexico from the 1920s to the 1950s, or South Africa from the 1920s onwards, appear in new forms by these migrants. These compact life histories add to recent work in microhistory and biography focused on itinerant lives, such as Harald Fischer-Tine's study of Shyamji Krishnavarma (1857–1930),[79] Satadru Sen's exploration of Benoy Kumar Sarkar (1887–1949),[80] or the collectively produced annotated translation of Gadadhar Singh's *Thirteen Months in China*, a book about China during the Boxer Rebellion, written in 1900.[81] All of these essays aim to grasp how life histories that intersect with unexpected places situate South Asian migrations into global histories.

The chapters assembled in this book show how the study of modern South Asian migration histories is most certainly not in a 'state of conceptual stagnation'.[82] The thematic sub-sections move the study of South Asian migrations outside either assimilation into the nation-state or Anglo-Atlantic-centric notions of globalization. By situating indentured labour migrations in a wider framework than merely indenture itself, and placing it alongside non-indentured labour migrations, and pursuing thematic approaches to the 'creativity' of migrants,[83] this study of South Asian migrations shapes both our current understandings of globalization and updates South Asian history outside a territorial frame. Such updates follow from the reflections of colonial India's heralded historian, Crispin Bates, who argues that descendants of Indian indentured labourers across various registers require a new historical framework. This framework would be a 'new story ... one in which the "stain" of indenture is expunged and their ancestors no longer depicted as mere victims ... who made at least as great a contribution to the development of the modern world as European migrants in the same period'.[84] Through empirically dense work on individuals such as Das, Khankoje and Govinden, as well as textured studies of consent, law, skilled/unskilled labour distinctions and the politics of food in indentured histories, we find new stories in which 'victims' in earlier historiographies did not only become 'entrepreneurs'. Rather, South Asian migrants have responded to and shaped significant contours of the modern world, from the rise and fall of formal indentured labour across the Indian and Atlantic Oceans, to the global regulation of labouring migrants after the end of formal indenture, and to struggles for citizenship and recognition in modern North America.

Any study of migration histories that attempts to switch between macro, micro and meso scales[85] cannot possibly exhaust all of the potential insights South Asian migration, as a field of study, offers to historians of globalization. Further empirical research on labouring, legal and biographical links to areas of the world compelled by this framework, such as work focused on Eastern Africa and Western Africa, have entered scholarly conversations about the nature and impacts of South Asian migrants within global histories.[86] Other areas not fully covered in this work include the significance of internal migrations within India, as recently explored by Chinmay Tumbe.[87] Tumbe's notable book offers a broad view of Indian migration with the goal of assessing the place of diversity within India, as well as how Indian migration has affected India over time. Other patterns of migrations in the era of the nation-state, such as contemporary Bangladeshi migrations to and from Malaysia, Singapore, Italy and South Africa or Indian migrations to Burma and Bhutan traversing colonial and post-colonial periods, compel potentially new historical insights applicable to the meaning of migration in global history. The frameworks offered in this collection – of labour histories via insights from indenture, legal histories from different scales and the importance of biography – provide interpretive strategies for writing migration histories in the future.

The image adorning the cover of this book, a visual depiction of 'Mother India' as envisioned in the specific form of the *Ghadar* party's messaging apparatus in 1914 on the Pacific coast of North America *may* conjure Indocentric notions of nationalisms within the framework of a migration history. As detailed study of migration histories from anywhere will show, the tension between particular cases and general patterns yields potential conceptual problems. In our present angle into migration histories, the potential presence of Indocentric and Indian nationalist conclusions – and Hindu nationalist sentiments within the broader Indian nationalist frame – loom large for scholars and general readers, especially as the histories examined in this book occurred before the term 'South Asia' was invented. However, the internally variegated lives of migrants in labouring, legal and microhistorical frameworks do not easily add up to an Indian nation-state, nor flow back to a conception of Hindu nationalism projected back in time. For the vast majority of people on the move in the modern world, some formal conception of India remained most salient for migrants as well as their interlocutors, even if such a conception masked many other forms of politics, connections and meanings. As Claude Markovitz's afterword to an edited volume about the Indian diaspora proposes,[88] the 'Indian' part of any diasporic, or migrant, historical framework should always remain closely scrutinized. However, rigorous exploration of particular cases, such as the Sindhi merchant communities studied by Markovitz, does not warrant the conclusion that 'India' should disappear from historical analysis of migration altogether. Although this image of 'Mother India' does refer to an ahistorical Indian national conception, it rather reminds readers and viewers of the specific context of such visualizations: struggles for honourable and just treatment of labourers, aspirations to and denials of citizenship and legal recognition of migrants from South Asia. Such processes not only occurred in but also shaped significant portions of the modern world. The variously themed chapters in this book offer a start to thinking creatively and purposefully about how such processes are incomprehensible without a systematic understanding of South Asian migrations in the modern world.

Notes

1   See Vivek Bald, Miabi Chatterji, Sujani Reddy and Manu Vimalassery, eds. *The Sun Never Sets: South Asian Migrants in an Age of U.S. Power* (New York: NYU Press, 2013) for a useful treatment of this topic through sub-sections on overlapping empires, migration from a global perspective and aspects of race, gender and labour in the North American context.
2   See Vijaya Ramaswamy, ed. *Migrations in Medieval and Early Colonial India* (New York: Routledge, 2016) for a recent overview of this facet of migration history. This volume includes sections about peasant, artisanal and merchant migrations in pre-modern histories. Chinmay Tumbe's *India Moving: A History of Migration* (Delhi: Penguin, 2018) includes a broad-based analysis of Indian migration from ancient times to the present, integrating older migrations with modern and contemporary variants. A significant essay on this topic situates South Asian mobility as part of a long historical process, interrupted by modern border practices, blurring our lines of vision into how mobile South Asians have been before modernity. See David Ludden, 'Presidential Address: Maps in the Mind and the Mobility of Asia,' *The Journal of Asian Studies* 62, no. 4 (November 2003): 1057–1078.
3   Sven Beckert and Dominic Sachsenmeier, 'Introduction' in *Global History, Globally: Research and Practice around the World*, ed. Sven Beckert and Dominic Sachsenmeier (London: Bloomsbury, 2018), 1.

4   These are found in two companion articles in *Global Perspectives*, a new online journal 'devoted to the study of global patterns and developments across a wide range of topics and fields', https://online.ucpress.edu/gp, accessed 3 April 2020. Two particular articles in this edition, Arjun Appadurai, 'Globalization and the Rush to History', and Dilip Menon, 'Walking on Water: Globalization and History', integrate cognate fields such as cultural studies and literary and art criticism into their reflections on the history of globalization.

5   Menon, 'Walking on Water: Globalization and History', 5.

6   In particular, his article 'Global Migration, 1846–1940' *Journal of World History* 15, no. 2 (June 2004): 155–189, situates Asian migrations into a global history of migrations. His book *Melancholy Order: Asian Migration and the Globalization of Borders* (New York: Columbia University Press, 2011) explores how modern border regimes in parts of the Global North resulted in large part from restricting Asian migration.

7   See Renisa Mawani, *Across Oceans of Law: The Komagata Maru and Jurisdiction in the Time of Empire* (Durham, NC: Duke University Press, 2018) and Radhika Mongia, Indian Migration and Empire: A Colonial Genealogy of the Modern State (Durham, NC: Duke University, 2018) for arguments that centre South Asian migrations, in various ways, inside a global history. These build upon Sunil Amrith's *Crossing the Bay of Bengal: Crossing the Bay of Bengal: The Furies of Nature and the Fortunes of Migrants* (Cambridge, MA: Harvard University Press, 2013) and *Migration and Diaspora in Modern Asia* (New York: Cambridge University Press, 2011).

8   Key touchstones for the history of migration in global history include Caroline B. Brettell and James F. Hollifield, eds., *Migration Theory: Talking Across Disciplines*, 3rd ed. (New York: Routledge, 2015) and Christiane Harzig and Dirk Hoerder, with Donna Gabbaccia, *What is Migration History?* (Cambridge: Polity, 2009). Both claim migration studies as an interdisciplinary field on its own.

9   See Adam McKeown, 'Periodizing Globalization' *History Workshop Journal* 63, no. 1 (March 2007): 218–230 and 'Global Migration, 1846–1940' *Journal of World History* 15, no. 2 (June 2004): 155–189. Key books include Dirk Hoerder, *Cultures in Contact: World Migrations in the Second Millennium* (Durham, NC: Duke University Press, 2002) and Patrick Manning, with Tiffany Trimmer, *Migration in World History*, 2nd ed., (New York: Routledge, 2013). See also Amit Mishra, 'Global Histories of Migration (s)' in *Global History, Globally: Research and Practice around the World*, edited by Sven Beckert and Dominic Sachsenmeier, 195–214.

10 As discussed in Bretell and Hollifield, the 'meso' scale – institutions and associations between the nation-state and individual – becomes essential in any serious history of migrations, requiring engagement across different types of sources.

11 See Jacques Revel, ed. *Jeux d'Echelle: La Micro-Analyse a l'Experience* (Paris: Editions EHESS, 1996), for a discussion of 'playing with the scales'. For an application of this approach to South Asian migrants in global history, see Harald Fischer-Tiné, *Shyamji Krishnavarma: Sanskrit, Sociology, and Anti-Imperialism* (Delhi: Routledge, 2014), especially 183–190.
12 Rachel Sturman, 'Indian Indentured Labour and the History of International Rights Regimes' *American Historical Review* 119, no. 5 (December 2014): 1439–1465, Sandro Mezzadra and Brett Nielson, *Border as Method, or, the Multiplication of Labor* (Durham, NC: Duke University Press, 2013).
13 Marilyn Lake and Henry Reynolds, *Drawing the Global Colour Line: White Men's Countries and the International Challenge of Racial Equality* (Cambridge: Cambridge University Press, 2008).
14 Mongia, *Indian Migration and Empire*.
15 See C.A. Bayly, *The Birth of the Modern World, 1780–1914: Global Connections and Comparisons* (Oxford: Blackwell, 2004) and *Remaking the Modern World, 1900–2015* (Oxford: Blackwell, 2019). A distinction lies between the 'making' and 'transformation' of the modern world, the latter approach to modern world history deployed by Jürgen Osterhammel, *The Transformation of the World: A Global History of the Nineteenth Century* (Princeton: Princeton University Press, 2015).
16 Osterhammel, *The Transformation of the World: A Global History of the Nineteenth Century*.
17 See Dipesh Chakrabarty, 'The Muddle of Modernity' *American Historical Review* 116, no. 3 (June 2011): 663–675. Chakrabarty distinguishes between institutional modernization and reflections on being, or inhabiting, modernity. This position drawn from modern history is a response to Sanjay Subrahmanyam, 'Hearing Voices: Vignettes of Early Modernity in South Asia, 1400–1750' *Daedalus* 127, no. 3 (Summer, 1998): 75–104. Notable in Subrahmanyam's definition of modernity as a global and conjunctural phenomenon is the inclusion, inter alia, of 'Indian textile traders in diaspora', 100.
18 Bayly, *Birth of the Modern World, 1790–1914: Global Connections and Comparisons*.
19 Of Wang Gungwu's many works, his most significant publications within this context feature *Don't Leave Home: Migration and the Chinese* (Singapore: Eastern Universities Press, 2003) and *The Chinese Overseas: From Earthbound China to a Quest for Autonomy* (Cambridge, MA: Harvard University Press, 2000). These two books offer empirically substantive approaches to the history of Chinese migration within global frameworks of intercultural encounter, the tensions and ambiguities built into migrant communities over time and space and the complex nature of assimilation into host societies. Important book chapters that remain significant for the broader field include 'Sojourning: The Chinese Experience in Southeast Asia', in *Sojourners and Settlers: Histories of Southeast Asia and the Chinese*, edited by

Anthony Reid (St. Leonards, NSW: Allen and Unwin, 1996), 1–14 and 'Migration and its Enemies', in *Conceptualizing Global History*, edited by Bruce Mazlish and Ralph Buultjens (Boulder, CO: Westview Press, 1993). His edited collection, *Global History and Migrations* (Boulder, CO: Westview Press, 1997), builds upon the work of Mazlish and Buultjens but also draws on concerns specific to Asian migrations in multiple frameworks.

20 Joya Chatterji, Claire Alexander and Annu Jalais, *The Bengal Diaspora: Rethinking Muslim Migration* (New York: Routledge, 2015).

21 Sunil Amrith, *Migration and Diaspora in Modern Asia* and *Crossing the Bay of Bengal: The Furies of Nature and the Fortunes of Migrants*.

22 His many articles exploring global history feature a number of critiques of the practice of world history in Anglophone scholarship. Two contributions that provincialize Atlantic world approaches to global history include his 2013 lecture at the College de France, 'On the Origins of Global History', https://books.openedition.org/cdf/4200?lang=en, as well as his 'Historicizing the Global or Labouring for Invention', *History Workshop Journal* 64 (Autumn 2007): 329–334.

23 Of his many works on this theme, see his 'Atlantic Paradigms and Aberrant Histories' *Atlantic Studies* 111, no. 1 (2014): 47–63 and his co-authored essay with Sanjay Subrahmanyam, 'On the History of Globalization and India: Concepts, Measures, and Debates' in *Globalizing India: Perspectives from Below*, ed. Jackie Assayag and C.J. Fuller (London: Anthem Press, 2005), 17–46.

24 See his 'Periodizing Globalization', 218–230 and 'Global Migration, 1846–1940'. Chapter Seven of *Melancholy Order: Asian Migration and the Globalization of Borders*, 'The "Natal Formula" and the Decline of the Imperial Subject, 1888–1913', 185–214, offers a close reading of one important moment in the history of South Asian migrations at the turn of the twentieth century.

25 A critique of the Atlantic model on the study of migration also appears within recent considerations of African diasporas and migrations. See Paul Zeleza, 'Rewriting the African Diaspora: Beyond the Black Atlantic' *African Affairs* 104, no. 14 (2005): 35–68, Idem, 'African Diasporas: Toward a Global History', *African Studies Review* 53, no. 1 (April 2010): 1–19.

26 Published by Harvard University Press, editors feature Eric Tagliacozzo, Peter Perdue and Helen F. Siu. Volume 1 (2015) offers snapshots of key years in Asian history from the mid-sixteenth century through to the mid-twentieth century and is titled 'Changing Times', 2 (2015), 'Connected Places', focuses on 'spatial assemblages' and features maritime and terrestrial connections across Asia from the Arab Middle East through the South China Sea and island Southeast Asia, inclusive of South Asian nodes in broader Asian networks. The third and final volume (2019), 'Itinerant People', looks at 'transient histories of "people on the move", through voluntary or involuntary circulation, either part of chosen paths

(such as migration) or the radials of coerced journeys (such as slavery or the dislocations wrought by conflict', 3.

27 Tagliacozzo, Perdue, and Siu, 'Introduction: Seekers, Sojourners and Meaningful Worlds in Motion', *Asia Inside Out* 3, no. 3.

28 Statistics of the total number of indentured labourers vary across sources, though the figure of 1.2 million is derived from Clarke, Peach and Vertovec, eds. *South Asians Overseas: Migration and Ethnicity* (New York: Cambridge University Press, 1990), 9.

29 Hugh Tinker, *A New System of Slavery: The Export of Indian Labour Overseas* (London: Oxford University Press, 1974).

30 Brij V. Lal, *Girmitiyas: The Origins of the Fiji Indians* (Canberra: Journal of Pacific History, 1983). Another key early historical work is Panchanan Saha, *Emigration of Indian Labour, 1834-1900* (Delhi: People's Publishing House, 1970). Along with studies of indentured labour, histories of Indian migrants in Britain as well as Anglophone Southeast Asia, such as G.S. Aurora, *The New Frontiersman: Indians in Great Britain* (Bombay: Popular Prakashan, 1976), N.R. Chakravarti's *The Indian Minority in Burma: The Rise and Decline of an Immigrant Community* (London: Oxford University Press, 1971) and K.S. Sandhu's *Indians in Malaya: Immigration and Settlement, 1786-1957* (Cambridge: Cambridge University Press, 1969) emerged in the 1960s and 1970s.

31 Ashutosh Kumar, *Coolies of the Empire: Indentured Indians in the Sugar Colonies, 1830 - 1920* (Delhi: Cambridge University Press, 2017).

32 Recent works include Ravi Ahuja, 'Mobility and Containment: The Voyages of South Asian Seamen, c. 1900-1960' in *Coolies, Capital, and Colonialism: Studies in Indian Labour History*, edited by Rana Behal and Marcel van der Linden (Cambridge: Cambridge University Press, 2006), 111-141, G. Balachandran, *Globalizing Labour? Indian Seafarers and World Shipping, c. 1870-1945* (Delhi: Oxford University Press, 2012), and Aaron Jaffer, *Lascars and Indian Ocean Seafaring, 1780-1860: Shipboard Life, Unrest, and Mutiny* (Rochester: Boydell Press, 2015).

33 The many works of Ashin Dasgupta on merchants in the Indian Ocean world showcase a pillar of this field; key works are collected in *Merchants of Maritime India, 1500-1800* (Aldershot: Ashgate, 1994) and *The World of the Indian Ocean Merchant, 1500-1800: Collected Essays of Ashin Dasgupta* (Delhi: Oxford University Press, 2001). Important works in this genre include Christine Dobbin, *Asian Entrepreneurial Minorities: Conjoint Communities in the Making of the World Economy, 1570-1940* (Abingdon: Routledge Curzon, 1996) and Mark-Anthony Falzon, *Cosmopolitan Connections: The Sindhi Diaspora, 1860-2000* (Leiden: Brill, 2004). Pedro Machado, *Ocean of Trade: South Asian Merchants, Africa and the Indian Ocean, c. 1750-1850* (Cambridge: Cambridge University Press, 2014) adds to the roster of works complicating histories of slavery through an Indian Ocean history. Claude Markovits, *The Global World of Indian*

Merchants, 1750–1947: Traders of Sind from Bukhara to Panama (Cambridge: Cambridge University Press, 2000) and Scott Levi, *The Indian Merchant Diaspora in Central Asia and its Trade, 1550–1900* (Leiden: Brill, 2002) engage with merchant networks across Western and Central Asia.

34 Of the many works in this area, significant highlights include Elleke Boehmer, *Indian Arrivals 1870–1915: Networks of British Empire* (Oxford: Oxford University Press, 2015), Michael Fisher, *Counterflows to Colonialism: Indian Travelers and Settlers in Britain, 1600–1857* (Delhi: Permanent Black, 2004) and Shompa Lahiri, *Indian Mobilities in the West, 1900–1947: Gender, Performance, Embodiment* (New York: Palgrave Macmillan, 2010). A classic work in this field is Rozina Visram, *Ayahs, Lascars and Princes: Indians in Britain, 1600–1947* (London: Pluto Press, 1986).

35 Representative works include Marina Carter's two major investigations in Mauritius such as *Servants, Sirdars and Settlers: Indians in Mauritius, 1834–1874* (Delhi: Oxford University Press, 1995) and *Lakshmi's Legacy: The Testimonies of Indian Women in 19th Century Mauritius* (Stanley Hill: Edition de l'ocean Indien, 1994).

36 Maritsa Poros, *Modern Migrations: Gujarati Indian Networks in New York and London* (Stanford, CA: Stanford University Press, 2010), Gijsbert Oonk, *The Karimjee Jivanjee Family: Merchant Princes of East Africa, 1800–2000* (Amsterdam: Pallas Publications, 2009) and *Settled Strangers: Asian Business Elites in East Africa* (New Delhi: Sage, 2013).

37 John D. Kelly, *A Politics of Virtue: Hinduism, Sexuality, and Countercolonial Discourse in Fiji* (Chicago: University of Chicago Press, 1991).

38 Claude Markovits, Jacques Pouchepadass and Sanjay Subrahmanyam, eds., *Society and Circulation: Mobile People and Itinerant Cultures in South Asia, 1750–1950* (London: Anthem, 2006).

39 See Gaiutra Bahadur, *Coolie Woman: The Odyssey of Indenture* (Chicago: University of Chicago Press, 2013), as well as 'Conjure Women and Coolie Women' *Small Axe* 22, no. 2 (2018): 244–253. Several poetic works attest to the notion of 'Coolitude', an appropriation of 'Negritude' that speaks to the condition of descendants of 'coolies'. On 'coolitude', see Marina Carter and Khal Torabully, *Coolitude: An Anthology of the Indian Labour Diaspora* (London: Anthem, 2002). Rajiv Mojabir's many works across genres of poetry, memoir and translation contribute a burgeoning archive to the many histories of indenture and its legacies manifested in artistic and poetic form. His translation of Lalbihari Sharma's *1916 I Even Regret Night: Holy Songs of Demerara* (Los Angeles: Kaya Press, 2018) offers an unprecedented act of historical retrieval and poetic commentary. His 'Coolitude Project' includes a host of literary and historical writings, http://www.rajivmohabir.com/coolitude-project.

40 Significant contributions that contextualize convicts from South Asia into multiple historical frames include Clare Anderson's *Convicts in the Indian Ocean: Transportation*

*from South Asia to Mauritius, 1815-53 (*New York: St. Martin's, 2000) and *Subaltern Lives: Biographies of Colonialism in the Indian Ocean World* (Cambridge: Cambridge University Press, 2012). Anand Yang's 'Indian Convict Workers in Southeast Asia in the Late Eighteenth and Early Nineteenth Centuries' *Journal of World History* 14, no. 2 (2003): 179–208, places Indian convicts into broader histories of global migration.

41 See Ashutosh Kumar, *Coolies of the Empire: Indentured Indians in the Sugar Colonies, 1830–1920*, as well as the AHRC-funded collaborative project between the University of Leeds and the University of Edinburgh, 'Becoming Coolies: Rethinking the Origins of the Indian Ocean Labour Diaspora, 1772–1920', http://www.coolitude.shca.ed.ac.uk/about-project.

42 Sujit Sivasundaram, 'The Indian Ocean' in *Oceanic Histories*, edited by David Armitage, Alison Bashford and Sujit Sivasundaram, eds. *Oceanic Histories* (Cambridge: Cambridge University Press, 2017), 31–61, provides a useful overview of the entire field. Recent narrative histories include Michael Pearson, *The Indian Ocean* (New York: Routledge, 2003) and Sugata Bose, *A Hundred Horizons: The Indian Ocean in an Age of Global Empire* (Cambridge, MA: Harvard University Press, 2006). Important considerations of labour history – from slavery, indentured labour and various forms of unfree labour – find detailed exposition and exploration in the many works of Gwyn Campbell. Two works in this genre hold serious implications for any history of South Asian migration in the Indian Ocean: Gwyn Campbell, ed., *The Structure of Slavery in Indian Ocean Africa and Asia* (London: Frank Cass, 2003) and *Abolition and its Aftermath in Indian Ocean Asia and Africa* (New York: Routledge, 2005). Palgrave Macmillan hosts an Indian Ocean World Series, which focuses on themes of slavery, textiles, monetary currency circulation, knowledge, science and many more topics. As of 2019, the series has published twenty-one books.

43 K.N. Chaudhuri, *Trade and Civilisation in the Indian Ocean: An Economic History from the Rise of Islam to 1750* (Cambridge: Cambridge University Press, 1985), *Asia Before Europe: Economy and Civilisation of the Indian Ocean from the Rise of Islam to 1750* (Cambridge: Cambridge University Press, 1990) and Satish Chandra, ed., *The Indian Ocean: Explorations in History Commerce and Politics* (Delhi: Sage, 1987).

44 See his 'Connected Histories: Notes Towards a Reconfiguration of Early Modern Eurasia', *Modern Asian Studies* 31, no. 3 (1997): 735–62 and 'Holding the World in Balance: The Connected Histories of the Iberian Overseas Empires 1500–1640', *American Historical Review* 112 (2007): 1359–1385.

45 Abdul Sheriff and Enseng Ho, eds., *The Indian Ocean: Oceanic Connections and the Creation of New Societies* (New York: Oxford University Press, 2014), Sunil Amrith, *Crossing the Bay of Bengal: The Furies of Nature and the Fortunes of Migrants* (Cambridge, MA: Harvard University Press, 2013), Fahad Bishara, *A Sea of Debt:*

Law and Economic Life in the Western Indian Ocean, 1780–1950 (Cambridge: Cambridge University Press, 2017), Nile Green, *Bombay Islam: The Religious Economy of the West Indian Ocean, 1840–1915* (Cambridge: Cambridge University Press, 2011) and Renisa Mawani, *Across Oceans of Law*.

46   Isabel Hofmeyr, 'The Black Atlantic Meets the Indian Ocean: Forging New Paradigms of Transnationalism for the Global South – Literary and Cultural Perspectives' *Social Dynamics* 33 (2007): 3–32. Three recent twenty-first century volumes advance South-South literary critical frameworks: Pamila Gupta, Isabel Hofmeyr and Michael Pearson, eds. *Eyes across the Water: Navigating the Indian Ocean* (Pretoria: Unisa Press, 2010), Isabel Hofmeyr and Michelle Williams, eds. *South Africa and India: Shaping the Global South* (Johannesburg: Wits University Press, 2011) and Gaurav Desai, *Commerce with the Universe: Africa, India, and the Afrasian Imagination* (New York: Columbia University Press, 2013).

47   Donna Gabbacia and Dirk Hoerder's edited volume, *Connecting Seas and Connected Ocean Rims Indian, Atlantic, and Pacific Oceans and China Seas Migrations from the 1830s to the 1930* (Leiden: Brill, 2011), integrates research as well as theoretical insight from Atlantic, Pacific and Indian Ocean histories. Chapters by Ulrike Freitag, Amarjit Kaur, Michael Mann, Claude Markovitz and Pamila Gupta provide insights from a diverse set of research agendas within Indian Ocean contexts.

48   See Vivek Bald, et al., *South Asian Migrants in an Age of U.S. Power*, Nayan Shah, *Stranger Intimacy: Contesting Race, Sexuality, and The Law in the North American West* (Berkeley, CA: University of California Press, 2011), Vivek Bald, *Bengali Harlem and the Lost Histories of South Asian America* (Cambridge, MA: Harvard University Press, 2012), Seema Sohi, *Echoes of Mutiny: Race, Surveillance, and Indian Anticolonialism in North America* (New York: Oxford University Press, 2014), Hugh Johnston, *The Voyage of the Komagata Maru: The Sikh Challenge to Canada's Colour Bar* (Vancouver, BC: UBC Press, 1989) and Renisa Mawani, Across Oceans of Law.

49   Sanjoy Chakravorty, Devesh Kapur and Nirvikar Singh, *The Other One Percent: Indians in America* (New York: Oxford University Press, 2017), Sunil Karma, *American Karma: Race, Culture, and Identity in the Indian Diaspora* (New York: NYU Press, 2007), Sandhya Shukla, *India Abroad: Diasporic Cultures of Postwar America and England* (Princeton: Princeton University Press, 2007), Amminah Mohammed-Arif, *Salaam America: South Asian Muslims in New York* (London: Anthem, 2002), Sunaina Maira, *Desis in the House: Indian American Youth Culture in New York City* (Philadelphia: Temple University Press, 2002), Vijay Prashad, *The Karma of Brown Folk* (Minneapolis: University of Minnesota Press, 2001), and Neilesh Bose, ed. *Beyond Bollywood and Broadway: Plays from the South Asian Diaspora* (Bloomington, IN: Indiana University Press, 2009).

50 Important works that explore the links between Asian migrations, settler colonialism and dispossession of Indigenous peoples include Bonita Lawrence and Enakshi Dua, 'Decolonizing Racism' *Social Justice* 32, no. 4 (2005): 120–143, which argues that immigrants of colour to settler colonial states, including a range of differentiation via class, origin and relations to the state, occupy the structural role of settler. A response from Nandita Sharma and Cynthia Wright, 'Decolonizing Resistance, Challenging Colonial States' *Social Justice* 35, no. 3 (2008–09): 120–138, offers a different view, questioning the notion that all migrants belong to the category of settler and also interrogating the grounds of nationalisms based on notions of indigeneity. A recent special edition of *BC Studies*, 24 (2019), '(Un)Settling the Islands: Race, Indigeneity and the Transpacific', edited by John Price and Christine O'Bonsawin, integrates the place of Asian migration in the history of British Columbia. A recent historical contribution that highlights the importance of South Asian migrants in North American histories features Rita Dhamoon, Davina Bhandar, Renisa Mawani and Satwinder Kaur Bains, eds. *Unmooring the Komagata Maru: Charting Colonial Trajectories* (Vancouver: UBC Press, 2019). This work is followed by Renisa Mawani, *Across Oceans of Law*, 2018 and Nayan Shah, *Stranger Intimacy: Contesting Race, Sexuality, and the Law in the North American West* (Berkeley, CA: University of California Press, 2012). Though Mawani touches on the issue of how particular Indian commentators in colonial India understood indigenous-settler relationships in early twentieth-century Canada, scholarship about migration and settler colonialism and dispossession of various indigenous and/or tribal groups in territorial South Asia remain largely disconnected from studies of migration and forms of settler colonialism outside territorial of South Asia.

51 See Kama Maclean, *British India, White Australia: Overseas Indians, Inter-colonial Relations, and the Empire* (Sydney: UNSW Press, 2020) and Samia Khatun, *Australianama: The South Asian Odyssey in Australia* (London: Hurst, 2018).

52 The study of settler colonialism as a component of imperial histories is a vast subfield and established traditions of scholarship in North American and Australian contexts have yielded diversified approaches to the subject. Two crucial articles include Patrick Wolfe's 'Settler Colonialism and the Elimination of the Native' *Journal of Genocide Research* 8, no. 4 (Dec. 2006): 387–409 and J. Kehaulani Kauanui's 'A Structure, Not an Event: Settler Colonialism and Enduring Indigeneity' *Lateral: A Journal of the Cultural Studies Association* 5, no. 1 (2016): https://doi.org/10.25158/L5.1.7, accessed 2 April 020. Margaret Jacobs 'Seeing Like a Settler Colonial State' *Modern American History* 1, no. 2 (2018): 257–270, clarifies the importance of the analytical usage of settler colonial frameworks for American history. Overviews of the field include Lorenzo Veracini's *Settler Colonialism: A Theoretical Overview* (Basingstoke: Palgrave Macmillan, 2010) and the same author's *The Settler Colonial Present* (Basingstoke: Palgrave Macmillan, 2015). Other significant works situating settler colonial histories within global historical

frameworks include Zoe Laidlaw and Alan Lester, eds. *Indigenous Communities and Settler Colonialism: Land Holding, Loss, and Survival in an Interconnected World* (Basingstoke: Palgrave Macmillan, 2015) and Lisa Ford, *Settler Sovereignty: Jurisdiction and Indigenous People in America and Australia, 1788–1836* (Cambridge, MA: Harvard University Press, 2011).

53 Claire Alexander, Joya Chatterji and Annu Jalais, *The Bengal Diaspora: Rethinking Muslim Migration* (New York: Routledge, 2015).

54 Alexander, Chatterji and Jalai, *The Bengal Diaspora*, 2.

55 See the review forum with contributions by Michael Keith, Nasar Meer, Pawan Dhingra, Victoria Redclift and Fatima Rajina, William Gould and Sean McLaughlin as well as responses from the authors themselves. The entire forum appears in *Ethnic and Racial Studies* 40, no. 3 (2017): 388–432.

56 See Tariq Ali, *A Local History of Global Capital: Jute and Peasant Life in the Bengal delta* (Princeton, NJ: Princeton University Press, 2018) for the most recent study of East Bengal's history within global historical frameworks. The special edition, 'Oral Histories of Decolonisation: Bengali Intellectuals, Memory and the Archive', in *South Asia: Journal of South Asian Studies* 41, no. 4 (2018): 827–913 explores Bengali Muslim histories within broader contexts of decolonization, including contributions by Kris Manjapra, Iftekhar Iqbal, Neilesh Bose, Vinayak Chaturvedi, Ananya Jahanara Kabir and Pramatha Banerjee. Other works situating Bengali Muslims into multiple historical frameworks include Neilesh Bose, *Recasting the Region: Language, Culture, and Islam in Colonial Bengal* (Delhi: Oxford University Press, 2014) and Iftekhar Iqbal, *The Bengal Delta. Ecology, State and Social Change, 1840–1943* (New York: Palgrave Macmillan, 2010).

57 See McLoughlin, 'Locating Muslim diasporas: multi-locality, multidisciplinarity and performativity', *Ethnic and Racial Studies* 40, no. 3 (2017): 425. Alexander, Chatterji and Jalais offer an extraordinary set of insights regarding the historical as well as living diversity of Islam in chapter 6, on 'Bihari piety' in the context of 'Bihari' migrants into what is now Bangladesh and the layered expressions of Islam over time.

58 Sugata Bose and Ayesha Jalal, 'Introduction: Islam is the Ocean' In *Oceanic Islam: Muslim Universalism and European Imperialism*, ed. Sugata Bose and Ayesha Jalal (London: Bloomsbury, 2020), 2.

59 *For God or Empire: Sayyid Fadl and the Indian Ocean World* (Stanford, CA: Stanford University Press, 2019).

60 Wilson Chacko Jacob, 'Of Angels and Men: Sayyid Fadl b. 'Alawi and Two Moments of Sovereignty', *Arab Studies Journal* XX, no. 1 (Spring 2012): 45.

61 See Jacob's analysis of *Idah al-Asrar al-'Alawiyya wa Manahij al-Sada al-'Alawiyya* (Visualizing the Secrets of the 'Alawis and the Pathways of the 'Alawi Sayyids) in such a context, 'Of Angels and Men', 50–60.

62 See Nile Green, 'Islam for the Indentured Indian: A Muslim Missionary in Colonial South Africa' *Bulletin of the School of Oriental and African Studies, University of London*, 71no. 3, 529–553 and 'Migrant Sufis and sacred space in South Asian Islam', *Contemporary South Asia*, 12, no. 4 (2003): 493–509.

63 See Brian Hatcher, *Hinduism Before Reform* (Cambridge, MA: Harvard University Press, 2020) for a historical and comparative critique of the term 'reform' for individuals such as Rammohan Roy and Sahajanand in the early nineteenth century. In Hatcher's account, both the larger frameworks of movement and mobility are crucial to the making of modern Hinduism. His study remains the only book that systematically compares these two crucial figures in the history of Indian religion.

64 Sunil Amrith, *Crossing the Bay of Bengal*.

65 Adam McKeown, 'Periodizing Globalization' *History Workshop Journal* 63, no. 1 (March 2007): 218.

66 As Arif Dirlik argues in an older yet resonant critique of world history, 'globalization may well appear to be a contemporary substitute for earlier paradigms of modernization – and even Westernization', in 'Confounding Metaphors, Inventions of the World: What is World History For'? *Education/Pedagogy/Cultural Studies* 22, no. 4 (2000): 326. A similar position is found in Vinay Lal, 'Provincializing the West: World History from the Perspective of Indian History' in *Writing World History, 1800–2000*, edited by Benedikt Stuchtey and Eckhart Fuchs (Oxford: Oxford University Press, 2003), 270–289, which also contains a reprint of Dirlik's essay.

67 See Amit Mishra's 'Global History of Migration (s)', in *Global History Globally*, 195–214 and 'Indian Indentured Labourers in Mauritius: Reassessing the "New System of Slavery" vs Free Labour Debate' *Studies in History* 25, no. 2 (2010): 229–251. In a piece that engages with Indian exceptionalism, see 'Sardars, Kanganies and Maistries: Intermediaries in the Indian Labour Diaspora during the Colonial Period', in Sigrid Wadauer, Thomas Buchner and Alexander Mejstrik (eds.), *The History of Labour Intermediation: Institutions and Finding Employment in the Nineteenth and Early Twentieth Centuries* (New York, Oxford: Berghahn Books, 2014), 368–387.

68 The term 'plantation complex' conventionally refers to plantations and large-scale economic and political systems that sustained them in the era of trans-Atlantic slavery from the seventeenth to the nineteenth centuries. See Philip Curtin, *The Rise and Fall of the Plantation Complex: Essays in Atlantic History* (New York: Cambridge University Press, 2012). A 'global plantation complex' refers to the associated social, economic, and political systems in India and the Indian Ocean drawing on plantations in the Atlantic world during and after the abolition of trans-Atlantic slavery in the 1830s. Kris Manjapra explores the history

of plantations in which he offers periods including the 1840s–1870s and the 1870s–1930s, both of which feature South Asian indentured labourers in various parts of the world within a history of plantations. He describes the age of abolition as a time when 'the plantation as an exploitative, racial, political-ecological complex began to expand and travel the face of the earth … the plantation complex, and the modes of racial labour command endemic to it, actually flourished in abolition's aftermath'. See his 'Plantation Dispossessions: The Global Travel of Agricultural Racial Capitalism', in *American Capitalism: New Histories*, edited by Sven Beckert and Christine Desan (New York: Columbia University Press, 2018), 361.

69 Crispin Bates, 'Some Thoughts on the Representation and Misrepresentation of the Colonial South Asian Labour Diaspora' *South Asian Studies* 33, no. 1 (2017): 8.

70 Richard Allen, 'Reconceptualizing the "New System of Slavery"', *Man in India* 92, no. 2 (2012): 225–245.

71 Ibid., 230.

72 Rachel Sturman, 'Indian Indentured Labor and the History of International Rights Regimes'.

73 These histories provide essential correctives to Atlantic-centric assumptions about slavery, abolition and free labor. See Gwyn Campbell, ed., *Abolition and its Aftermath in Indian Ocean Africa and Asia*, (passim). Of particular relevance is Gwyn Campbell, 'Introduction: Abolition and its Aftermath in the Indian Ocean World', 1–28 and Indrani Chatterjee, 'Abolition by Denial: The South Asian Example', 150–168. Other significant works on the topic feature Chatterjee, 'The Locked Box in Slavery and Social Death', in *On Human Bondage: After Slavery and Social Death*, edited by John Bodel and Walter Scheidel (Boston: Wiley-Blackwell, 2016), 151–166, Richard Allen, 'Re-conceptualizing the New System of Slavery', and Clare Anderson, 'Convicts and Coolies: Rethinking Indentured Labour in the Nineteenth Century', *Slavery and Abolition: A Journal of Slave and Post-Slave Studies* 30, no. 1 (2009): 93–109.

74 'Expatriate patriots' such as Gandhi, Tagore and Subhas Bose are explored in Bose, *A Hundred Horizons*, 148–192.

75 See her 'Conjure Women and Coolie Women' and Saidiya Hartman's 'Venus in Two Acts', *Small Axe* 12, no. 2 (2008): 1–14.

76 New York: W.W. Norton & Co., 2019.

77 Ben Zachariah, 'A Long Strange Trip: The Lives in Exile of Har Dayal' *South Asian History and Culture* 4, no. 4 (2013): 574–592.

78 Omar Ali, *Malik Ambar: Power and Slavery across the Indian Ocean* (New York: Oxford University Press, 2016), Sanjay Subrahmanyam, *The Career and Legend of Vasco Da Gama* (Cambridge: Cambridge University Press, 1998), idem, *Three Ways to be Alien: Travails and Encounters in the Early Modern World* (Waltham, MA: Brandeis University Press, 2011), idem, *Europe's India: Words, Peoples,*

Empires, 1500–1800 (Cambridge, MA: Harvard University Press, 2017) and Ananya Chakravarti, 'Mapping "Gabriel": Space, Identity and Slavery in the Late Sixteenth-Century Indian Ocean' *Past & Present* 243, no. 1 (May 2019): 5–34.
79 Fischer-Tine, *Shyamji Krishnavarma: Sanskrit, Sociology, and Anti-Imperialism.*
80 Satadru Sen, *Benoy Kumar Sarkar: Restoring the Nation to the World* (Delhi: Routledge, 2015).
81 Gadadhar Singh, *Thirteen Months in China*, ed. and trans. Anand Yang, Kamal Sheel and Ranjana Sheel, eds. (New York: Oxford University Press, 2017).
82 Allen, 'Reconceptualizing the "New System of Slavery"', 236.
83 See Crispin Bates, 'Some Thoughts on the Representation and Misrepresentation of the Colonial South Asian Labour Diaspora', 18.
84 Ibid., 18.
85 See Brettell and Hollifield, *Migration Theory: Talking Across Disciplines*, 'Introduction', 1–36.
86 Innovative research agendas linking South Asian migrations to frameworks of globalization feature exploration of migrations and connections that engage with historical anthropology, memory studies and paradigms of decolonization in comparative perspective. Sana Aiyar's *Indians in Kenya: The Politics of Diaspora* (Cambridge, MA: Cambridge University Press, 2015), explores how nationalism for East African Indians held multiple registers and trans-regional sentiments. For work that crosses historical frontiers of the expulsion of Asians from Uganda in historical anthropology, see Anneeth Kaur Hundle, 'The Politics of (In)security: Reconstructing African-Asian Relations, Citizenship and Community in Post-Expulsion Uganda', PhD diss., University of Michigan, 2013 and 'Unsettling Citizenship: Race, Security and Afro-Asian Politics in Contemporary Uganda', conference paper, University of Victoria, 27 October 2017. In Western African contexts, the work of Shobana Shankar on West African and Indian entanglements pursues such an agenda too. See her 'A Tale of Two Gandhis: Complicating Ghana's Indian Entanglements' in *Afro-South Asian in the Global African Diaspora*, edited by Omar Ali, Kenneth X. Robbins, Beheroze Schroff and Jazmin Graces, forthcoming. Another line of future inquiry in this domain features a focus on mercantile capital outside frames of nation or territoriality, as advocated by Dilip Menon in 'Not just Indentured Labourers: Why India Needs to Revisit its pre-1947 History of Migration,'https://scroll.in/article/856271/not-just-indentured-labourers-why-we-should-revisit-the-history-of-migration-from-pre-1947-india, first published 16 January 2018.
87 Tumbe, *India Moving*, 2018.
88 Claude Markovitz, 'Afterword: Stray Thoughts of a Historian on "Indian" or "South Asian" "Diaspora (s),"' in *Global Indian Diasporas: Exploring Trajectories of Migration and Theory*, ed. Gijsbert Oonk (Amsterdam: Amsterdam University Press, 2007), 263–272.

Part One

Impacts of Indentured Labour

1

Gokhale, Polak and the end of Indian indenture in South Africa, 1909–1911

Goolam Vahed

Indian indenture resulted from two distinct but converging factors: the labour shortage on plantations that followed the emancipation of slaves in the British Empire in 1833 and a new phase of imperialism that resulted in the expansion of European settlers and capital into new parts of the world, such as Natal and Fiji, which had not known slavery. Around 1.2 million Indians emigrated as indentured workers, mainly to British colonies in a 'massive, micro-managed state-controlled enterprise'[1] for purposes of 'facilitation' rather than 'restriction' of labour migration.[2] Despite several commissions across the Empire that exposed labour abuses,[3] there was little pressure to end indenture within India itself until the early twentieth century. Sustained agitation only materialized in the period after 1910, when indentured emigration entered Indian nationalist discourse in a significant way as an attack on British imperial rule itself.[4]

Natal was the first colony where pressure was applied to end indenture and this chapter examines the complex set of factors that drove this process as well as the key figures involved. While the figure of Mohandas K. Gandhi, the future Mahatma, understandably dominates the historiography of Indians in South Africa during this period, the influence of two other individuals, the South African–based Jewish lawyer and Gandhi's accomplice Henry Polak, and to a lesser extent Indian nationalist leader Gopal Krishna Gokhale, was key to ending indentured emigration to Natal. Until now, the involvement of Polak in particular in ending indenture has been overlooked and a key contribution of this chapter is to examine his critical role. This chapter also argues that those seeking to end indentured migration to Natal had different motives. Natal was set apart from other colonies/countries that received indentured labour in that its white minority government was itself looking to end its reliance on this labour supply and was actively seeking alternative sources. At the same time, anti-colonial leaders like Gandhi, Gokhale and Polak, though working towards the same end, had different motivations for wanting an end to indenture. This chapter provides a brief overview of indentured migration to Natal, then discusses anti-Indian legislation which rendered Indians as second-class citizens, and finally focuses on the sustained campaign in India to end indentured emigration to Natal.

The 'Indian problem'

The annexation of Natal by the British in 1843 was followed by large-scale immigration of mainly British settlers who found success with sugar production, but whose enterprise was hampered by the shortage of a stable, low-cost labour force because the indigenous Zulu had access to land and were not willing to labour on sugar plantations.[5] Colonists were aware of the success of Indian indenture in Mauritius and petitioned the British for Indian labour. Between 1860 and 1911, 152,641 indentured migrants arrived in Natal. Tayal,[6] Desai and Vahed,[7] and others have chronicled the appalling living and working conditions of the indentured as well as the lives they made in South Africa. From the mid-1870s, indentured workers were followed to Natal by free migrants from Gujarat on the west coast of India. As they and the ex-indentured population spread throughout the colony, white settlers saw them as constituting an economic and political threat and pressured for legislation to restrict Indian trade, residence and immigration rights.[8]

After Natal achieved self-government in 1893, the new government dealt with the perceived 'Asiatic Menace' by passing laws 'to establish expensive registration taxes and pass systems, and to restrict commercial activities and property holding for postindenture Indians'.[9] Formal Indian political leadership was provided by the merchant class who formed the Natal Indian Congress (NIC) in 1894 under Gandhi's leadership. The NIC's strategy was primarily constitutional and included petitions to government officials and private persons in Britain, Natal and India, as well as letters to newspapers arguing for the rights of non-indentured Indians.[10] This strategy failed to stem the tide of racist legislation.

As Indians made their way from Natal to the Cape, the Orange Free State and the Transvaal, these governments also passed measures to restrict Indian trade and residence rights. The Free State adopted legislation in 1891 prohibiting

Indian settlement in that colony; the 1906 Immigration Act introduced a literacy test that made migration to the Cape extremely difficult; and Law 3 of 1885 – amended in 1886 – restricted Indian trade and residence rights in the Transvaal. The British used the treatment of Indians in the Transvaal as part justification for going to war with the Boers in what would come to be known as the South African War (1899–1902). Lord Landsdowne told a meeting in Sheffield in 1899: 'Among the many misdeeds of the South African Republic I do not know that any fills me with more indignation than its treatment of these Indians'.[11]

To the consternation of Indians, however, the British pursued anti-Asiatic policies in the postwar period. Lord Alfred Milner, the British High Commissioner and Governor of the Transvaal and Orange River Colony, was an advocate of white supremacy. He told the Johannesburg Municipal Congress on 18 May 1903: 'The white man must rule, because he is elevated by many, many steps above the black man; steps which it will take many centuries to climb, and it is quite possible that the vast bulk of the black population may never be able to climb at all'.[12] As Radhika Mongia has pointed out, the first decade of the twentieth century witnessed the transformation of '"Asiatics" into new kinds of nationality-bearing "Indians" and "Chinese"', and 'the category of "British subject" was also undergoing a thorough redefinition' to exclude 'racialised subjects' from citizenship in 'white-settler colonies of the British empire'.[13] Racist controls resulted in the adjective 'white' being attached to 'settler' colonies.[14]

Anti-Asiatic legislation in the Transvaal climaxed with the Asiatic Law Amendment Ordinance of 1906, which Gandhi termed the 'Black Act' as it required Indians to register by providing fingerprints. Gandhi went to London in 1906 to canvas against the law. His delegation, led by London-based Sir Lepel Griffin, Chairman of the East India Association, met with John Morley, the Secretary of State for India, on 22 November 1906. Griffin urged Morley to stop indentured migration to Natal 'until the status of their fellow-subjects in South Africa is altered'.[15] The British acted duplicitously in vetoing the 'Black Act' in December 1906 but allowing the law to be passed when the Transvaal was given self-government under General Louis Botha on 1 January 1907. The British government approved the Transvaal Registration Act on 9 May 1907 and on 11 May Gandhi announced that Indians would embark on a passive resistance campaign against it. The Act came into effect on 1 July 1907.

Gandhi's satyagraha campaign began in December 1907. He himself was arrested on 27 December and sentenced to two months' imprisonment. The matter was raised at the Surat conference of the Indian National Congress (INC) which was held a few days after his arrest; the INC's discussion of the issue caused alarm among British rulers. *The Register*, an Adelaide-based newspaper, reported from London on 3 January 1908 that British officials feared that it could lead to

> a spread of the boycott of British goods and a revival of sedition (Swadeshi Movement). It must have the effect of strengthening the agitation against British rule. Indignation is expressed towards the British government for not having vetoed a law which is denounced as insulting to Indian peoples. Ministers are characterized as either servile and weak in their attitude to the colonies, or hypocritical in their professed determination to defend the King's Asiatic subject against injustice.[16]

As prisons began filling up in the Transvaal, General Jan Christiaan Smuts, the Colonial Secretary and Education Secretary in General Botha's government, met with Gandhi on 30 January 1908 and they reached a compromise, which Gandhi understood to mean that the Act would be repealed if Indians registered voluntarily.[17] But Smuts did not repeal the Act and was accused by Gandhi of 'foul play'. At a mass meeting at the Hamidia Mosque in Johannesburg on 16 August 1908, around 2,000 Indian registration documents were burnt and the passive resistance movement recommenced. Gandhi was imprisoned between February and May 1909. In all, 3,000 people were arrested, and fifty-nine were deported to India in April 1910 and a further twenty-six in June 1910. In addition to registration, the Botha regime also passed an Immigration Act which virtually ended further Indian entry into the Transvaal.[18]

While the satyagraha movement was ongoing, the colonies of Natal, Transvaal, Orange Free State and the Cape began discussions about forming a Union of South Africa. Indians were concerned about their fate and two delegations went to London in 1909, one from the Transvaal headed by Gandhi and another from Natal under the auspices of the NIC, while Gandi sent Polak to India as a one-man delegation to publicize the grievances of Indians in South Africa. Nationalist fervour was gathering momentum in India and Indian nationalists took a keen interest in what was going on in the colonies. The treatment of Indians in South Africa in particular was a rallying point for many in the INC.

The Indian context

The INC, formed by Indian moderates in 1885, took a keen interest in the treatment of Indians in the Transvaal due, in part, to the close relationship between Gandhi and Gokhale, but also because they believed that Indians' patriotism to the Empire was not rewarded with equal treatment. Moderates argued that Queen Victoria's Proclamation of 1858 stipulated that Indians were subjects of the Crown entitled to 'the equal and impartial protection of the Law', and thus citizens of the British Empire, and it was within the framework of Empire that they were claiming their rights.[19] In reality, however, there was a colour line in the Empire as India was not only treated unequally in comparison to self-governing dominions such as Australia, New Zealand and Canada – even though it contributed the most financially to the Empire – but within each of these 'white' states, Indians were discriminated against because of their race.[20]

Gandhi's associate Polak was an English Jew who had arrived in the Transvaal in 1903. He was sub-editor of a newspaper, *Transvaal Critic*, when he became acquainted with Gandhi through the latter's work during the plague epidemic of 1904. Polak wrote that 'there was a quality of character within him which marked him out amongst his followers'.[21] They found much in common and Polak joined Gandhi in his legal practice and spent time at the Phoenix Settlement as editor of *Indian Opinion*, the newspaper that Gandhi had started in 1903. Polak was intimately connected with the struggles of Indians in South Africa and was sent to India in 1909 to publicize their grievances. He reached Bombay on 21 July 1909 and spent the rest of the year in India.

During his stay in India, Polak met with Gokhale, the moderate Indian nationalist who arranged meetings for him in Madras and Bombay. It was through Gokhale that the plight of Indians in South Africa initially came to the attention of India and dominated nationalist discourse long before that of any other colony. Gokhale was born in 1866 in the Bombay presidency to a Brahmin family, graduated from Elphinstone College in 1884, and joined the INC in 1889. The Indian Councils Act of 1892 allowed limited representation in legislative councils and Gokhale was one of the first to take advantage.[22] He became joint secretary of the INC in 1895, and was elected to the Bombay Legislative Council in 1897, and to the all-India Imperial Legislative Council from 1902.[23]

Gokhale was arguably 'the most widely recognised Indian nationalist of this period', both in India and England, and had influence among the Indian populace and their government.[24] He was a moderate who was influenced by the Round Table group which advocated closer links between Britain and India.[25] Until the first decade of the twentieth century, Gokhale and other moderates, mostly professionals, 'did not question the continuance of British rule …. They wanted more Indian participation in the legislative councils … and deliberately stood aside from the intense and widespread social cultural reform activities of the day'.[26]

Lord Curzon's measures, such as the Calcutta Corporation Act in 1899, which reduced Indian employment; the Universities Act of 1904, which placed Indian education under government control; and the partition of Bengal in 1905 undermined nationalists.[27] Bengal, Punjab and parts of Madras and Maharashtra were witness to the Swadeshi Movement between 1905 and 1908, which ushered in the first acts of terror. However, Congress remained in moderate hands because Pherozeshah Mehta transferred the Congress session of December 1907 from Nagpur to Surat, where they were able to avert a radical takeover.[28] As president from 1906, Gokhale led a moderate INC, while the radical faction was led by Bal Gangadhar Tilak who actively opposed colonial rule. Tilak had the backing of Lala Lajpat Rai in the Punjab and Bipin Chandra Pal in Bengal, forming what came to be known as the 'Lal-Bal-Pal triumvirate'.[29]

As a young barrister, Gandhi met with Gokhale in October 1896 when he had returned to India to publicize the problems of Indians in Natal and to take back his family. He published *The Green Pamphlet* which outlined the discrimination faced by Indians and toured Bombay, Madras, Poona and Calcutta to speak publicly on this issue. They met on 12 October 1896 in Poona. The final report of the Congress meeting stated that though many Indians were 'equally competent with the white settlers in point of wealth and ability', they were discriminated against 'for no other reason than that some of the Indians have to work as coolies'.[30]

Gandhi next met Gokhale when he returned to India in 1901 to start a law practice in Bombay. He attended a meeting of the INC in Calcutta in December 1901, where he moved a resolution in support of the rights of Indian South Africans. Gandhi was nervous about presenting the resolution and only did so with Gokhale's prompting.[31] Gandhi spent the month between January and February 1902 with Gokhale in Calcutta and Gokhale became Gandhi's political mentor. When Gokhale visited South Africa in 1912, Gandhi said at the welcome ceremony in Cape Town on 26 October, that the 'name of Mr. Gokhale was sacred to him; Mr. Gokhale was his political teacher, and whatever he had been able to do in the service of his fellow countrymen in South Africa was due to Mr. Gokhale'.[32]

Gokhale arranged for Polak to meet with lawyers, nationalist leaders, newspaper editors and industrialists, as well as address public meetings. The treatment of Indians in South Africa was given much publicity within Indian nationalist circles. According to the twenty-second Congress Report, 1906, one speaker considered it ironic that 'so long as the Indians were subjected to mistreatment by strangers, the British Government was quite prepared to protect them'. It appears Indians were better off under the Boers for 'our condition is made distinctly worse and more humiliating and all this done by our English rulers'.³³ This fed into the broader question of imperial citizenship. According to the report of the twenty-fourth INC meeting, 1909:

> Congress speakers warned of the disillusionment with Empire citizenship that would result from further insults. We have to complain of the treatment meted out to us within the British Empire, and by the limbs and bones of the same body politic – in a way by our own kith and kin! Is this condition favourable for the growth of a feeling in the Indian heart that he is a member of the same Empire and a partner in its destiny, to which some of his oppressors belong?³⁴

Pressure from Indian nationalists led to important changes in British governance of India. Fearing restlessness amongst Indian nationalists, John Morley, Secretary of State for India and Lord Minto, the Viceroy, introduced minor constitutional changes to appease younger, Western-educated leaders.³⁵ The Indian Councils Act 1909 – or the Minto-Morley Reforms – gave Indians a limited number of seats in the Legislative Council, where they could put questions and move resolutions, and had limited power over budget discussions.³⁶ On the whole, however, there was little political activity in the years from 1909 to the First World War as most of the 'extremists' were imprisoned. Moderates did little other than 'make eloquent speeches' and the treatment of Indians in South Africa was a key platform of their politics. Ray argues that after the split in the INC in 1907,

> the moderates were eager to fasten on to an issue in which they could be seen to be backing Indian interests and opposing tyranny. The indenture issue gave the opportunity for them not only to do this, but also to condone – at a safe distance – the tactics of passive resistance and active opposition to government which they were hesitant to espouse in India. Thus, throughout the first decade of the century, against the background of the Moderate-Extremist conflict; the issue of Indians in South Africa grew in importance in the Congress.³⁷

Moderates were primarily concerned about the treatment of free Indians; indentured migrants were thrown into the discussion as a bargaining chip. Ray argues that for moderate Indian politicians, indentured emigration to Natal

> was ideal for their purposes. It struck at injustice, but at enough distance not to conflict with the interests of the Government of India or bring the loyalties of those who demanded stoppage into question. It was a national issue which

had been widely publicized, but was conveniently free of any communal taint; the Muslim League and the Indian National Congress were here in agreement.[38]

The reports of the INC from 1902 onwards show that members wanted to stop indenture to punish white settlers. Indeed, the INC passed a resolution in 1905 calling on the governments of India and Britain 'to insist by prohibiting, if necessary, the emigration of indentured labour and adopting other retaliatory measures, on the recognition of the status of emigrants as British citizens in all the colonies'.[39] At the 1908 Congress, Dr U.L. Desai urged Congress to deny white settler colonies Indian labour, without which they would 'be in a hopeless mess both financially and politically, for I know what stamina these spendthrift, pleasure loving, lazy and unreasonable colonials have'.[40]

Polak in India

Polak played a critical role in popularizing the issue of indenture in middle class Indians' consciousness. He worked tirelessly, travelling from city to city holding meetings, drafting petitions, establishing contact with nationalists and helping to raise funds. The problems of Indians in South Africa and the emerging figure of Gandhi and his strategy of non-violent resistance, were given wide publicity. Meetings in Bombay and Calcutta were organized by Gokhale's Servants of India Society, which had been formed in 1905 on the basis of self-sacrifice; Gandhi's friend from London, Pranjivan Mehta, hosted Polak in Rangoon; while G.A. Natesan did likewise in Madras.

Polak met with Congress leaders such as Sir Pherozeshah Mehta and B.M. Malabari, editor of the *Indian Spectator*. It was Gokhale's Madras branch of the Servants of India Society that introduced Polak to Natesan, who organized meetings in Madras as well as in nearby towns like Tiruchi, Tuticorin and Madurai from where many indentured migrants had come to Natal. Natesan was born in 1873, graduated from Presidency College, Madras, in 1873 and started his own publishing company, G.A. Natesan & Co. in 1897. He became involved in Congress politics and the struggle for Indian independence from early on in life.[41] Aside from Polak's booklet on the problems of Indian South Africans, Natesan published a second pamphlet on the Transvaal problem, *The Tragedy of Empire: The Treatment of British Indians in the Transvaal;* distributed a biography of Gandhi penned by the Reverend J.J. Doke of Johannesburg; gave extensive coverage to the struggle in his monthly publication in English,

The Indian Review, which he started in 1900; and solicited funds from the likes of the Nizam of Hyderabad, the Maharaja of Mysore and the Maharaja of Bikaner for Gandhi and the struggle in South Africa.[42]

Polak's *The Indians of South Africa: Helots within the Empire and How They are Treated*, provided an account of the laws affecting Indians and Gandhi's passive resistance campaign, and contained extracts from speeches by Indian statesmen on the South Africa question, as well as a damning indictment of indenture itself. Polak linked the struggle in the Transvaal with the treatment of Indians in the Empire, writing that Indians there ...

> understood that upon their efforts depended whether or not this race-virus should infect the rest of South Africa and the rest of the Empire, whether India herself would not have to suffer and drink deep of the cup of humiliation. What of all this has India realized? Have the bitter cries from the Transvaal Indians penetrated to the ears of their brethren in the Motherland?[43]

Polak described the system of indenture as having

> evil effects upon Indian and European alike. Nowhere else in South Africa is the customary mental attitude of the Europeans towards the Indians so contemptuous .... The Indian contract labourer is often, to him, a being of a sub-human order ... a mere chattel, a machine, mortal, a commercial asset to be worked to its fullest capacity .... Between the master and the servant there can be no human relationship save such as may often be observed between an owner and his cattle .... Because the slave wears a gold collar round his neck and is clothed in silks or satins, he is no less a slave ....[44]

Polak's book was widely circulated in India and generated enormous anger as it highlighted in searing language the horrific treatment of workers, the social ills resulting from the shortage of women, lack of medical treatment, the extraordinarily high suicide rate, and a legal system that was weighted heavily in favour of employers. Protectors failed to provide 'protection' to workers, nor did magistrates who

> born and bred in an atmosphere of semi-slavery and tainted with the Colonial prejudice against and contempt for indentured labourer, and perhaps himself an employer of contract labour, may be a friend of the particular employer concerning whom complaint is made and who may be in a position to bring social pressure to bear .... In most cases every possible excuse is advanced for the brutality of employers accused of assault. The penalty is quite disproportionate to the offence .... Too often, it appears there is one law for the European employer and another for the Indian employee.[45]

The book detailed some of the most flagrant cases of ill-treatment of indentured workers recorded in Natal, and was the most widely circulated critique of indenture before Andrews and Pearson's 1916 account of indenture in Fiji. It is best summed up by this line: 'The life of an indentured Indian in Natal – what is it? In many instances a hell upon earth'.[46] Polak reinforced the point that by importing indentured workers, Natal was

> adding to the intensity of popular prejudice existing against all Indians all over South Africa, thus preventing the removal of disabilities weighing heavily upon the resident Indian population, and imposed only because of the fear of an Asiatic invasion drawn from this source.[47]

Aside from official commissions of inquiry, this was the first real indictment of Indian indenture. Polak urged the raising of funds for the cause in South Africa, and called for additional pressure to be put on the Indian government to end indenture and the establishment of an organization to canvass support for Indians in South Africa. Gandhi wrote in October 1909 that 'a very fine cable-report of the Bombay mass meeting appeared in the local newspapers. People's feelings were roused to a high pitch by Mr. Polak's speech'.[48] After Polak addressed a meeting in Calcutta on 10 October 1909, an Indian South African League was formed to organize support for Indians in South Africa and resolutions were passed calling on the Indian government to stop indentured labour to Natal.[49]

The INC conference of 1909

Polak addressed the twenty-fourth session of the INC conference in Lahore on 29 December 1909. Indenture was high on the agenda as the Union of South Africa Bill had been passed without guarantees for Indian, African and Coloured ('non-White') South Africans. More broadly, the treatment of the indentured raised the question of the status of Indians in the British Empire. The two dominant figures in Indian moderate politics spoke about indentured migration, ex-president Gokhale and incumbent Madan Mohan Malaviya, who would subsequently become Chancellor of Benares Hindu University from 1919 to 1940. Malaviya was concerned that the 'intensity of feeling throughout the country' would put moderates on the defensive for collaborating with the British unless they did something. He argued that the Government of India was

> bound in honour and duty to their Indian fellow subjects to take steps now to actively resent and to retaliate the treatment which is accorded to them in South

Africa. (Hear, hear.) And the least they ought to do is to withdraw all facilities for enlisting indentured labour in South Africa, until the white colonists there agree to recognize Indians as their equal fellow subjects. (Cheers.)[50]

Gokhale argued that the status of Indians abroad affected their status within India itself. While the Government of India's representations to the Transvaal government met with no success, 'happily for us the means of retaliation are in the hands of the Government of India. Natal wants Indian labour, they do not want any free Indians there. The Government of India have got to say that they have either to stand the free Indian or do without the indentured labour.'[51] Gokhale moved for a resolution calling on the Indian government to abolish indentured emigration to Natal in retaliation for the racist policies against Indians, to implore the imperial government to stop moves towards a white Union in South Africa and to raise funds for the struggle of Indians in South Africa.[52] Surendra Nath Banerjee, another high profile leader, described the Union of South Africa Act as 'unduly straining Indian loyalty', while the laws in the Transvaal were 'barbarous and savage', although 'passed by an avowedly Christian government'. Following appeals, 'extraordinary scenes followed' as 'jewels and money were thrown at his feet. Thousands of pounds have been collected for transmission to the Transvaal'.[53]

Polak's tour led to intense agitation amongst political leaders and organizations and the press in India against the treatment of Indians in the Transvaal and increasingly against indenture. Theosophist Annie Besant organized a meeting against indenture in Benares. Newspapers like *The Leader* in Allahabad, *The Advocate* in Lucknow, and the *Madras Mail* gave extensive coverage to Polak's book and lectures on the ill-treatment of Indians in South Africa.[54] Sir Sultan Muhammad Shah, the Aga Khan III, presiding at the annual session of the All-India Moslem League in Delhi in December 1909, called on the imperial government to stop indentured emigration to Natal unless the Transvaal government changed its policies towards Indians, whom he described as 'martyrs'.[55]

The Natal and Transvaal governments demonstrated no intention of changing their policies. During negotiations over Union, the only question on which Natal agreed with the Transvaal and the Orange Free State was the denial of franchise to people of colour. Natal Prime Minister F.R. Moor stated that 'the white and black races in South Africa would never be amalgamated. The history of the world proved that the black man was incapable of civilisation'.[56] The South African Union, which came into being on 31 May 1910, consolidated white hegemony.

Gokhale's resolution and the termination of indentured labour to Natal

Acting on the Congress resolution, Gokhale tabled a resolution in the Viceroy's Legislative Council on 25 February 1910 empowering the Governor-General 'to prohibit the recruitment of indentured labour in British India for the colony of Natal'.[57] Gokhale argued passionately in moving the resolution:

> The whole of the Indian problem in South Africa has arisen out of supply of indentured labour to South Africa .... A continued influx of indentured labour into South Africa, and the consequent inevitable annual additions to the ranks of the ex-indentured tends to steadily lower the whole position of the free Indian population, and the feeling of contempt with which the indentured Indian is generally regarded comes to extend itself to not only to the ex-indentured but even to traders and other Indians of independent means. The struggle of free Indians to maintain themselves becomes more and more acute by these constant additions.[58]

Gokhale underscored the high suicide rate amongst the indentured, difficulties with trading licences and the lack of educational facilities in Natal, as well as the restrictive legislation against Indians in the Transvaal, Cape Colony and Orange Free State. He described the policy of the Natal government as 'an utterly selfish and heartless one and the only way in which relief can be obtained is by the Government of India adopting a stern attitude towards the Colony in return'.[59] Gokhale argued that the threat to stop indentured labour would help to secure 'from the Natal Government fair terms generally for the Indian community resident in the Colony'. It would also force the colony to keep its African labour in the province, thus creating a labour shortage in the Transvaal whose government would have to reconsider its own attitude to Indians. Gokhale urged that the resolution be adopted as 'no single question of our time has evoked more bitter feelings throughout India ... than the continued ill-treatment of Indians in South Africa'.[60] As Ray observes, Gokhale 'was apparently more interested in the indentured labourers' potential political value than in whether they were victims of an unfair system'.[61] Even Polak, in his scathing indictment of indenture, considered the treatment of Indians in the Transvaal as the prime problem involving Indians in South Africa. He wrote:

> The writer has dealt very lengthily with the question of indentured Indian immigration into Natal, largely because he holds it to be an Imperial scandal second only in importance, in South Africa, to the treatment of the Transvaal Indians.[62]

Fourteen Indian members of the Viceroy's Legislative Council spoke in support of Gokhale's resolution which was unanimously adopted, though the system of indenture as a whole was not challenged. Sir Vithaldas Damodar Thackersey reminded members that 'no question attracted greater attention throughout the length and breadth of India than the question of the position of Indians in South Africa' and the Indian government had to act for the good of both India and the workers.[63] Mohammed Ali Jinnah, a rising star in Congress who would later join the All-India Muslim League, and lead the struggle for a separate Muslim state, was the Calcutta Council's Muslim member from Bombay. He came into conflict with Viceroy Minto when he spoke to the resolution. Jinnah said that it 'was a most painful question – a question which has roused the feelings of all classes in the country to the highest pitch of indignation and horror at the harsh and cruel treatment that is meted out to Indians in South Africa'.[64] Minto reproached Jinnah for his use of the words 'cruel treatment' which, he said, was 'too harsh to be used for a friendly part of the Empire'. Jinnah responded: 'My Lord! I should feel much inclined to use stronger language. But I am fully aware of the constitution of this Council, and I do not wish to trespass for one single moment. But I do say that the treatment meted out to Indians is the harshest and the opposition in this country is unanimous'.[65]

The resolution calling for the passing of a law that would allow the Governor-General to prohibit recruitment of indentured emigration to any colony that did not treat free Indians fairly, was passed unanimously. The India-based *The Empire* newspaper voiced regret that 'no European member seized the opportunity of identifying his community with the irresistible case for justice and reparation to the Indians in South Africa .... The impression that outsiders will naturally and inevitably derive from the reports is that the European population in this country is either indifferent or hostile to the measure ....'[66] On the other hand, in Natal, the white-owned *Natal Advertiser's* editorial of 26 February 1910 voiced disgust 'with the manner in which members of those white British governments have not hesitated to take sides with the alien inhabitants of India against their white British compatriots of South Africa'. Halting indenture would not cause whites in South Africa to 'budge one inch from the perfectly just' policies they were implementing to prevent the country being 'overrun and swamped by unlimited hordes of inferior Asiatics'.[67]

In order to terminate indentured emigration to Natal, the Indian Emigration Act of 1908 had to be amended as it only gave the Governor-General power to prohibit indentured emigration to any country if 'sufficient grounds' existed to do so. These grounds related specifically to the treatment of indentured and not free Indians. On 28 March 1910, Sir Benjamin Robertson, Member for Commerce and Industry, introduced a Bill to amend the Act to grant the Governor-General the power to stop indentured emigration 'for any reason he may consider sufficient', including the treatment of free Indians. The House adopted this motion[68] and the Bill passed its final reading in July 1910.

This went against the conclusion of the Sanderson Committee, which had been appointed in March 1909 by the Secretary of State for the Colonies to investigate indentured emigration to the colonies. It reported in June 1910 that Indians should only be allowed to indenture in colonies where they could settle in an independent capacity after completing their indentures and that reindenturing should be prohibited.[69] However, the committee did not see a problem with the indentured system in general and advocated for its continuance as the indentured could earn more in these colonies than was possible in India.[70]

The Government of India issued notification under the Indian Act XIV of 1910 prohibiting emigration to Natal with the date to be decided upon following negotiations with the Natal government.[71] An editorial in *Indian Opinion* was optimistic that stopping indenture would lower the Indian population proportionate to the white population and free Indians could thus expect 'to get the laws about passes, etc., repealed, and there will be fewer attacks on traders'.[72]

The Indian government had hoped that South Africa would liberalize its laws towards Indians to avoid the termination of indenture. However, F.R. Moor, the last prime minister of Natal, and Minister of Commerce in the Union of South Africa, at a public meeting on 23 August 1910 clarified that the government would not change its policies. He said at this meeting that 'We are not going to allow these Indians to come to this country to inundate South Africa and to have all these so-called rights granted to them because of the industries in Natal at the present time'.[73] At another meeting a few days later, he assured employers that alternative labour would be found for the coastal industries in Natal.[74]

The colonies in which the indentured had first arrived had undergone a profound shift. By the first decade of the twentieth century, whites were in the ascendency politically, economically and militarily, with the discovery of gold and diamonds and resultant changes in the colonial economies and global markets, making this part of the world important to Western economies. The result was the passing, with British approval, of various taxes and restrictive land legislation that forced Africans onto the labour market. This included legislation that prevented Africans from settling in urban areas and the Land Act of 1913 that reserved around thirteen per cent of the land for over eighty per cent of the population. Desperate for work to pay taxes and unable to move to the cities,

Africans were forced to work on farms and mines.⁷⁵ Many of the workers in Natal came from Pondoland and those in the Transvaal from Mozambique, underscoring the multidirectional and transnational connections of what was in effect a global migrant labour system.

On 3 January 1911 it was announced that 'in the absence of any guarantee that the Indians will be accepted as permanent citizens of the South African Union after the expiration of their indentures', the Governor-General in Council would introduce a notice on 1 April prohibiting further emigration of indentured labour to Natal from 1 July 1911. On 4 January 1911, Lord Harcourt, Secretary of State for the Colonies, relayed the message to Lord Gladstone, the Governor-General of South Africa.⁷⁶ The announcement evoked 'a feeling of sincere satisfaction' in Gokhale, who saw it as proof that the Indian government would not hesitate to 'take decisive action for the furtherance of their interests, even though it should inflict some injury on a British Colony'.⁷⁷

Indian Opinion welcomed the decision for wherever in a 'foreign land, the coolie exists, there all Indians must surely be dragged down, politically, socially and economically, to the "coolie" level. All are "coolies" alike'.⁷⁸ The end of indenture would thus raise the status of the free Indian population. The NIC convened a public meeting on 7 January 1911, where Chairman Dawud Mahomed said that they had gathered to rejoice because 'our Motherland has made it plain that she will no longer submit to the intolerable indignities that our European fellow-colonists have attempted to impose upon us.' Indians could, 'for the first time, look whites squarely in the face, firm in the knowledge that henceforth we are free men, untainted with the poison of a slavish environment.'⁷⁹ The NIC submitted a memorial to the Secretary of State for the Colonies on 15 May 1911 offering the 'respectful thanks of the British Indian community of Natal' for the 'decision to stop the supply of indentured labour to Natal'. It also expressed hope that the treatment of free Indians would improve because 'most of the troubles that British Indians throughout South Africa have had to undergo have been largely due to an artificial increase in the Indian population of South Africa, brought about by the introduction of this class of labour'.⁸⁰

The white-owned *Natal Mercury* (4 January 1911) provided a sober reminder that 'public opinion in South Africa is strongly opposed to the free admission of Asiatics' and, with the exception of employers of indentured labour, most whites welcomed the stoppage of indenture.⁸¹

Polak spent a few months at Gandhi's Phoenix Settlement when he returned from India. He wrote to the *Natal Mercury* that all 'self-respecting Indians in South Africa' would 'heartily rejoice' at the Indian government's decision. They regarded the action 'to be in the nature of a Nemesis for the injustices that have been practiced everywhere in South Africa against them'. Whites who were concerned about industries in Natal, 'should have thought of this before they took up the pleasant pastime of Indian-baiting.'[82] Polak left Natal at the end of April 1911. At a farewell reception for him at the Union Theatre in Durban, NIC chairman Dawud Mahomed commended Polak whose 'self-sacrifice and marvellous zeal in their cause had stirred the hearts of the Indian people'. The NIC presented him with a commendation that read:

> Your admirable and useful work in India on behalf of the Indians in South Africa, and especially the procuring of the stoppage of the recruitment of Indian servile labour for Natal, in which you were so largely instrumental, will ever remain bright in our memories, nor do we think that our Motherland, for whose honour your task was undertaken, will be unmindful of it.[83]

Gandhi himself noted that Polak had 'no other interests apart from the problem of South African Indians .... If the Indian community produced a number of persons like him, India would be free soon. In doing his own duty, Mr. Polak has served to remind us of our duty'.[84] He raised over one lakh of rupees (100,000) for passive resisters.[85]

The end of indentured emigration to South Africa

The treatment of Indians in South Africa aroused great anger in India and withholding indenture was seen as a means of 'punishing' white South Africa. Indian nationalists questioned how they could be patriotic to an empire in which they were politically subordinated.[86] Indians in South Africa believed that the termination of indenture would reduce the Indian population as a proportion of the total population, and thus resolve the Indian question because whites would no longer view Indians as a demographic threat. But as McKeown points out, across the Empire, 'race and the ideal of self-government had worked together to make the national community more attractive than empire as a form of political membership in a modern world of free migration'.[87] The result was that more legislation would be passed that would make the conditions of Indians even more intolerable across the Empire. This theme is developed more fully in Marina Martin's excellent chapter in this volume on how the identity of Indian migrants in South Africa was shaped by the changing dynamics between the 'metropole' and the colonial settler peripheries.

The years following the end of indentured emigration to Natal would also see pressure ramped up to suppress indenture in its entirety. In fact, it became a central platform of nationalist rhetoric. Once more, Polak was at the heart of the agitation, as he undertook another tour of India from December 1911 to September 1912. At an INC meeting in Calcutta on 26 December 1911, which was attended by Polak and Sorabji Shapurji of the Transvaal, a resolution was passed: 'Whilst thanking the Government of India for the prohibition of indentured Indian labour for South Africa, this Congress is strongly of opinion that, in the highest national interests, the system of indenture is undesirable and should be abolished ....'[88] Polak also addressed the Seventh Indian Industrial Conference in Calcutta on 29 December 1911, where president M.B. Dadabhoy of Nagpore stated that indenture should be stopped because 'the Indian is not wanted by white colonists except as a cooly. It is far better, far more dignified, to sweat at home than to drudge abroad'. A resolution proposed by N. Subba Rao was passed unanimously: 'in the highest interest of the country, the system of Indian indentured labour is undesirable and should be abolished'.[89]

In the Imperial Legislative Council debate on 4 March 1912, Gokhale showed the transformation in his own thinking as he came to see indenture as inherently bad and introduced a resolution to terminate it altogether. He argued this time that indentured emigration resulted in 'national degradation .... Wherever that system prevailed the Indian, no matter what his position, was a mere coolie'. Gokhale therefore introduced a resolution to terminate indenture entirely:

> Two years ago this Council adopted a Resolution recommending that the Governor-General should obtain powers to prohibit the recruitment of indentured labour in this country for the Colony of Natal .... It is true that the Resolution of two years ago was adopted by this Council principally as a measure of retaliation rendered necessary by the continued indignities and ill-treatment to which our countrymen were subjected in South Africa .... I respectfully invite the Council today to go a step further and recommend that the system of indentured labour should now be abolished altogether.[90]

Pandit Madan Mohan Malaviya, another longstanding critic of indenture, considered it 'a matter of deep shame and pain that any one of them, man or woman, should be subjected to those indignities and cruelties which have been heaped upon Indians in many of these colonies'. The system, he said,

> cannot be mended, the best thing is that it should be ended, and that without delay .... What will the whole world avail the emigrant if he lost his soul by going to those lands? He is subjected to moral degradation; he is subjected to national

degradation; he is utterly demoralised, placed under conditions in which he has to live a life of sin and shame; whilst he ceases to be a free man and virtually becomes a slave – a slave of the worst type? .... The evil lies in the system being what it is, and the remedy lies in its total abolition.[91]

Sir Gangadhar Rao Chitnavis said that 'on account of this system India has fallen in the estimation of the civilized world .... Times have changed and we now ask why India, alone among all the countries of the world, should be subjected to this indignity'.[92] Mazharul Haque warned that 'the people of India feel very keenly about it (indenture). They think they are disgraced in the eyes of other countries inasmuch as India is the only country which supplies indentured labour. It is certainly nothing else but a very bad form of slavery'.[93]

Despite these fervent attacks, the white members of the Imperial Council saw little that was wrong with indenture. Typical was the Honourable Mr Clarke who asked, 'what degradation was it to an Indian labourer to do agricultural work in a Colony, the same kind of work he had in his own country'. He did not think it a 'great hardship that when a coolie refused to work he should be punished'. For Clark, indentured labour 'opened out to the more adventurous spirits a new life in a new land where they might hope to attain a state which they could never hope to attain in their own country'.[94] The resolution was rejected, twenty-two voting for and thirty-three against, but Gokhale was adamant that it would

> not be the end of the matter. This motion will be brought forward again and again, till we carry it to a successful issue. It affects our national self-respect, and therefore the sooner the Government recognize the necessity of accepting it, the better it will be for all parties.[95]

The Indian press was 'indignant' at the rejection of Gokhale's resolution. The *Indian Social Reformer* stated that Clarke 'enlarged at such length and with so much eloquence on the blessings enjoyed by the indentured labourers that it might almost seem that the Honourable Member, had he not been condemned by an unkind fate to be a member of the Government of India, would himself have preferred to be an indentured labourer'.[96] An editorial in *The Leader* of Allahabad stated that Gokhale 'was simply overwhelming .... The impression left in our mind by the debate and the voting is that indentured labour is doomed .... The whole of India object with one voice. All this points to but one conclusion. The system ought to go, it must go, it will go'.[97]

Following the debate in the Legislative Council, Polak toured the East Coast of Madras, visiting places like Berhampore, Vizianagram, Vizagapatam, Ellore, Masulipatam, Guntur, Coconada, Rajahmundry and Bezwada between 7 and

15 March 1912, and receiving 'a most cordial reception, and resolutions were passed condemning the treatment of South African Indians, calling on the government for redress, and condemning the system of indentured recruitment and requiring its abolition'.[98] On 26 March 1912, Polak addressed a meeting convened by the Indian South African League at the YMCA Auditorium, Madras where other speakers included Natesan and V.S. Srinivasa Sastri, who would be appointed in 1927 as the first Indian Agent-General to South Africa. Natesan moved a resolution 'deeply regret[ting] the rejection of the Hon'ble Mr. Gokhale's resolution' and being 'emphatically of opinion that the system of indentured recruitment is opposed to the best interests of the Indian people, and requests the Government to take early steps to give effect to the strong feeling on the subject aroused throughout the country'.[99]

The move to terminate indenture continued to gather momentum. Polak attended the sixth United Provinces Provincial Conference at Cawnpore on 5 April 1912, which also passed a resolution calling for the 'total abolition of indentured labour at [as] early a date as possible ... in the highest national interests'.[100] He was at the Madras Provincial Conference held at Kumbakonam on 9 May 1912 where a resolution was passed that 'the indenture system of recruiting labour in India for British Colonies has resulted in untold misery and suffering to the labourers and is injurious to the self-respect of the Indian people [and] has provoked universal indignation in the country'.[101] At the Vizapatam District Conference on 27 May 1912, in Polak's presence, C.Y. Chintamani called

> for the total abolition of the indenture system, which does not differ much from what was more plainly called slavery in a less civilised age. .... We, the educated Indians, who speak not merely for ourselves but for our inarticulate countrymen, [must] keep up an active agitation against the system, agitation to which fresh life was imparted by my friend, Mr. Polak, to whom you rightly accorded a warm reception in this hall.[102]

Notwithstanding widespread condemnation of indenture, Edwin Montagu, the Under-Secretary of State for India, stated in the House of Commons on 22 July 1912 that the government had no intention of stopping indentured immigration 'and thereby to inflict serious injury on Crown colonies and at the same time to debar British Indian subjects from employment overseas'.[103] Following a meeting in Bombay on 31 July, where 'leading Indians were present', a memorial was submitted to the Governor-in-Council, Simla, dated 1 August 1912, which stated on the question of indenture: 'The conscience of India protests against the maintenance of a system that demoralizes its victims, that embodies an economic and social injury both to India and to the countries that avail themselves of this semi-servile labour, and that lowers Indian prestige in the eyes of the civilised world'.[104]

Having aroused national indignation, Polak returned to Natal on 4 September 1912. He was met at the Port of Natal by leading officials of the NIC, whose president, Abdul Karim Haji Adam thanked him on behalf of Indians; and Polak and his wife Millie were garlanded by Parsee Rustomjee, while Ambaram Maharaj recited a poem honouring Polak. Forty telegrams of thanks were received from Indian organizations across the country. The Polaks stayed with another NIC member Ismail H. Moosa, on the Berea.[105] The *Indian Opinion* editorialized that:

> Mr Polak, by his tact, ability and perseverance, has been able to rouse public opinion in India in such a manner that probably there is no question which occupies so much attention and commands such unanimous advocacy as the South African Indian. His persistent effort has enabled the Honourable Mr. Gokhale to achieve the brilliant result he did on the Indian question. His advocacy filled the exhausted passive resistance chest and, thanks to his unremitting zeal, the Government of India is posted up with the fullest particulars of our grievances.[106]

End of indentureship

Although Gokhale's resolution had been defeated, nationalists in India continued to agitate against indenture. As Ray points out,

> In the India of the teens the system was universally damned – by Indian politicians and the British Government; by the "Westernized" Parsis of Bombay and the orthodox Marwaris of Calcutta; by Hindus and Muslims, "Moderàtes" and "Extremists", rajas and village spokesmen. The issue of Indian indentured emigration was almost the only point on which Indian politicians and their patrons were agreed.[107]

Nationalist agitation was helped by increased condemnation of indenture from the colonies themselves. Ms H. Dudley, a pioneer missionary in Suva, Fiji, wrote a lengthy letter to the magazine *India* on 4 November 1912, highlighting the social evils caused by the paucity of women, which ranged from the murder of women, to prostitution, and called on the editor 'not to cease to use your influence against this iniquitous system till it be utterly abolished'.[108] Religious and cultural organizations such as the Arya Samaj in Uttar Pradesh, and the Marwaris in Calcutta, who formed an 'Indenture Cooly Protection Society', began circulating pamphlets and holding public lectures against indentured emigration from 1914.[109] A major coup for the Indenture Cooly Protection Society was securing the support of an indentured migrant, Totaram Sanadhya, who had spent twenty-one years in Fiji before returning to India in 1914 and publishing a book, *Fiji Dwip Me Mere Ikkish Varsh*, chronicling abuses in the system.

In most of these discourses, women were central, being 'constructed as both innocent victims and guilty migrants, insiders and outsiders'.[110] A powerful story was that of Kunti, who claimed to be raped by a white overseer and whose story was published in 1913. Kunti returned to India in 1914 and canvassed against indenture on behalf of the Indenture Cooly Protection Society.[111] Gupta observes that the figure of the indentured woman gave the campaign to end indenture 'an ethical edge, whereby stereotypes of morality, sexuality, national honour, sisterhood and exploitation could be promulgated in print and press'.[112] Reports on the treatment of free Indian labour in Ceylon and Malaysia, and indentured labour in Fiji,[113] were seized upon by nationalists 'as further evidence of the inability of the British Imperial Government to take care of its subjects properly'.[114]

The Government of India was aware of the nationwide anger against indenture but, as Riyad Koya also shows in this volume, 'abolition as such was never effected'. Instead, World War One resulted in indenture being terminated by default in March 1917 because of the military and labour needs of the British. The Secretary of State for the Colonies sent a message to the Government of India on 10 March 1917 that recruitment for indenture was illegal under the Indian Defence Act since labour was needed in India itself, and on 17 March 1917, the (Indian) Imperial Legislative Council gazetted that the movement of people out of India for unskilled work was suspended for the duration of the war and for two years thereafter. That, effectively, was the end of indentured emigration even though the system only officially ended on 1 January 1920 as a result of nationalists' pressure in India.

Conclusion

Pressure to end indentured labour migration to British colonies increased with the rise of Indian nationalism in the early twentieth century. Natal was an exception to the general pattern. The treatment of free Indians in South

Africa provoked great anger in India, in part because of Gandhi's links to prominent Indian nationalists and the publicity generated in India by his satyagraha campaigns. Indian nationalists hoped that stopping the supply of indentured labour would reduce the overall Indian population in South Africa and change white policies towards Indians. Thus, the treatment of the free Indian population, rather than that of indentured Indians, was what initially prompted agitation against indenture. An individual who was arguably more directly active than Gandhi in India on the indenture question was Polak, his able lieutenant. Polak had two long stints in India. His 1909 tour of India was critical in rallying sentiment on the Indian question in South Africa, which was instrumental in ending indentured emigration to South Africa in 1911, while his 1911/1912 tour led to consensus among Indian nationalists and large segments of the educated middle classes that the indentured system as a whole should be scrapped. This chapter highlighted Polak's overlooked role in these processes while also examining the nuanced reasons for various stakeholders wanting to end indentured emigration to South Africa. In the South African case, the white minority government itself had arranged alternative African labour supplies and so was pleased to end Indian labour migration, despite protests from sugar planters. Indenture did not end immediately following Polak's tour of 1912 because of the (British) Indian government's insistence that the economies of the colonies should not be threatened. The system eventually ended because of the wartime needs of the British.

Notes

1 Radhika Mongia, *Indian Migration and Empire. Colonial Genealogy of the Modern State* (Durham: Duke University Press, 2018), 26.
2 Ibid., 55.
3 See Radhika Mongia, 'Impartial Regimes of Truth', *Cultural Studies* 18, no. 5 (2004): 749–768.
4 Ashutosh Kumar, 'Songs of Abolition: The Anti-Indenture Campaign in North Indian Public sphere', in *Indian Diaspora. Socio-Cultural and Religious Worlds*, ed. P. Pratab Kumar (Leiden: Brill, 2015), 38.
5 K. Atkins, 'The Cultural Origins of an African Work Ethic and Practices: Natal, South Africa 1843–75' (Madison: University of Wisconsin Press, 1986).
6 M. Tayal, 'Indian Indentured labour in Natal, 1860–1911', *Indian Economic and Social History Review* XIV, no. 4 (1977): 519–549.

7   Ashwin Desai and Goolam Vahed, *Inside Indian Indenture. A South African Story 1860-1911* (Cape Town: HSRC Press, 2010).
8   Goolam Vahed and Surendra Bhana, *Crossing Space and Time in the Indian Ocean: Early Indian Traders in Natal – A Biographical Study* (Pretoria: UNISA Press, 2015), 23-40.
9   Adam M. McKeown, *Melancholy Order. Asian Migration and the Globalization of Borders* (New York: Columbia University Press, 2011), 75.
10 Maureen Swan, *Gandhi. The South African Experience* (Johannesburg: Ravan Press, 1985), 51.
11 L.E. Neame, *The Asiatic Danger in the Colonies* (London: George Routledge & Sons, 1907), 59-60.
12 C. Headlam, *The Milner Years. South Africa 1899-1905, Volume 2* (London: Cassel, 1933), 175.
13 Mongia, *Indian Migration and Empire*, 110.
14 Ibid., 143.
15 Mohandas K. Gandhi, *Collected Works of Mahatma Gandhi*. 98 volumes. Electronic Book (New Delhi: Publications Division, Government of India, 1999), vol. 6, 141.
16 *The Register*, 3 January 1908.
17 *Indian Opinion*, 1 February 1908.
18 Ashwin Desai and Goolam Vahed, *The South African Gandhi. Stretcher-Bearer of Empire* (New Delhi: Navayana and Stanford: Stanford University Press, 2016), 119-133.
19 See Sukanya Banerjee, *Becoming Imperial Citizens: Indians in the Late-Victorian Empire* (Durham: Duke, 2010).
20 Radica Mahase, '"Abolish Indenture" and the Indian Nationalist discourse in the Early 20th Century', in *Historical Diversities. Societies, Politics and Cultures. Essays for V.N. Datta*, eds. Kundun Tuteja and Sunitha Pathania (Delhi: Manohar, 2008, 1-21), 12.
21 H.S.L. Polak, 'South African Reminiscences', *Indian Review* (October 1926): 621-30, 622.
22 Barbara D. Metcalf and Thomas R. Metcalf, *A Concise History of Modern India* (Cambridge, UK: Cambridge University Press, 2001), 135.
23 Ramachandra Guha, *Makers of Modern India* (New Delhi: Penguin Books India, 2010), 98.
24 Karen A. Ray, 'The Abolition of Indentured Emigration and the Politics of Indian Nationalism, 1894-1917', D. Phil diss., Department of History, McGill University, 1980, 37.
25 Ibid.
26 Metcalf and Metcalf, *A Concise History of Modern India*, 137.

27 Sumit Sarkar, *Modern India, 1885–1947* (Delhi: Macmillan, 1983), 106.
28 Ibid., 127.
29 Metcalf and Metcalf, *A Concise History of Modern India*, 150.
30 Ray, 'The Abolition of Indentured Emigration', 25.
31 Radhey Sharma Verma, 'Gophal Krishna Gokhale and his contribution to the struggle for People of Indian Origin in South Africa', *Proceedings of the Indian History Congress*, 70 (2009/2010): 863.
32 *India Opinion*, 2 November 1912.
33 Ray, 'The Abolition of Indentured Emigration', 28.
34 Ibid., 29.
35 Bridglal Pachai, *The International Aspects of the South African Indian Question, 1860–1971* (Cape Town: C. Struik, 1971), 24.
36 Sumit Sarkar, *Modern India, 1885–1947* (London: Macmillan, 1983), 139.
37 Ray, 'The Abolition of Indentured Emigration', 31.
38 Ibid., 58.
39 *Indian Opinion*, 6 January 1906.
40 Ray, 'The Abolition of Indentured Emigration', 34.
41 See Prabha Ravi Shankar, *G.A. Natesan and National Awakening* (Bibliophile South Asia, 2015).
42 Gandhi, *Collected Works*, vol. 11, 189.
43 H.S.L. Polak, *The Indians of South Africa. Helots Within the Empire and How They are Treated* (Madras: G.A. Natesan & Co., 1909), 21.
44 Ibid., 22–23.
45 Ibid., 30, 36.
46 Ibid., 43.
47 Ibid., 54.
48 *Indian Opinion*, 16 October 1909.
49 Shankar, *Natesan*, 177.
50 in Ray 'The abolition of indentured emigration', 37.
51 Ibid., 39.
52 Pachai, *South African Indian Question*, 54.
53 *The Mercury* [Hobart, Tasmania], 1 January 1910.
54 Ray, 'The abolition of indentured emigration', 50–52.
55 *Indian Opinion*, 5 February 1910.
56 in E.H. Brookes and C. de B Webb, *A History of Natal* (Pietermaritzburg: University of Natal Press, 1965), 240.
57 *Indian Opinion*, 9 April 1910.
58 Ibid.
59 Ibid.
60 Sanjeev Sabhlok, 'Gokhale's finest hour: persuading the British to abolish indentured labour, 1910–12', 16 May 2015. Available online: http://www.

sabhlokcity.com/2015/05/gokhales-finest-hour-persuading-the-british-to-abolish-indentured-labour-1911/ (accessed 11 April 2017).
61 Ray, 'The Abolition of Indentured Emigration', 59.
62 Polak, *The Indians of South Africa*, 61.
63 *Indian Opinion*, 16 April 1910.
64 Stanley Wolpert, *Jinnah of Pakistan* (Oxford: Oxford University Press, 1984), 33.
65 Ibid.
66 *Indian Opinion*, 23 April 1910.
67 in *Indian Opinion*, 5 March 1910.
68 in *Indian Opinion*, 14 May 1910.
69 *Indian Opinion*, 23 July 1910.
70 Mahase, '"Abolish Indenture"', 10.
71 Brookes and Webb, *History of Natal*, 286.
72 *Indian Opinion*, 2 April 1910.
73 *Indian Opinion*, 27 August 1910.
74 *Indian Opinion*, 3 September 1910.
75 An excellent work that highlights the plight of Africans under white minority rule in South Africa is Sol T. Plaatje's *Native Life in South Africa* (Johannesburg: Ravan Press, 1995. Original 1916). Plaatje was one of the finest South African journalists of the time and an African National Congress (ANC) leader who, in this volume, records the effects of the Land Act on African peoples and his failed visit to England to obtain redress from the British imperial government.
76 National Archives Repository (South Africa), Government Gazette (GG) 88, 15/89, January to May 1911.
77 *Indian Opinion*, 11 February 1911.
78 *Indian Opinion*, 25 February 1911.
79 *Indian Opinion*, 14 January 1911.
80 Gandhi, *Collected Works*, vol. 11, 403–04.
81 *Natal Mercury*, 4 January 1911.
82 *Indian Opinion*, 7 January 1911; republished *Indian Opinion*, 14 January 1911.
83 *Indian Opinion*, 6 May 1911.
84 *Indian Opinion*, 1 July 1911.
85 Shankar, *Natesan*, 187.
86 Mahase, '"Abolish Indenture"', 12.
87 Adam M. McKeown, *Melancholy Order. Asian Migration and the Globalization of Borders* (Columbia: Columbia University Press, 2011), 212.
88 *Indian Opinion*, 17 February 1912.
89 *Indian Opinion*, 24 February 1912.
90 *Indian Opinion*, 13 April 1912.
91 Ibid.
92 *Indian Opinion*, 8 June 1912.

93 *Indian Opinion*, 15 June 1912.
94 *Indian Opinion*, 13 April 1912.
95 K.G. Gokhale, *Speeches and Writings of Gopal Krishna Gokhale*, eds. R.P. Patwardhan and D.V. Ambekar (New Delhi: Asia Publishing House, 1962), 350, 358.
96 *Indian Opinion*, 20 April 1912.
97 *The Leader*, 5 March 1912.
98 *Indian Opinion*, 11 May 1912.
99 *Indian Opinion*, 5 June 1912.
100 *Indian Opinion*, 25 May 1912.
101 *Indian Opinion*, 3 August 1912.
102 Ibid.
103 *Indian Opinion*, 28 September 1912.
104 *Indian Opinion*, 19 October 1912.
105 *Indian Opinion*, 14 September 1912.
106 *Indian Opinion*, 7 September 1912.
107 Ray, 'The Abolition of Indentured Emigration', 1.
108 *Indian Opinion*, 18 January 1912.
109 Kumar, 'Songs of Abolition', 39.
110 Charu Gupta, '"Innocent" Victims/"Guilty" Migrants: Hindi Public Sphere, Caste and Indentured Women in Colonial North India', *Modern Asian Studies* 49 no. 5 (2015): 1345–1377, 1345.
111 Ibid., 1345.
112 Charu Gupta, 'Saving "Wronged" Bodies: Caste, Indentured Women And Hindi Print-Public Sphere In Colonial India', *Proceedings of the Indian History Congress* 75 (2014): 716–722, 716.
113 C.F. Andrews and W.W. Pearson, *Report on Indentured Labour in Fiji: An Independent Enquiry* (Calcutta: Star Printing Works, 1916).
114 Mahase, '"Abolish Indenture"', 15.

2

Imperial labour: Labour, security and the depoliticization of oil production in the Arabian Peninsula

Andrea Wright

In June 1932, workers at the Bahrain Petroleum Company (BAPCO) discovered oil in Bahrain, at what is today known as the Awali oilfield.[1] The discovery of oil at Awali was the first time oil was found in one of the countries of the Arabic-speaking Gulf. This find by BAPCO, a Canadian subsidiary of the American-owned Standard Oil of California (SoCal), came seven years after the Sheikh of Bahrain granted the first oil concession. It also came days after SoCal sold half of its shares of BAPCO to Texaco, another American oil company. Today, forty per cent of the world's proven oil reserves are located in the Arabic-speaking Gulf and almost one-quarter of the oil consumed annually comes from Bahrain, Kuwait, Qatar, Oman, Saudi Arabia and the United Arab Emirates.[2] The consequences of oil production in the Arabic-speaking Gulf have impacted politics, social life and economics in the Gulf, and continue to have reverberations throughout the Arabian Sea and, indeed, the world.

Almost six years after oil was discovered in Bahrain, the workers at the Awali oilfield held their first organized strikes.[3] The fact that workers went on strike in order to agitate for better working conditions is not surprising. What is surprising is that these strikes involved a coalition of workers that included Bahrainis, other Arab workers and Indians. After Bahrainis, British Indians were the largest nationality working at BAPCO. The 352 British Indians at BAPCO comprised thirteen per cent of BAPCO's workforce and outnumbered all Americans, Canadians and British workers combined.[4] These Indians in Bahrain were just a few of the increasing numbers of Indians working in the Gulf and, by 1950, approximately 15,000 Indians worked in oil and related industries in the Arabic-speaking Gulf.[5] Even more surprising is that worker strikes to effect change in their working conditions today are extremely rare. In Dubai on 10 March 2015, a few hundred South Asian construction workers took to the streets to protest their working conditions. Within hours, the Dubai police issued a statement that the workers had returned to work. This chapter examines the processes that have led such large numbers of South Asians to work as labourers in the Gulf historically and today, and labourers' precarious position in the Gulf. The reason for this is often attributed to an economic model of scarcity and surplus: the Gulf has a surplus of oil and a scarcity of workers, and South Asia has a surplus of workers but a scarcity of jobs. In contrast, I argue that colonial labour mobilities, racialized hierarchies and attempts to evacuate politics from the oilfields all contributed to the large numbers of South Asians working in the Gulf.

Over the course of the twentieth century, Middle Eastern oil became increasingly associated with 'national security'. In attempts to secure Britain's rights to Gulf oil and control over oil production, oil companies and the British administration in the Gulf mobilized the apparatuses used to move Indian indentured labour in the nineteenth century in order to move contract labour from India to the Gulf's oilfields in the twentieth century. In her investigation into the connections between colonialism, slavery, liberalism and trade, Lisa Lowe shows how the colonial logics of labour were shaped by colonial subjugation, liberal philosophy and racialized divisions of humanity. Central to colonial governance and the moves from slavery to indenture to contract labour were the contradictory tensions between the liberal ideology of 'free' labour and the racial categorizations that characterized some peoples as 'unfit for liberty'.[6] According to Lowe, with the 1807 Slave Trade Act, 'the category of "freedom" was central to the development of what we could call a modern racial governmentality in which a political, economic, and social hierarchies ranging from "free" to "unfree" was deployed in the management of diverse labors of metropolitan and colonized people'.[7] Liberal ideologies and racialized hierarchies worked in conjunction with the techniques and technologies developed to regulate colonial migration. These techniques and technologies informed contemporary understandings of individual liberty, and, as Radhika Mongia demonstrates, the signing of contracts becomes 'the definitive element of "freedom"'.[8] This chapter traces these colonial logics into the twentieth and twenty-first centuries and attends to the central role of colonial infrastructure in shaping contemporary labour precarity. In the case of migrant labour to the Gulf, the interplay of labour, security and imperialism elucidates the enduring legacy of these apparatuses in shaping the necropolitics of contemporary neoliberal security regimes.

Oil security

One factor in the connection between oil and security may be traced to the early twentieth century when militaries shifted from coal to oil power. For the British, Winston Churchill's decision in 1911 to use oil to power the British navy revitalized the British navy, increased Britain's dependence on oil and led to deep connections between oil and the military.[9] During the first half of the twentieth century the British government had a controlling stake in many of the oil companies operating in the Gulf, but their interest in the Gulf was largely strategic. As Britain was not the only country interested in the Gulf's oil reserves, the British felt their oil interests were threatened by both the American and Russian governments' oil projects in the region. Pan-Arab movements argued for an end to British colonialism; and hostile foreign powers attempted to halt oil production as a means of harming British military capacities.

While the British held oil concessions for the majority of the Gulf, with the exception of Saudi Arabia, foreign oil companies continued to try and make inroads into the Gulf's oil industry. In the 1920s, two American companies gained oil concessions in the Gulf. Profiting from the fact that they, unlike many of the other oil companies in the Middle East, had not signed the Red Line Agreement, the Gulf Oil Corporation of Pennsylvania (Gulf) and the Standard Oil Company of California (SoCal) were able to negotiate concessions in Bahrain and Saudi Arabia.[10] In Kuwait, in 1934, joint concessions were negotiated by the Anglo-Persian Oil Company and Gulf. British administrators had mixed feelings on the involvement of American oil companies in the Gulf and wanted to stop Americans from moving farther south into the Gulf. To prevent additional American involvement in the Gulf, in the 1930s the British administration there advised Gulf rulers to give concessions to British instead of American oil companies. In addition, the British government 'actively supported' companies that had partial British ownership by, for example, providing manpower, as oil companies vied for oil concessions in the Trucial Coast and Oman.[11] Another way the British administration attempted to curb American influence was by insisting that British subjects, including persons from British India, staffed oil projects. The circulation of British managers throughout the Empire meant that many of the British managers of oil companies had begun their careers in British India before moving across the Arabian Sea.[12] In addition, Indians had experience working in oil and developing British oil projects, including Burmah Oil, where 6,000 Indians were employed in 1904.[13]

The British administration's efforts to control who worked on Gulf oil projects and who owned oil companies operating in the region reflects Britain's interest in the Gulf as a strategic 'buffer zone' protecting colonial India.[14] As emphasis was on this strategic importance, from 1933 to 1945 the British colonial administration showed little interest in worker strikes, and the treaties they had signed with the Gulf rulers detailed that the Gulf rulers ran the internal workings of their sheikdoms. Strikes did occur during this period, and a broad coalition of workers of differing religions, nationalities and ethnicities participated. For example, the strikes at the Awali oilfield in Bahrain in 1938 were inspired by ideas of Arab nationalism that were 'spreading across the increasingly well-educated Bahraini population, and reform movements [that] were emerging in Kuwait and Dubai'.[15] These strikes were not only by Sunni and Shi'a Bahrainis but also involved Indians; together, the strikers sought equal pay for Bahrainis and Indians. Some of their demands were met, but not that of equal pay. There was another strike in 1943 that did more to further worker demands.[16] While disruptive to oil production, these strikes garnered relatively little colonial attention as compared to strikes in the 1950s and 1960s.

The British administration's focus shifted from the strategic value of the Arabic-speaking Gulf to its potential as a source of oil in the late 1940s and early 1950s. During that period, Iran briefly nationalized its oil industry and many of the Arabic-speaking Gulf States began exporting oil in larger quantities.[17] Strikes were, at times, costly for oil companies. Concerns over labour agitations came to the fore in 1951, when British oil assets in Iran were nationalized. This nationalization was spurred in no small part by the worker strikes at the oil refinery at Abadan. After Iran's nationalization of the oil industry, British oil companies and government officials showed an interest in acquiring a workforce that could be controlled or replaced. For example, while Indians participated in collective action at Abadan, those who went on strike or organized politically were easily deported and new workers hired.[18] Because, from the late 1940s through the early 1970s, oil company managers could replace Indian and Pakistani employees who disrupted worksites, workers from these countries came to be increasingly hired for unskilled or semi-skilled positions.

Colonial apparatuses

The hiring of workers from the subcontinent was not simply because of the manpower needs of the oil industry and the dictates of colonial authorities.

Rather, the ease with which unruly workers were fired and new workers hired by oil companies was due to, what one British intelligence officer described as, the 'labour recruiting organisation in India'.[19] This recruiting organization was instrumental in mobilizing thousands of Indians for work in the Gulf and was composed of government representatives, oil company recruiters and local recruiters. This organization is structurally the same as that which today moves Indians to the Gulf. While useful for the oil industry, this organization was not developed first by oil company managers, but by the British colonial government in India to move indentured labourers during the nineteenth century. Beginning in the 1830s, the British Raj enacted emigration policies as a means to manage the movement of indentured labourers out of India. Indentured labour was important for the provision of labour throughout the British colonies after the 1807 Slave Trade Act, the 1833 Slavery Abolition Act and the eventual banning of slavery in territories held by the British East India Company in 1843. From the 1830s onwards, India was one of the largest sources of indentured labour in the world.[20] As chapters in this volume by Goolam Vahed, Ashutosh Kumar and Riyad Koya demonstrate, the movement of indentured workers provides insight into how concepts, such as freedom, rights and labour, were shaped in a global context.

As the indenture labour system was implemented to supply labour throughout the British Empire, British officials required that indentured labourers sign contracts as a means of ensuring that indenture was not slavery. Concerns quickly arose around the issue of consent and whether indentured labourers were able to consent to the terms of their contracts. Particularly, both British government officials and the British public worried that those who were hiring indentured labourers were not honest about the working conditions labourers would face. In addition, it was believed that extreme poverty restricted individuals' options; for example, during times of famine, there was a marked increase in the number of people taking work as indentured workers. Finally, once indentured workers left India, they often had constraints on their ability to return at the end of their contracts, and it was not uncommon for plantation owners to refuse to pay for their return passage to India.

In an attempt to ensure that indentured labour was not a new form of slavery, the British colonial government in India institutionalized a bureaucratic structure called the Protector of Emigrants. The Protector of Emigrants was set up to ensure that migrants were not coerced and were healthy and treated fairly in their destination country.[21] The Protector of Emigrants was also to oversee recruiting agents; those who facilitated the emigration of Indians as indentured labourers throughout the British colonial empire. These agents were often British businessmen based in port cities who worked with Indian subagents based in the interior of India. The recruiters were overseen by 'protectors' who were responsible to the British colonial authorities for the welfare of migrants. The Protector of Emigrants system was enacted with an underlying assumption that more laws would result in better conditions for indentured labourers but this was not necessarily the case. As Mahdavi Kale's work on indenture shows, colonial planters and metropole capitalists argued that there were labour shortages after the abolishment of slavery and pressured British Parliament to relax labour policies. By the 1840s, few protections for 'freed peoples' rights and liberties' remained.[22] In this context indenture was an 'imperial labour reallocation strategy' and 'a site where hierarchies of empire were enunciated, contested and inscribed'.[23] Similarly to the colonial regulations against slavery that Johan Mathew explores, the Protector of Emigrants system focused on the transaction of indentured labour, rather than the conditions of labour.[24]

In 1917, due to pressure from Indian nationalists, indentured labour ended. At this time, the British colonial authorities rewrote the emigration laws with the Emigration Act of 1922. Similar to earlier emigration acts, consent and freedom were key concerns. Competing concerns over the freedom of citizens to emigrate and the desire to protect vulnerable citizens continued to be an issue after India's independence in 1947. The tension between freedom and protection underlay Indian government officials' debates over how the newly independent state should regulate emigration and implement the Emigration Act of 1922. Bureaucrats at that time were aware that the Gulf was becoming the largest employer of overseas Indian workers and working conditions on oil projects in the Gulf were often poor, with limited options for potential emigrants due either to poverty or lack of education.[25] Although government officials did not want to impede the freedom of citizens they simultaneously argued that protecting citizens was a central obligation of the state. For the nascent Indian nation, and today, the question of how the rights of individuals are best ensured by the government was, and continues to be, a pressing issue. The rights of citizens to emigrate and, in particular, an individual's ability to consent to contracts and to make their own choices is sometimes viewed to be in conflict with government's duties to protect its citizens.[26] In the end, the government decided to continue the Protector of Emigrants system. As this system was adopted and subsequently modified by the Indian state, citizens were unevenly impacted based on their gender, education and job category.[27]

Today, the Indian government has laws and processes to oversee Indian migrant labour to the Gulf precisely because it wants to ensure that potential migrants are freely consenting to their contracts and do not experience labour abuses while abroad. These laws require that potential emigrants who the government classifies as the most 'vulnerable' to abuse, receive permission from the government before they are legally able to emigrate. For male potential emigrants, they are considered vulnerable if they have not studied through tenth class and wish to migrate for work to one of seventeen countries, including all of the countries of the Arabic-speaking Gulf.[28] This system of protecting vulnerable workers is overseen by the Protector General of Emigrants, based in New Delhi, and the system is managed by local Protector of Emigrant offices. In order to negotiate the bureaucratic structures associated with the Protector of Emigrants offices, approximately ninety-five per cent of labour migrants go through recruiting agents who facilitate the paperwork and help workers acquire permission to emigrate.[29]

While the emigration regulations are intended to protect vulnerable Indians working abroad, the system has potential for abuse. An investigation by the Indian Central Bureau of Investigation estimated that workers in Protector of Emigrant offices illegally collect INR 64 crore, or over USD 12 million every year, from migrants who are seeking emigration clearance.[30] In addition, some agents charge migrants fees that are over the amount allowed by the Indian government. This 'nexus formed between erring government officials and recruiting agents' means that Indians hoping to work in the Gulf often borrow large amounts of money at high interest rates from moneylenders.[31] Once they reach the Gulf, Indian migrants may experience harsh working conditions and they have little legal or political recourse. In many examinations of Indian migrant workers in the Gulf, scholars have argued that corrupt individuals or 'traditional' cultural practices are the cause of contemporary worker precarity.[32] This chapter shifts focus from a localized specificity of the Gulf and India in order to understand contemporary labour as deeply imbricated in imperialism and colonial labour mobilities. This perspective demonstrates that legacies of colonial labour and contemporary neoliberal security regimes are central factors shaping workers' experiences. Much like the period of indenture, the alleged protection afforded by these regulations often does not lead to better working conditions for Indian migrants. Indeed, as the following example illustrates, continuing racialized labour hierarchies and the conflation of contracts and freedom often means that workers experience increased precarity.

Complaints by workers at Aden

While bureaucrats argued that emigration regulations protected workers, in the 1950s, workers often claimed that they were more vulnerable due to these regulations and the recruitment process associated with them. Examining complaints made by Indian workers at British Petroleum's Aden Refinery construction project exemplifies how the recruiting process, in conjunction with racialized labour hierarchies present at oil projects, curtailed the rights of workers and undermined worker requests for better labour conditions. In 1953, 350 Indian employees at the Aden project went on a 48-hour hunger strike.[33] The workers' grievances fell into two main categories: living conditions and racial discrimination.[34] In regard to their living conditions, workers reported that the food was of poor quality and 'unpalatable to Indian taste', the latrines were unacceptable and their housing was of poor quality and lacked fans.[35] Workers argued that the cause of their poor living and working conditions was racial discrimination by oil company managers. One worker said that he worked a minimum of ten hours a day, but more often worked twelve or fourteen hours and was given no credit for overtime. He described spending all day in the hot sun and, upon asking for a transfer, was refused. When he resigned, he said that the European worker who replaced him was given a 'fat' salary and assistants.[36] Such discrepancies in the treatment of Indians and Europeans were compounded by the racial segregation of living and leisure spaces at the refinery. Explicit racism was also reported, and Indians said their nationality was abused in the most 'insulting of terms'.[37] From the perspective of the Indian employees, the discrimination they faced was based on their skin colour.[38]

Workers argued that discriminatory oil company practices acted in collusion with the recruitment and emigration process in India to exploit workers. Workers reported that they were not told about the working conditions in Aden. They also claimed that the recruiting system was trying to 'mak[e] capital' off workers, thereby implying that the contractors, local recruiters and, perhaps, even the government were charging workers high rates for jobs in the Gulf or emigration permission.[39] In addition, the recruitment system was used by company management to control worker behaviour. Indians reported that they were 'terrified of victimization' due to a 'spy system' used by the company control employees. This spy system consisted of six Indian informants who provided the company with information about other Indian workers.[40] Workers feared the company was using this spy system to compile a 'blacklist' of those suspected to have led the strike and that the employees on the list would be 'sent packing'.[41]

When the Indian government reopened recruitment shortly after the strike, this fear became more pronounced.[42] This was because Indian workers at the refinery knew that, with reopened recruitment, disgruntled workers could be dismissed and, using the recruitment system, easily replaced by workers who would not complain.

The response of both company management and the Indian government relied on employment contracts to undermine worker complaints. When workers appealed to the Indian government as a means to address their labour situation, the government temporarily halted recruitment for the Aden Refinery construction project but, after pressure from British Petroleum and contractors, quickly reopened it. The other response adopted by Indian bureaucrats, both in this and subsequent cases, emphasized informing potential emigrants of working conditions. This information, some bureaucrats argued, would ensure migrants were 'freely consenting' to their contracts which would alleviate the government from further responsibility. For example, bureaucrats in New Delhi asked that the Protector of Emigrants in Bombay warn workers of the situation abroad so that they might choose not to go in the first place.[43] The warning was accompanied by a form signed by the worker that he was aware of the risks, understood the terms of the contract and accepted those terms 'without reservation'.[44] The result, officials hoped, would be to dissuade those workers who were likely to 'feel disgruntled and make complaints on returning to India' from migrating.[45] Here, the practices of both the Indian bureaucrats and oil company managers relied on the signing of a contract as evidence of the free labour.

For their part, oil company managers argued that the conditions were the same for all workers and were not different from those laid out in the employment contracts. Instead, managers argued that Indian employees simply needed to adapt and claimed that Indian employees were 'reactionary' and likely to 'infect other employees with radical ideas'.[46] Management also attempted to legitimate the discrepancies in pay based on global inequalities. One manager argued that the company was 'in no way responsible for the different standards of living and comparative wage scales throughout the world'.[47] Thus, within this context, contracts legitimated working conditions. In the aforementioned case and others, managers argued workers should not have signed contracts and travelled to Aden if they were unhappy with the terms. Through such an argument, the managers claimed that the differences in treatment and pay of employees were based on the nationality of the employee, even as management simultaneously refused to deal with employees through national employee unions. This argument was, and continues to be, common in the oil industry in the Gulf,[48] and it attempted to naturalize differences between American or British management and workers hired from the Middle East or South Asia, thereby ignoring how colonial racial hierarchies shape oil company management.[49] This argument also omitted to acknowledge how racism and racialized hierarchies were mobilized by managers in the Gulf to control the workforce and was justified, as I describe in the next section, with an argument that echoed the colonial discourse of some peoples being 'unfit for freedom'.

Depoliticizing the oilfields

Over the course of the 1950s and 1960s, the ability of Indian workers to participate in collective action at Gulf oil projects became increasingly curtailed. In part, this was due to the efficiency of the labour recruiting system. This system and subsequent restrictions on worker collective action gained legitimacy through contracts that were approved by the Indian government. The robust nature of the recruiting system ensured that there was a large number of Indians available to work abroad. This situation led one oil company manager to instruct his staff to hire Indians and Pakistanis because they 'can be fired without any problem at all'.[50] During the 1960s, a series of strikes by *khalījī* workers in Qatar, Abu Dhabi and Bahrain, were characterized as threats to national security and, as a result, Gulf governments, British administrators and oil companies worked together to reduce the impact of future strikes. Frustrated by lost revenue and fearful of nationalization projects, oil companies increasingly focused on the stability of the workforce – both in the oilfields and in the industries providing support for oil production. Workforce stability – as oil company managers and British administrators argued – was the central feature of political stability. The result was an evacuation of politics from the oilfields through the replacement of *khalījī* workers with precarious South Asian workers who, today, compose the majority of labourers at oil projects.

In late May and early June 1963, the *khalījī* workers – or workers from countries in the Arabic-speaking Gulf – at the oil projects in Abu Dhabi held a series of strikes. These strikes began at the onshore projects of Abu Dhabi Petroleum Company (ADPC)[51] and ADPC's sub-contractors.[52] Located over 100 kilometres west of Abu Dhabi City, the strikes were centred at Jebel Dhanna, Tarif and Murban. On 21 May at Jebel Dhanna, workers guarded the gates to the camps and refused entry to company officials. The strike was well-organized, non-violent and the order to strike was 'passed around quickly and obeyed absolutely'.⁵³ At other oil projects in Abu Dhabi, the strikes were more volatile. In Tarif, the oil company office was 'besieged' by around 100 workers with sticks and, when a British agent visited the Tarif offices, he and his companions faced a crowd of thirty workers 'armed with stones and iron bars'. The unrest radiated out to smaller camps and at a nearby camp called Santa Fe, the expatriate staff, mostly Americans, were 'besieged in the offices and mess-hall' and property was destroyed or stolen.⁵⁴ Beginning 31 May, the strikes spread offshore and workers at Abu Dhabi Marine Areas Ltd (ADMA)⁵⁵ at Das Island also began to participate in the strikes. Here, too, violence erupted: two British managers were beaten and two Indian clerical staff were injured.⁵⁶

Oil company managers and government agents in the Gulf feared the strikes were influenced by pan-Arab movements. If successful, managers and agents feared the nationalization of oil and attributed the cause of these strikes to outside forces. One piece of evidence the British administration for the outside coordination of the strikes was that the workers at ADMA and at ADPC made a similar series of demands.⁵⁷ Onshore, these demands included a wage increase, paying locals the same as other Arab employees – 'equal pay for equal work' – and hiring local men for work currently done by expatriates, in particular hiring locals for the semi-skilled positions held by the Lebanese and other 'northern' Arabs. Workers also demanded the dismissal of unpopular managers. At Das Island, worker demands were almost exactly the same as the demands at Jebel Dhana, with a few key differences. First, at Das Island, there were more Indians and Pakistanis working in technical and managerial positions and, therefore, the foreigners identified by the striking *khalījī* workers included not only Arabs from outside the Gulf but also Indians and Pakistanis.⁵⁸ The workers at Das Island, like Jebel Dhanna, also requested that all jobs be given to nationals, and, going a step further, asked for educational programmes in order to make this possible.

Rumours and speculation fuelled the British administration and the oil companies' perspectives on the strikes and their potential consequences.⁵⁹ Believing the strike in Tarif was completely unexpected and 'without any real cause', one British government official wrote that 'everyone in the management of the oil company seems convinced that trouble is being deliberately stirred up by agitators from outside but no one seems to know what the motives for this are'.⁶⁰ While there was no direct evidence that the strike was instigated by external forces, some of the Abu Dhabi workers had been employed elsewhere in the Gulf and this lent weight to the fear that these workers 'may well have come under hostile influence'.⁶¹ In the months after the strikes, rumours of potential strikes abounded. For the British, these rumours were spurred by fears that the radio broadcast *Sawt al-Arab*, or 'Voice of the Arabs', which discussed worker salaries and conditions, was instigating workers to strike. The main problem, according to this radio broadcast, was that foreigners were being given better jobs and higher pay than nationals.⁶²

In Jebel Dhanna, the managers of the oil companies, for their part, also believed that the strike had no cause and was instigated by outside troublemakers.⁶³ However, when one looks at the strikes from the perspective of the workers themselves, another framing emerges: We can see a politics of locality in which Abu Dhabi locals mobilize under an understanding of a *khalījī* network that moved across state boundaries. The networks defined by the workers were not confined to the geographic boundaries established to ease oil concessions. At Jebel Dhanna the strikes were attributed to the company's proposal to fire seven workers. Only two of these workers were Abu Dhabians. The most influential of the men the company wanted to fire were three Awamir from Hadhramaut, part of the Aden Protectorate. This claim for a *khalījī* locality defined by kin and exchange relations was also reflected in workers' demands for autonomy from both the British administration in the state and the oil companies' control over oil projects. Even after work at Jebel Dhanna resumed, workers remained resistant to British or oil company authority. Workers threatened management with violence and told them they would inform the sheikh of any bad practices by management and he would then deport the managers.

Securing the oilfields

The British attributed these strikes to pan-Arab movements attempting to destabilize the rule of both the British and local governments. This perspective meant that the strikes were engaged with as threats to the security of oil company property, British access to oil and the stability of the Abu Dhabi government. In contrast, workers' requests during the strike indicated their desire to be trained for better positions in the company, while their actions indicated that they saw their complaints rooted in local politics. For example, workers wanted to only negotiate with Abu Dhabi's ruler, Sheikh Shakhbut, indicating that they saw him as a legitimate authority in the emirate. At Tarif, workers refused to discuss their demands with the company there, and insisted that they would only speak with Sheikh Sultan, the son of Sheikh Shakhbut.⁶⁴

This demand by the workers to speak directly with the ruler or one of his sons was repeated at other sites, for example, the workers at Das Island who wanted to negotiate directly with another of the ruler's sons, Sheikh Said. Such appeals revealed the workers' understanding of the ruler as an advocate for their rights, as well as an authoritative figure with regard to work negotiations. The prestige workers assigned to the ruler and members of the royal family was such that even representatives of the sheikh, unless actually related to him, were not always accepted as authorities; for example, a representative for Sheikh Sultan was unable to prevent workers from striking at the Santa Fe camp.[65]

While the workers may have understood the sheikh to be the legitimate authority figure, the British characterized the ruler's response to these strikes as largely ineffective.[66] Early in the days of the strikes at ADPC, Sir William Luce, the British Political Resident in Bahrain, met with the ruler to impress upon him that 'his primary responsibility [was] to enforce law and order'. Sir Luce attempted to clarify to the ruler the British government's position on the strikes. He told him, the 'British were not concerned with industrial disputes between workers and their employers or with breaking strikes, but we were concerned with the security of lives and property of people under our jurisdiction who were working in his State'. He continued that if the ruler was unable to maintain order and the British 'saw that the lives and property of those to whom we have an obligation were thereby imperiled, I should not hesitate to take such steps necessary to protect them'. Sir Luce wrote that he was confident that Sheikh Shakhbut would take the appropriate action, and he believed having the British interfere in the matter would hurt the ruler's reputation and standing among the populace.[67]

Despite these warnings from Sir Luce, the strikes continued and it was perceived that both property and British persons were threatened. The continued strikes were attributed to the ineffectiveness of Sheikh Shakhbut; this was compounded by the inability and reluctance of the Abu Dhabi police to restore order.[68] In part, the British claimed the Abu Dhabi police were ineffective because they lacked training and leadership[69] but they were also seen as identifying with the workers and supporting their cause. At the Tarif strikes, the police 'fraternised with the strikers, shaking hands and rubbing noses with them'.[70] And at Das Island, the police were completely absent during the strike on the island, something the British attributed to police solidarity with the strikers.[71] Sheikh Shakhbut was 'disturbed' by accounts of the unsatisfactory performance of his police force during the strikes; he had hoped the police would be more effective in controlling workers. This was particularly alarming for Shakhbut because the strikes were thought to be spurned by pan-Arabism, a movement that both he and the British feared would shift governmental control in the Gulf if it succeeded. Seeing threats to the internal security of the state by striking workers, Shakhbut agreed to hire a Bahraini police officer to train the Abu Dhabi police force for three months, with particular attention to be paid to security duties.[72] Later, in October 1963, in order to improve the police force, the British administration proposed that a riot squad be trained and stationed near Jebel Dhanna. They also suggested that the police force's salaries and conditions of service be regularized.[73]

Security measures were not limited to police intervention as the military was also mobilized during the strike. For example, in order to ensure effective protection of British property and persons, the British administrators sent two units of the Trucial Oman Scouts (TOS) to the area, in case there was additional trouble.[74] The TOS were instructed to interfere only if the Abu Dhabi police force 'failed and the Europeans and other foreign nationals' lives are threatened'. The TOS were also instructed not to stop the strikes, but rather 'to guard each installation and to form a defended centre in each area, where European and other foreign national staff can take shelter if the police are overwhelmed'.[75] The British also sent HMS *Striker* in the vicinity of Das, but 'out of sight of the Island'. The Striker was to act as a backup in case the TOS lost control of the onshore situation. In anticipation of such an event, plans were drawn up for Sir Luce to order a landing party from the Striker onto the island.[76] Through these types of policies and moving of personnel, the British administration sought to develop a security apparatus that could be used to protect the lives of Europeans in the Gulf and the property of oil companies.

A central concern shared by the British administration, the oil companies and the ruler was how to best manage the local population of workers. Both day-to-day operations and broader, industry-level changes were creating new problems and contributing to growing worker dissatisfaction. For example, after construction ended at these oil projects, the number of workers needed to maintain the oil projects decreased significantly and resulted in the dismissal of most workers from their jobs. It was feared that local workers, upon termination, would cause trouble and stop oil production. The termination of *khalījī* employees was especially problematic.[77] The British administration saw any method of operating that did not use a maximum number of local labourers as likely to stir unrest. Thus, in the 1960s, there were twice the number of men in a shift than would be the case in North America because such a practice was seen as beneficial for Gulf relations.[78]

In 1966, after another series of strikes by *khalījī* workers in Abu Dhabi, the Director of Labour, Sayyid A. Hijazi, dissatisfied with the current condition of labour laws in Abu Dhabi decided to implement a series of reforms. These reforms included Abu Dhabi joining the International Labour Organization, labour education that would inform workers of their rights, the recognition of trade unions, the opening of more labour offices in the oilfields, and creating a Department of Social Affairs.[79] The British administration objected to both these reforms and similar reforms that were proposed in Qatar after a series of strikes by local workers. In particular, the British administration worried that these reforms would open Abu Dhabi to disruptive outside influences, such as pan-Arab groups.

In conversations with Sayid Hassan Jumaa, a high-ranking Abu Dhabi government employee, a British administrator elaborated the problems with trade unions and the reasons that Arab nations 'had never had the ability' to develop industrial movements. First, trade unions had become the only civilian institution with political significance and this was because Arab countries were unable to evolve adequate political institutions. Second, 'in the traditional evolutionary Arab states, it was difficult for trade unions to develop on Western European lines because industry was either relatively unimportant to national security or it was all-important'. Third, Arab nations were 'paternalist in nature', meaning that they protected the rights of workers without workers themselves having to agitate for changes. Finally, given the 'the lack of developed political institutions and the banning in many countries of political groups opposed to the ruling regime, the trade unions became a target for infiltration by political forces seeking some form of expression'. When asked if the Abu Dhabi government should try to help develop these unions, the administrator insisted that the change should happen slowly; 'there was certainly no case for formation of trade unions in a primitive society such as existed in Abu Dhabi' he argued. A better solution, according to the British, was a system of Joint Consultative Committees for the oil industry, such as those in Qatar.[80]

This characterization of Abu Dhabi and other Gulf States as 'primitive societies' was used by British administrators to reinforce an understanding of sheikhly rule that relied upon the rulers distributing wealth amongst the population and differential treatment between national and foreign workers. According to this view, the labour reforms that the Director of Labour wanted to implement were 'quite unsuitable for a primitive society in an early stage of evolution'.[81] This rhetoric by British administrators repeats the discourse that oil companies developed at oil sites in countries as diverse as 'Mexico, Iran,

Venezuela, Colombia, Nigeria, [and] Saudi Arabia'. In these countries, local populations asked oil companies for development and training. The companies responded with the nineteenth-century idea that 'long, slow tutelage' was best for the development of native populations.[82] These oil company policies mobilized the racialized labour hierarchies of colonialism that categorized some peoples as 'unfit for liberty'. In the Gulf, this view reinforced the role of the sheikh in a 'tribal society' to distribute money, provide social services and protect the nationals in a paternalistic fashion.[83] While this view of labour relations was contested and debated amongst Abu Dhabi governmental employees, the British administration's insistence upon tightening measures in order to ensure the stability of the sheikhs or the internal security of the state most often won out.

Conclusion

From an oil company perspective, the strikes in Abu Dhabi were evidence that nationals and other *khalījī* workers who were able to make claims upon the nation for rights were potentially destabilizing. Furthermore, the authority of the sheikhs was not always absolute and the consequences of strikes meant the loss of money for oil companies. Managing local workers also required heavy investment in policing and armed forces. In contrast, South Asians, already present in large numbers in higher level jobs, were thought to be ideal workers to replace *khalījī* workers. An effective recruiting system meant that there was a large number of South Asians available to work abroad. This situation led one oil company manager to instruct his staff to hire Indians and Pakistanis because they 'can be fired without any problem at all'.[84] In contrast, the firing of *khalījī* workers led to strikes that the British had difficulty ending without military intervention. Finally, both the British government and local rulers feared that local dissatisfaction on the jobsite would encourage *khalījī* workers to support pan-Arab or Islamist groups that wanted a change in governance. Thus, during the 1960s, labour laws in the Gulf were rewritten to favour employers and *khalījī* workers increasingly began jobs in local government.

Today, non-*khalījīs* are excluded from the political and cultural milieu of the Gulf States, and foreigners' ability to access state resources and participate in governance is limited. For Indian migrants to the Gulf, this means that there are no strong labour laws to protect them and there are legal structures that formalize their exclusion. Increasing securitization and the use of the colonial infrastructure used to move indentured workers facilitated the evacuation of politics from the Gulf's oilfields. During this time, the composition of labourers in the workforce shifted from local nationals to South Asians, with the explicit hope by oil company managers and colonial bureaucrats that workforce stability would be created. This shift was not merely a consequence of the new wealth from oil production or industry manpower needs. Rather, colonial racial hierarchies, labour mobilities and infrastructures continue to shape emigration policies and contracts. These colonial legacies are also deeply imbricated in neoliberal security regimes. Today, the consent of workers, in conjunction with the securitization of the state around oil, means that workers have limited rights and the loss of these rights is framed as consensual and necessary.

Notes

1 Today, all of Bahrain's proven oil reserves, 125 million barrels, are located in the Awali field, although there is the potential for offshore oil production. See: Energy Information Administration, U.S. Department of Energy.
2 International Energy Statistics, US Energy Information Administration. http://www.eia.gov/countries/data.cfm. Last visited 8/16/19.
3 Jane Kinninmont, 'Bahrain' in *Power and Politics in the Persian Gulf Monarchies*, ed. Christopher Davidson, (New York: Columbia University Press, 2011), 35.
4 Annual Report of the Bahrain Petroleum Co. Ltd 1940. National Archives of India [NAI], External Affairs, Near East Branch, 1941. F 360-N/41.
5 I.J. Seccombe and R.I. Lawless, 'Foreign Worker Dependence in the Gulf, and the International Oil Companies: 1910–50' *International Migration Review* 20, no. 3 (August 1986): 564–565.
6 Lisa Lowe, *The Intimacies of the Four Continents* (Durham: Duke University Press, 2015), 7, 36, 39.
7 Ibid., 24.
8 Radhika Mongia, *Indian Migration and Empire: A Genealogy of the Modern State* (Durham: Duke University Press, 2018), 7, 16.
9 Rashid Khalidi, *Resurrecting Empire: Western Footprints and America's Perilous Path in the Middle East*, (Boston: Beacon Press, 2010), 83. Timothy Mitchell, *Carbon Democracy*, (London, Verso, 2011).
10 The Red Line Agreement, signed in 1928, was an agreement between French, British and American oil companies regarding the oil resources in the former Ottoman Empire. Importantly for this discussion, it did not have power over oil companies that had not signed the agreement. This allowed for some American oil companies excluded from the agreement to pursue oil concessions where other companies were unable.

11 Seccombe and Lawless, 'Foreign Worker Dependence in the Gulf, and the International Oil Companies', 550–551.
12 For example, ever since the founding of the Anglo-Persian Oil Company (later AIOC), Indians had worked for the company, and British businessmen often moved from working in industries in India to positions as managers at APOC. Seccombe and Lawless, 'Foreign Worker Dependence in the Gulf, and the International Oil Companies', 558.
13 T A B Corley, *A History of the Burmah Oil Company, 1886–1924* (London: Heinemann, 1983).
14 James Onley, *The Arabian Frontiers of the British Raj* (Oxford: Oxford University Press, 2007).
15 Jane Kinninmont, 'Bahrain', 35.
16 Ibid., 36–37.
17 Mitchell, *Carbon Democracy*.
18 Thomas letters to General Headquarters, 10 July 1946. NAI, MEA, Middle East Branch [ME], 1946. 10-(91)-ME/46.
19 Thomas letter to General Headquarters, 24 August 1946. NAI, MEA, ME, 1946. 10-(91)-ME/46.
20 Sugata Bose, *A Hundred Horizons: The Indian Ocean in the Age of Global Empire*, (Cambridge: Harvard University Press, 2009), 75. See also: Marina Carter, *Servants, Sirdars, and Settlers: Indians in Mauritius, 1834–1874*, (Oxford: Oxford University Press, 1995); Crispin Bates, 'Coerced and Migrant Labourers in India' *Edinburgh Papers in South Asian Studies* 13 (2000): 2–33; Mahadavi Kale, *Fragments of Empire: Capital, Slavery, and Indentured Labor in the British Caribbean* (Philadelphia: University of Pennsylvania Press, 2010); Anand A Yang, *The Limited Raj: Agrarian Roots in Colonial India, Saran District, 1793–1920*, (Berkeley: University of California Press, 1989).
21 Thomas R Metcalf, *Imperial Connections: India in the Indian Ocean Arena* (Berkeley: University of California Press, 2008), 136–137, 144.
22 Kale, *Fragments of Empire*, 6–7
23 Kale, *Fragments of Empire*, 6, 10.
24 Johan Mathew, *Margins of the Market: Trafficking and Capitalism across the Arabian Sea*, (Berkeley: University of California Press, 2016), 54.
25 Report on the Working of the Indian Emigration Act (VII of 1922) for the year 1951. NAI, MEA, S.E.A. Section. 2/54/6551/10003; Lanka Sundaram, 'Effects of Emigration on the Economic Situation of the Population of Selected Asian Countries of Emigration (with reference to India),' 10 September 1954. NAI, MEA, Emigration, 1954. F. 13-9/54-Emi; Skilled workers engaged by the Bahrain Petroleum Co., Bahrain. NAI, MEA, Emigration, 1948. F. 22-8/48-Emi.
26 For a discussion of the 'liberal individual' and the centrality of an individual's possession of his own person, see: Wendy Brown, *States of Injury: Power and*

Freedom in Late Modernity, (Princeton: Princeton University Press, 1995); Georg Wilhelm Friedrich Hegel, *Phenomenology of the Spirit*, trans. A. V. Miller, (Oxford: Oxford University Press, 1977); Lisa Lowe, *The Intimacies of Four Continents*, (Durham: Duke University Press, 2015). For a discussion of the centrality of the state to ensure rights see Hannah Arendt, 'Decline of the Nation State and the End of the Rights of Man' in *Origins of Totalitarianism*, (New York: Harcourt, 1973).

27 Indian Emigration Act, 1922 – Considerations of Amendments of, to extend its provisions to journeys by air and by land, unaccompanied domestic servants, etc. NAI, MEA, Emigration, 1954. F. 17–6/54-Emi; Annual Report on the Working of the Indian Emigration Act VII of 1922 and the Rules framed thereunder for the port of Calcutta for the year 1952. NAI, MEA, Emigration Section, 1953. F. 17–6/54-Emi; Material required by Sri Lanka Sundaram MP for a paper on the 'Effect of Emigration'. NAI, MEA, Emigration, 1954. F. 13–9/54-Emi; "Report on the Working of the Indian Emigration Act (No. VII of 1922) for the Year 1952". NAI, MEA, Emigration, 1953. F. 17–6/54-Emi.

28 Women who have not matriculated face even greater restrictions and are unable to legally emigrate if they are under thirty years of age. For more on this topic, see: Andrea Wright, '"The Immoral Traffic in Women": Regulating Indian Emigration to the Persian Gulf' in *Borders and Mobility in South Asia and Beyond*, eds., Reece Jones and Md. Azmeary Ferdoush, (Amsterdam: Amsterdam University Press, 2018), 145–166.

29 S Irudaya Rajan, V J Varghese, and M S Jayakumar, 'Looking Beyond the Emigration Act 1983: Revisiting the Recruitment Practices in India', in *Governance and Labour Migration*, (Routledge: India, 2010), 280.

30 Chandrani Banerjee, 'The Clay Pigeons', *Outlook India*, September 21, 2010.

31 Rajan, Varghese, and Jayakumar, 'Looking Beyond the Emigration Act 1983', 251–252; Andrea Wright 'Migratory Pipelines: Labor and Oil in the Arabian Sea' (PhD diss., University of Michigan, 2015), 219–223.

32 Anh Nga Longva, *Walls Built on Sand: Migration, Exclusion, and Society in Kuwait*, (Boulder, CO: Westview Press, 1997), 100, 103–105; Andrew Gardner, *City of Strangers: Gulf Migration and the Indian Community in Bahrain*, (Ithaca, NY: Cornell University Press, 2010), 37.

33 Telegram to Embassy of India, Cairo. NAI, MEA, Emigration, 1953. F.23–9/52-Emi.

34 Letter to POE, Bombay, from BP, 10 June 1953. NAI, MEA, Emigration, 1953. G/16307.

35 Extract from Monthly Report No. 5 of 1953. NAI, MEA, Emigration, 1953. F.23–9/52-Emi.; Letter to the Secretary, MEA, from Thadani, 10 June 1953. NAI, MEA, Emigration, 1953. 2954/53-Emi.; Letter to Ghatge, 26 March 1953. NAI, MEA, Emigration, 1953. F.23–9/52-Emi.

36 Extract from Monthly Report No. 5 of 1953; Letter to the Trade Commissioner, Aden, from Bechtel and Wimpey, 20 May 1953. NAI, MEA, Emigration, 1953. F.23–9/52-Emi.

37 Letter to the Secretary, MEA, from Thadani, 10 June 1953. NAI, MEA, Emigration, 1953. 2954/53-Emi; Letter to Indian Trade Commission from Indian Employees Committee, 4 July 1953. NAI, MEA, Emigration, 1953. F.23–9/52-Emi; Letter to POE, Bombay, from BP, 10 June 1953. NAI, MEA, Emigration, 1953. G/16307; Letter to the Secretary, MEA, from Thadani, 10 June 1953. NAI, MEA, Emigration, 1953. 2954/53-Emi.

38 Letter to the Trade Commissioner, Aden, from Bechtel and Wimpey, 20 May 1953. NAI, MEA, Emigration, 1953. 2954/53-Emi.

39 Letter to Indian Trade Commission from Indian Employees Committee, 4 July 1953. NAI, MEA, Emigration, 1953. F.23–9/52-Emi.

40 In response to these allegations, the Commissioner 'gave [the Indian employee] a short lecture on building national character, for communicating to his colleagues [at the refinery].' Extract from Monthly Report No. 4 of 1953. NAI, MEA, Emigration, 1953. 2954/53-Emi.

41 Letter to Secretary, MEA, from Commissioner, 27 June 1953. NAI, MEA, Emigration, 1953. 2779/53-Emi.

42 Telegram to Foreign Office, New Delhi, 8 July 1953. NAI, MEA, Emigration, 1953. 27321/53-Emi.

43 Skilled workers engaged by the Bahrain Petroleum Co., Bahrain. NAI, MEA, Emigration, 1948. F. 22–8/48-Emi.

44 Annual Report on the Working of the Indian Emigration Act VII of 1922 and the Rules Issued Thereunder during the Year Ending 31st December 1952, of the Ports of Bombay, Porbandar, Bedi Bunder and Port Okha. NAI, MEA, Emigration, 1953. F. 17–6/54-Emi.

45 Skilled workers engaged by the Bahrein (*sic*) Petroleum Co., Bahrain. NAI, MEA, Emigration, 1948. F. 22–8/48-Emi.

46 Report of Dr Chand, Embassy of India, Baghdad, 22 April 1954. NAI, MEA, Emigration (originally in AWT section), 1953. F.6–6/53-Emi/D.2049/AWT/54.

47 Report Dated 30 July 1953 from Messrs Middle East Bechtel Corporation and George Wimpey & Co., Ltd., Aden. NAI, MEA, Emigration, 1953. F.6–6/53-Emi.

48 Letter to POE, Bombay from E.E. Evans, Recruiting Agent, Arabian American Oil Co, 30 March 1954. NAI, MEA, Emigration, 1953. F.6–6/53-Emi.

49 For example, Vitalis outlines the work undertaken to maintain colour lines at the oil projects in Dhahran, Saudi Arabia. See, Robert Vitalis, *America's Kingdom: Mythmaking on the Saudi Oil Frontier*, (New York: Verso, 2009), 98–105.

50 'Review of the Events in Qatar in 1964', British Political Agency, Doha, 2 January 1965. *Political Diaries of the Arab World: Persian Gulf [PG]* (24), 359–368.

51 ADPC was a subsidiary of Iraq Petroleum Company (IPC) established in 1939 to hold Abu Dhabi oil concessions. The major shareholders of IPC in the 1960s were British Petroleum (previously named the Anglo-Iranian Oil Company), Deutsche Bank, Shell and the British Government. (http://www.adnoc.ae/content.aspx?newid=27&mid=27)
52 J.E.H. Boustead, Memo to HM Political Residency, Bahrain, 28 May 1963. *Records of the* Emirates [*RE*] (1963), 568.
53 The main players at Jebel Dhanna were ADPC and the consultants at the Jebel Dhanna project, Eastern Bechtel Corporation. J.E.H. Boustead, Record of a visit to Jebel Dhanna, 29 May 1963. *RE* (1963), 573–576.
54 J.E.H. Boustead, Report of Visit to Tarif, 28 May 1963. *RE* (1963), 569–570.
55 Today this company is ADMA-OPCO (Abu Dhabi Marine Operating Company). It is a subsidiary of Abu Dhabi National Oil Company (ADNOC).
56 Report of Strike on Das Island, 3 June 1963, *RE 1963*, 578–580. Telegram No. 324 From Bahrain to Foreign Office, 1 June 1963. *RE* (1963), 564.
57 Report of Strike on Das Island, 3 June 1963.
58 Ibid.
59 Rumours were also circulating among workers. For example, the precipitating event at Das Island may also have been the arrest of an Awamir employee who was stealing cars and joyriding them around the camp at night. A British manager apprehended the man, but as the manager spoke no Arabic, the Awamir was taken to the Arab Affairs Officer. Upon his release, the Awamir told his colleagues he was beaten by the Arab Affairs Officer, who was Lebanese, in the UK camp. Report of Strike on Das Island, 3 June 1963.
60 J.E.H. Boustead, Memo to HM Political Residency, Bahrain, 28 May 1963.
61 Confidential Memo from Bahrain to Foreign Office, 30 May 1963.
62 D. Slater to P.W. Summerscale, Political Residency Bahrain, 29 July 1963. *RE* (1963), 586-7; D. Slater to F.D.W. Brown, Political Residency Bahrain, 12 August 1963. *RE* (1963), 588.
63 J.E.H. Boustead, Record of a visit to Jebel Dhanna, 29 May 1963.
64 Ibid.
65 J.E.H. Boustead, Report of Visit to Tarif, 28 May 1963.
66 Confidential Memo from Bahrain to Foreign Office, 30 May 1963.
67 W.H. Luce to Foreign Office, 5 June 1963. *RE* (1963), 567.
68 Confidential Memo from Bahrain to Foreign Office, 30 May 1963.
69 J.E.H. Boustead, Memo to H.M. Political Residency, Bahrain, 28 May 1963.
70 J.E.H. Boustead, Report of Visit to Tarif, 28 May 1963.
71 Report of Strike on Das Island, 3 June 1963
72 Confidential Annex to Abu Dhabi Monthly Diary, No. 7 of 1963, 1–31 July. *PG* (24), 159.

73 F.D.W Bron Letter to Political Residency, Bahrain, 16 October 1963. *RE* (1963), 613.
74 Confidential Memo from Bahrain to Foreign Office, 30 May 1963; Telegraph No. 322, From Bahrain to Foreign Office, 31 May 1963. *RE* (1963), 563.
75 J.E.H. Boustead letter to Political Residency, Bahrain, 30 May 1963. *RE* (1963), 571.
76 Telegram No. 324 From Bahrain to Foreign Office, 1 June 1963.
77 D. Slater to Political Residency, Bahrain, 15 September 1963. *RE* (1963), 589–590.
78 State of Qatar, 'Report on Labour, Industrial and Social Developments: Assessment and Recommendations', 6 December 1968. LAB13/2164. *Records of Qatar [RQ]* (2), 675–8.
79 D. Slater to Political Residency, Bahrain, 15 September 1963. *RE* (1963), 589–590.
80 'Note of a discussion with Syed Hussan Jumaa', 5 December 1967. FCO 8/70. *RE* (2), 302–304.
81 A British administrator reported that when he told this to Hijazi, who had a degree in sociology from a university in London, Hijazi was 'extremely frustrated and angry'. The administrator seemed to be at a loss as to why. R.L. Morris to British Embassy Beirut, 'Abu Dhabi: Report on Labour, Social and Industrial Developments'.
82 Robert Vitalis, *America's Kingdom: Mythmaking on the Saudi Oil Frontier*, 40.
83 R.L. Morris to British Embassy Beirut, 'Abu Dhabi: Report on Labour, Social and Industrial Developments'.
84 'Review of the Events in Qatar in 1964', British Political Agency, Doha, 2 January 1965. PG (24): 359–368.

3

Legal discourse on 'coolies' migration from India to the sugar colonies, 1837–1922

Ashutosh Kumar

In the 1880s, a conflict started on a ship between Indian indentured labourers and the colonial authorities regarding the provisions of rice and chapati (made of flour). A group of Gorakhpuri indentured labourers demanded chapati instead of rice in their meal. After an inquiry, a new provision of legislation stipulated that rice and chapati be provided to labourers on the board the ship. In another case, the colonial government decided to keep live goat and sheep on board and appointed a Muslim butcher to slaughter them in the traditional *halal* way. Both cases show the bargaining power of indentured labourers with the Empire. A close look at emigration legislation demonstrates how parts of the indenture system were distinctive within the overall history of global migration. In this chapter, I explore the scope of freedom and bargaining power in the larger framework of indentured legislation on the strength of little-known archival sources in the discussion of global labour migration in the age of nineteenth-century imperialism.

The nineteenth century has been marked as a phase of global labour migration.[1] Indentured migration was primarily begun to overseas European sugar colonies in the Pacific, Caribbean and Indian Oceans, where parts of pre-existing economies focused on slavery. The demand for labour, especially

---

In this chapter, I have used the phrase 'legal discourse' in terms of actual contract of indenture, its evolution and framing under the British colonial regime, which had legal value in the British colonial judiciary and courts.

This chapter is an elongated version of a contribution to a special forum scheduled to appear in the *Journal of World History* on indenture and its legacies in world history, edited by Neilesh Bose. I am grateful to Neilesh Bose and two anonymous reviewers for their comments and insights on this chapter.

on the sugar plantations after the abolition of slavery by the British Empire in 1833, was the primary drive for this process. Those who served in this system had to sign a legal contract, which was generally for five years, to work on the sugar plantations of overseas colonies. This form of contract, apart from listing wages, mentioned facilities of accommodation, hospital and free return passage back home after another five years, among other provisions.[2] Until 1917 – when the system was abolished – almost 1.3 million people had been recruited to work within this system.[3] From the late nineteenth century, alongside this system of indenture, the *kangani* (headman or foreman/overseer) and *maistry* (foreman or master workman) systems of migration also oversaw labourers to Southeast Asian regions. Under these systems, a headman or *sirdar* who himself was an immigrant working on a plantation organized labourers from his village and adjoining areas to work on plantations. He was empowered to pay passage and other expenses of all labourers. It was based on trust, leaving no room for a legal contract signed between the headman and the labourers regarding wages, accommodation, food, medical and other necessities. Thus, labourers were completely dependent on the headman for their security and needs. The expenses incurred in bringing labourers to the plantations were treated as a loan which labourers had to pay back during their employment.[4] Brutal working conditions and incidents of violence attracted the attention of anti-slavery activists as well as humanitarians who were responsible for the abolition of slavery from the British Empire. Many of these activists denounced indentured labour as a new system of slavery. Such activists visited people brought from India to the sugar colonies of the Caribbean and the Pacific and produced evidence of brutality, violence and deception. As the system was much more visible due to less attention paid to other systems, it became a source of debate in academic treatments of labour and migration. In recent years the focus of the debates has centred on the legal dimension of the indenture system. This essay focuses on such dimensions; on the freedom, agency and bargaining power of the indentured migrants compared to other forms of labour migration in colonial India. Given that absolute 'freedom' is impossible, I approach the issues in terms of a relative level of 'freedom' involved in a particular system. While recognizing the role of the contract in the capitalist need to regulate labour, this essay argues that contracts in the indenture system showed a higher degree of freedom and bargain than other prevalent forms of labour migration at the time.

Historiography of labour emigration laws

The specific impact of labour emigration laws with particular reference to indentured labour comprises an area of research not fully explored in the history of colonial India.[5] Historians have largely focused on the labour legislation in colonial India and on the lack of 'agency' and bargaining power in the making and functioning of labour legislation. Hugh Tinker sees the labour emigration from India as a coercive labour system with recruitment through fraud, coercion and misrepresentation. By focusing on the taxing measures on indentured workers, Tinker asserts that it was a device to put *coolies* in 'a state of modified slavery'; a term used by the Anti-Slavery Society members.[6] Legal historians have argued that the labour laws of the nineteenth century essentially provided poor relief, increased subordination, enforced harsher terms and provisioned no legal remedy for accidents at the workplace to the wageworkers.[7] Robert J. Steinfeld portrays indenture as an 'unfree labour' and argues that the planters used bodily coercion to implement the labour contract. In the context of nineteenth-century Britain and America, Steinfeld argues that harsh remedies were applied to enforce the labour contracts such as prison terms in the British case and wage forfeiture in the American case.[8]

In the context of colonial India, Peter Robb has argued that the state regulations related to labour were not successful in India. According to him there were three significant elements in Indian labour relations which made state measures unsuccessful: first, the role of intermediaries who controlled the labourers; second, identities such as caste and religion in the labour market; and third, the tide of dependence.[9] Some scholars have argued that the labour laws in colonial India advocated the welfare measures as state concerns and colonial government opted it.[10] However, Prabhu Mohapatra found that the early labour regulation (1814–60) by the British in colonial India reflected the cultural baggage of 'master and servant' laws of Great Britain in which breach of contract was criminalized. According to Mohapatra, the labour laws of the Assam Plantations institutionalized a system of voluntary servitude through the introduction of various labour laws.[11]

This topic also holds a place in global history. Scholars working within this field have tended to homogenize the various kinds of long-distance migrations in the nineteenth century by depicting it as a 'global' phenomenon. World historians, such as Adam McKeown, have argued that not only in the nineteenth century but even in the twentieth century, one cannot define labour migration in terms of push and pull factors, nor in terms of legislation in the context of European needs or fleeing of peasants due to overpopulation pressure.[12] McKeown has argued that most of the migrations were voluntary in nature and channelled through networks of kith and kin. He presumed that indentured labour was unfree or coerced and, therefore, an aberration from the dominant trend of global migration in the post-slavery world. Prabhu Mohapatra, offers a different view on the nature of South Asian labour migrations. According to him 'even in the absence of (and after the abolition of) a formal indenture system, the great bulk of Asian migration flows seem not to have led to the installation of "free" and non-coerced migration but rather that indenture acted as a template for the "contract" and debt-bonded migration of free labourers'.[13] This is evident in the bulk of migration under *kangani* and *maistry* systems (non-indentured) from India to Southeast Asia and Ceylon.[14] Contrary to McKeown and Mohapatra, Crispin Bates and Marina Carter argue that in so many cases of indentured migration 'returnees, sirdars and recruits created out of indenture a dynamic that operated clearly outside the planter/ administrator worldview'.[15] In the context of the emergence of transnational human rights concepts and law, Rachel Sturman recently traced its links to the regulations of the official British system of Indian indentured labour. Sturman maintained that these rules and regulations of the indenture system not only protected but also ensured the humanity of labourers through strict scrutiny and interventions. Indentured laws and regulations were sought to protect the labourers' humanity not only by distinguishing indenture from slavery, but by prompting a framework of laws and regulations that was oriented towards the provision of welfare. Various problems faced by the colonial authorities in securing labourers' rights – such as coercion, exploitation and neglect – and the efforts to overcome these problems formed the early conceptual and administrative frameworks that shaped the emergence of modern international labour regulations.[16]

Recent scholars have also discussed the ideas of freedom and contracts in terms of liberalism and its limits. In *The Intimacies of the Four Continents*, Lisa Lowe argues that the eighteenth and nineteenth century ideology of political liberalism, which advocated European emancipation, universal rights and promotion of wage labour and free trade, was the foundation for colonialism to ensure the subjugation of colonial subjects. Citing the cases of early nineteenth century workers transported from Bengal to the Caribbean, she argues that the notion of 'free' migration was simply a strategic deployment of liberalism. She further argues that the whole business of 'coolie trade' was just a changing role for the US and Britain from natural competitors to partners in the nineteenth century.[17] In similar ways, Radhika Mongia explored the formation of the nation-state in India and the notion of state sovereignty and argued that the development and state regulation of colonial labour migration between 1834 and 1917 was part of the process of changing from a colonial state to a nation-state. Mongia contended that the state regulation of indentured labour facilitated the recruitment by promise of 'agency', voluntariness and freedom in the signing or thumbing the contract.[18]

The aforementioned scholars overlook the pre-existing structural social subjugation of Indian lower caste populations, who formed the largest component of the emigrants. In the age of liberalism such emigrants found a way to leave their feudal bondage on a short-term contract. One of the blank spots in colonial Indian history has been the subject of the bargaining power of subaltern subjects. Labourers in the *kamiati*, *kangani* or *maistry* systems certainly did not have bargaining power.[19] Indenture, for the first time, provided not only the power of bargain but also an aspiration to social equality in terms of the rule of law under British rule in India.[20] For them, becoming contractual workers (*girmitiya*) would have provided more freedom relative to other systems of labour. Excluded from all the previous scholarship is the specific nature of contract inside the indenture system. While there were no legal contracts involved in the *kangani* or *maistry* systems, the indenture system had a legal contract, mentioning terms and conditions for validation in front of a magistrate.

Indentured vs non-indentured

As mentioned in the introduction, two major forms of labour migration streams in nineteenth-century India were the indentured and *kangani* or *maistry*. Even though the introduction of the indenture contract betrayed an intimate motive for enticing indentured labourers to ensure the availability of a labour force, the legal framework also included the space to bargain and to secure signatories' rights compared to other forms of labour migration. In terms of recruitment, the indenture system was highly organized and employers were principally the large companies situated in the British sugar colonies. Recruiters were broadly divided into two classes: licensed and unlicensed. Licensed recruiters may be again subdivided into head recruiters, commonly called subagents and ordinary recruiters. Ordinary recruiters were either subordinate to a head recruiter or independent. We thus get the following diagram:

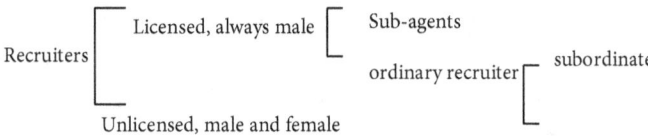

Unlicensed male and female independent agents had subagents in the countryside under them and these subagents had recruiters under them. The business of a subagent was to collect emigrants brought in by recruits from all parts of the territory over which his operations extended. Sometimes he had outposts which were controlled by a subordinate recruiter.[21] Grierson notes that below the recruiter there were *arkatis* (unlicensed men), who would bring coolies to the recruiter.[22] *Arkatis* were not employed universally, but rather in such places only where recruiters were few and the chances of obtaining *coolies* high. At ports of embarkation such as Calcutta and Madras, coolies were presented to a magistrate to enquire about their willingness to work on indenture contract. There labourers had to sign a legal contract which had all the terms and conditions written in English as well as in Indian languages such as Hindi, Urdu, Bangla, Telugu, Tamil etc. Once signed, an emigration pass would be issued to each intending labourer.[23]

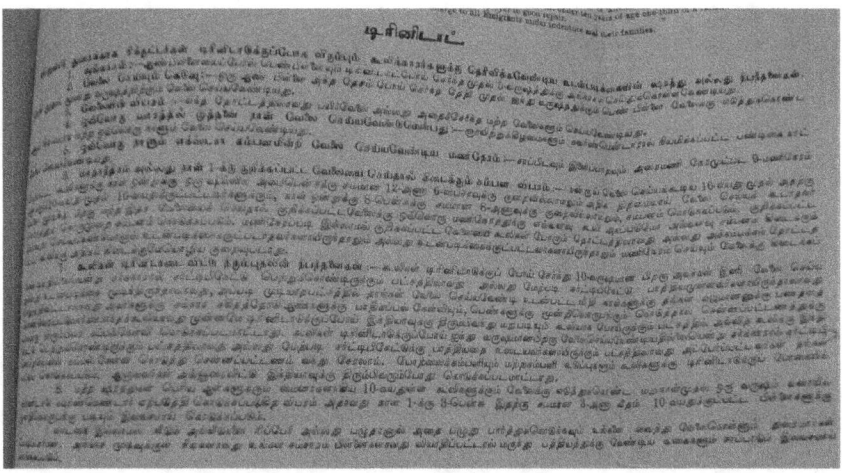

Figure 3.1 Original Copy of Terms of Service in Tamil for Trinidad. Source: National Archives of London.

Legal Discourse: The Sugar Colonies 1837–1922   91

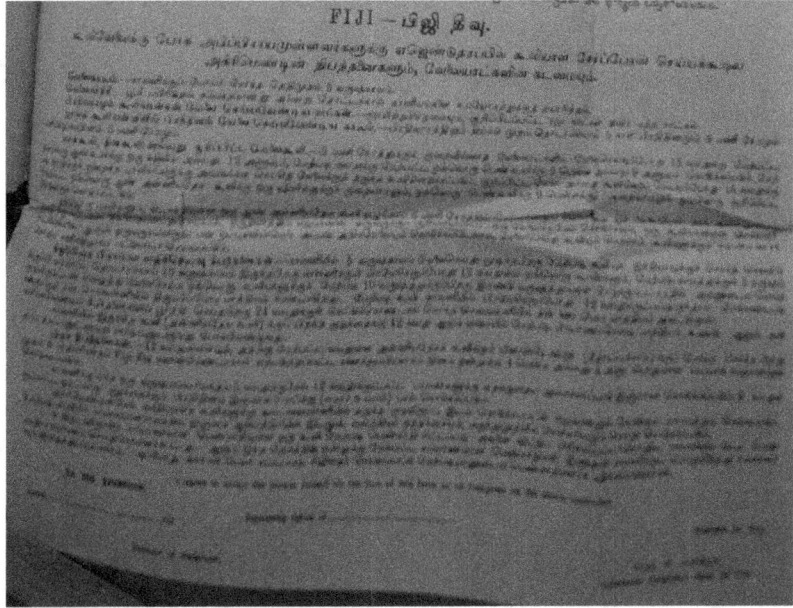

Figure 3.2 Original Copy of Terms of Service in Tamil language for Fiji. Source: National Archives of London.

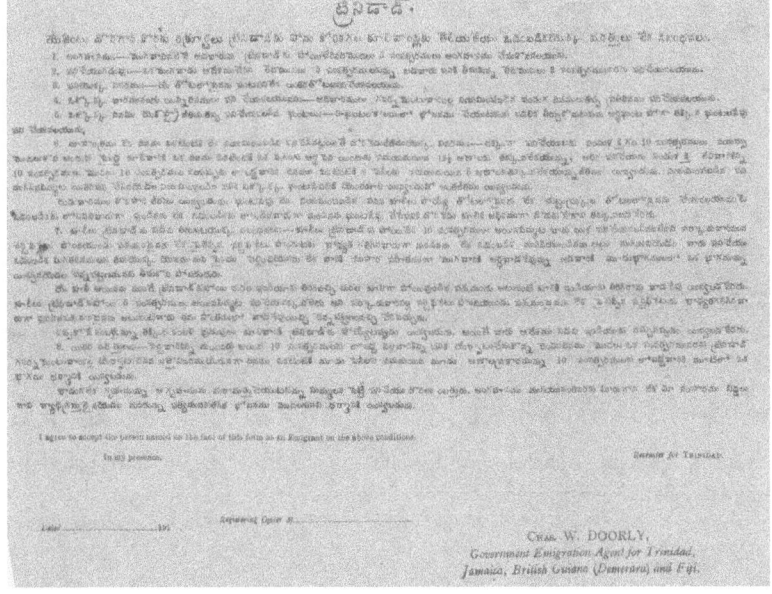

Figure 3.3 Original Copy of Terms of Service in Telugu language. Source: National Archives of London.

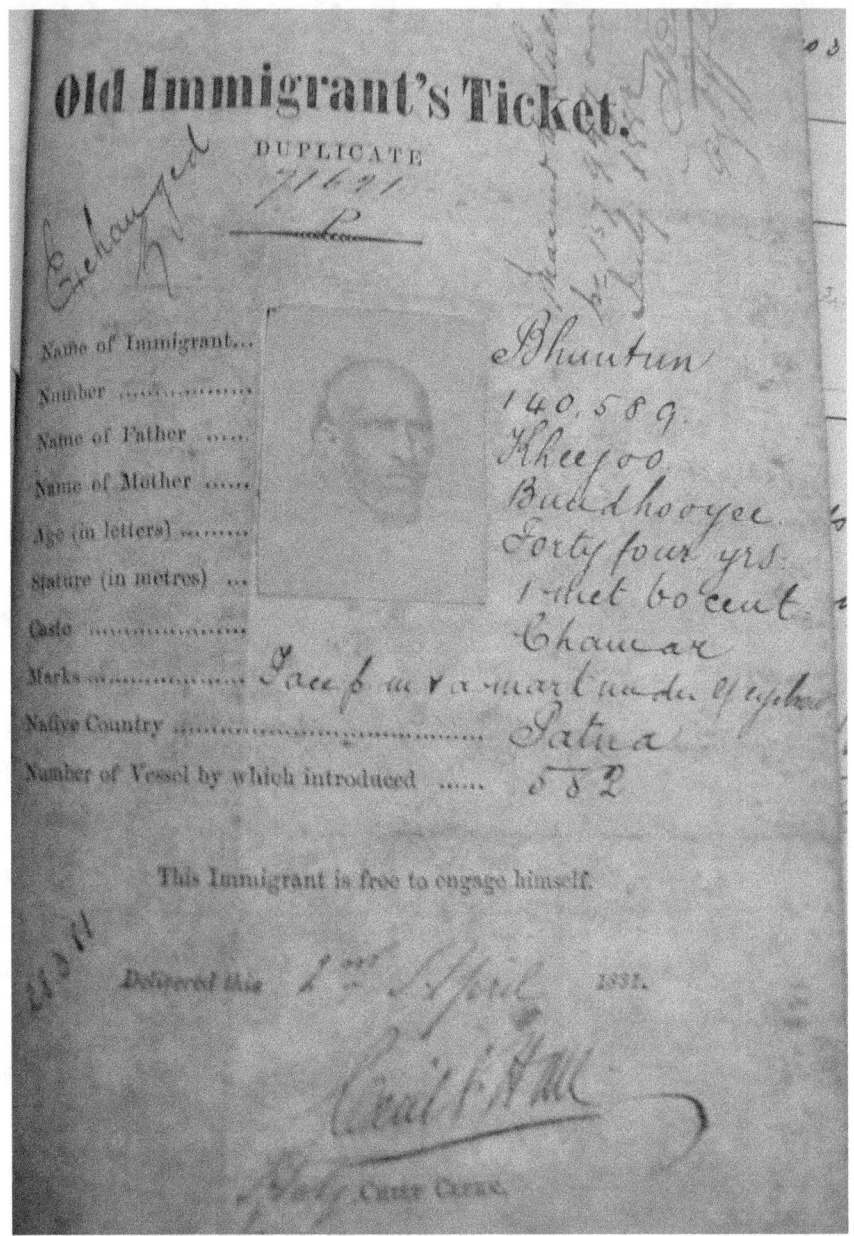

Figure 3.4 A Picture of an old immigrant's ticket, PA-16, NAM. Source: National Archives of Mauritius.

Figure 3.5 a) Original Copy of Terms of Service for Natal. Source: National Archives Depot, Pietermaritzburg

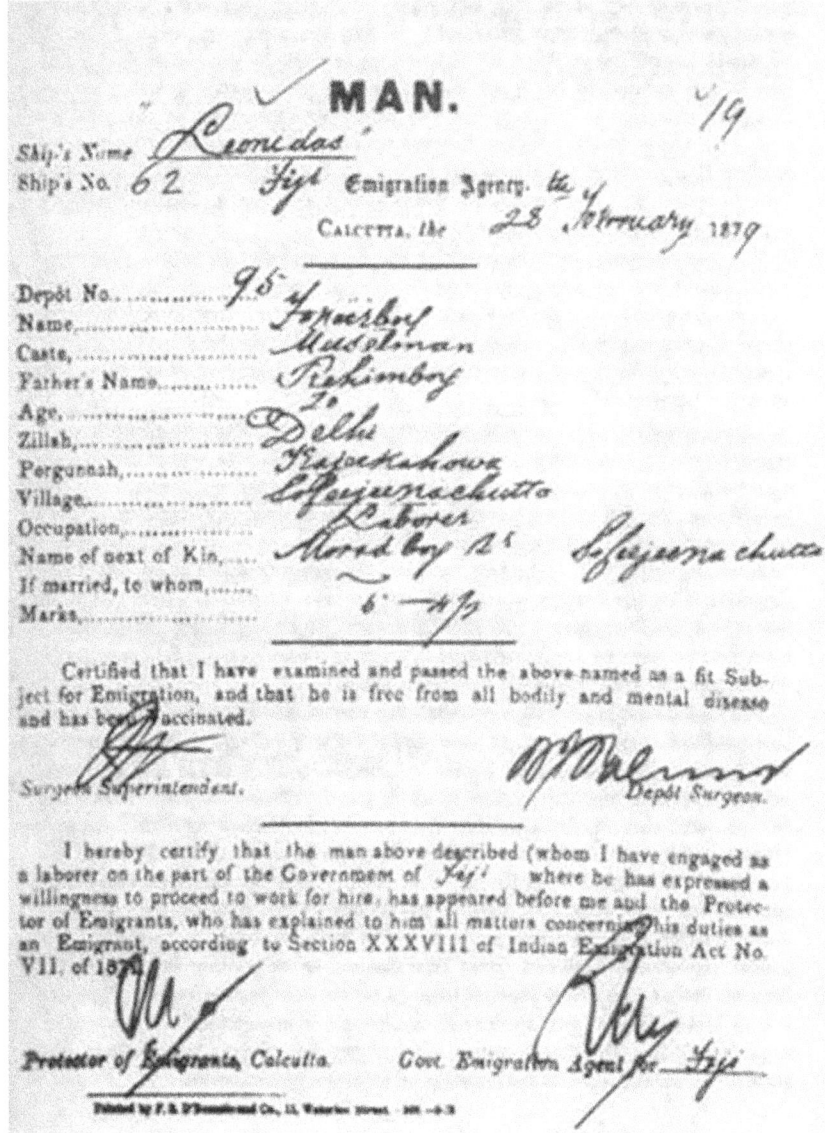

Figure 3.5 b) Emigration Pass for Men for Fiji. Source: National Archives Depot, Pietermaritzburg

WOMAN. 1729

Ship's Name Pronah?

Ship's No. 176

Fiji Emigration Agency,

CALCUTTA, the 5th April 1882.

Depôt No. 202

Name, Soleni

Caste, Brahmin

Father's name, Shadonul

Sex Female.

Age, 25

Zillah, Joypore

Pergunnah or Thanna,

Village, Neemnathana

Occupation, Laborer

Name of next-of-kin, Dhoonul Br Neemnathana

If married, to whom,

Height, 4–10½

Marks, Slightly Pock marked face.

Certified that I have examined and passed the above-named as a fit Subject for Emigration, and that she is free from all bodily and mental disease, and has been Vaccinated.

Surgeon-Superintendent.

for Depôt-Surgeon.

I hereby certify that the woman above described (whom I have engaged as a labourer on the part of the Government of Fiji, where she has expressed a willingness to proceed to work for hire) has appeared before me and the Protector of Emigrants, who has explained to her all matters concerning her duties as an Emigrant, according to Section XXXVIII of Indian Emigration Act No. VII. of 1871.

Protector of Emigrants, Calcutta.

Govt. Emigration Agent for Fiji.

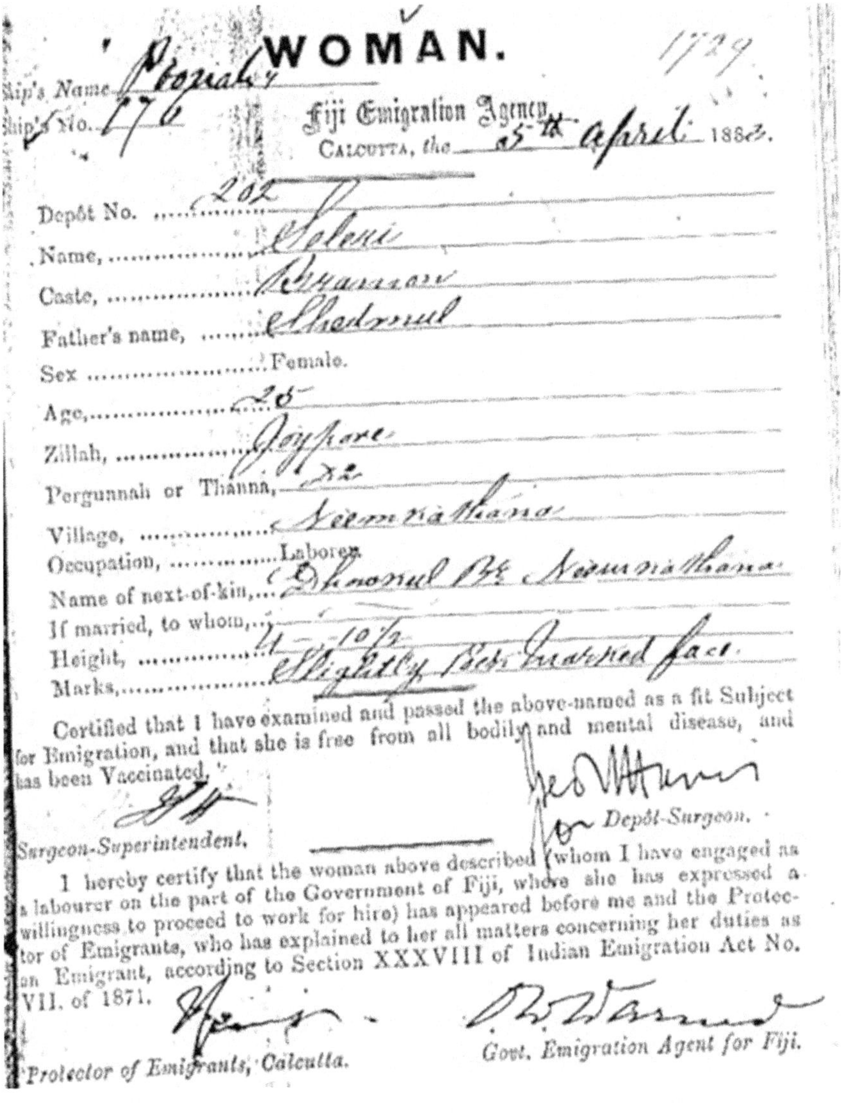

Figure 3.5 c) Women's emigration pass for Fiji. Source: National Archives Depot, Pietermaritzburg

These snapshots show the details of the terms and conditions offered by the indenture system. It has always been at the centre of the arguments by critics of the indenture system that the language of 'contract' was complicated and elite in nature making it difficult for an illiterate labourer to understand. Until now, most historians have simply assumed that the actual contract and terms of services on which illiterate labourers put their thumb impression to agree for work were only available in the 'colonial language' – especially English – and not very useful for determining the specific nature of this labour system. However, the contracts mention the period of contract, the nature of work, holidays, the amount of rations to be available, salary, medical facilities and dwelling and clothing in numerous languages of labourers such as Bangla, Hindi, Urdu, Tamil, Telegu, Malayali as well as other Indian local languages of catchment areas of labourers. Apart from these, passes were issued to male and female indentured labourers which contained all possible information about the emigrants. Apart from these, laws were passed in the legislative council of India which regulated the indentured migration.

The identification of such sources prompts the question of whether the employers fulfilled the indenture contracts. Did the labour regime and state fulfil their promises? To understand this issue, one needs to dig deep into the experience of indentured labourers. Recently, works on the memoirs and testimonies of the indentured workers have emerged.[24] The fulfilment of terms and conditions by the plantation regime differed depending on the social background of the labourers.[25] To be more specific, many labourers of the lower social strata of society in India found the regime sufficient at fulfilling the contract. On the other hand, those who enjoyed a higher social strata found the regime suppressive. Interestingly, in memoirs on experience as indentured labourers, evidence of high caste labourers lying about their social status has been uncovered. For example, Totaram Sanadhya and Baba Ramchandra, two high caste indentured labourers in Fiji lied on the written official paper that they do not belong to the Brahmin caste.[26]

Regarding non-indentured labour migration streams, from 1880 the *kangani* method of recruitment began for rubber, tea and coffee plantations within imperial South and Southeast Asia. The recruitment was mostly conducted in south Indian villages. Under the *kangani* system, no legal contract comparable to the indenture contract ever emerged. Every part of life on plantations was dependent on the *kangani*, who was recruiter as well as worker on the same plantation. In the absence of any detailed documentation, it is difficult to trace the exact number of people involved at each level of the system or to assess precise views on their treatment on the plantations. Some historians have argued that the *kangani* system was better than indentured migration. According to Arasaratnam, in this type of system the *kangani* could be expected to exercise greater care in the choice of labourers. That aside, since the *kangani* was from the same village and community, there may have been a greater willingness to volunteer as emigrants. Therefore, the danger of abuses may have been less than in a system of outright coercion. Since all labourers brought to plantations by *kangani* had to work under him, this process reduced the hardship resulting from the migration.[27]

However, during periods of high demand for labour, the *kangani* would extend their recruitment to areas beyond their villages, community and castes and could induce labourers to fulfil their obligations and personal interests. In the absence of any regulatory measures, the *kangani* would put labourers in debt-bondage by providing cash advances to the intending emigrants.[28] The advances were not only limited to intending emigrants for their passage but to their families left behind at home as well as pocket money to sustain them during the initial days at the destination colonies.[29] Since labourers had no legal contracts, in cases of any discrepancy it was impossible to get justice through the courts or other legal means. This state of affairs enabled *kanganies* to place labourers in continuous indebtedness as well as control the freedom of employment and mobility for many labourers. In many cases, *kanganies* compelled labourers to move along with them from one estate to another against their wishes.[30] Since there was no legally defined contract between the *kangani* and the labourer, employers were not bound to provide facilities of food, medical and other facilities. Furthermore, the system provided no means to control such fraud and coercion in recruitment, whereas in the indenture system, a legal process ensued in the case of any discrepancy between labourers and employers. In cases of fraud and coercion, legal provisions emerged as pivotal in the prosecution of such cases. Scholars and labour historians who have argued that recruiters of the indentured were involved in fraud have not looked at the data relating to cases filed and convictions against the recruiters. In some examples of recruitment in northern India, the data show that during the period 1878–82, there were 262 licensed recruiters and 40,028 emigrants registered in the North-Western Provinces and Oudh excluding those rejected by medical officers, deserters and rejections by registering officers. During the same period twenty-eight cases were initiated against recruiters of which eighteen were dismissed and ten convicted.

Emigrants Registered in the North-Western Provinces and Oudh during 1878–82 and Criminal Charges against Recruiters

Station	Number of emigrants registered	Criminal cases instituted against recruiters		
		Number of cases instituted	Dismissal	Convicted
Benaras	5,064	6	2	4
Cawnpore	3,983	4	4	–
Lucknow	3,676	–	–	–
Fyzabad	3,201	–	–	–
Allahabad	3,007	3	2	1
Agra	2,748	2	–	2
Ghazipur	2,085	–	–	–
Bareilly	1,957	2	–	–
Muttra	1,928	1	1	–
Aligharh	1,744	–	–	–
Gorakhpur	1,697	2	2	–
Farukhabad	1,034	1	1	–
Azamgarh	734	–	–	–
Etawah	638	–	–	–
Basti	614	–	–	–
Mainpuri	603	–	–	–
Bulandshahr	586	1	1	–
Gonda	508	2	2	–
Moradabad	500	1	1	–
Sultanpur	441	–	–	–
Jaunpur	363	1	1	1
Fatehpur	352	–	–	–
Unao	307	–	–	–
Shahjahanpur	300	–	–	–
Barabanki	299	1	–	1
Meerut	260	–	–	–
Mirzapur	255	–	–	–
Hardoi	239	–	–	
Banda	228	–	–	–
Bahraich	175			
Etah	166	1	1	–
Budaun	136	–	–	–

Station	Number of emigrants registered	Criminal cases instituted against recruiters		
		Number of cases instituted	Dismissal	Convicted
Sitapur	91	–	–	–
Pratapgarh	59	–	–	–
Ballia	27	–	–	–
Raibaeli	23	–	–	–
Total	40,028	28	18	10

Source: Pitcher Report, Appendix iii, p.43.

Apart from the convictions of the recruiters who were involved in fraud and coercion, the government did cancel licences of recruitment on suspicion of fraud in recruitment. The following table shows the Colonial Recruiting Licences granted and cancelled from 1880 to 1902 in Northern India.

Colonial Recruiting Licences Granted and Cancelled[31]

year	No. granted	No. cancelled	% cancellation	No. recruited	Average no. per recruiter
1880–81	559	11	2.0	15,430	27.6
1881–82	452	14	3.1	11,539	25.5
1877	345	3	0.9	6,882	19.9
1888	511	4	0.8	10,325	20.2
1889	171	15	2.1	16,813	23.4
1890	768	20	2.6	23,813	30.0
1891	1,003	22	2.2	25,613	25.5
1892	857	2	0.2	17,225	20.1
1893	866	8	0.9	15,046	17.4
1894	1,023	6	0.6	26,707	26.1
1895	838	13	1.6	17,315	20.7
1896	755	12	1.6	16,439	21.8
1897	539	3	0.6	12,315	22.8
1898	701	27	3.9	9,334	13.3
1899	801	43	5.4	14,051	17.5
1900	1,088	27	2.5	18,489	17.0
1902	1,415	37	2.6	13,807	9.8

As Brij Lal has argued, the cases of fraud and deceit that reached the official record were perhaps only the 'tip of the iceberg'. In light of the long history of indentured emigration, it would be fair to suggest that the elaborate machinery set up to govern recruitment was effective in many cases. Cases of fraud were certainly far fewer than it would appear from impressionistic and oral evidence.[32] Such measures were not possible for non-indentured migrants.

Space for bargain under the indenture system[33]

What was possible for indentured migrants becomes clear through an analysis of regulations regarding food provisions on ships. On the 11 July 1881, the colonial office sent a letter to the Secretary of State relating to the diet of coolies on board emigrant vessels regarding rice and flour according to the distinction between rice eaters and flour eaters. The office suggested that cooked rations of rice and – when practicable – flour be issued alternately to the coolies.[34] Edward Wingfield of the colonial office wrote this letter to the Secretary of State, after receiving a note from a surgeon superintendent who had experienced discontent on a recent voyage from Calcutta to Trinidad with emigrants recruited principally from the North-Western Provinces. Some emigrants demanded chapati instead of rice in their meal. Protests emerged after failure to issue both types of rations, as there were both rice eaters and flour eaters on the ship. An enquiry was conducted and it was decided 'that each class might throughout be provided with its accustomed food-supply', meaning that a diet of flour and rice should be issued alternately.

In 1860s another conflict emerged between the labourers and the ship authorities on the issue of preserved meat. From the beginning of the indenture system, there was provision for meat on the menu during the sea journey. The idea of preserved meat was completely new for both Hindu and Muslim Indians. Therefore, such preserved meat created discontent among the emigrants as it created suspicion of not being *halal* for Muslims and the possibility of beef being served to Hindus. Given the dietary rules in Islam, which allow only the consumption of the meat of an animal ritually butchered in compliance with Halal rules, in addition to Hindu proscriptions against the consumption of beef, both groups were suspicious of preserved meat on board the ship. To resolve this problem arising from such practices, the authorities introduced a live sheep and goat on board the boat, along with a Muslim butcher who was to slaughter them in the *halal* way.[35] From that point, mutton was to be preserved with a portion of the bone attached to it. Bigger bones would be an indication that the animal was a cow instead of a goat.[36] The colonial state incorporated these provisions into the Emigration Acts 1864 and 1883.

The aforementioned cases give a view of indenture that differs from the standard emphasis on the negative excesses of the system. Historians and scholars have maintained that the workers who signed the contract of indenture were unable to bargain or (re)negotiate for their better living conditions. Hence, they supposedly had no 'free choice', pointing to the conclusion that contractual relations between employers and the employees were not, in fact, voluntary.[37] However, the creation of an arena of dietary space from a point of view of the labourers showed their bargaining capacity as well as the limitations of colonial systems of power.[38] In India of this time, prominent social hierarchies associated with caste often barred inter-dining and inter-marriage.[39] High and low castes were defined by the food they consumed, with one's purity being contingent on the purity of one's food. Indian religious texts have categorically described the eating rules for various castes. High castes enjoyed refined dishes while low castes lived on sustainable and simple food.[40] In Indian society, to remain unpolluted and conserve the hierarchy, high castes maintaining these rules would not eat food prepared by the lower castes; neither would high and low castes dine together.[41] The fulfilment of such dietary demands of indentured emigrants who had previously experienced hierarchy throughout their life in India shows their bargaining capacity in the colonial system of indentured labour.

Here, it is also important to note that while the colonial government introduced the rule of providing habitual food and addressing dietary demands on ships, it completely flouted the caste rules with regard to inter-caste dining. Munshi Rahman Khan, an indentured labourer in Surinam discussed the practices of dining on the ship during the journey from countryside to central depot and from the central depot at embarkation point to the destination depot in the colonies. He revealed that at the central depot in Calcutta, people forgot about caste hierarchy while eating.[42] In an interview, returned indentured labourers informed Grierson, in early 1880, that 'a man can eat anything on board ship, a vessel being like the Temple of Jagannath, without caste restrictions'.[43] The only arrangement permitted by the colonial authorities on the ship was the Brahmin *Bhandaries* (cooks) and *topazes* (sweepers), from the low caste. Basil Lubbock described this arrangement as follow:

They [Bhandaries] were usually chosen from men of high caste, Brahmins when possible ... The topazes, commonly called "sweepers" in India, were of course men of low caste, but they were well paid for their duties.[44]

James M. Laing, an experienced Surgeon Superintendent on a 'coolie' ship also instructed ship officials to appoint Brahmins, the men of high caste, as *Bhandaries*, if possible.[45]

The question of freedom and coercion in the indentured contract

Historians and scholars have explored the issues of freedom and unfreedom in very abstract ways. Integrating the history of indentured labour into this matrix brings a complication to the assumptions about the history of freedom and labour.[46] In its nature and genesis, labour has never been fully free in the abstract sense. However, historians and theorists have marked a change in the context of labour in the nineteenth century. They have noted the appearance of new terminologies such as 'will' or 'consent' in the labour contract laws.[47] In the context of nineteenth-century Britain, David Lieberman noted a transformation from the 'master and servant' law into legal contract law. However, in the context of indenture, some scholars have seen its genesis in the master and servant law of the British as it incorporated criminalization of breach of contract by employee.[48] Some scholars have focused on the imposed circumstantial necessity by the planters on their plantations, which depicts the unfree nature of the regime. However, these scholars have not provided any study of indentured labour laws at the point of origin in India and the components of freedom or unfreedom in these laws.

Recently, Radhika Mongia provided a significant perspective to the history of indentured Indian migration. Mongia argues that the indentured contract had no foundation in any existing law. By exploring the debate among the stakeholders of indentured migration, Mongia found that from the very beginning of the system it was 'plagued by opposition, doubt, and anxiety regarding the "freedom" of the emigrants'. Hence, in an effort to ensure freedom, the whole system was placed under state regulation and became a massive, micro-managed, state-controlled enterprise.[49] While discussing contract and consent, Mongia argues that before the nineteenth century, while contract had a concept of consent or will it also included many other important elements such as equality in exchange and the absence of fraud, duress or mistakes. In the case of such criteria failing, the law could deem it invalid. In other words, 'consent in and of itself did not make a contract binding'. In the nineteenth century, according to Mongia, a contract was defined as binding and enforceable in terms of will or consent. The best example of such a contract in the actual historical records of colonial India was the indenture contract.[50]

However, I argue against the assumption that the indenture contract was binding and enforceable in terms of will or consent. In the actual clauses of indentured contracts, there existed space and scope to breach the contract legally at any point in time. Apart from that, the indentured contract featured checks and balances for both parties, that is, both labourers and planters. The first legislation on indentured emigration arrived in 1837. Emigration Act 7 of 1837 stipulated that no emigrant could be transported without a permit which was granted by the officer authorized for that purpose. The memorandum of contract had to be in English *and the mother tongue of the native or some language understood by the labourer* that specified the nature, terms and wages of service. A fine of Rs. 200 or thirty days' imprisonment was imposed for every Indian worker who embarked without a permit.

After this important legislation, twenty-seven years later in 1864, the comprehensive Act XIII was introduced. In this Act, provisions were made specifically to prevent abduction, kidnapping and involuntary emigration by bringing these under the ambit of the Indian Penal Code. There was also a provision for emigration agents to pay money to the emigration department of the colonial government in case the labourer was not in satisfactory condition – due to bad health etc. – to board the ship. Failing this, the protector had the right to recover money from the emigration agent at an interest rate of six per cent. At the same time, it also provisioned through section 44 of the Act that those emigrants who refused or neglected to proceed without sufficient cause were liable for punishment under section 492 of the Indian Penal Code.[51]

New clauses defined the offence in the Emigration Act of 1883. According to the Act:

> 93. (1) if any emigrant deserts before arrival at depot, or refuses without reasonable cause to proceed to the depot, he shall be punished with fine which may extend to twenty rupees, or to the cost incurred in entering into an agreement with, registering and conveying him to the depot, whichever is greater, and, in default of payment of the fine, with imprisonment which may extend to one month. (2) Any fine levied under this section may, in the discretion of the convicting magistrate, be paid to the Emigration Agent or recruiter by whom the cost was incurred.

> 94. (1) If any emigrant– (a) deserts from depot, or (b) without reasonable cause, refuses or neglects to embark when called upon to do so by the Emigration Agent, he shall be punished with imprisonment for a term which may not extend one month, or with fine which may extend to 50 rupees, or to double the amount of the cost incurred in entering into an agreement with, registering and conveying him to the depot, and maintaining him therein, or with both. (2) Any fine levied under this section may, in the discretion of the convicting Magistrate, be paid to the Emigration Agent or recruiter by whom the cost was incurred'

Section 44 of the Emigration Act, 1864 made the refusal to embark without sufficient cause a criminal act under section 492 of the Indian Penal Code and section 93 (1) and 94 (1) of the Emigration Act 1883. While these sections did not allow the intending emigrant full 'freedom' to breach the contract at the embarkation point, at the same time, the law formally allowed a registered emigrant the 'freedom' not to board a ship after undergoing one month's imprisonment or paying a sum of Rs. 50. Anti-slavery activists as well as Indian nationalists interpreted this law as coercive and unfair, as an example of 'unfreedom'. But as I have enquired elsewhere, would it be a high price to pay the sum incurred by their journey down to Calcutta for having a life of hell – if it was – for five to ten years in the sugar colonies? After the full abolition of indentured contract in January 1920,[52] the next Emigration Act emerged in 1922. In Sinha's words, the Emigration Act of 1922 gave the abolition of indenture official imprimatur.[53] At this point, the colonial state relinquished its previous role in the actual terms of the contract for those who were emigrating overseas.

Conclusion

Historians have homogenized the nineteenth-century labour regimes and experience. The indenture system of labour has often been interpreted as extremely coercive and an unfree form of labour in legal terms. On the other hand, recent particular studies of global migration, such as that of McKeown, diminish the significance of indentured migrants from India within a global framework.[54] His work also argues that the indentured migration was an involuntary form of migration, compared to European labour migrations.[55] In a recent article, Rachel Sturman has tried to highlight for the first time the significance of indentured contracts where she indicates how various watchdogs made the system highly protective to ensure humanity towards labourers. Following Sturman's pivotal work, I have explored how the presence of the contract in the indentured migration system forms a crucial site for the exploration of debates about freedom in the context of global labour history.

The indenture contract uniquely provided a space for bargain by labourers, as we have seen in the context of provisioning implemented through laws. It also gave space for breach of contract by labourers at final embarkation points. In other words, it was not necessary for labourers to perform the contract once they had signed it. They had the space to cancel the contract by either providing a valid reason or by paying an amount decided by the contract or going to jail for a period determined in the contract. The various cases show that indentured labourers even used this space to bargain or to cancel the contract. A study of various clauses of the indentured contract shows that the regulatory clauses were based on the best possible measures to take care of both labourers and the planters. This made indenture a special case in comparison to other forms of labour migration from the Indian sub-continent abroad such as the *kangani* and *maistry* systems of migration. The indentured migration system then offered certain labourers, particularly those in socially subordinate positions in colonial India, limited mobility out of a feudal regime of work into a capitalist regime of work.[56] Such an experience of the indenture system became an important pathway for a broad sector of labourers, especially members of lower caste groups, towards a new system, but definitely not one of slavery.

Notes

1. See G. Balachandran, *Globalizing Labor? Indian Seafarers and World Shipping, c. 1870–1945* (New York: Oxford University Press, 2012); Adam McKeown, *Melancholy Order: Asian Migration and the Globalization of Borders* (New York: Columbia University Press, 2011); and David Northrup, *Indentured Labor in the Age of Imperialism, 1834–1922* (New York: Cambridge University Press, 1995). All place the nineteenth century at the centre of a new form of labour migration.
2. For details on the indenture system, see Ashutosh Kumar, *Coolies of the Empire: Indentured Indians in the Sugar Colonies, c.1830–1920* (Cambridge: Cambridge University Press, 2017).
3. For the end of the indenture system, see, Ashutosh Kumar, 'Indian Nationalist and the End of the Indenture System', Occasional paper, History and Society, No. 48 (Nehru Memorial Museum and Library, 2014); and Karen A. Roy, 'The abolition of Indentured Emigration and the Politics of Indian Nationalism, 1894–1917', unpublished PhD thesis (McGill University, Canada, 1981). Other relevant articles include Ashutosh Kumar, 'Anti-Indentured Bhojpuri Folksongs and Poems from

North India' *Man in India: An International Journal of Anthropology* 90, no. 4 (2013): 509–519 and the same author's 'Songs of Abolition: Anti-Indentured Campaign in Early-Twentieth Century India' in *Indian Diaspora: Socio-Cultural and Religious Worlds*, ed. P. Pratap Kumar (Leiden: Brill, 2015), 38–51.

4   For the *kangani* and *maistry* system, see S. Arasaratnam, *Indians in Malaysia and Singapore* (London: Oxford University Press Institute for Race Relations, 1970). For a description and operation of the *maistry* system in Burma, see N.R. Chakravarti, *The Indian Minority in Burma* (London: Oxford University Press Institute for Race Relations, 1971). For British Malaya, see K.S. Sandhu, *Indians in Malaya: Immigration and Settlement, 1786–1957* (Cambridge: Cambridge University Press, 1969) and P. Ramasamy, 'Labour Control and Labour Resistance in the Plantations of Colonial Malaya' *Journal of Peasant Studies* 19 (1992): 87–105. On Sri Lanka, see Frank Heidemann, *Kanganies in Sri Lanka and Malaysia: Tamil Recruiter-cum-Foreman as a Sociological Category in the Nineteenth and Twentieth Centuries* (Munich: Anacon, 1992) and Patrick Peebles, *The Plantation Tamils in Sri Lanka* (London: Leicester University Press, 2001).

5   In-depth studies of colonial legal history in India are rare though the field has shown signs of revival in recent years. An important milestone in the field is Radhika Singha, *A Despotism of Law: Crime and Justice in Early Colonial India* (Delhi: Oxford University Press, 1998). See also Sanjay Nigam, 'Disciplining and Policing the Criminals by Birth, Part 1: The Making of a Colonial Stereotype – The Criminal Tribes and Castes of North India' *The Indian Economic and Social History Review* 27, no. 2 (1990): 131–164 and 'Disciplining and Policing the Criminals by Birth, Part 2: The Development of a Disciplinary System, 1871–1900' *The Indian Economic and Social History Review* 27, no. 3 (1990): 257–287. Classic works include David Washbrook, 'Law, State and Agrarian Society in Colonial India' *Modern Asian Studies* 15, no. 3 (1981): 649–721and Anand A. Yang, ed., *Crime and Criminality in British India* (Tucson, AZ: University of Arizona Press, 1985).

6   Hugh Tinker, *A New System of Slavery: The Export of Indian Labor Overseas, 1830–1920* (Oxford: Oxford University Press, 1974), 84.

7   Willy Forbath, 'The Long Life of Liberal America: Law and State-Building in the U.S. and England' *Law and History Review* 24, no. 1 (2006): 179; Amy Stanley, *From Bondage to Contract: Wage Labor, Marriage, and the Market in the Age of Slave Emancipation* (Cambridge: Cambridge University Press, 1998), and Christopher Tomlins, 'A Mysterious Power: Industrial Accidents and the Legal Construction of Employment Relations in Massachusetts, 1800–1850' *Law and History Review* 6, no. 2 (1988): 375–438.

8   Robert J. Steinfeld, *Coercion, Contract and Free Labor in the Nineteenth Century* (Albany: SUNY Press, 2001).

9   Peter Robb, 'Introduction: Meanings of Labour in Indian Social Context' in *Dalit Movements and the Meanings of Labour in India*, ed. Peter Robb (Delhi: Oxford University Press, 1993).

10 See, for instance, Michael Anderson's 'Work Construed: Ideological Origins of Labour Law in British India' in *Dalit Movements*, 91.
11 Prabhu P. Mohapatra, 'Regulated Informality: Legal Constructions of Labour Relations in Colonial India, 1814–1926' in *Workers in the Informal Sector: Studies in Labour History 1800–2000*, ed. Jan Lucassen and Sabyasachi Bhattacharya (New Delhi: Macmillan India/SEPHIS, 2005), 11.
12 Adam McKeown, 'Global Migration, 1846–1940' *Journal of World History* 15, no. 2 (2004): 155–189.
13 Prabhu Mohapatra, Eurocentrism, Forced Labour, and Global Migration: A Critical Assessment, *International Review of Social History*, Vol. 52, p. 112.
14 Prabhu Mohapatra, 'Eurocentrism, Forced Labour, and Global Migration: A Critical Assessment' *International Review of Social History* 52, no. 1 (2007): 112.
15 Crispin Bates and Marina Carter, 'Enslaving Life, Enslaving Labels: A New Approach to the Colonial Indian Labor Diaspora' in *New Routes for Diaspora Studies*, eds. Sukanya Banerjee, Aims McGuiness and Steven C. McKay (Bloomington, IN: Indiana University Press, 2007), 73.
16 Rachel Sturman, 'Indian Indentured Labor and the History of International Rights Regimes' *American Historical Review*, 119, no. 5 (2014): 1439–1465.
17 Lisa Lowe, *The Intimacies of Four Continents* (Durham, NC: Duke University Press, 2015).
18 Radhika Mongia, *Indian Migration and Empire: A Colonial Genealogy of the Modern State* (Durham and London: Duke University Press, 2018).
19 For details on the *kamiati* system, see Gyan Prakash, *Bonded Labor: Genealogies of Labor Servitude in Colonial India* (Cambridge: Cambridge University Press, 1990).
20 Caste discrimination in this historical context had been present in practices of dining, marriage and other elements of social life. For further analysis of social equality and indenture, see Kumar, *Coolies of the Empire* and the same author's 'Feeding the Girmitiya: Food and Drinks on the indentured Ships to the Sugar Colonies' *Gastronomica: The Journal of Critical Food Studies* 16, no. 1 (Spring 2016): 41–52.
21 Revenue and Agriculture Department (Emigration) Part A, Progs.9–15, August 1883, Major D.G. Pitcher and George A. Grierson enquiry into emigration (hereafter Grierson Report), Para 43–46, 10.
22 *Arkati* is the Bhojpurisation of the English recruiter.
23 It is important to note here that not all potential recruits made it to the sugar colonies, as the authorities rejected many due to their physical make-up. As Brij Lal has shown, almost 40 per cent of recruited labourers faced rejection due to unfitness. See, Brij Lal, *The Girmitiya: The Origin of the Fiji Indians* (Canberra: Journal of Pacific History, 1983).
24 See Kathinka Sinha-Kerkhoff, Ellen Bal and Alok Deo Singh, *Autobiography of an Indian Indentured Labourer. Munshi Rahman Khan (1874–1972)* (Delhi: Shipra Publications, 2005), Brij V Lal, Yogendra Yadav and Ashutosh Kumar, ed., *Bhootlen*

Ki Katha: Girmit Ke Anubhav by Totaram Sanadhya (Delhi: Rajkamal Prakashan, 2012), and Kumar, *Coolies of the Empire,* especially chapter 6.

25 On this aspect of the indenture system see Kumar, 'Feeding the Girmitiya: Food and Drinks on the indentured Ships to the Sugar Colonies'.

26 See the analysis on the hiding of actual caste on the original legal contract form of indenture by Brahmin Indians in Kumar, *Coolies of the Empire*, chapter 7.

27 Arasaratnam, *Indians in Malaysia and Singapore,* 16.

28 See Ritesh Kumar Jaiswal, 'The "Other" System of Indian Migration: A Case Study of *Kangani* and *Maistry* System in Ceylon and Burma, 1880s–1930s,' Unpublished M.Phil. diss., Department of History, University of Delhi, 2014.

29 Jaiswal, 44.

30 Jaiswal, 101.

31 Lal, *Girmitiyas,* 54, and the same author's *Chalo Jahaji: On a Journey through Indenture through Fiji* (Canberra: ANU Press, 2012), 86. Lal obtained data from the Proceedings Reports of the various years listed.

32 B.V. Lal, *Girmitiyas,* op. cit. p. 55.

33 This section draws partially from my article 'Feeding the Girmitiya: Food and Drink on Indentured Ships to the Sugar Colonies'.

34 Proceedings of Bengal Government, General Department, Colonial Emigration 1881. National Archives of India [Hereafter NAI].

35 Government of Bengal [hereafter GoB], Emigration Proceedings [hereafter EP], June 1869. Extract from the report of James Crosby, Immigration Agent, No. 179, Friday 19 February 1869, on the immigrant ship the Winchester to West Indies. NAI

36 GoB, EP, No. 10, July 1870. From Geoghegan, Under-Secretary to the GoI Home Department to GoB, dated Simla 29 October 1869 in Enclosure No. 1 of letter from T.W.C. Murdoch to Sir F. Rogers, Simla, dated 16 July 1869. NAI.

37 Two particular contributions that integrate the history of India into this debate feature Michael Anderson, 'India, 1858–1930: The Illusion of Free Labour' and Prabhu Mohapatra, 'Assam and the West Indies, 1860–1920: Immobilising Plantation Labour' in *Masters, Servants and Magistrates in Britain and the Empire, 1562-1955,* ed. Douglas Hay and Paul Craven (Chapel Hill and London: University of North Carolina Press, 2004), 422–454 and 455–480. Other important works include Prabhu P. Mohapatra, 'Regulated Informality: Legal Constructions of Labour Relations in Colonial India, 1814–1926' and Gail Omvedt, 'Migration in Colonial India: The Articulation of Feudalism and Capitalism by Colonial State' *Journal of Peasant Studies* 7, no. 2 (1980): 185–212.

38 For a detailed discussion of 'space' and limits of colonial power, see Kumar, 'Feeding the Girmitiya: Food and Drinks on the Indentured Ships to the Sugar Colonies.'

39 The subject of caste and food appears in the long literature on anthropological treatments of caste and social life. Jack Goody, *Cooking, Cuisine, and Class: A Study in Comparative Sociology* (Cambridge: Cambridge University Press, 1982) remains an authoritative study on the subject in a comparative sociological and historical context. Recent work assessing the enduring importance of a comparative sociological perspective on food and social hierarchies includes J. Klein and Murcott, eds., *Food Consumption in Global Perspective: Essays in the Anthropology of Food in Honor of Jack Goody* (Basingstoke: Palgrave Macmillan, 2014).
40 Goody, *Cooking, Cuisine, and Class*, 115
41 Goody, 116.
42 See Kumar, 'Feeding the Girmitiya: Food and Drinks on the Indentured Ships to the Sugar Colonies.'
43 Kumar, 'Feeding the Girmitya,' 47.
44 Basil Lubbock, *Coolie Ships and Oil Sailors* (Glasgow: Brown, Son & Ferguson, 1935), 58.
45 James M. Laing, '*Handbook for Surgeons Superintendent of the Coolie Emigration Service*,' (1889), CO 885/5/32.
46 Robert Grafstein, 'The Theory of Freedom,' *Social Science Quarterly* 70, no. 4 (1989): 851–854.
47 Morton Horwitz, 'The Historical Foundation of Modern Contract Law' *Harvard Law Review* 87, no. 5 (March 1974): 917–956, James Gordley, *The Philosophical Origins of Modern Contract Doctrines* (Oxford: Clarendon, 1991), and P. S. Atiyah, *An Introduction to the Law of Contract* (Oxford: Clarendon Press, 1995).
48 Michael Anderson, 'India, 1858–1930: The Illusion of Free Labor'.
49 Mongia, *Indian Migration and Empire*, 25–26.
50 Ibid., 41–42.
51 The provision of section 44 was not in the draft of the Emigration Act 1864. Instead, there was only a provision for emigration agents to pay money in case the labourer was not in a condition to board the ship. Failing this, the protector had the right to recover money from emigration agent at a six per cent interest rate. After an objection by the emigration agent, the refusal to embark without sufficient cause was included in section 492 of the Indian Penal Code. For a detailed discussion of this issue see Kumar, *Coolies of the Empire*.
52 The abolition of the indenture system formally occurred in 1917, but all indentured labourers literally enjoyed freedom from contracts on 1 January 1920.
53 Mrinalini Sinha, 'Premonitions of the Past' *The Journal of Asian Studies* 74, no. 4 (2015): 31.
54 McKeown, 'Global Migration, 1846–1940'.
55 In his reply to McKeown, Prabhu Mohapatra points out that McKeown's argument of European transatlantic migration being economically driven, voluntary, and

'free' was Eurocentric as non-European migration in the same period was largely indentured or involuntary. Mohapatra disagrees with McKeown only on the issue of causation of such involuntary migration from Asia. According to Mohapatra, 'free migration' was itself a product of government regulations in many instances and the segmentation of free European and unfree Asian migration streams was not a product of natural conditions but a result of political intervention not only by governments but by powerful employers, both European and non-European. See his 'Eurocentrism, Forced Labour, and Global Migration: A Critical Assessment'.

56 Most of the labourers in pre-colonial India worked under a bonded system of labour. Ian J. Kerr in his recent research shows that many communities in pre-colonial India were involved in labour work such as Banjaras, Waddars, Woddas or Woddaru, a tribe of Telinga origin, etc. See Ian J. Kerr, 'On the Move: Circulating Labour in Pre-Colonial, Colonial, and Post- Colonial India' *International Review of Social History* 51 (2006): 85–109. However, the bulk of labourers who migrated under the indenture system were not from these groups and hailed from those areas where feudal labour bonds were active. See Prakash, *Bonded Histories*.

Part Two

Law in Migration Histories

4

Slavery, abolitionism, indentured labour: The problem of exit and the border between land and sea in colonial India

Riyad Sadiq Koya

In May 1871, newspaper reports of the kidnapping of a young woman in Allahabad provoked a flurry of official letters. In an article entitled 'An Indian Slave Trade', the *Pioneer of India* relayed an account of a young woman returning home after finding there was no corn to grind at her place of work. A man 'accosted' her on the road, offering her work to grind corn. Taken to a serai within the city, she was confined with several other women and children. Her pleas to return home to her infant child were met with 'blows and cuffs'. The 'kidnappers' informed her that 'she would be sent to Jamaica, where she would get twelve rupees a month besides clothes'. The next day, her sister located the serai, 'and began to weep and beat her breast before the door'. The sister was also confined, but by means of 'vociferous howling', was able to force her own release.

The young woman's sister sought the assistance of two missionaries, who inquired after the women and children at the serai. An 'agent', described as a 'scoundrel', claimed that the women inside had given their 'consent' to travel to Jamaica. The women denied the agent's claims and rushed onto the street. Some twenty 'wretched women' were then presented before the magistrate, who effected their release. The agents, led by Buldeo, were subsequently placed on trial. The 'kidnappers' were revealed to be 'Jamaican Emigration Agents' in the employ of Bird and Company, a noted Calcutta managing agency.

My thanks to Neilesh Bose, Sandria Freitag, David Gilmartin, Renisa Mawani, Barbara D. Metcalf, Thomas R. Metcalf, Radhika Mongia and three anonymous reviewers for their comments on earlier drafts of this paper, first presented at the Association of Asian Studies meetings in 2018. A shorter outtake from this article will appear in the *Journal of World History* 31, no. 1 (March 2021).

Officials at the Colonial Office and the Colonial Land and Emigration Commission (CLEC) reviewed excerpts of the *Pioneer of India* reports, printed by the *Standard* in London. Clinton Murdoch of the CLEC doubted the veracity of the account, noting that his office had not been informed about the incident. He further stated that 'such a transaction' was 'impossible' by the terms of Act XIII of 1864, which regulated the emigration of indentured labour. The thirtieth section of the Act required that emigrants appear before a magistrate with their recruiter. If the magistrate suspected 'fraud, misrepresentation, or a failure to understand the terms of engagement', registration could be refused. The Colonial Office sent the newspaper clippings and Murdoch's letter to the India Office which, in turn, forwarded the papers to the Government of India, querying if an 'amending Act' was required.[1]

I suggest that the events at Allahabad illustrate the significance of the border between land and sea for colonial South Asia.[2] This border was charged with a history of slave trafficking and unfree labour migration in the Indian Ocean world.[3] As the East India Company became a territorial power on the South Asian subcontinent, it confronted reports of the kidnapping of British Indian subjects by foreign powers.[4] Consequently, the Company sought to prohibit the trafficking of slaves overseas. In the nineteenth century, as India became a key source of labour for colonial plantations in the British, French, Dutch and Danish empires, new border practices were devised to regulate the emigration of Indian labourers. In contradistinction to the problem of entry that transpired in the early twentieth century with debates about the exclusion of British Indian subjects, border practices in colonial South Asia were distinctively concerned, I argue, with the problem of 'exit'.

The border between land and sea in colonial South Asia was subject to continuous revision or 'recalibration'.[5] Slave trafficking had provoked novel border practices to prohibit the exit of enslaved British Indian subjects. The abolition of slavery in the British Empire in 1833 occasioned new border practices to regulate the departure of British Indian subjects to Mauritius. Ostensibly under contracts of indenture, allegations persisted that British Indian subjects were kidnapped or that recruiters fraudulently represented the terms of the labourers' engagements. To guarantee the 'voluntariness' of overseas emigration, the Government of India passed a series of emigration acts between 1837 and 1908. These acts implemented permits, passes and registration procedures to 'materialize' the consent to the contract of indenture.[6] In certain cases, such as that of the young woman at Allahabad, consent proved less tangible.

While Indian emigration legislation insistently regulated the departure of indentured labourers overseas, other occupations and further migration streams to Ceylon and Malaya were exempt from regulation. Adapting the work of Sandro Mezzadra and Brett Neilson, I argue that this 'division of labour' constituted a 'multiplication of labour'.[7] The concept of the 'multiplication of labour', I suggest, invites a reassessment of the distinction between regulated and non-regulated labour migration which has partitioned the study of South Asian migrations. In contrast, I argue that the border between land and sea constituted 'differentially regulated' migration streams. At the beginning of the twentieth century, the problem of entry became entangled with the problem of exit when new immigration restrictions were imposed on British Indian subjects. The subsequent campaign for the abolition of indentured labour, I argue, prompted a further recalibration of the border between land and sea.

Slave trafficking in the Indian Ocean World

Scholarship on Indian Ocean slavery has existed in the shadow of the more extensive literature on the Atlantic slave trade. A range of scholars have wrestled with the question of the comparability of slavery in the Indian Ocean world and the 'chattel' slavery of the Atlantic worlds.[8] Extant scholarship stresses that Indian Ocean slavery was a variegated institution, with slaves ensconced as domestic labourers or concubines, engaged either in agricultural production, conscripted to military service or as servants in elite households. Indian slaves in particular were widely trafficked by ships in the employ of various European trading companies, including the East India Company.[9]

As Company officials assumed territorial rule over the Mughal province of Bengal in the late eighteenth century, they made a key distinction between domestic slavery and 'foreign' slave trafficking. Company policy broadly confirmed the ownership of already existing slaves, particularly domestic slaves, even to the point of facilitating the recovery of fugitive slaves.[10] Such a policy helped to secure the loyalty of native elites, while at the same time preserving domestic slavery in elite European households.[11] More broadly, Company officials perceived domestic slavery to be deeply entangled in caste and religion. Chatterjee argues that colonial officials conceptualized Indian slavery as a 'fixed ritual' rather than a 'political-jural' status.[12] Insofar as 'indigenous' slavery was imbued with a 'religious' aura, Company officials were reluctant to intercede in relationships of bondage and dependency.

Company officials were, however, decisive when it came to 'foreign' slave trafficking. As Allen has documented, the Company was itself deeply engaged in coastal slave trafficking in South Asia from the seventeenth century, though he finds diminished evidence of Company slave voyages by the late eighteenth century.[13] Fighting for military supremacy on the South Asian subcontinent, however, Company officials were keen to deny military labour to other European powers. Chatterjee further argues that the prohibition on foreign slave trafficking was 'mercantilist', the Company conserving 'both slave-holding and financial resources'.[14]

Accounts of slave trafficking often alleged that natives of India had been 'kidnapped' by foreign powers. Allen cites a report from 1622 in which slaves were believed to have been 'stollen upon the highwayes' by Dutch slave traders. British officials reported that 'country people' feared attending local markets as a result.[15] Allen notes that children in particular were vulnerable to the 'sweet words' of recruiters promising food and clothing.[16] Reports of the kidnapping of children continued into the early nineteenth century.[17] Major recounts substantial concerns about internal markets for kidnapped children and slaves within native states, posing jurisdictional problems for the Company state.[18] Young women, she notes, 'could also be subject to deceptive strategies of acquisition'.[19]

Major argues that Company officials became particularly preoccupied by the movement of slaves across 'borders'. Noting widespread concern about the kidnapping of slaves for both foreign colonial settlements and internal slave markets, she writes:

> The borders between EIC [East India Company] possessions and those of Indian princes, or other European companies, were neither static nor distinct in this period and people could move, or be moved, across these porous boundaries with relative ease. Moreover, conflicts with Mysore in the south, as well as ongoing tensions between the EIC and its European rivals, exacerbated fears of instability and disorder. In the circumstances, the unregulated exportation of colonial subjects as slaves was deemed inimical to the peace, stability and profitability of the country.[20]

Major's invocation of 'borders' here suggests the constant process of recalibration, as Company officials negotiated ongoing military conflicts, treaty relations with native states and the threat of foreign ships engaging in coastal raids to kidnap and enslave a population increasingly understood as 'British subjects'.

Measures taken by the Company to redress slave trafficking consistently invoked a border between land and sea. The first such measures were the 1774

Bengal Regulations issued by the administration of Warren Hastings. Allen notes that these measures were explicitly targeted at the 'the practice of Stealing children', a 'Savage Commerce' by which French and Dutch ships conveyed such children 'out of the country' – presumably overseas.[21] These same regulations, however, confirmed slave ownership on the possession of a deed signed by a native jurisconsult. Proclamations in Calcutta in 1789 and Madras in 1790 against slave trafficking similarly left 'domestic' ownership undisturbed.

The Company's protection of slavery as a 'domestic' institution within British India led to important divergences from imperial policy. The abolition of the slave trade in 1808 raised the question of prohibiting 'land-based' slave trafficking within the subcontinent.[22] As Chatterjee notes, Company officials construed abolition to apply solely to the African slave trade, and concluded that British Admiralty Courts charged with prosecuting illegal trafficking were confined to the removal or importation of slaves by sea.[23] Nevertheless, a local Act, Bengal Regulation X of 1811, was passed to prohibit 'the movement of slaves for sale, by land or sea'. Its application, however, was not extended to previously owned slaves, leaving undisturbed the domestic households of 'chiefs and nobles'.[24] Similarly, the imperial Slave Trade Felony Act of 1811 was circumvented by limiting its application to slaves imported by sea.[25] The Governor-General, Lord Minto, promulgated the Act only to port areas, refusing to circulate the Act to inland districts.[26]

The Company took the further step of negotiating an explicit exemption from the Slavery Abolition Act of 1833. It argued, successfully, that in contrast to Atlantic chattel slavery, Indian slavery was 'mild'. 'Domestic' slavery persisted, with 'delegalization' by Act V of 1843 failing to abrogate the rights of masters, including the pursuit of fugitive slaves.[27] Slavery had been prohibited at the border between land and sea. A new experiment in Mauritius, however, would complicate the problem of exit and occasion a significant recalibration of the border.

Consent at the border

Prior to the abolition of slavery, Indian labour was widely dispersed throughout the Indian Ocean world. Indian labour was heterogeneous: sailors, military recruits, domestic servants, convict labourers, slaves, artisanal workers and indentured labourers. The demand for labour was especially voluminous in the Mascarene Islands, where French administrators had initiated plantation agriculture since the 1720s.[28] The French demand for slaves extended to Madagascar, the Swahili Coast and to coastal South Asia; many of the kidnapping accounts that haunted the Malabar and Coromandel coasts involved French slaving ships.[29] A system of *engagisme* (engagement), involving the procurement of labour under contract, emerged in Réunion as early as the eighteenth century.[30] After the British assumed control of Mauritius and Réunion in 1810, French planters continued to pursue an illicit traffic in slaves. Some of this traffic was disguised under contract.[31] British abolitionists mobilized against the 'clandestine' trade in the late 1820s, focusing their attacks on the first British governor of Mauritius, Robert Farquhar.[32]

Given its connection to illicit slave trafficking and potentially fraudulent engagements, Mauritius was an unlikely 'test case' for free labour after the abolition of slavery.[33] Scholars typically date the inauguration of the indentured labour system to an early shipment of thirty-nine labourers, under contract, to Mauritius in 1834.[34] A Government of India official, John Geoghegan, described the contracts as 'liberal on paper', requiring a five-year commitment of service, with a wage of five rupees a month and 'liberal rations and clothing'.[35] Between 1834 and 1837, Geoghegan estimated that 7,000 indentured labourers arrived in Mauritius, about 'one-half of the whole number' were '"hill coolies", i.e. Dhangars, Kols, or Santhals' and that 'not more than 200 at the outside' of the labourers are women.[36]

The large scale traffic of Indian labourers after abolition raised questions about the efficacy of the border between land and sea. The use of contracts appeared to distinguish indentured labour from slavery. If British Indian subjects were not enslaved, how might their departure be prohibited? Mongia discusses an important effort by Mauritius to prohibit the entry of Indian immigrants. The power to prohibit entry, Governor William Nicolay reasoned, would enable him to regulate the bourgeoning traffic of Indian labourers. In 1835, he forwarded two ordinances to the Colonial Office authorizing such prohibition. A local planter, Hollier Griffiths, objected that the British sovereign did not hold the power to prohibit the entry of a British subject to British territory. While the ordinances ultimately were disallowed, the correspondence gestured to a prevailing uncertainty as to the limits of sovereign power with respect to exit and entry.[37] Given these limits upon entry controls in Mauritius, the Government of India would improvise new exit procedures.

In Calcutta, growing concern was expressed about the travel of Indian labourers overseas. The Government of India's exit procedure with respect to the

Mauritius trade was limited to a brief interview with local police to ascertain the voluntariness of the engagement.[38] The Law Commission was considering new legislation to regulate the embarkation of native seamen, menial servants and passengers 'embarking on their own account'.[39] To these cases, the Government of India added a fourth case, that of 'Dangur coolies and others, hired to proceed to Mauritius and elsewhere, as labourers on sugar estates'.[40] The Law Commissioners recommended new legislation only in the case of indentured labourers. These deliberations led to the passage of Act V of 1837.

Act V of 1837 instituted a new permit requirement prior to the departure of the labourer for service overseas. The permit was to be issued by an officer authorized by the presidency government. Act XXXII of 1837 repealed Act V while re-enacting its provisions to encompass the Madras and Bombay presidencies.[41] The 1837 Acts applied to contracts 'without the Territories of the East India Company', confirming the combined presidencies as a distinctive territorial space. The Act referred to 'Natives of India', sanctioning a particular form of political belonging. The permit was to be acquired by any Native of India who sought to 'embark' aboard a 'Vessel' – implying travel overseas. The Act denoted the 'Port' where the Native of India embarked upon such vessel.[42] The regulation of the process of embarkation by the new legislation recalibrated the space of the border.[43]

The 1837 acts reiterated the earlier land/sea distinction developed to prohibit coastal slave trafficking. However, where the earlier acts had prohibited departure, the new legislation embraced what Mongia has termed a 'logic of facilitation'.[44] The existence of a contract for hire, coupled with the permit confirming the consent of the labour, appeared to distinguish the new system of indentured labour from the slave trade. Revelations of a parallel stream of indentured labour to British Guiana, however, mobilized abolitionist opinion in both India and England. The controversy led to the appointment of formal inquiry committees in Mauritius and Calcutta to investigate charges of kidnapping, fraud and deceit in the recruitment of labourers.

Abolitionists questioned the voluntariness of the overseas labour contract. In 1838, protests mushroomed in London and Calcutta.[45] A parliamentary speech by Henry Brougham is exemplary: ' ... I hold it to have been wickedly, deceitfully, fraudulently, crimpingly, kidnappingly done, and with the purpose of inveigling and cheating, and carrying away the natives of Asia after the most approved practices of Slave trading, in their nefarious proceedings on the African coast'.[46] In Calcutta, a meeting of 'prominent citizens' passed a resolution claiming that the labourers 'do not understand, and are not capable of understanding, the terms of the contract into which they are said to enter ...'[47] The kidnapping charges that had haunted the earlier regime of slave trafficking had resurfaced in public discourse. Such charges were confirmed by the 1840 report of the Dickens Committee from Calcutta.[48]

Abolitionists appeared to win a decisive victory with the passage of the Government of India's Act XIV of 1839. The new Act suspended indentured emigration by imposing a criminal fine on any person making a contract with or aiding a 'Native of India' to emigrate for employment overseas as a 'labourer'.[49] In Mongia's terms, the Government of India returned to a 'logic of constraint', which had previously been embraced to prohibit slave trafficking.[50] As I discuss below, the terms of this prohibition provoked confusion over the applicability of the ban to non-indentured labour migration.

A period of intense lobbying followed the 1839 prohibition upon the emigration of indentured labour. Planters in Mauritius proposed new safeguards for the 'efficient protection' of labourers.[51] The revival of indentured migration was given a key boost by J.P. Grant's 'minute' dissenting from the conclusions of the Dickens Committee. Grant argued that indentured labour could be successfully regulated and proposed a series of measures to promote 'free emigration'. Crucially, Grant argued that the rights of labourers as British subjects were at stake. He wrote:

> It is, as I conceive it, no less a question than this, whether the whole of the labouring population of the vast, portion of Her Majesty's territories entrusted to the government of the East India Company ought, or ought not, to be as free as the rest of Her Majesty's subjects in respect to the disposal of their labour, and their right of going about.[52]

Grant thus framed the revival of indentured emigration as a question of political belonging. British subjecthood imbued the Indian labourer with mobility: a right to cross borders that superseded abolitionist objections to the 'new system of slavery'.

The 1839 suspension was followed by the emergence of a publicly regulated system of indentured labour. Whereas the private trade had provoked the abolitionist lobby, public regulation effected a more settled, mundane process of amending previous legislation, adding new rules or consolidating previous ordinances.[53] The procedures used to guarantee consent at the border between land and sea were subject to continuous revision as new cases of kidnapping, fraud and deceit came to the attention of officials in India and London.

The space of consent

In the early stages of the indentured labour system, as with previous efforts to prohibit slave trafficking, border practices were concentrated within the space of the port. The initial exit procedure was limited to a police interview. The 1837 Acts upgraded the interview to a permit. With the shift to a publicly regulated system, Indian emigration legislation instituted new spaces of authority for the protection of emigrants. By 1864, however, ongoing concerns about the voluntariness of emigration prompted the extension of border practices to inland recruiting districts. The enhanced role of the district magistrate extended the space of consent.

Indentured emigration was revived by Act XV of 1842. The Act provided for the appointment of a colonial Emigration Agent to supervise recruitment.[54] This appointment was made by the governor of Mauritius, and confirmed by the presidency government. The Emigration Agent issued a 'Certificate or Pass' to the 'Emigrant' after ascertaining whether she had been induced to emigrate. The Emigration Agent was charged with the selection of the migrants, ascertaining the 'good health' of the Emigrant, and that he or she were not 'incapacitated from labour by old age, bodily infirmity or disease'. The border was recalibrated to accommodate colonial authority over the recruitment and selection of labourers for export overseas.

Act XXI of 1843 provided for the Government of India to appoint its own official, the Protector of Emigrants, to superintend the recruitment of British Indian subjects. The Protector was to countersign the certificate prior to embarkation.[55] This arrangement was carried forward by Act XXI of 1844, authorizing emigration to British Guiana, Jamaica and Trinidad.[56] Similar arrangements were preserved in the case of emigration to Saint Lucia and Grenada (Act XXXI of 1855), Saint Vincent (Act XII of 1860), Natal (Act XXIII of 1860), Saint Kitts (Act XLI of 1860), Seychelles (Act XXII of 1862) and the Danish colony of Saint Croix (Act VII of 1863). The Protector's authority was limited to counter-signing the pass or certificate generated by the Emigration Agent. The sequence of the acts is revealing: only after the signature permitting entry is rendered does the counter-signature permit exit.

Act XIII of 1864, authored by Henry Sumner Maine, significantly recalibrated the space of the border between land and sea.[57] The Act required that the Emigration Agent establish a depot which would be licensed by the Protector of Immigrants. At the depot, the newly appointed Medical Inspector of Emigrants examined intending emigrants to confirm their fitness for emigration. As noted by Murdoch in the Allahabad case, a new registration procedure was initiated in the district of recruitment. The recruiter was required to present the 'intending emigrant' before the district magistrate for inspection. The name of the emigrant, along with the father's name, age and village or place of residence was entered into a register. The district magistrates' power to refuse registration, exercised in the Allahabad case, would become a serious point of contention with colonial emigration agents.[58] Recruiters or designated agents were required to accompany intending emigrants from the recruitment district to the emigration depot. The consent of the 'intending emigrant' was subject to multiple, spatially discrete, points of inspection.

The role of the Emigration Agent was substantially modified by the 1864 Act. The powers of the Emigration Agent ostensibly had been exercised on 'foreign soil'. Authority and jurisdiction was reapportioned, as the border between land and sea resembled a 'mixed jurisdiction'. The appointment of the Emigration Agent was subject to the approval of local governments. The Act required the Emigration Agent to inspect the registration of the emigrants upon arrival at the depot. The Emigration Agent then issued a pass, still counter-signed by the Protector. The Protector, however, could refuse to permit the embarkation of emigrants deemed unfit for the voyage. The Protector also licensed all recruiters. While the Protector had acquired new power to oversee the process of exit, recruitment was at the initiative of the Emigration Agent. Indeed, the Emigration Agent deployed a substantial recruitment apparatus, stretching from depots at ports of embarkation to sub-depots and agency houses in inland districts. The inquiries following from the Allahabad case highlighted the informality of this apparatus and the controversial role of unlicensed subagents.

While the emigration depot appeared to be a smoothly regulated space, the space of inland 'labour catchment areas' (LCAs) was sharp, jagged, marked by 'border struggles'.[59] A key struggle concerned the recruitment of women. Investigations by D.G. Pitcher and George Grierson uncovered contentious debates over women's consent. Despite the publicity concerning the Allahabad case, fears of kidnapping persisted, with unscrupulous recruiters accused of the enticement of women. As a result, Pitcher observed that magistrates refused to register women unaccompanied by husbands.[60] Grierson argued, however, that the 'native woman' had the capacity to consent.[61] Sen documents objections by district magistrates that consent obtained by fraud or deceit amounted to 'kidnapping'. Others argued that women should not be permitted to emigrate without the consent of their husbands, a position adopted by Act VI of 1901, governing inland emigration to Assam.[62] Pitcher also reported widespread complaints that magistrates described emigration as crossing the *kala pani* or 'black waters'. The term invoked a religious boundary enforcing the loss of caste and religion and fears of 'transportation' of convict labour.[63]

Multiple, overlapping forms of recruitment occurred in any particular catchment area. Grierson noted, for example that the districts in Bihar that supplied much of the emigration for overseas plantations were also fertile recruiting grounds for 'inland emigration'.[64] Similarly, Lalita Chakravarty notes that in 1910 the Bengal jute industry, the tea gardens of Assam and the colony of Mauritius recruited from the same 'Eastern' catchment area and that emigration to Africa overlapped with recruitment for the Bombay cotton mills. She concludes: 'Those people who migrated from the LCAs to overseas destinations under [the]contract system were exactly those who came as "free" labourers to factory gates'.[65]

Competition between recruiters sometimes fomented corrupt practice. Chakravarty has argued that the market for what she terms 'unskilled labour' often featured practices of 'bribery and usury' by a 'labour-lord'. The labour lord, in her definition, included the sardar, the jobber, the kangany and recruiters – sometimes termed 'labour intermediaries' – who helped to recruit labourers to a specific location or for a specific industry.[66] While emigration law referred to the recruit as an 'intending emigrant', some portion of that intention was contrived by the recruiter. Although recruitment often was based on previous kinship and village networks, there is also ample evidence of encounters with recruiters on the road, in the bazaar, at a fair, on pilgrimage or at a festival. Such encounters suggest that contact with a recruiter or subagent was new and unexpected. Depending upon the recruiter encountered, the emigrant might be guided to 'emigrate' to Assam, Trinidad, Fiji, Calcutta or Bombay. An element of chance, even capriciousness appeared to guide the emigrant to her final destination, despite attempts to legislate the voluntariness of the engagement.[67]

Multiplying labour and differential inclusion under Indian emigration law

The literature examining the regulation of indentured labour has largely associated Indian emigration law with the indentured labour system. I wish to pull together the various strands of 'overseas' and 'inland' emigration into a single inquiry. The experience of competition in the recruitment of labourers in the labour catchment areas suggests certain correspondences between these various forms of migration. Whether by recruiters, subagents, managing agencies, *kanganies* or *maistries*, recruitment was plagued by allegations of kidnapping or, alternatively, fraudulent engagement. The shared problem of exit led to frequent borrowing of features between these 'systems'. Henry Maine, for example, adapted the procedure of inland district registration from Bengal Act III of 1863, regulating recruitment for Assam.[68] In turn, aspects of the 'Mauritius model' were selectively adapted to regulate overseas emigration to Ceylon and Malaya, and 'inland emigration' to the tea gardens of Assam.[69]

The division of these various migration streams occurred at the border between land and sea. The instrument of division was Indian emigration law. By exempting specific occupations or excluding particular migration streams from state regulation, emigration law multiplied labour. That is, 'labour' was not a singular category for purposes of recruitment. The differential regulation of various occupations and labour migration streams multiplied different forms and experiences of labour migration. Mezzadra and Nielson's concepts of the 'multiplication of labour' and 'differential inclusion' illuminate how emigration law divided Indian 'labour' into multiple streams of migration, accommodating new global processes by recalibrating the border between land and sea.

As the Law Commission first reviewed the special case of emigration to Mauritius, two other 'cases' were under consideration. The first was that of sailors, the second domestic servants. As Michael Fisher has illuminated, a large traffic of sailors and domestic servants was extant in Britain from the late eighteenth century.[70] The Company was increasingly concerned at the high cost of return passages for sailors and servants found 'destitute' in Britain. Increasingly it required a deposit or 'security' prior to the departure of such employees from British India. The Mauritius government also had raised concerns about the prevalence of vagrancy and destitution among labourers who had completed their contracts.

Although scholars write of an 'indentured labour system', the term 'indenture' does not appear in Indian emigration legislation. The term used in the 1837 Acts is 'contract of service'. The use of this particularly capacious category indicates the persistence of the idea of 'labour as service' deep into the nineteenth century.[71] Sailors and domestic servants departed British India under contracts of service. Given extant provisions for a 'security' posted upon departure, the 1837 Acts included a specific exemption for both 'Native Seamen' and 'Menial Servants': 'nothing' in the Acts was made to apply to their cases. The 1837 Acts divided labour: a distinction between those rendering service within British India and those overseas, and occupational distinctions with respect to contracts of service. A further division was also implied – those 'embarking on their own account' were 'free'.

The exemption of 'native seamen' and 'menial servants' was applied in subsequent legislation. The 1839 Act, notably, maintained this exemption. Act XV of 1842, narrowly tailed to apply only to emigration to Mauritius, did not require the exemption. A similar arrangement prevailed for Act XXI of 1843, which opened emigration to British Guiana, Jamaica and Trinidad. The consolidating Act of 1864 recovered the earlier exemptions of 'Native seamen' and 'menial servant'.[72] Act VII of 1871 maintained these definitions and exemptions, while Act XXI of 1883 exempted only domestic servants.

By the early twentieth century, the Government of India was contemplating new 'cases' to be brought under Indian emigration law. A shift is apparent from exemption to inclusion under the protective umbrella of state regulation. One such case was that of individuals engaged in 'public entertainment' in England or Europe. The general provisions of the revised Act continued to apply to the new category of 'unskilled labour' replacing the earlier category of 'labour for hire'. However, a new chapter XIV was added to the 1902 Act empowering local governments to regulate the emigration for the 'purpose' of '(a) of working as an artisan or (b) of any exhibition or entertainment or (c) of service in any restaurant, teahouse or other places of public resort'.[73] The prospective employer was required to state in detail the conditions of work to the local government. A form of differentiated regulation was established by this new procedure, which was carried forward to Chapter XI of Act XVII of 1908.[74]

Also of relevance was the evolving definition of 'emigration', a key instrument in regulating the border between land and sea. Act XV of 1842 was the first to use the term 'emigration', which in turn was first defined by Act XIII of 1864: 'The word "Emigrate" shall denote the departure of any Native of India out of British India for the purpose of labouring for hire in some other place; and the word "Emigrant" shall denote any Native of India under engagement to emigrate'.[75] Act XXI of 1883 introduced further refinements: 'emigrate and emigration denote the departure by sea out of British India of a Native of India under an agreement to labour for hire in some country beyond the limits of India other than the island of Ceylon or the Straits Settlements'.[76] Section 105 of the 1883 Act also provided for departure by land 'under a contract to labour for hire in some country beyond the sea' other than Ceylon or the Straits Settlements.[77] In 1896, the words 'under a contract' were changed to 'under, or with a view to entering into, an agreement' to accommodate recruitment of labour for the construction of railways in Uganda.[78] Also left outside these definitions of 'emigration' was the phenomenon of 'inland' emigration, which was regulated instead by a series of emigration acts applicable to Assam.[79]

The exclusion of Ceylon and the Straits Settlements from the definition of emigration in the 1883 Act divided overseas labour service into what have been known conventionally as 'regulated' and 'non-regulated' migration streams. The geographical destination of the emigrant was crucial to effecting differential inclusion with respect to the state regulation of mobility. As noted, the emigration acts issued from 1842 up to 1864 were narrowly tailored to facilitate emigration to a specific colony. Jurisdictions not named by these individual acts were excluded from indentured emigration. These acts were consolidated by Act XIII of 1864, which included a list of colonies to which emigration was permitted and provided a notification procedure for legalizing emigration to new destinations.

Though not formally a part of the system of indenture, 'non-regulated' emigration was authorized within the Indian Ocean world. Up to 1864, no mention was made of Ceylon or the Straits Settlements in emigration legislation. For example, the Government of India passed Act XIII of 1847 clarifying that emigration to Ceylon was exempted from penalties under Act XIV of 1839. Emigration to the Straits Settlements was regulated by passenger Acts passed in 1857 and 1859.[80] In anticipation of administrative separation, the Straits Settlements were excluded from the list of permitted colonies in the 1864 Act.[81] After administrative separation from India in 1867, Act XIV of 1872 excluded emigration to the Straits Settlements from the new emigration Act, Act VII of 1871. These exceptions facilitated differentially regulated migration. Act V of 1877 inaugurated Government of India regulation of Straits Settlements migration, though on terms distinct from those under Act XVII of 1871 or, later, Act XXI of 1883. The 1883 Act again excluded both Ceylon and the Straits Settlements from the definition of 'emigration'. The form and experience of migration to both destinations remained distinct from that authorized for the indentured labour system.

From 1837, the Company asserted jurisdiction over British Indian subjects to establish the terms of their emigration. 'Emigration' was not, however, a uniform category; it was selectively applicable. Occupational exemption and geographical exclusion divided Labourers into distinctive streams of labour migration. Different forms of 'engagement' – as an indentured labour, a native seaman, a domestic servant or a public entertainer – imbued the 'Native of India' with the capacity to cross some borders, but not others. Indentured labourers could migrate to distant colonies in the Caribbean or Pacific – or labour in the tea gardens of Assam. A domestic servant might be eligible for service in Britain; a 'lascar' could render labour while at sea. Non-indentured – or 'differentially regulated' – agricultural labour predominated in substantial migration streams to Ceylon and what became British Malaya. Conditions of mobility were 'bordered' by inclusion, exemption or exclusion from the category of the emigrant.

The 'abolition' of indentured labour

The campaign for the abolition of indentured labour, I argue, may be understood as a significant recalibration of the border between land and sea. Indian labour had flowed across borders on the presumption of shared British subjecthood. Yet as dominion governments began to articulate their own conceptions of local citizenship, British Indian subjects were increasingly excluded from political and civic life. Dominion governments imposed a range of disabilities including access to trading licences, exercise of the municipal franchise, ownership of immoveable property, residential segregation and rights of exit and entry.[82]

The passive resistance campaign in South Africa played a key role in mobilizing Indian nationalist opinion against the indentured labour system. Many of the grievances articulated by passive resisters related to the status of Indian merchants, who had followed indentured labourers to Natal, before moving into other provinces of South Africa, including the Transvaal.[83] The Transvaal government's attempt to compel the registration of all 'Asiatic' subjects provoked passive resistance in 1906. Ongoing negotiations on the rights of entry and exit for the 'free' or 'passenger' migrants in South Africa were thrown into disarray by a series of legal judgements putting into question the legal status of Indian marriages.[84] These judgements suggested that Hindu and Muslim forms of marriage were inadmissible under South African law as the personal laws under which they were conducted sanctioned polygamy. This finding incited Indian public opinion, with Mohandas K. Gandhi writing that Indian women had been rendered as 'concubines' by the judgements.[85] The refusal to legally recognize Indian forms of marriage gave a decided 'religious' hue to the border between South African and India.

The campaign for the abolition of indentured labour was instigated as 'retaliation' for the treatment of Indians overseas. In 1910, a leading moderate nationalist, Gopal Krishna Gokhale, moved a resolution at the imperial Indian

Legislative Council calling for the prohibition of recruitment of indentured labour for Natal. A second resolution in 1912 called for the prohibition of all recruitment for the indentured labour system. Rachel Sturman observes: '... while elite nationalists deplored the exploitation and oppression of Indian labourers abroad, their criticism of the system nonetheless focused on the fact that it created a global image of Indians as "coolies".'[86] Indeed, Gokhale claimed that indentured labourers lowered the 'position' of Indians in general in South African society.[87] Moving his second resolution, he argued that the 'monstrous system' of indentured labour was a 'great blot on the civilization of any country that tolerates it'.[88]

Gokhale and other Indian abolitionists claimed that indenture, which 'bordered' slavery, should be abolished and not regulated. Gokhale stated: 'It is true that it [indenture] is not actual slavery, but I fear in practice in a large number of cases it cannot be far removed from it'. He continued to insist that indenture 'must really border on the servile', given that the labourers were transported to a 'distant land' where they were 'entirely ignorant' of the 'language, customs, social usages and special civilization' of their employers.[89] The premise of ignorance certainly underestimated the information networks developed by indentured migrants over the several decades that the indenture system operated.[90] It recapitulated, however, earlier concerns that consent was invalid if obtained by fraud or deceit.

Gandhi, returned to India from the passive resistance campaign in South Africa, repeatedly insisted that indenture bordered slavery. In an early speech, he quoted a South African official's assessment that indenture was 'perilously near to slavery'. He commented that the 'mental state' of the recruiters 'must be miserable', having sent overseas 'so many of their countrymen as semi-slaves'.[91] Gandhi termed indenture a 'remnant of slavery'.[92] He later argued that indenture could be described as 'slavery for a limited period'.[93] Gandhi also called indenture 'temporary slavery'.[94] Here it was the length of the contract, and not the consent of the emigrant, that distinguished indenture from slavery.

A vernacular abolition campaign emerged in the labour catchment areas, where concerns about kidnapping, fraud and deceit in recruitment persisted. The vernacular press widely publicized an account of Kunti's escape from a European overseer in Fiji.[95] An autobiographical account by Totaram Sanadhya, an ex-indentured labourer recently returned from Fiji, decried the sexual abuse of women on Fiji's plantations, inspiring several literary works.[96] Continued allegations of the abduction of women by recruiters animated a village-level campaign against recruitment.[97] A pamphlet, 'Save Yourself From

Depôt-Wallahs' apprised against the defilement of religion 'under pretense of service' and against the 'inducing talks' and 'cajoling' of *arkatis*. 'Escape the Deceivers' warned that overseas employment was not a 'service', but a 'woe', and that travel overseas would destroy caste.[98] The popular campaign articulated a border between land and sea, emphasizing the loss of caste and religion and the degradation of Indian women.

Literary representations of the plight of indentured women further articulated the border between land and sea. In her examination of writings on indenture in Hindi, including Kunti's narrative, the poetry of Maithili Sharan Gupt and Premchan's story 'Shudraa', Charu Gupta observes:

> ... there appeared a symbiotic relationship between indentured women, water, and virtue. Jumping or drowning in the water was a metaphor for both the preservation of the woman's chastity and the punishment of the 'unchaste' woman. It was like a 'trial by water', which signified both an escape for 'innocent' victims, as in the case of Kunti, and drowning as 'shame' for their apparent transgression, promiscuity, and sexual impurity. The 'good' victims were assisted and protected by the water, while the 'bad' women were punished by drowning.

Gupta continues to make a broader point about the sea:

> The sea was also borderless and unidentifiable, where certainties of place, nationality, and identity were dissolved. The force of the flowing water, particularly the ordeal of the sea, not only disturbed ideas of borders and national belonging, but also embodied the cruelties of indenture, loss of humanity, tears, struggles, and death. The sea passage, equated with the mythology of the *kala pani* (black water), figured large in the arguments of the anti-migration lobby. Its symbolic association with barriers, transitions, and journeys separated women from their family and drove them away from their land and nation. However, water was also fluid, and no space was proof against its invasive power.[99]

The *kala pani* myth, earlier detected in Pitcher's investigations of labour recruitment in the 1880s, thus persisted into the last years of the indentured labour system.

In March 1916, Madan Mohan Malaviya, who had assumed leadership in the Legislative Council after Gokhale's death, introduced a resolution asking that 'early steps' be taken to abolish indentured labour. Malaviya's introductory speech resonated with the popular campaign. He noted that the opening of recruitment depots 'gave rise to complaints of kidnapping and other objectionable practices'.[100] He argued that 'simple, illiterate, ignorant, village people' were 'inveigled into entering a very solemn agreement'. Like Gokhale, he stressed that colonial employers did not understand the 'language, custom and manners' of labourers.[101] He also related his own experience rescuing women from depots.[102] Malaviya drew upon the report issued by the Anglican missionaries C.F. Andrews and W.W. Pearson on conditions of indenture in Fiji, to emphasize the 'violent interference' with the religion of labourers and the immorality that prevailed on plantation estates.[103]

The 'early steps' proposed by Malaviya's resolution were taken unhurriedly. Recruitment was temporarily suspended under Defence of India Act rules in 1917. An interdepartmental conference in London sought to contrive a new system of 'assisted' emigration. Gandhi renounced the resultant report: 'In India itself if the scheme is adopted', he wrote, 'we are promised a revival of the much-dreaded depots and emigration agents, all no doubt on a more respectable basis, but still of the same type and capable of untold mischief'.[104] Gandhi and Andrews mounted a popular campaign for the cancellation of contracts in Fiji by 1920. Meanwhile, both Fiji and British Guiana sent delegations to India seeking approval for their own schemes for assisted emigration. It was only in 1921, however, that the Government of India proposed to revise the 1908 Act, opening the possibility for a final, legal abolition of indenture.

Act VII of 1922, Sinha argues, 'put the official imprimatur on the abolition of indenture'.[105] The 1922 Act also recalibrated the border between land and sea. First, the apparatus of recruitment was decommissioned, 'unmixing' jurisdictions at the border. The office of the Emigration Agent, the emigration depots and the licensing of recruiters were eliminated. Second, the scope of regulation was enhanced to encompass both skilled and unskilled labour. Unskilled work was defined simply to include 'engaging in agriculture'. 'Skilled work', formerly defined as departure by sea 'for certain purposes' under the 1908 Act, included clerks and shop assistants. In the enhanced regulation of 'skilled labour' under the 1922 Act, earlier exemptions were transmuted into new chapters outlining distinctive – and differential – procedures for state regulation. The 1922 Act extended what Mongia terms the state monopoly over mobility.[106] However, Indian emigration law continued to divide and multiply labour, relying particularly on the category of skill while continuing to permit labour emigration within the Indian Ocean World. A new exemption was articulated for military labour.[107]

Was indentured labour 'abolished' in 1922? The Act made emigration for unskilled work lawful only after notification by the Governor-General in Council and the approval of both houses of the legislature. The political bar was high for any new scheme of emigration, but there was no specific legal bar for unskilled labourers to be 'assisted' to emigrate to overseas colonies. Sinha summarizes the legislation: 'In the name of protecting workers from abuses in the colonies, the Act curtailed the mobility of labour'.[108] Rather than 'abolition', this curtailment, I argue, constituted a recalibration of the border between land and sea.

Conclusion

Negotiations for emigration to British Guiana and Fiji failed in the early 1920s. The notoriety of the previous system precluded the approval of large scale labour migration by the Indian legislature, even under revised terms. In a peculiar way, the posture of the Indian legislature mimicked the politics of Asiatic exclusion. Dominion governments refused the immigration of unskilled labour; the Indian nationalists campaigned to prohibit the emigration of unskilled labour. The 1922 Emigration Act installed the Indian legislature as the ultimate guarantor of the voluntariness of emigration, nationalizing the border between land and sea. The containment of the 'unskilled' by recalibration of the border between land and sea offered ironic proof of India's enhanced sovereign status and provisional entry into the Westphalian system of nation-states.

Labour migration within the Bay of Bengal, however, continued, subject to enhanced state regulation. State regulation was similarly extended to new occupational groups, including labour deemed to be 'skilled'. Certain 'non-national' aspects of the recruitment apparatus were discarded, while other features crucial to the identification and selection of emigrants were retained. These features had been crucial to the facilitation of emigration. Just as crucial was the persistence of the multiplication of labour, evidenced by the sharp distinction between skilled and unskilled labour. As histories of Gulf migration demonstrate, the border between land and sea continues to produce multiple forms of labour mobility subject to differential state regulation.

To close, I return to the case of the young woman in Allahabad. What was her experience of the border between land and sea? The border materialized with her examination before the magistrate. That examination had proved not her consent, but her 'kidnapping'. It seems she was freed to return home to her infant son. We know nothing of her subsequent life history – did she find adequate work? Did she later emigrate? Was she married? Her 'case' became known by the name of her recruiter, Buldeo. Murdoch presumed that case was 'impossible'. Her experience of the process of recruitment – the roadside encounter with the subagent, the 'blows and cuffs' delivered at the serai, the terror of confinement – may not have been typical. It was, I insist, an experience of 'emigration'.

Significantly, a trace of the young woman's experience was recorded. In that reporting, we have a glimpse of the precariousness of consent for those who crossed the border between land and sea.

Notes

1   See National Archives of India (hereinafter, 'NAI'), Agriculture, Revenue and Commerce Department, Emigration Branch, August 1871, Part A, Index Nos. 15–22. These papers were also transferred to the Legislative Department. See NAI, Legislative Department, August 1871, Part A, Proceedings Nos. 30–33.
2   For an important consideration of migration and maritime worlds, see Renisa Mawani, *Across Oceans of Law: The Komagata Maru and Jurisdiction in the Time of Empire* (Durham and London: Duke University Press, 2017).
3   For histories of slavery and abolition in the Indian Ocean world, see William Gervase Clarence-Smith, ed., *The Economics of the Indian Ocean Slave Trade* (London and New York: Routledge, 1989); Gwyn Campbell, ed., *The Structure of Slavery in Indian Ocean Africa and Asia* (London and Portland, OR: Frank Cass, 2004); Gwyn Campbell, ed., *Abolition and its Aftermath in Indian Ocean Africa and Asia* (London and New York: Routledge, 2005); Richard Allen, *European Slave Trading in the Indian Ocean, 1500–1850* (Athens, OH: Ohio University Press, 2014).
4   See Andrea Major, *Slavery, Abolitionism and Empire in India, 1772–1843* (Liverpool: Liverpool University Press, 2012) and Indrani Chatterjee, *Gender, Slavery and Law in Colonial India* (New Delhi: Oxford University Press, 1999). For longer histories of slavery in South Asia, see Utsa Patnaik and Manjari Dingwaney, eds., *Chains of Servitude: Bondage & Slavery in India* (Madras: Sangam Books, 1985) and Indrani Chatterjee and Richard M. Eaton, eds., *Slavery & South Asian History* (Bloomington and Indianapolis: Indiana University Press, 2006).
5   Sandro Mezzadra and Brett Nielson argue that 'spatial formation' of the nation-state has been 'recalibrated' by 'global processes'. See *Border as Method, or, the Multiplication of Labor* (Durham and London: Duke University Press, 2013), 63. I have been provoked to consider the 'imaginary' of borders by Étienne Balibar, 'The Borders of Europe' in *Cosmopolitics: Thinking and Feeling Beyond the Nation*, eds. Pheng Cheah and Bruce Robbins (Minneapolis and London: University of Minnesota Press, 1998), 217.
6   In arguing for an 'agrarian imaginary', Neeladri Bhattacharya, citing Cornelius Castoriadis, argues that 'imaginaries' are ideas 'formed through material processes and embodied in material things'. Bhattacharya, *The Great Agrarian Conquest: The Colonial Reshaping of a Rural World* (Ranikhet: Permanent Black, 2018), 1–2.

7   Mezzadra and Neilson, *Border as Method*, 22.
8   See, for example, Suzanne Miers, 'Slavery: A Question of Definition', in Ibid., 1–16.
9   See Allen, Chapter 4, 'Carrying Away the Unfortunate from India and Southeast Asia, 1500–1800', in *European Slave Trading*.
10 Chatterjee, *Gender, Slavery and Law*, 176.
11 Major, *Slavery, Abolitionism, and Empire*, 5.
12 Chatterjee, *Gender, Slavery and Law*, 7.
13 Allen, *European Slave Trading*, 35.
14 Chatterjee, *Gender, Slavery and Law*, 181–182. My thanks to Barbara Metcalf for asking me to clarify this point.
15 Allen, *European Slave Trading*, 121.
16 Ibid., 122.
17 Ibid., 191–192.
18 See Chapter 5, '"Open and Professed Stealers of Children": Slave-trafficking and the Boundaries of the Colonial State", in Major, *Slavery, Abolitionism and Empire*.
19 Ibid., 156.
20 Ibid., 72.
21 Allen, *European Slave Trading*, 183. Allen argues that abolitionist concerns about the trafficking of children have not yet received adequate scholarly attention. Ibid., 212.
22 Major, *Slavery, Abolitionism and Empire*, 169.
23 Chatterjee, *Gender, Slavery and Law*, 183.
24 Major, *Slavery, Abolitionism and Empire*, 170.
25 Ibid., 171.
26 Ibid., 172.
27 Chatterjee, *Gender, Slavery and Law*, 213–214.
28 For an account, see Richard B. Allen, *Slaves, Freedmen, and Indentured Laborers in Colonial Mauritius* (Cambridge: Cambridge University Press, 1999) and Meghan Vaughan, *Creating the Creole Island: Slavery in Eighteenth Century Mauritius* (Durham and London: Duke University Press, 2005).
29 Major, *Slavery, Abolitionism and Empire*, 52.
30 See Alessandro Stanziani, *Sailors, Slaves, and Immigrants: Bondage in the Indian Ocean World, 1750–1914* (New York: Palgrave Macmillan, 2014), 73. Stanziani stresses the 'interaction' between the 'notions' of *engagisme* and indentured labor. Ibid., 5.
31 Ibid., 76.
32 See Anthony J. Barker, *Slavery and Antislavery in Mauritius, 1810–33: The Conflict between Economic Expansion and Humanitarian Reform under British Rule* (New York: St. Martin's Press, 1996).

33 Allen, *European Slave Trading*, 194, citing I.M. Cumpston, *Indians Overseas in British Territories, 1834–1854* (London: Dawsons of Pall Mall, 1969), 85.

34 John Geoghegan believed that the 'first instance' of 'emigration' occurred to Bourbon in 1830. See *Parliamentary Papers* 1874 (314), 'Copy of Mr. Geoghegan's Report on Coolie Emigration from India', 2.

35 Ibid., 2.

36 Ibid., 2.

37 See Mongia's discussion of this episode in *Indian Migration and Empire: A Colonial Genealogy of the Modern State* (Durham and London: Duke University Press, 2018): 29–32. See also Mongia's earlier article, 'Historicizing State Sovereignty: Inequality and the Form of Equivalence', *Comparative Studies in Society and History* 49, no. 2 (2007): 399–403.

38 See No. XXVII, Extract, Public Letter No. 3 of 1837, Government of India (hereinafter, 'GOI') to Court of Directors, 18 January 1837, in *Papers Respecting the East-India Labourers' Bill* (London: By Order of the General Court, 1838), 176.

39 See No. XXXIII, Extract, India Public Consultation of 5/25/1836, No., Letter from F. Millett, Esq., Secretary India Law Commission, to H.T. Prinsep, Esq., Secretary to the GOI, General Department, 6 May 1836, in Ibid.

40 No. XXXIII, No. 157, Letter from H.T. Prinsep, Esq., Secretary to the GOI, to F. Millet, Esq., Secretary to the India Law Commission, 25 May 1836, in Ibid.

41 Sarup, *Indentured Labour*, 257–260.

42 For the text of Act V and Act XXXII of 1837, see Sarup, *Indentured Labour*, 257–260.

43 Mongia emphasizes the 'spatial locations of migration controls' as 'iterations of the border'. See *Indian Migration and Empire*, 67.

44 Ibid., 1.

45 For the Calcutta debates, see Purba Hossain, 'Protests at the Colonial Capital: Calcutta and the Global Debates on Indenture, 1836–42', *South Asian Studies* 33, no. 1 (2017): 37–51.

46 Brougham and Vaux, Henry Brougham, Baron, 'Lord Brougham's speech in the House of Lords … March 6, 1838, upon the eastern slave trade' (London: James Ridgway and Sons, 1838), 45. The Making of the Modern World, accessed 30 December 2013.

47 As cited by by Panchanan Saha, quoting from the *Bengal Hukuru*. See Saha, *Emigration of Indian Labor (1834–1900)* (Delhi: People's Publishing House, 1970), 87.

48 As noted by Cumpston, *Indians Overseas*, 31. Saha also stresses widespread kidnapping prior to the enforcement of the 1837 Act. Saha, *Emigration of Indian Labour*, 80.

49 Sarup, *Indentured Labour*, 261.

50 Mongia, *Indian Migration and Empire*, 2.
51 See Charles Anderson, *Outlines of a Plan Submitted to Her Majesty's Government for the Purpose of Establishing an Authorized Committee to Regulate and Carry on the Introduction of Indian Laborers at Mauritius ...* (London: Nichols, Printer, 1840).
52 J.P. Grant, 'Minute on the Cooly Question', in *Parliamentary Papers*, 1841 Session 1(427), 'Copies of Papers Respecting the Exportation of Hill Coolies'.
53 For recent discussion of Indian emigration legislation, see Mongia, *Indian Migration and Empire*; Ashtosh Kumar, 'Regulating Indenture', in *Coolies of the Empire: Indentured Indians in the Sugar Colonies, 1830–1920* (Cambridge: Cambridge University Press, 2017); and Rachel Sturman, 'Indian Indentured Labor and the History of International Rights Regimes', *American Historical Review* 119, no. 5 (December 2014): 1439–1465.
54 Sarup, *Indentured Labour*, 262–270.
55 Ibid., 271.
56 Ibid., 272–277.
57 Ibid., 316–341.
58 Kumar, *Coolies of the Empire*, 62–63.
59 On labour catchment areas, see Lalita Chakravarty, 'Emergence of an Industrial Labour Force in a Dual Economy-British India, 1880–1920,' *Indian Economic and Social History Review* 15, no. 3 (1978): 251.
60 Basdeo Mangru, ed., *Kanpur to Kolkata: Labour Recruitment for the Sugar Colonies* (Hertford, Hertfordshire: Hansib Publications, 2014), 49.
61 Basdeo Mangru, ed., *Colonial Emigration from the Bengal Presidency* (Hertford, Hertfordshire: Hansib Publications, 2014), 75.
62 Samita Sen, 'Unsettling the Household: Act VI (of 1901) and the Regulation of Women Migrants in Colonial Bengal,' *International Review of Social History* 41 (1996): 142–143; 144–146.
63 Mangru, *Kanpur*, 47–48. For the connection between convict and indentured labor, see Clare Anderson, 'Convicts and Coolies: Rethinking Indentured Labour in the Nineteenth Century,' *Slavery and Abolition* 30, no. 1 (2010): 93–109.
64 Mangru, *Colonial Emigration*, 20.
65 Chakravarty, 'Emergence,' 253–254. On the shift in recruitment for the jute industry from Bengal to Bihar and the United Provinces, see Dipesh Chakrabarty, *Rethinking Working Class History: Bengal 1890 to 1940* (Princeton, NJ: Princeton University Press, 1989), 102–105.
66 Ibid., 251. Chakrabarty explores the role of the sardar as a 'supplier and supervisor of labor' in the Calcutta jute industry. See *Rethinking Working Class History*, 96–100. For a recent treatment of sirdar and the recruitment of indentured labour, see Crispin Bates and Marina Carter, '*Sirdars* as Intermediaries in Nineteenth

Century Indian Ocean Indentured Labour Migration' *Modern Asian Studies* 51, no. 2 (2017): 462–484.
67 Sunil Amrith similarly notes the role of "fate, chance, and decision" in the recruitment of laborers by the kangani. See Amrith, *Crossing the Bay of Bengal: The Furies of Nature and the Fortune of Migrants* (Cambridge, MA and London: Harvard University Press, 2013), 118.
68 'Statement of Objects and Reasons,' in NAI, Legislative Department, October 1863, Part A, Proceedings Nos. 11–12.
69 On the adaptation of the 'Mauritius model' to Assam, see Varma, *Coolies of Capitalism: Assam Tea and the Making of Coolie Labour* (Berlin: De Gruyter Oldenbourg, 2017), 7.
70 Michael Fisher, *Counterflows to Colonialism: Indian Travelers and Settlers in Britain 1600–1857* (Delhi and Ranikhet: Permanent Black, 2004).
71 Alessandro Stanziani argues this point in *Bondage: Labor and Rights in Eurasia from the Sixteenth to the Early Twentieth Centuries* (New York and Oxford: Berghahn Books, 2014).
72 Sarup, *Indentured Labour*, 316.
73 See 'Extract of the Proceedings of the Council of the Government of India, March 19, 1902, Appendix U' in The Indian Emigration Act, 1902 (X of 1902), NAI, Legislative Department Proceedings, October 1902, Nos. 11–42, Part A. This Act is not included in the Sarup compilation.
74 Sarup, *Indentured Labour*, 610–612.
75 Ibid., 316. "Act XIV of 1839 used the term 'emigrating, Sarup, *Indentured Labour*, 261." Technically, the Act XV of 1842 was the first to use the term "emigration."
76 Sarup has published the rules under the 1883 Act, and not the Act itself. See *A Collection of the Acts Passed by the Governor General of India in Council in the Year 1883* (Calcutta: Printed by the Superintendent of Government Printing, 184), p. 8 of the Act.
77 Sarup, *Indentured Labour*, 44.
78 NAI, Revenue and Agriculture Department, Emigration Branch, July 1896, Part A, Proceedings Nos. 18–55.
79 For discussion see Varma, *Coolies of Capitalism*; Rana P. Behal, *One Hundred Years of Servitude: Political Economy of Tea Plantations in Colonial Assam* (New Delhi: Tulika Books, 2014); Jayeeta Sharma, *Empire's Garden: Assam and the Making of India* (Durham and London: Duke University Press, 2011).
80 Kernial Singh Sandhu, *Indians in Malaya: Immigration and Settlement, 1786–1957* (Cambridge: Cambridge University Press, 1969), 77.
81 David Chanderbali, *Indian Indenture in the Straits Settlements* (Leeds: Peepal Tree Press, 2008), 88.
82 For broader histories of race and immigration in the British Empire during this period, see Marilyn Lake and Henry Reynolds, *Drawing the Global Colour*

Line: White Men's Countries and the International Challenge of Racial Equality (Cambridge: Cambridge University Press, 2008) and Jeremy C. Martens, *Empire and Asian Migration: Sovereignty, Immigration Restriction and Protest in the British Settler Colonies, 1888-1907* (Crawley, Western Australia: UMA Publishing, 2018).

83 Surendra Bhana, *Setting Down Roots: Indian Migrants in South Africa, 1860-1911* (Johannesburg: Witwatersrand University Press, 1990).

84 Radhika Mongia, 'Gender and the Historiography of Gandhian Satyagraha in South Africa,' *Gender & History* 18, no. 1 (2006): 130-149; Mongia, *Indian Migration*, chapter 3.

85 Gandhi, 'The Marriage Question,' *Indian Opinion*, 1 October 1913, *Collected Works of Mahatma Gandhi* (hereinafter '*CWMG*'), Vol. 12 (Publications Division, Government of India, 1964), 224-227.

86 Sturman, 'Indian Indentured Labor', 1464. Amrith concurs that "respectable" Indian merchants and lawyers were "tainted" by their association with indentured laborers. Amrith, *Crossing the Bay of Bengal*, 140.

87 Gopal Krishna Gokhale, 'Indentured Labour For Natal' in *Speeches of Gopal Krishna Gokhale,* 3rd edition (Madras: G.A. Natesan & Co., 1920), 510.

88 Gokhale, 'Indentured Labour', Ibid., 520-521.

89 Gokhale, 'Indentured Labour for Natal', Ibid., 510.

90 As emphasized in the work of Marina Carter.

91 Gandhi, 'Speech on Indentured Labour at Bombay', *CWMG*, Vol. 13 (Publications Division, Government of India, 1964), 131-132.

92 Gandhi, 'Indentured Labour,' Ibid., 248; 'Letter to C.F. Andrews,' Ahmedabad, June 30, 1916, Ibid., 284.

93 Gandhi, 'Speech at Surat on Indenture,' 26 February 1917, Ibid., 349.

94 Gandhi, 'Indian Colonial Emigration', *Indian Review*, September 1917, Ibid., 515.

95 Brij V. Lal, 'Kunti's Cry: Indentured Women on Fiji Plantations,' *Indian Economic and Social History Review* 22, no. 1 (1985): 55-71.

96 Mrinalini Sinha, 'Totaram Sanadhya's *Fiji Mein Mere Ekkis Varsh*: A History of Empire and Nation in a Minor Key' in *Ten Books That Shaped the British Empire*, Antoinette Burton and Isabel Hofmeyr, eds. (Durham and London: Duke University Press, 2014), 182-183.

97 Shobna Nijhawan reports widespread discussion of such abductions at an Allahabad conference in 1917. Nijhawan, 'Fallen Through the Nationalist and Feminist Grids of Analysis: Political Campaigning of Indian Women against Indentured Labour Emigration' *Indian Journal of Gender Studies* 21, no. 1 (2014): 116-117.

98 The texts of these pamphlets are located in NAI, Commerce and Industry Department, Emigration Branch, December 1916, Part A, Proceedings Nos. 43-54.

99 Charu Gupta, '"Innocent" Victims/"Guilty" Migrants: Hindi Public Sphere, Caste and Indentured Women in Colonial North India', *Modern Asian Studies* 49, no. 5 (2015): 1363.
100 Malaviya, 'The Abolition of Indentured Labour', *Speeches and Writings of Pandit Madan Mohan Malaviya* (Madras: G.A. Natesan & Co., 1919), 324.
101 Ibid., 327–328.
102 Ibid., 333.
103 Ibid., 331, 342; C.F. Andrews and W.W. Pearson, 'Report on Indentured Labour in Fiji: An Independent Inquiry' (1916).
104 Gandhi, 'Indian Colonial Emigration', *Indian Review*, September 1917, *CWMG*, Vol. 14, 515.
105 Sinha, 'Premonitions', 831.
106 Mongia, *Indian Migration*, 1.
107 Radhika Singha, 'Finding Labor from India for the War in Iraq: The Jail Porter and Labor Corps, 1916–1920', *Comparative Studies in Society and History* 49, no. 2 (2007): 445.
108 Sinha, 'Totaram Sanadhya's *Fiji*', 185.

Who is Asiatic? Drawing the boundary in the legal and political framing of Indian South Africans, 1860–1960

Marina Martin

This chapter examines how political and legal decisions led to a particular construction of the South African classification 'Asiatic' between 1860 and 1960. Looking at the political and legal scaffolding of the Asiatic classification allows us to reach beyond the so-called 'Indian Question' – that is, the question of Indian South African rights around settlement – to the way in which Indian South African identity transitioned from British subjecthood to 'Asiatic'. Importantly, the political dimension of the Asiatic classification also reveals how the category was partitioned and fenced in, while other conceivable 'Asiatic' groups were excluded from the classification for political and economic reasons. This discussion provides a critical appraisal of the way in which identity was politicized and how boundaries between groups, though highly subjective, were cemented by law. It also contributes to debates on discourses of immigration, the language of exclusion and legitimacy not only on colour lines but also on the prevailing economic and political status quo.

Introduction

It is hard to pin down when the term 'Asiatic' first crept into British colonial documentation. The label strikes at the heart of the issues surrounding intra-imperial migration, and the weakness of imperial citizenship, especially in the face of the growing autonomy of white settler colonies such as South Africa. Despite its wider connotations in twenty-first century literature, 'Asiatic' primarily became used by the British in Africa to refer to Indians and Chinese migrants. There was a colour consciousness embedded within the term, to be used as a marker separating so-called 'whites' from 'non-whites'. However, it was more stringently used than this because native Africans were not included in this category, nor were Jewish migrants or Mediterraneans. It would also be too simplistic to say the category was merely a non-European or Asian designation; this is evident in the South Africa government literature from the 1930s. From this point officials began a process of selectively excluding categories of migrants from the designation, who would normally be construed as people of colour or Asian from a geographic standpoint. Diplomatic representations from various countries to remove their citizens from the category, reveal the primacy of economic and political considerations that shaped the parameters of the Asiatic category.

The question of who should be defined as Asiatic provides one of the biggest insights into the implications of legislative interventions to shifting identities and discourses around legitimacy, citizenship, exclusion and alienation. While the Durban Riots of 1949 highlighted territorial lines between Indians, Africans and Europeans, diplomatic dialogues and legislative discussions around the classification 'Asiatic' show how these lines were created and reinforced. This paper discusses some of the key ways in which the category 'Asiatic' was shaped within the Union of South Africa, and the basis on which various groups sought to exclude themselves from the category.

There were several factors that shaped the category of Asiatic. First one needs to turn back to the roots of the term. Why did this category arise in the first place? Why the distinction between Asiatic and non-Asiatic? Why did the identity of British subject not take primacy? There is no easy answer to this question. In essence, the term Asiatic is a compendium of different events and forms of legislation. There was no clear fixed definition. The term evolved over time to mainly refer to South African Indians and the Chinese, but at a certain point in time it also comprised other groups, such as the Japanese, Turks and Egyptians. The Asiatics Land and Trading Amendment Act of 1919 defined the category as follows:

'"Asiatic" means any Turk and any member of a race or tribe whose national home is in Asia, but shall not include any member of the Jewish or the Syrian race or a person belonging to the race or class known as the Cape Malays.'[1]

However, in the 1887 Report of the Indian Immigrants Commission, otherwise known as the Wragg Commission, the authors state from the outset: 'The words "Indian Immigrants", as used in this report, do not mean or include those persons who in Natal are usually designated "Asiatics" or "Arab traders".'[2]

In this report, a distinction is made between the Indian indentured labourers who fulfilled the labour requirements of British plantations in the colony, and more affluent traders who emerged from different parts of British India. On the other hand, because the impetus for doing business in the colony was seen to be driven by 'Indian immigrants', the two were seen as corollaries of each other and it was perceived as desirable to keep the numbers of Indian immigrants down.

What happened to the British imperial subject?

An examination of the term through a 1903 despatch conveys the idea that while Indians were included under the banner of Asiatics, a conceptual difference was drawn between 'British Indians' and other Asiatics.[3] In essence, 'British Indian' was a subcategory, but distinct from other Asiatics because of its implicit membership of the Empire.

In his communication with the colonial metropole, the Governor of the Transvaal reports that British Indians 'claimed for themselves absolute equality of treatment with all other British subjects' with respect to European agitation for more stringent measures against Asiatics. The British imperial distinction between British Indians and other Asiatics, along with the European settler view of disregarding this distinction is revealing. It points not merely to the relationship between the colonial government and Indians as British subjects, or to the relationship of European settlers with Indians, but also to the pressures of governing a colony that gave primacy to its European settler population.

How the label British Indian gave way to Asiatic in the white settler context is best explained by referring to what Daniel Gorman described as the fragility of imperial citizenship.[4] Gorman reached into the heart of imperial imaginings of citizenship across empire and demonstrated how its ideological foundations were fractured by the newly constituted political formations of the soon-to-be dominions. Describing the settlement colonies as early incarnations of nation-states, he argued that a common British identity was unable to take root. Undoubtedly, vast distances between the British colonies and the metropole would have played a role in loosening ties with Britain. Before the advent of the electric telegraph links, communication across the British Empire would have taken significant time.

The different groups already present in the colonies would also have played a part. In the case of South Africa, there was a previously established Dutch descended settler community, which nursed their own grievances towards the British following two successive Boer wars in the late eighteenth and early nineteenth centuries. They also felt a growing sense of antipathy towards Indian migrants with whom they felt no common British tie.

The sense of entitlement and racial hierarchy felt by the European settler population is demonstrated through an 1884 Dutch petition that was translated by an English official in 1899 to underscore European settler attitudes towards the presence of other racial groups in the colony. The year 1884 was the year in which the London Convention[5] – a treaty relinquishing British suzerainty over the South African Republic – took effect.

> We fear that if His Lordship (Lord Derby, then Secretary of State) should be of opinion that Asiatics should enjoy the same privileges as Europeans who came to settle in this State, this would be in conflict with our constitution, which recognises only two races of men, white and coloured; and the clause in the constitution relative to this matter remained unaltered during the time of the British Government.[6]

The 1903 Governor's despatch also demonstrates the shift in the British imperial position towards British Indians due to mounting anti-Asiatic sentiment by European settlers. The desire to appease the European population was clearly greater than British Indian discontent. One way of explaining this is to consider the vision of the colony held by the imperial government at the outset. On the one hand, the colonial government wished to achieve levels of prosperity attained by colonists in New Zealand, North America and Australasia. On the other hand, it recognized that the climate and soil were not conducive to the kinds of agricultural activities employed in those territories. Financial inducements, like free passage, preferential land schemes – such as those in other white settler colonies – would not be enough, but rather elevating the rank of the white working class immigrant by having the native population waiting on him. Evidently, maintaining the status of the white settler population was important from the beginning.[7] That being so, Gorman's argument that non-whites were excluded or marginalized, not merely out of racism, but with a view to building 'cultural unity', seems to hold water.[8] Rather than being part of imperial design, Gorman argues that the nebulous nature of imperial citizen against the far more concrete backdrop of state structures, was a prime driver of inequalities of rights and benefits amongst imperial subjects.

Citizenship scholars tend to regard the British concept of citizenship as having been weak, with no definition provided until the Nationality Act of 1948, which then applied to the colonies as well as the United Kingdom.[9] On the other hand, the diffuse nature of that citizenship posed problems, encouraged fragmentation but also provided the ground for claims of inclusion for smaller 'self-defining' communities.[10] Importantly, status and laws were therefore uneven across empire. Cooper provides the example of the high profile Somerset case of 1772, which ruled slavery illegal in England but not across the empire, and observes that 'norms in one part of the empire could disrupt other parts'.[11] It is not difficult to see why Indian membership as British imperial subjects, with attendant claims for equality in South Africa, rested on very thin ice.

The Bombay-based Imperial Indian Citizenship Association was formed in 1914 in an attempt to make these claims for equality.[12] This, however, was the primary idiom from which India's elite drove their aspirations for equal legal rights.[13] Some scholars have critiqued Gandhi's actions in South Africa – the symbol of the most prominent challenge to Indian inequity – on the basis of this imperial dialogue.[14] There is, however, a growing body of work that is drawing greater attention to the ways in which Indian imperial subjects, particularly the elites in the Indian subcontinent, were driven to couch their demands for rights in the language and forums that formed part of the ideological foundations of empire.[15] As white supremacy and the burgeoning nation-state rendered this language obsolete, Indian elites, as spearheaded by Gandhi and the Indian National Congress, had changed course by the late 1920s, desirous of the rights and autonomy of the dominions.[16] Following the Balfour Declaration of 1926, which ceded greater political and diplomatic autonomy to the white settler colonies, we can comprehend how the language of inter-imperial relations changed considerably. This happened in two ways: directly, through domestic pressures boiling over into colonial governance; but also because colonial officials were influenced by what other white settler colonies were doing.

Despite differences across the white settler colonies, officials were looking overseas at immigration policies that were being employed towards non-whites and borrowing from them. In some ways, white settler colonies felt greater affinity towards each other than they did with imperial ideology in the metropole. When Australia introduced the 1896 New South Wales Coloured Races Restriction and Regulation Bill, the colony of Natal's Attorney General, Harry Escombe, urged the Colonial Office in London to follow suit. This was in stark contrast to the position of 1887, when government commissioners voiced strong opposition to restrictive legislation that targeted Indians, particularly in view of its repercussions for British rule in India.[17] The Natal parliament had already passed its own measures contravening the Colonial Office by 1894, divesting Indians of the franchise.[18] Mounting hostility towards Indians, particularly free (passenger) Indians, found expression in the creation of the 1897 Natal Immigration Restriction Act. Although Indians were not mentioned by name in the Act, strict quarantine and European language requirements were devised to delineate the 'prohibited immigrant'. According to Maartens, in describing excluded classes, the Colonial Office borrowed virtually word for word from the American *Immigration Act* of 1891, with additional quarantine and European language provisos ensuring the effective exclusion of Indians without explicitly doing so.[19]

Many of the mechanisms for restricting 'Asiatics' were shared across white settler colonies and later dominions through these kinds of legal transfers.[20] As they did so, the language of restriction shaped the nature of how prohibited persons like Indians were seen. 'Asiatic', as a category, took on a new form of currency. This kind of legal parlance was also influenced in the early 1900s by immigration restrictions occurring in the United States, particularly towards Chinese immigrants who, as with Australia, were attracted to the goldfields from around 1840 onwards.[21] It was also part of a transnational movement across the self-governing colonies for 'whiteness' as an ideologically based racial identification.[22]

The build-up to white supremacy as a framework happened in phases and as a corollary to the disintegration of 'British Indian' subjecthood and the more frequent usage of 'Asiatic'. When Indian immigrants came into competition with the white settler trading community and even outperformed them, white settler status was threatened. Many of the colonial official reports investigating economic conditions detail how Indian shopkeepers were able to operate with better profit margins as well as through servicing the needs of the native population, something white shopkeepers were unwilling to do.[23] It would be inaccurate to say that racial hostility towards the Indian immigrant population was premised on a vision of a 'white colony' alone. The economic history and tensions between white settlers who sought to preserve access to resources against growing affluence in the Indian immigrant population, served as a tinderbox for much of the legislation.[24] As early as 1885, the Wragg Commission reported that white colonists increasingly saw free Indians – time-expired indentured labourers and passenger Indians – as rivals and competitors either in agriculture – for instance, market gardening – or in the commercial sphere.

These kinds of attitudes towards Indians by white settlers permeated other British ruled areas of Africa, and inflected narratives between African native populations and Indians. One common narrative consisted of the idea that

Indians had deprived native Africans of their livelihood and even their birthright. In East Africa, and in particular Kenya, some scholars have attributed this to the 'middleman' thesis, in which Indians were employed by the British first as labourers to build railroads, but who then stayed on as lower-level administrators and commercial middlemen.[25] This kind of narrative was undoubtedly one of the primary reasons leading to the infamous Durban Riots in 1949.

Alongside this trend, white settler aspirations for legitimation of their own identity, particularly in view of the presence of native black populations, led to the drawing up of primitive ethnological classifications of 'yellow', 'black' and 'brown' races in South Africa.[26] Ethnological classifications such as these masquerading as scientific ideas, metaphorically and literally coloured waves of migration and 'helped to nurture a sense of acquired indigeneity on the part of white South African settlers'.[27]

Monitoring of the European versus the Indian population began relatively early on in Durban. This kind of monitoring was not merely limited to population numbers but rather focused on comparisons of land ownership, interest rates for mortgages and distribution of housing. Radhika Mongia interprets the colonial state's apparatus for monitoring migration as 'a circuit of connections and contestations between imperial and colonial state formations'.[28] These contestations moved beyond monitoring, spilling out to create the emergence of layer upon layer of anti-Indian legislation in subsequent years. All of this anti-Indian legislation fed into the classification of Asiatic. As a category, it contained a number of connotations, shaping a supposed racial group through restricted access to resources.

In 1924 and 1925, an attempt was made by parliament to restrict the rights of Indians in Natal to purchase property outside certain areas, but the outcry raised by Indians was so great that the bill was dropped. Instead, between 17 December 1926 and 12 January 1927, a Round Table Conference between representatives of the Government of India and the Union Government took place in Cape Town. The resulting agreement, known as the Cape Town Agreement or Gentlemen's Agreement, put in place an assisted emigration scheme aimed at inducing Indians to repatriate. However, the numbers which chose to use the scheme were small. The Cape Town Agreement also marked the beginning of a series of significant diplomatic interventions on behalf of Indian South Africans by the Government of India. Protest towards anti-Indian legislation took a much more prominent place on the stage of foreign diplomacy.

In May 1927, at the request of Gandhi, the Government of India appointed V.S. Srinivasa-Sastri as its first Agent-General – later known as the High

Commissioner – in South Africa. Sastri had been part of the delegation representing the Indian Government for the Round Table Conference. Earlier on, in 1922, he had also been a representative to the dominions of Australia, New Zealand and Canada in a bid to improve the condition of Indians domiciled in those countries. Later, between 1930 and 1932, Sastri represented the Government of India to discuss constitutional reform at a series of sessions making up the Round Table Conference in London. In this way, the parameters of the Asiatic category were further shaped by the Indian government's negotiations. This was because the category explicitly targeted Indians even though it mopped up other ethnic groups. So, whatever interventions the Indian government made were a response to anti-Indian rulings and, in turn, the interventions made by the Indian government evoked further responses from the Union government.

Indian migrants were an amorphous group when they first arrived in South Africa. They had no clear sense of 'Indianness'. The first indentured labourer migrants had clearly left an India that was a British colony, but on arriving in South Africa, their membership as British Indians was so undermined by white settler attitudes that a type of Indianness began growing instead. As Parvathi Raman points out this 'loose sense of community and notion of Indianness' was also partly framed by a sustained relationship with India.[29] However, it was also developed through India's political interventions in South Africa, as well as segregation and discrimination enacted via legislation.

Indian penetration and the Broome Commission

In successive years until his return to India in 1929, Sastri was instrumental in having a number of segregation bills withdrawn. Nevertheless, segregation laws were still passed against Indians. Despite the 1927 agreement, anti-Indian agitation took on fresh vigour in the form of 'Indian Penetration' – a storm of resentment about Indians allegedly encroaching on European residential areas in Durban. Although only the white poor were eligible for subsidized municipal housing developments, 'Indian Penetration' anti-Indian agitation pamphlets illustrated that Indians occupied the vast majority of such housing. In trade, the state began monitoring licences held by Europeans and Indians, respectively. Once again, these pamphlets stated that Indians had 'ousted' Europeans in rural areas in the Transvaal, and that they held disproportionately higher numbers of licences elsewhere relative to their population size. On the back of this pressure cooker of anti-Indian sentiment, in 1940 the Union Government appointed the first Broome Commission to investigate 'Indian penetration'.

The Broome Commission concluded that Indian penetration was not taking place, but this failed to appease European settler discontent. The Durban City Council immediately disregarded the findings and sought to induce the Minister for the Interior to introduce legislation restricting Indians from purchasing property outside specific areas.

By the end of 1942, Justice Broome headed a second commission to enquire into the same issues reported on in the first Broome Commission. Even though this second commission failed to find any veracity in the report that Indians had engulfed urban areas of Durban, the City Council convened the third Broome Commission.

As a result of three Broome Commissions, the Smuts Government forged the Pretoria Agreement of 19 April 1944. This government had been navigating between the Indian government's opposition to anti-Indian legislation, as well as opposition in some quarters within Smut's own party against the backdrop of populist white settler demands for measures to be taken against further 'penetration' of Indians and reduce economic competition.[30]

Diplomacy and the Asiatic Land Tenure and Indian Representation Bill 1946

The Act that left one of the most significant imprints on carving out territory was the Asiatic Land Tenure and Indian Representation Bill of 1946, also known as the 'Ghetto Bill'. The Act, which commenced on the 6 June, massively restricted Indian property ownership in 'white' areas of Natal. While this Act became notorious for sealing the fate of Indian South Africans in the annals of history, scholars have written little about the diplomatic negotiations undertaken by countries other than India and South Africa in the decades preceding and following the formation of this Act. To understand these negotiations, it is necessary to grasp the overarching significance of 'Indian penetration'.

As seen in the earlier discussion, 'Indian penetration' was a complex multifaceted issue. It consisted of a struggle for dominance between white settlers and Indian settlers over the resources of land and property, with white settlers vying for primacy of claims and Indian settlers negotiating for equality. Alongside this, the primacy of white settler claims was not merely economic but intermingled with notions around the superiority of 'white races' and their respective civilizations. Victorian sensibilities were largely intolerant of Indian social traditions and practices.[31] These ideas provided the thrust for large-scale racial-spatial engineering, into which townships were born. Segregation of this kind further increased the sense of racial difference and injected irrational, even 'pathological metaphors such as crime, epidemic disease and public health'[32] into the narrative. If there was any substance to these metaphors, they were largely self-fulfilling. Stripped of the right to attractive land and property, townships were always at the periphery of proper infrastructure and services.

The Indian government closely monitored the resulting reports of all three Broome Commissions and attempted through various negotiations to redress the tightening discrimination directed at Indian South Africans. For this reason, the formation of the Ghetto Act was a massive blow to the status of Indian South Africans, not least because it signalled a failure to break through the status quo at the diplomatic level. When examining this failure, it is important to understand that India's struggle to achieve Dominion status in its relationship with Britain weakened its negotiating position with South Africa. This constituted the third facet of Indian penetration.

With this backdrop in mind, we can perceive the mindset of other countries that sought to distance themselves from the Asiatic category. The four countries of China, Japan, Egypt and Turkey surfaced as individual files within the diplomatic papers negotiating for an exclusion from the 'Asiatic' category. These diplomatic negotiations took place over the course of several decades. We can learn much about how the international community viewed the Asiatic category from the diplomatic archives.

Arguments put forward by the four countries varied in terms of their approach towards Indian South Africans as well as the political externalities that they could draw on to influence South Africa. As these groups attempted to exclude themselves from the 'Asiatic' category, their views about Indian South Africans also crystallized. The diplomatic dialogues additionally present an international perspective of South Africa's segregationist policies as well as the political context in which they took place. For the South African government, there were a series of priorities that informed who was included or excluded from the category. For those who negotiated with the government, the power of their representation was the decisive factor.

South Africa decided to exclude the Japanese from the Asiatic classification because of a Gentleman's Agreement forged in 1930 to facilitate financially attractive transactions with Japan. The Union of South Africa opted to do this because the number of Japanese trickling into South Africa was exceedingly small, and the government considered them to be of a comparably better class than the Chinese. Compounding this, the agreement entailed admitting only Japanese wholesale merchants and buyers of South African produce for export, along with staff on the recommendation of the Japanese Consul, and these numbers were to be restricted to a 'reasonable limit'.[33] This is not to say the Japanese never experienced discrimination, but by the 1960s, post-war economic activity led to an 'honorary white' designation.

It is unclear when China's interventions began, but the diplomatic papers reveal negotiations as early as 1929 with the reported expulsion of Chinese merchants from South Africa. According to the Chinese chargé d'affaires, specific societies came into existence for the express purpose of expelling Asiatics.[34]

While there were multiple forms of discrimination towards the Chinese, the Chinese government did not call for a dismantling of the term 'Asiatic', but purely for exemption. However, the major drive for exemption was in response to the Asiatic Land Tenure and Trading Act of 1939. As part of their negotiations China compared what it saw as more favourable treatment of the Chinese in Great Britain, other dominions and even the USA. Referring to the precedent of favourable treatment towards Jews and Syrians in 1919 by the Governor-General, China sought a similar exemption. They argued that the Chinese should be differentiated from Indians for several reasons. First, Indians were British Empire members, and their treatment was an internal affair of the British Empire which had nothing to do with China. It was further contended that the alleged 'penetration' that drove legislation, did not apply to the Chinese.[35]

The Government of China also attempted to use the events of World War II and the issue of alliances as a lynchpin for preferential treatment. Resenting the preferential treatment accorded the Japanese in South Africa, China stressed their dangerous nature. In contrast they presented themselves as faithful allies of Great Britain and drew attention to the US's sympathetic attitude towards China.

Finally, China argued that the notion of being European was contentious. It argued that the perceived distinction between Asiatics and Europeans was subject to the vagaries of geography and interpretation.[36] The 1961 document reveals the Chinese response to the Japanese receiving more privileges than the Chinese. The Chinese Ambassador approached the Republic of South Africa seeking the same privileges as the Japanese.[37]

Turks were originally included within the definition of 'Asiatic', but after significant lobbying, also from the Egyptian government on behalf of Turks, the Asiatic Laws Amendment Act of 1948 excluded Turks. There were two main arguments made by Turks in their own negotiations; first they asserted they were European, and also light-skinned enough to pass off as European. Second, they indicated that their shared position vis-à-vis Soviet Russia would come under pressure if South Africa continue to discriminate against Turks.[38]

Curiously, South Africa perceived Egypt as sympathetic to India in its foreign policy. However, Egypt appears to have had more leverage than either the Chinese or Turks by threatening embarrassment to the Union of South Africa if Egypt severed diplomatic ties. This had the desired effect of exemptions because of Egypt's membership of the Arab League. Through this membership, Egypt threatened the Union government's Pan African schemes by exerting influence on the large Muslim population in Africa.[39] Nevertheless, darker skinned Egyptians were still to be judged with reference to South African racial groups.

Conclusion

This discussion examines how political and legal decisions led to a particular construction of the South African classification 'Asiatic' between 1860 and 1960. It also contributes to debates on discourses of immigration and the language of exclusion and legitimacy, not only on colour lines but also on the prevailing economic and political status quo. As British imperial citizenship disintegrated it was replaced by the growing autonomy of the white settler colonies and the language and legislation that cut across the colonies rather than the London-based Colonial Office. The ideological fragility of the concept of imperial citizenship was a key factor spurring the rise in usage of the label 'Asiatic' as distinct from British Indian.

As the analysis reveals, there was no clear definition of 'Asiatic'. British colonials originally forged the legislative parameters of the category in response to white settler attitudes originally towards the two main immigrant non-European groups, namely, the Indians and Chinese. A class dimension also seeped into the category; and this paper places the close relationship between Indian indentured servitude/bonded labour and the evolution of the category 'Asiatic', within the dual historical context of settler colonialism and empire building. It was, nevertheless, a flexible category evolving over time to ring-fence access to the resources of land, property and commercial opportunity. Unsurprisingly therefore, the diplomatic negotiations centred on the matter of exclusion.

By studying the diplomatic papers of these countries, a picture of how these various groups saw themselves emerges, in stark contrast to the South African view. They also provide an insight into how legislation created and cemented group identity politics, by privileging specific aspects of 'race' according to economic and political prerogatives. This construction of spurious identities had the effect of manipulating the social and political landscape and drove further scaffolding around the category. Going back even further, the paper exposes how British colonials fostered racial categories as part of their administrative drive across the Empire, and the forces that led to differentiation across not only the British colonies – particularly other white settler colonies with Dominion status – but also across the continent of Africa. An examination of empire would be incomplete without understanding how the discourses of membership created narratives that resonated in other parts of the world and future work will delve into this.

The term 'Asiatic' was fundamentally a compendium of different events and forms of legislation. It reflected white settler attitudes towards Indians, the evolving status of Indians as they shifted from British subjects fulfilling an economic purpose, to undesirable settlers competing for resources. Alongside this, it reflected state-building measures away from colonial prerogatives as South Africa gained more autonomy from the UK, diplomatic priorities and the effort outwardly to position its segregationist policies as a domestic issue in the international arena.

Notes

1 Act No. 37 of 1919, Asiatic Land and Trading Amendment Act of 1919.
2 'Report of the Indian Immigrants Commission 1885–1887', known as the Wragg Commission, (PMB) NCP/8/3/28/1887
3 'Despatch from the Governor of the Transvaal respecting the position of British Indians in that colony', (PMB) BPP/Vol.74/Cd1864/1903
4 Daniel Gorman, *Imperial Citizenship: Empire and the Question of Belonging* (Manchester: University of Manchester Press, 2006).
5 The London Convention took effect on 27 February 1884.
6 Correspondence between the High Commissioner and the State President in 1899 on the Asiatic Question, (PMB) BPP/Vol83/No.1/1899
7 Report on Crown Lands and European Immigration, Colony of Natal, 1876, (PMB) NCP/ADD/2/1/1876
8 Daniel Gorman, 'Wider and Wider Still? Racial Politics, Intra-Imperial Immigration and the Absence of Imperial Citizenship in the British Empire' *Journal of Colonialism and Colonial History* 3, no. 3 (2002): https://muse.jhu.edu/article/38080.
9 Frederick Cooper, *Citizenship, Inequality and Difference: Historical Perspectives* (Princeton: Princeton University Press, 2018), 55.

10 Michelle Everson, '"Subjects", or "Citizens of Erewhon"? Law and Non-Law in the Development of a "British Citizenship", *Citizenship Studies* 7, no. 1: 83.
11 Cooper, ibid.
12 Niraja Jayal, *Citizenship and its Discontents: An Indian History* (Cambridge, MA: Harvard University Press, 2013).
13 See Jayal, *Citizenship*; Ashwin Desai and Goolam Vahed, *The South African Gandhi: Stretcher-Bearer of Empire* (Stanford: Stanford University Press, 2016); and Sukanya Banerjee, *Becoming Imperial Citizens: Indians in the Late Victorian Empire* (Durham: Duke University Press, 2010).
14 See Desai and Vahed, *The South African Gandhi*, as a notable example.
15 See Banerjee, *Becoming Imperial Citizens*, for a discussion on four high profile elite Indian imperial subjects.
16 See, for instance, Sunil Amrith, 'Empires, Diasporas and Cultural Circulation' in *Writing Imperial Histories*, ed. Andrew Thompson (Manchester: Manchester University Press, 2013).
17 See Robert Huttenback, *Racism and Empire: White Settlers and Colored Immigrants in the British Self-Governing Colonies 1830–1910* (Cornell: Cornell University Press, 1976), 22. See also, Jeremy C. Maartens, *Empire and Asian Migration: Sovereignty, Immigration Restriction and Protest in the British Settler Colonies, 1888–1907* (Crawley: UWA Publishing, 2018), 87–88.
18 Maartens, *Empire and Asian Migration*.
19 Maartens, 99–100.
20 See Daniel Ghezelbesh, 'Legal Transfers of Restrictive Immigration Laws: A Historical Perspective' *International and Comparative Law Quarterly* 66, no. 1 (January 2017): 235–255.
21 See Mae Ngai, *Impossible Subjects: Illegal Aliens and the Making of Modern America* (Princeton: Princeton University Press, 2004).
22 See Marilyn Lake and Henry Reynolds, *Drawing the Global Colour Line: White Men's Countries and the International Challenge of Racial Equality* (Cambridge: Cambridge University Press, 2008).
23 'Report of the Indian Immigrants Commission 1885–1887', (PMB) NCP/8/3/28/1887; See also the later 1909 commission called the Clayton Commission, (PMB) NCP 8/3/82/1909.
24 See K. Buchanan and N. Hurwitz, 'The Asiatic Immigrant Community in the Union of South Africa' *Geographical Review* 39, no.3 (July 1949): 448.
25 See Gijsbert Oonk, 'South Asians in East Africa (1880–1920) with a Particular Focus on Zanzibar: Toward a Historical Explanation of Economic Success of a Middlemen Minority' *African and Asian Studies* 5, No. 1 (2006): 57–90.
26 Saul Dubow, 'South Africa and South Africans: Nationality, Belonging, Citizenship' in *The Cambridge History of South Africa, Vol.2: 1885–1994*, eds.

Robert Ross, Anne Kelk Major, and Bill Nasson (Cape Town: Cambridge University Press, 2012), 17–65.
27 Dubow, 'South Africa and South Africans', 25.
28 Radhika Mongia, *Indian Migration and Empire. A Colonial Genealogy of the Modern State* (Durham, NC: Duke University Press, 2018), 2.
29 Parvathi Raman, 'Being Indian the South African Way: The Development of Indian Identity in 1940s' Durban' in *Rethinking Settler Colonialism. History and Memory in Australia, Canada, Aotearoa New Zealand and South Africa*, ed. A.E. Coombes (Manchester: Manchester University Press, 2006), 193.
30 Jean Van der Poel, ed., *Selections from the Smuts Papers: Volume 6, December 1934– August 1945* (Cambridge: Cambridge University Press, 1973).
31 Maynard Swanson, 'The "Asiatic Menace": Creating Segregation in Durban, 1870–1900' *The International Journal of African Historical Studies* 16, no. 3 (1983): 404.
32 Ibid., 402.
33 'Position of Japanese in the Union with Regard to Residential and Trading Rights', (NAP) BTS 19/2/2, Vol. 1.
34 'Position of Chinese in the Union with Regard to Residential and Trading Rights', (NAP) BTS 19/2/1, Vol. 1, File 1.
35 Ibid.
36 'Position of Chinese in the Union with Regard to Residential and Trading Rights', (NAP) BTS 19/2/1_Vol.1, File 2.
37 'Position of Chinese in South Africa Relating to Residential and Commercial Law', (NAP) BTS 19/2/1_PL.
38 Position of Turks Under the Asiatic Land Tenure and Indian Representation Act", (NAP) BTS 19/2/4.
39 'Egyptians: Position of in the Union of South Africa', (NAP) BTS 19/2/5 Vol. 1. Key (PMB) Pietermaritzburg Archives, South Africa (NAP) National Archives Pretoria, South Africa

Part Three

Historical Biography

6

Taraknath Das: A global biography

Neilesh Bose

Though cited frequently in histories of South Asian migrants[1] in the United States of America, the itinerant Indian nationalist and political activist Taraknath Das (1884–1958), has yet to find a detailed place in the historiography of modern globalization. Das spent significant time in the US-Canada borderlands in the western part of North America, attended a military academy in Vermont and applied for and received US citizenship just before Asian exclusion acts were passed barring South Asians from citizenship. He participated in nearly each major anti-colonial Indian movement in North America before the Great War. Finally, Das was likely one of the first politically active South Asian migrants in Canada to link the various struggles of South Asians in British Columbia to the larger struggle of Indian nationalists throughout the world in the early twentieth century. These efforts of Das just before the First World War correspond in time to rising 'expatriate patriots' such as Mohandas Gandhi in South Africa and Shyamji Krishnavarma in England and France, in the early twentieth century. In the words of an eminent scholar of Indian migration, Das was 'the first important political activist to give a convergent orientation to the aspirations of the Indian communities in the north of the American continent'.[2] This chapter will explore how Das' movements, writings and politics in the first two decades of the twentieth century comprise the seeds of a global biography. Global microhistory is the site of excitement in certain circles but, much like global history, cautious reservation too.[3] A 'global biography' is not simply the story of a peripatetic life nor a life whose history shows mixing across lines of difference. Rather, global biography assists the uncovering of broad-based macro-level changes – in this case, the relationship between long-distance nationalism and hardening imperial surveillance – within the purview of an individual's life. Recent studies in biography have generated a rich trail of precedents for considering how a particular life not only illuminates larger structures of power but also offers a look at both subjectivity and structure, and ambiguities of self-presentation and realities of power at various levels of state, family and religion.[4] Global-biographical turns have occurred in early modern contexts that emphasize both external factors and aspects of self-fashioning.[5] Modern interventions in microhistory by Marc Gamsa;[6] Desley Deacon, Penny Russel and Angela Woollacott;[7] and Harald Fischer-Tine[8] all build upon such foundations to consider external determinants of the modern world, such as imperial governance, immigration restrictions, racial mixing and passing and textured histories of lived cosmopolitanisms.[9] Das' life forms the substance of a global biography insofar as his life focused on two major elements of the modern world system. One included the borders of settler states like the US and Canada through the vantage point of non-white immigrants at the cusp of formal exclusion. The other featured the meaning and form of Indian nationalism outside of India.

Das' life included significant portions of time in North America as a worker of odd jobs, a student and a political organizer. He entered via Seattle in 1906 – he travelled to Asia and Europe during the Great War, but returned to stand in the 'Hindu-German Conspiracy' Trial of 1916 and was jailed until 1918 – before heading to Europe in 1925 with his wife Mary Keating Morse. He returned to the USA in 1938 and stayed throughout World War II, with only one trip back to India in 1952 after which he returned a widower and died in New York in 1958. This chapter will focus on four aspects of this trans-regional life. The first section will detail his entry into North America and activities amongst Indian migrants in the US and Canada from 1906 to 1913. His work from 1913 through 1917, during the formation of the Ghadar Party, a global anti-colonial organization started in San Francisco, comprises the second portion. The final two sections will consider his writings during this time period as well as drawing a comparison to another figure of the time, Mohandas Gandhi who, during the early twentieth century, engaged in similar activities but in Southern Africa.

Das in North America, 1906–1913

South Asians have entered historical studies of North American history primarily through consideration of community histories, interracial intimacies and entanglements with immigration restrictions, as well as overseas surveillance and the growth of political intelligence.[10] In the context of migration in the colonial period, the numbers of South Asians entering British Columbia in the early twentieth century pale in comparison to other regions, as millions migrated to Malaya, the Straits Settlements, Sri Lanka and Burma over the 1834–1930 period, whereas approximately 80,000 migrated to Canada, Australia, Hawaii, Mexico, Panama and Argentina. The numbers of migrants in British Columbia begin to grow from 1904 in very small increments and over 2,000 appear in the watershed year of 1907, but the total number until the 1920s hovered at around five thousand. The political significance of the relatively small numbers of migrants in the Pacific Northwest – though broadcast in the popular press as being about 10,000 – outweighs the limited numbers compared to other parts of the world. This significance is drawn from the fact that key locations on the Pacific Coast – Vancouver, Victoria, Seattle, Portland, Astoria, San Francisco – were hotbeds of radical labour politics as well as the birthplace of the *Ghadar* party, a trans-regional anti-colonial political organization that published newspapers and political pamphlets as well as procured arms to build a revolution against the British Empire. The most politically visible portion of these migrants was in the borderland regions in the Pacific Northwest. There were various types of migrants in the Pacific Northwest at the turn of the twentieth century. Labourers worked in Vancouver and throughout British Columbia in Mill Side, Fraser River Mill, New West Minster, Port Moody, Abbotsford and Port Haney, as well as large numbers in Portland and Astoria, Oregon. Significant numbers of students at universities were in Seattle at the University of Washington as well as in Pullman, Bellingham and Corvallis across the Pacific Northwest.[11]

Taraknath Das entered the Pacific Northwest, replete with Asian migrants of various origins, in 1906. The son of Kali Mohan Das, an employee of the Check Office in Calcutta, Taraknath Das was born in 1884 in Majhipara, north of Calcutta. His upbringing as a student in secondary school and college included study circles with revolutionary groups, such as the well-known revolutionary society, *Anushilan*, formed in 1903. From then he attended numerous meetings of young revolutionaries, including Jatin Mukherjee, a leader of *Yugantar*, a revolutionary group that planned assassinations and offered training in physical culture in order to overthrow the British in India. At one meeting called by Mukherjee, Taraknath Das, along with others was instructed to travel abroad to Japan and other parts of the world, including the United States of America, to attain education, military training and resources for promoting the cause of Indian independence. In 1905, he left for Japan, took courses at the University of Tokyo and worked with pan-Asianists and other Indian nationalists there. Under pressure from the British government to curtail seditious activity, the

Japanese authorities encouraged Taraknath Das to leave Japan. In the summer of 1906, he boarded the *Tango Maru*, which arrived in Seattle on the 12th July of that year.[12] In Washington, he worked on the railroads and in odd jobs before then moving to San Francisco. From this northern Californian base he found in Washington and Oregon a burgeoning community of Indian labourers working in lumber and shingle mills, small-scale agriculture, celery farms and various seasonal labour.

At the time of Das' entry onto the Pacific Coast, India saw the rise of several political organizations begun in the early twentieth century that had focused on self-help, moral regeneration, social service, physical culture and nationalist anti-colonial politics. In both the Bengal and Bombay Presidencies, key regions of the colonial state, organizations such as *Anushilan* and popular nationalist figures like Bal Gangadhar Tilak – the Marathi nationalist who was sentenced to eighteen months imprisonment for seditious writings in the Marathi paper *Kesari* – had spurred into action a new world of extremists taken to political violence and planning for revolution. Outside India, Indian revolutionary centres emerged in Paris, London and New York and with Das, parts of the Pacific Coast of North America. In 1907, India itself was alight with nationalist agitation of various sorts in the wake of the 1905 partition of Bengal, including various individuals and organizations who were noticed by the colonial state in Bengal, Madras, Bombay, Punjab and various other parts of central and northern India. In addition to core groups such as the *Anushilan Samiti*, James Campbell Ker, personal assistant to the Director of Criminal Intelligence, noted eight examples of 'sedition' published in India, including publications like *Bande Mataram* and *Yugantar*, as well as five examples of 'sedition' published outside India.[13] Prominent nationalists seen as dangerous to colonial India were listed in England, France, America, Germany and Turkey. Das' entry into the Pacific Northwest coincides with the opening of the Indian colonial state's documentation of the multifaceted global tendrils of anti-colonial organizations, newspapers and individuals seen as posing a threat to colonial India.

In early 1907, Das got a job as a laboratory helper at Berkeley and was also admitted as a special student in chemistry. At the end of the spring 1907 semester, he passed the civil service examination for the position of interpreter in the Bureau of Immigration and Naturalization Service of the USA. He served in that post in Vancouver from May of that year. From this point onward, as an employee of the US but living in Vancouver, he began shuttling between Vancouver, Victoria and various points in San Francisco, Seattle and different areas in Oregon. However, British Columbia is where his actual work as an Indian revolutionary began, as he witnessed and then responded to two particular riots in September 1907, including the Vancouver riots against Asians.[14] Interviewed by the *Daily Province* of Vancouver, Das enters the Canadian record by mentioning that Indians were fleeing the high taxes and oppressive conditions in India.

Due to the rising numbers of Indian immigrants in 1906, the BC (British Columbia) legislature, on March 27, 1907, unanimously voted to disenfranchise all South Asians. In April 1907, South Asians were denied the vote in Vancouver municipal elections. South Asians were excluded from serving on juries, being employed by the public service or getting work on public works contracts. Less than a year from when he entered the province, a Canadian Order in Council mentioning the 'Continuous Journey' legislation was issued. The Continuous Journey legislation was an amendment to the Immigration Act, passed on 10 April 1908, stating that the Government of Canada may prohibit the landing of any immigrant that did not come to Canada by continuous journey from the country of which they were a native or citizen.[15] This amendment resulted in the reduction of large numbers of Indian immigrants into Canada. This was successful, as only twenty-nine immigrants from India – and all of them return residents – entered Canada from 1909 to 1913, compared to several thousand in 1907 and 1908.[16] Though the numbers reduced because of this legislation, earlier arrivals had created small communities in Victoria and Vancouver that became the base for political agitation in local and global terms. In both of these cities, South Asian communities began to form in this period, inclusive primarily of Punjabi Sikhs, who began a *Khalsa Diwan* society in Victoria in 1912. Most early migrants found work in forest industries and lumber mills in Victoria and Vancouver. For a history of consciousness and activism based around Canadian immigration law and the exclusion of South Asians, British Columbia is the origin point of both legislative actions as well as organized Indian protest against them, as one part of the growing trans-regional Indian nationalism of the era.

After the Bellingham riots of September 1907, in which a mob of white men attacked South Asians in their homes, the small but growing communities of South Asians on the Pacific Coast began to organize and take refuge in Vancouver.[17] In this context, Das started the *Free Hindusthan*, a newspaper modelled after pre-existing Indian nationalist publications circulating in India, England and France and also the first South Asian publication of any kind in Canada. Models included the *Bande Mataram* published in Calcutta, another *Bande Mataram* published in Geneva and the *Indian Sociologist*, published in Paris.[18] Listed as the 'manager' of the paper, the first edition in April included long pieces about famine in India, designating causes in British policy, articles about Indian religion, the German revolution of 1848 and lengthy analysis of the challenges facing the movements of Indian labourers across imperial spaces. Published in the press room of the Socialist Party of Canada, which published the *Western Clarion*, the first issue appeared in April 1908. This led to the appearance of Das and the *Free Hindusthan* on the radar of the British Empire's Criminal Intelligence division as files on him and copies of the paper appeared in Ottawa and the India office in London. As C.J. Stevenson-Moore noted in the first report about the issue, 'its object is to create the impression among Canadians that there will be serious danger to the Empire if Hindus are shut out of Canada as they are shut out of Australia'.[19] Two thousand copies were printed and sent to India, the United States and South Africa. Given the seditious nature of the paper, the British administration in India immediately banned the paper, which led to scrutiny of his position at the US Immigration and Naturalization Services and his resignation on 18 April 1908. He then moved publication to Seattle in the middle of 1908 and then to New York for the editions of 1909 and 1910. Das held connections to political colleagues in Indian anti-colonial movements who were operating in New York and allied with Irish nationalists there. One such ally was George Freeman, who assisted him in shifting his operation to New York, and whose paper *Gaelic American* offered funds and resources enabling him to resume publication later in 1909 from New York.[20]

Free Hindusthan demonstrated a wide-ranging consciousness of the treatment of Indian migrants in South Africa, Fiji and Australia and inserts British Columbia into this context. In an analysis of how 500 'Hindusthanees', mostly Sikh veterans, sold their homes for passage money, but were denied entry and thus were rendered without shelter and forced into starvation, the paper mentions how the 'treatment we get in British Columbia is heart-rending'.[21] With the sub-heading of 'An Organ of Freedom, and of Political, Social and Religious Reform', the paper included a clear line about resistance to tyranny on the cover page of each edition. In the first issue in April 1908, this statement was 'Resistance to tyranny is obedience to God'. From the second issue in July 1908, this changed to 'Resistance to tyranny is service to humanity and a necessity of civilization'. The paper included updates regarding news about political prisoners and political activity in India. These updates included the hanging of Kanai Lal Dutt, the murderer of an informer, Gossain, on 10 November 1908, reported in the November–December 1908 edition; whereabouts of various revolutionaries, like Harilal Gandhi in South Africa, or Birendranath Dutt Gupta in Calcutta, or Vinayak Savarkar and their movements and arrests.

One of the most pressing issues covered by the paper was the topic of famine, mentioned in detailed terms in each issue of the paper. In the November–December 1908 edition, pictures of victims of British rule, stark images of Indians emaciated from starvation were published above the bold statement that the *Free Hindusthan* 'advocates [the] liberation of Hindusthan, that millions may be saved from the starvation caused by legalized pillage of India by the British government'.[22] In an anonymous piece, likely authored by Taraknath Das, famine is presented as the result of British policy, citing the authority of the economist Robert Ellis Thompson, declaring that British-made famines would ravage Hindusthan until she asserts her independence.[23]

Like other newspapers of the time, especially the *Indian Sociologist*, references to Western political theorists and historical figures appeared in most issues and justified the call for revolution in India. Each edition of *Free Hindusthan* appeared with quotations by Herbert Spencer on freedom as well as references to Mazzini and John Stuart Mill. Regarding Mill, each edition held a 'Thought for the Month' and the July 1908 edition's thought was Mill's: 'rebellions are never really unconquerable until they have become rebellions for an idea'. The final edition, issued in April 1910, carried a story titled 'Our Right to Create a Revolution in India'. Citing inspiration from Abraham Lincoln and Giuseppe Mazzini, the author mentions that

> we assert that we have power enough to create a revolution, because the history of India has seen many a revolution and she can have another one in this time of dire need. If creating a revolution is within our power, how to touch the vital point of the source of national energy, so that a motion of uncontrollable force may sweep the name and vestige of national slavery from the face of India, is the vital question.

What activated the attention of the criminal intelligence office was the continual mention of Indians in North America. Initially produced and sent from Vancouver, the paper functioned as a source of information about Indians in Canada to the broader audience of Indian revolutionaries throughout the world. In the second edition, a brief essay titled 'Our Position in Canada' Das mentions how Indians are kept out of each dominion of the British Empire as 'the gates of Australia are shut against us and South Africa is already a forbidden land. Our attempt to breathe air in South Africa is so disagreeable that several educated people and merchants are put in prison'. The goal of setting the situation of Indians in Canada into a broader context continues in the same edition in 'Hindusthanees in England', with details about political meetings and locales of political organizations. In the third edition in November–December 1908, he offers a look at how in Victoria, Sikhs convened a mass meeting in protest and sent a cable to Morley, Minto and Laurier. According to the paper, Sikhs in Victoria strongly protested against the orders of deportation from Canada to British Honduras[24], fearing the same treatment rendered to their countrymen in the Transvaal and Mauritius. It mentions how they are afraid that retired Sikh soldiers would be inspired by the idea of political freedom and that 'we know that in the sugar plantations of Fiji and other islands, our people are kept in a worse condition than those of slaves of past days'. According to the author, 'the reason for sending Sikhs from Canada to British Honduras is to put them in a system of contract labour that they will lose their idea of free-will and independent labour'.

It was becoming clear to authorities that this paper was appealing to Sikhs in Canada through a link to ongoing nationalist developments in India. The September 1908 edition published a letter from a Sikh student in the US:

> The Feringhi (foreigners) are going to interfere in all our business if we remain calm and quiet. The time is not very far when they will come to settle our social and family questions, such as marriage and protection of women. The man who supports British rule to make Khalsas slaves of foreign rulers is a traitor to all Khalsas and to our sacred religion. Every true Khalsa must do his best to free the nation from such slavery.[25]

In October 1908, it argues that Indian militaries were essential to maintaining British rule in 1857–58, like the Nepali Gurkhas and Sikhs, but this may change if 'we preach the sense of Hindu honour among the Nepalese, to stimulate their national desire to get a place among international powers'. Finally, the paper's November–December 1909 edition mentions a meeting on 3 October 1909 in the Sikh Temple of Vancouver. At this meeting, Natha Singh made a speech, published in the FH, mentioning that medals won by Sikh warriors in the British Empire were symbols of slavery. For Natha Singh, 'the medals they wore signify that they fought for the British as mercenaries against the cause of our fellow countrymen, or some free people. The medals acquired by serving in the British army ought to be regarded as medals of slavery'.[26] The paper, to the eyes of the British authorities, encouraged Sikhs in Canada to link their struggles to those in India. This latter point, along with the mention of sympathetic figures in the United States of America like William Jennings Bryan[27] caught the attention of both the Immigration Inspector William Hopkinson and the Governor of British Honduras E.J. Swayne, both of whom commented on the severity of critiques emanating from *Free Hindusthan*. Swayne mentioned that the 'general tenor is theosophical but from time to time contains articles setting forth the so-called unfair treatment of Hindus in Vancouver, and has reference to agitation in Bengal, and in tone is anti-British'.[28]

In the fall of 1908, Das left the northwest to attend Norwich University, a military training academy. Correspondence show how he was monitored as someone advocating war against a state with which the US was at peace, that of the British Empire. Suspended in 1909 because of his advocacy of war against their ally, the British Empire, he returned to Seattle and earned a BA in political science. In 1910, he began researching an MA on employer liability law, worked with labourers in Berkeley, and earned an MA in 1911. In this period, he served as an interpreter from Hindi and Punjabi in the St. John's trial in the spring of 1910, in which a few individuals and members of the police implicated in attacks on Indian labourers stood trial in St. John's, Oregon.

In 1911 after Das applied for and failed to receive citizenship in Seattle for the second time, the British Empire dispatched the Anglo-Indian immigration official William Hopkinson to his case. Hopkinson started following Das intently and declared him an anarchist in collusion with Canadian radicals. With a base in San Francisco, Canadian colleagues and Indian informants and spies in Vancouver, Hopkinson learnt that Das spent considerable time in Oregon as he registered the Bandon Clay Products Company, through gifts from a family, the Degassens of Oregon. News leaked that he planned to use this company as a front for training militant revolutionaries.

Das, Ghadr, and anti-colonialism, 1913–1917

In 1913, along with the newly arrived Har Dayal and others like Santokh Singh and Sohan Singh Bakhna, Das started the Pacific Coast Hindusthan Association, later known as the *Ghadr Party*. The party saw a rise of infiltration from Hopkinson and his network, first captivated by Das and then Dayal, which by 1914 held a 'Bengali house' and a 'Punjabi house' in its San Francisco core location but branches throughout the networks in Oregon, Washington and California as well as various regions throughout the world. In January 1914, Das submitted another application for citizenship in San Francisco. Despite Hopkinson trying his best to declare Das an anarchist and alert local authorities of the dangers he posed to the United States, Das received citizenship in June that year. As a newly naturalized US citizen, he immediately travelled to Canada to help those trapped in the *Komagata Maru*, held immobile in Vancouver's port since May of that year, due to recently passed legislation that only admitted immigrants who entered on a continuous journey, making it nearly impossible for Indians to enter Canada.

In 1914, the US also convened hearings on bills aimed at restricting the immigration of 'Hindu labourers'. Only visible in recent years to the US and Canadian authorities, Indians were tied to anarchism and radicalism in the official imagination. Additionally, by the 1917 Immigration Act that created a 'Barred Zone' including all of Asia, Indians were linked to both labour and insurgency in both countries. After leaving the US as a citizen in 1914, Das spent the next three years in various points northwest, as well as in Europe. In the spring of 1917, he was tried on sedition and allegations of conspiracy in the Hindu-German Conspiracy Trial along with and forty-two others, ranging from Ghadrites like Santokh Singh and Bhagwan Singh, and Germans like the former consul-general Franz Bopp. A relative high point in the spectacular rise of the nexus of surveillance showcases, the trial alleged a conspiracy that referred to a series of planned revolutionary uprisings from 1914 to 1917 by the Ghadr party, the Berlin India Committee and Indian revolutionaries. The nearly year-long trial cost $450,000, and included 150 witnesses summoned to testify against the Indian and German alleged conspirators, resulting in a six-hour jury deliberation which found Das and twenty-eight others guilty. Das was imprisoned in Leavenworth Prison in Kansas for a year alongside anarchists of various types, labour leaders, Germans like Bopp, and other radicals from around the world.

On 5 June 1918, Das entered Leavenworth as inmate 12489 with Bopp and von Shack, in leg irons and handcuffs. During the time of Das' imprisonment, the population there swelled to include criminals, court-martialled soldiers, German immigrants of various types, Mexican revolutionaries, socialists, anarchists and IWW members making up a total of approximately 400 other 'foreigners'. Separated from his fellow Ghadri-ites, he listed his religion as 'Vedantist' and occupation as professor of political science. Leavenworth was the place of his longest continual residence since he arrived in the US in 1906, and his prison file shows extensive meetings with folks like Bopp, anarchists of various stripes, IWW members like Haywood and conscientious objectors like Brent Dow Allison. After he served his time from June 1918 to October 1919, he was based both on the East Coast and in NY, as well as Germany in the interwar period, and worked for Indian independence along with his wife, Mary Keating Morse, classified as white, who worked for and was one of the founding members of the NAACP.

Das' early writings, 1917–1922

As did his counterpart Shyamji Krishnavarma who, like V.D. Savarkar, worked in London, Paris and Geneva, Das followed the tenets of European politics and posed the US as a role model for the future of India. Das' *Is Japan a Menace to Asia* was published in 1917. It was cited as evidence in the Hindu-German Conspiracy Trial as proof of his conspiracy, in which he wrote and agitated against the British Empire with the aid of German support. As a reflection of his early training in politics and formal political science at the University of Washington, and his Indian nationalism, he argued that Japan's rise to power was not a menace to Asia. Das shows that Japan's rise to power in the early twentieth century, noting the imperialism in Korea, aggression in China and role in Asian politics was not a 'menace to Asia' but rather a force of containing European aggression. Written from the explicit point of view of an insider in the global colour line of his moment, he mentioned how Japan's rise was a check to 'white men's countries' in Australia, Canada and South Africa. This is where Das by 1917 had lived experience in this kind of a settler colonial world, through his work as an interpreter in the immigration service and at numerous trials in BC and Oregon.

A focus on Asia preceded his book *India in World Politics*, a work that upholds the model of the United States of America as an exemplary republican form. This 1923 book started before he was jailed in March 1918 and completed while in jail. With fifteen chapters the book covers India's role in the British Empire to the Central Asian context, China relations, Anglo-French, German, Russian and Turkish relations, military relations, Suez Canal and the Persian Gulf and how Anglo-relations with Afghans, Japanese, Chinese and Americans, are all impacted by India. It is a consideration of the future of India as a world power. Approximately fifteen years after the appearance of Gandhi's seminal *Hind Swaraj*, Das' text reads in the opposite direction, a look outward, as opposed to the world of the self. With a foreword by the noted American man of letters, transcendentalist, sympathizer with Indian independence and scholar of English literature, Robert Morss Lovett, the work begins with an assessment of the importance of India to the British Empire and, like Gandhi in *Hind Swaraj*, notes how central the idea of empire is to the British and to Indians alike. His consistent mentions of the US constitution – as the 'greatest document of the world' – show his political leanings and were interpreted by Das as an inspiration to Chinese nationalists and to Indian nationalists. Das' work in these years fit clearly into the third of three discourses on Indian pan-Asianist thought as outlined by Fischer-Tine and Stolte in their landmark study, 'Imagining Asia in India: Nationalism and Internationalism (ca. 1905–1940)'.[29] Das approached the idea of India in a manner defined not by a spiritual antithesis to the Western world, nor an aspiration to a 'Greater India' but through a quest for independence following Japanese precedents.

In 1923, after the publication of *India in World Politics*, his citizenship was under scrutiny as the US government set upon him to revoke his citizenship and expel him from the country. Mysteriously, they could not find him. Even though he was a registered student in Georgetown's School of Foreign Service in 1923 and 1924, he eluded agents on his tail, as he had foiled Hopkinson a decade earlier. He then escaped to Europe after his 1924 marriage to Morse, after a whirlwind one year of writing a thesis, accepted in 1925. He lived most of the interwar years in Germany and Italy, and returned to the US after the war, to die in New York in 1958.

In his formative years, Das remarked on how Indian migrants held the sorts of skills required to succeed in an agrarian frontier. In many venues, Das wrote about the US as a model; about how American republicanism could be a guideline for an independent India. This United States was one in which Das was part of its settler expansion in the West. He did not see the dispossession that Western expansion depended on, but rather embraced the official notion of democracy on the frontier.

Das and Gandhi

The impetus to most of Das' writing and politics derived from restrictions against immigration into the US and Canada at the turn of the century. The cause of restricting immigration to Canada from India was part of a longer imperial history of the British Empire seeking to regulate and reduce immigration from India into various settler dominions within the Empire, including South Africa, New Zealand and Australia. South Africa is another key node in the broader network of imperial policies – as well as circuits of growing anti-colonialism – into which Das fit during the early twentieth century. Das' life and work in the Pacific Northwest, where BC played a pivotal role, compares to the work of Mohandas Gandhi (1869–1948), who began to develop a politics of anti-colonial protest and nationalism in the settler spaces of South Africa in the 1890s and 1900s. Both deployed similar techniques and methods of initiating institutions and newspapers that endured long after their departure from

Canada and South Africa. Though not exactly planned from the onset, both landed in a space where they found Indian workers exploited, harassed and the targets of violence and discrimination. Furthermore, both emerged at a time when the basis for immigration restrictions circulating throughout the Empire targeted Indians. Canada and South Africa, along with Australia and the United States shared an investment in the 1897 Natal Act passed in British Natal, which mandated a literacy test in a European language for all migrants entering Natal, cited by Australia and Canada numerous times in the first two decades of the twentieth century.

In 1907, the year Das entered British Columbia, Mohandas Gandhi had lived in British South Africa for nearly fourteen years. The Southern African region holds a long history of an Indian presence, stretching back to the seventeenth and eighteenth centuries, when the Dutch East India Company would purchase and transport slaves originating from India into their Cape Town settlement. In terms of the British Empire, Indians had been noticeably present since 1860, when the first batch of indentured labourers sailed across the Indian Ocean into the port of Durban, to work primarily on sugar cane plantations but also in other sorts of agricultural and manual labour, as well as for private estates. By the time of Gandhi's arrival in 1893, nearly 100,000 labourers had arrived in South Africa, and of these several thousand Indian traders and professionals arrived as 'passenger' Indians – those who paid their own passage. Gandhi belonged to this latter category. Before he arrived in the British-controlled portions of Southern Africa, the neighbouring South African Republic, in which Johannesburg served as the home of business, mining and capital accumulation, passed Law 3 of 1885, which named all the 'native races of Asia', and banned them from owning property, prohibited them from exercising franchise and mandated registration of all Asiatics. In 1894, one year after Gandhi entered the region, the British Empire sought to appease its growing European settler community by passing a range of laws targeting Indians in the settler colony of Natal. In 1894 it barred Indians from franchise. In 1895, it imposed a three pound tax on all ex-indentured labourers who failed to return, with punishment of deportation. Finally, in 1897, it passed a law restricting immigration based on education, health, age and literacy in a European language – the Natal Formula – which effectively barred any new Indian migrants from entering the country.

In these years, Gandhi began to organize politically and in 1894 formed the Natal Indian Congress with many of his business and trader colleagues there who met monthly, and was galvanized primarily by the disenfranchisement of Indians proposed that year and passed into law in 1896. In the 1890s, his politics then were based on Indians' right to franchise in the settler state of British South Africa. This occurred in the context of rising and violent opposition to Indian presence in the region as, on disembarkation in Durban after one trip back from London in 1897, a crowd of white youths were so agitated that they nearly beat him to death.[30] Nonetheless, for Gandhi, imperial citizenship maintained its allure and throughout the various wars which the British Empire fought in the 1890s against African groups like the Zulu, as well as during the Boer War of 1899–1902, he supported and volunteered for the war efforts.[31] In the first decade of the twentieth century, his politics began to shift away from petitions and associations and into journalism, organizing and communal living.

With the support of the Natal Indian Congress, and other notable Indians, Gandhi assembled a small staff and printing press and began the *Indian Opinion* in 1903, a newspaper published in Gujarati, Hindi, Tamil and English. In 1904, Gandhi relocated the publishing office to his settlement in Phoenix, near Durban, a communal living experiment in which all would share the labour of maintaining the space equally without regard to gender, race or caste. Read by Das and many associates in India and North America, it provided an inspiration for the *Free Hindusthan*. In the first few years, the newspaper was moderate and kept reiterating its faith in British law, but also began to highlight the plight of indentured labourers in South Africa, the poor conditions in which they worked, and how they were treated on estates, including cases of severe punishment, mental breakdown and suicide.

Just as a large component of Gandhi's politics in his South Africa period (1893–1915) derived from his exposure to indentured labourers, Das began to politically develop into an anti-colonial organizer through his exposure to labourers in BC. His organization of South Asian labourers and students to oppose racist treatment and immigration legislation, and his assistance to Indian migrants to Canada appear as analogues to the work of Gandhi. Both men appear on two sides of the growing nationalist movement that opposed British rule. Both men were activists but Gandhi transformed into a theorist of non-violence and created a political message that separated itself from the older nationalist approaches from the days of *Anushilan* in Bengal. *Indian Opinion* was an inspiration for Das and *Free Hindusthan* also circulated amongst Indians in South Africa.[32] Whereas Gandhi was building a new approach to non-violence in the years just before the First World War, Das continued with older messages of organized revolution.

As an indication of how Indian nationalism in the early twentieth century existed in multiple registers, this split between Das' older approach and the newness of Gandhi occurred most clearly in correspondence between Das, Count Leo Tolstoy – the famous Russian writer and Christian pacifist – and Mohandas Gandhi. At the moment of the launch of *Free Hindusthan*, on 24 May 1908, Das sent a letter to Tolstoy, asking for advice about the independence struggle and for help in publicizing *Free Hindusthan*. After receiving this and another letter in July 1908, with a copy of the first issue, Das received a lengthy response from Tolstoy.

Tolstoy offered a long and detailed response titled 'Letter to a Hindoo' on 14 December 1908. In his ornate letter, adorned with citations from the Vedas and several mentions of Krishna, Tolstoy offered an assessment of Das' position on resistance to tyranny – as discussed in *Free Hindusthan* – with a recourse to religion. Tolstoy proposes that the reason for the domination of 200 million people by a small alien group lies in the lack of a 'reasonable religious teaching which by explaining the meaning of life would supply a supreme law for the guidance of conduct and would replace the more than dubious precepts of pseudo-religion and pseudo-science with the immoral conclusions deduced from them and commonly called civilization'.[33] As a response to Das' embracing resistance to aggression, Tolstoy claims that 'you, an adherent of a religious people, deny their law, feeling convinced of your scientific enlightenment and your right to do so, and you repeat (do not take this amiss) the amazing stupidity indoctrinated in you by the advocates of the use of violence'.[34] As a way out of the predicament of this indoctrination, Tolstoy advocates a peaceful resistance to the violent deeds of the administration, the law courts, the collection of taxes and soldiering. With this, Tolstoy claims, no one will be able to enslave you.[35] Tolstoy's position adheres to a new perspective of a growing modern theory of non-violence, developed in this period by Gandhi in South Africa. Gandhi's own ideas were developing partially in relation to his engagements with Tolstoy in 1909 and 1910.

Das then engaged in a detailed reply, published as a series of four articles in *Twentieth Century Magazine* in 1910. This magazine, an early twentieth-century English language periodical published in Boston, was likely in Das' orbit through his connections with sympathizers in the USA, like Jabez Sunderland and Robert Morss Lovett. He disagreed vehemently with Tolstoy's conclusion that India's slavery was due to Indian complicity. He disagreed with Tolstoy's contention that 'in the absence of true religious consciousness and the guidance of conduct flowing from it, lies the chief, if not the sole cause, of enslavement of the Indian people by the English'[36] by arguing that true religious consciousness comes from a manifestation of love with non-resistance. This is not, for Das, true, as he argues that the idea of non-resistance 'has led the people of India to dullness and fatalism, and fatalism has led them to ignorance and superstition, and there is the remote cause of our downfall'. Like Tolstoy, Das cites Krishna, for a different purpose, as he shows that Krishna taught in the Gita 'to give up your lethargy and effeminacy and rise up to fight the battle for the right'. He further centres Krishna in his formulation of righteousness, such that 'whenever righteousness is dwindled by the acts of the unrighteous, I [Krishna] incarnate myself in the shape of popular spirit to save the followers of the right and truth and destroy the evil'.[37] For Das, resistance to tyranny was consistent with the spirit of love.

From 1909, when Gandhi begins to write to Tolstoy from London, he reveals that he has been reading Tolstoy's writings for some time and they informed his emergent ideas about Indian nationalism, violence and non-violence. In his first letter, dated 1 October 1909, Gandhi mentions that he has been given his 'Letter to a Hindu', an English translation of Tolstoy's response to Das. Gandhi in his *Indian Opinion* printed the letter Tolstoy sent to Das, and this led to the christening of the Tolstoy Farm in Johannesburg with his friend Hermann Kallenbach. A year later, on a ship between England and South Africa, he wrote the soon-to-be blockbuster *Hind Swaraj*, a short but powerful critique of industrialization, the violence of Western civilization, and violent methods used by young revolutionaries. This book is a short but remarkable account about the state of politics in the world at the time, the assumptions behind modern education, science, law and medicine and a sketch of revolt against the ideologies of colonial rule. Echoing Tolstoy's 1908 declaration in his letter to Das, in the context of arguing that the rule of violence only begets slavery and subordination to an endless cycle of violence, 'it is not the English who have enslaved the Indians, but the Indians who have enslaved themselves'.[38] This notion of Indian complicity in the manners of colonial rule emerged as a centrepiece of Gandhi's detailed critique of Indian nationalism as it existed at the time and his evolving ideas of non-violent political action.

When Das entered British Columbia in 1907, the province was engaged in creating immigration rules based on identifying and restricting Indian migrants within the British Empire. The travails of British Columbia follow about a decade later than the same exact politics of exclusion in Natal, the white settler colony on the eastern edge of British South Africa. From the 1890s, the British Empire in Natal had been confronting detailed agitations and protests against Indian migration, out of a fear of Indians out-competing white traders as well as a racialized opposition to Indians. The colonial office in London aimed, however, not to inflame sentiments amongst nationalist Indians who may have viewed policies affecting Indians in one of the British Empire's colonies as ammunition for their opposition to British Indian rule. The 1897 Immigration Act, which restricted immigration based on a literacy test, was itself based on US immigration legislation founded partially on US Southern state laws aimed at curbing suffrage of African-Americans. This 'Natal Act' became the standard for restricting Asian immigration into white settler colonies. Canadian representatives introduced the act eight times in the BC provincial legislature.[39] Das lived and worked in BC at the very same time that the global circuits of exclusionary legislation aimed at Indian migrants coalesced throughout the British settler imperial dominion world.

Conclusion

At one level Das is comparable to Mohandas Gandhi and Shyamji Krishnavarma, but he is the only 'expatriate patriot' who spent substantive time in the Pacific Northwest of North America, and outlasted the colonial world order that shaped most of his life and politics. As such, his vantage point helps put together a view of the history of globalization not from the subaltern margins within South Asia, but from nationalist perspectives reared in India but developed in tandem with struggles elsewhere. Biography as a genre entails a constant engagement with the close tracks of an individual's life as well as their interaction with the worlds they encounter. Das' worlds featured the world's most powerfully present in many iterations of the political present – empire sometimes not named as nation-state – nation-states behaving as modern empires in their manners of immigration restrictions and exclusions. Studying Das may confirm at one level the relationship between modern empires and the nationalisms produced out of critiquing such empires, they also show the cracks, fade-aways and unpredictable turns that such a person took in the course of a life. Das' nationalism originated from well-documented origin points in the hotbeds of nationalist Bengal, though most of his life was spent in the corners of North America at a time when he played rather unexpected roles in struggles invisible to most of his compatriots elsewhere in the world.

Studying Das is not important for the sake of simply digging out yet another individual from the storehouse of early twentieth-century border-crossers, but rather to explore the entangled history between expatriate patriots like Das, expanding settler states and claims made on behalf of a nationalism. Doing so through following his tracks may put the idea of the United States, as a republican form, into our considerations of long-distance nationalism. By including this vector of Das' itinerary, we find that many long-distance nationalists were, for a time, echoing aspects of liberal imperialism through a push for assimilation, recognition and citizenship. A revolutionary anti-colonialism did not, therefore, resist all aspects of imperialism. Living and working in the United States and Canada at the turn of century, Das internalized a great deal of such imperialism even while confidently supporting the cause of Indian independence.

Notes

1. In the twenty-first century, the term 'South Asian' refers to those whose origins lie in the Indian subcontinent. In the United States of America and Canada during the period under review the official term frequently used to refer to all South Asians was 'Hindu', though that designation included members of all religions including Sikhs, the majority of such migrants who entered BC at that time. This term of that time emerged from the ongoing discussions of 'Hindus' as a race from 'Hindustan', cemented in the 1911 Dictionary of Races used by the US Immigration Service to categorize migrants from what is now called South Asia. One therefore could be a Sikh or a Muslim – and also be a 'Hindu'. Government officials as well as South Asians consistently used this term to refer to all South Asians in official published writing. Rajani Kanta Das, author of *Hindusthanee Workers on the Pacific Coast* (Berlin: DeGruyter, 1923), remarks on this distinction in his work and chose to use the term 'Hindusthanee' to refer to all South Asians resident at the time.
2. Brij Lal, 'East Indians in British Columbia, 1904–14: A historical study in growth and integration' MA Thesis, University of British Columbia, 1976, 58.
3. Tonio Andrade coined the term 'global microhistory' in Tonio Andrade, 'A Chinese Farmer, Two African Boys, and a Warlord: Toward a Global Microhistory' *Journal of World History* 21, no. 4 (December 2010): 573–591. A critique of Andrade, warning against caricature, 'at the of risk finding ourselves in a world populated by faceless globetrotters, colourless chameleons and invisible boundary crossers', can be found in John-Paul A. Ghobrial, 'The Secret Life of Elias of Babylon and the Uses of Global Microhistory' *Past & Present* 222 (February 2014): 58.
4. Prominent examples include Natalie Zemon Davis, *Women on the Margins: Three Seventeenth-Century Lives* (Cambridge, MA: Harvard University Press, 1995); Jonathan Spence, *The Question of Hu* (New York: Knopf, 1988); Sanjay Subrahmanyam, *Three Ways To Be Alien: Travails and Encounters in the Early Modern World* (Waltham, MA: Brandeis University Press, 2011); and Linda Colley, *The Ordeal of Elizabeth Marsh: A Woman in World History* (New York: Pantheon, 2007).

5 Barbara Taylor's position on biography, that focuses both on 'inward as well as outward ... on the constitutive elements of human subjectivity as well as its external determinants' informs recent scholarship on the genre. See Barbara Taylor, 'Separations of the Soul: Solitude, Biography, History' *American Historical Review* 114, 3 (June 2009): 651. This approach is deployed by Ananya Chakravarti in *The Empire of Apostles: Religion, Accommodation, and the Imagination of Empire in Early Modern Brazil and India* (Delhi: Oxford University Press, 2018) and 'Mapping "Gabriel": Space, Identity and Slavery in the Late Sixteenth-Century Indian Ocean' *Past & Present* 243, no. 1 (May 2019): 5–34.

6 Mark Gamsa, 'Biography and (Global) Microhistory' *New Global Studies* 11, no. 3 (2017): 231–241.

7 Desley Deacon, Penny Russell, and Angela Woollacott, *Transnational Lives: Biographies of Global Modernity, 1700–present* (Basingstoke: Palgrave Macmillan, 2010).

8 Harald Fischer-Tine, Shyamji Krishnavarma: *Shyamji Krishnavarma: Sanskrit, Sociology, and Anti-Imperialism* (Delhi: Routledge, 2014).

9 Scholars in the field of South Asian history who are mindful of the 'biographical illusion', that of Pierre Bourdieu's warning that lives are not continuous, coherent wholes, include Ben Zachariah, 'A Long Strange Trip: The Lives in Exile of Har Dayal' *South Asian History and Culture* 4, no. 4 (2013): 574–592.

10 See Hugh Johnston, *The Voyage of the Komagata Maru: The Sikh Challenge to Canada's Colour* Bar (Vancouver: UBC Press, 2014) and Norman Buchigani, Doreen Marie Indra and Ram Srivastava, *Continuous Journey: A Social History of South Asians in Canada* (Toronto: McClelland and Stewart, 1985) on the history of South Asian migration in Canada. For the USA, see Vivek Bald, *Bengali Harlem and the Lost Histories of South Asian America* (Cambridge, MA: Harvard University Press, 2013); Nayan Shah, *Stranger Intimacy: Contesting Race, Sexuality, and the Law in the North American West* (Berkeley, CA: University of California Press, 2011); and Seema Sohi, *Echoes of Mutiny: Race, Surveillance, and Indian Anticolonialism in North America* (New York: Oxford University Press, 2014).

11 See *Span of Life* 5, no. 3, March 1912, a magazine featuring articles by prominent South Asian migrants such as Guru Ditt Kumar, whose 'Hindus in the United States: Activities of the Hindu students and labourers on the Pacific Coast' offers a panoramic summary of the different groups of South Asians in the Pacific Northwest at the time.

12 See Tapan Mukherjee, *Taraknath Das: Life and Letters of a Revolutionary in Exile* (Kolkata: National Council of Education, 1998), as well as the biographical sketch by Ranendranath Das and Tapan Mukherjee in Christian Bartolf, ed., *Letter to a Hindu: Taraknath Das, Leo Tolstoi, and Mahatma Gandhi* (Berlin: Gandhi Information Zentrum, 1997), 66–78. For further details see his petition for

naturalization in the United States of America, dated 8 February 1908 as well as Ranendranath Das, *Taraknath Das—Ein Lebensbild des indischen Revolutionärs, Freiheitskämpfers und Gelehrten* (Berlin: Taraknath Das-Stiftung, 1996).

13 James Campbell Ker, *Political Trouble in India, 1907–17* (Calcutta: Superintendent Government Printing, 1917), chapters 1 and 2, pp. 1–25. Ker was the personal assistant to the Director of Criminal Intelligence, C.P. Stevenson-Moore. He created a compilation of confidential reports between 1907 and 1917. These are contained in the India Office Records (hereafter, IOR), /L/PJ/12/1, with the American and Canadian material culled from Circular No. 5 of 1908, 'Note on the Anti-British Movement among Natives of India in America' and Circular No. 12 of 1912, 'Indian Agitation in America'.

14 See John Price, '"Orienting" the Empire: Mackenzie King and the Aftermath of the 1907 Race Riots' *BC Studies* 156 (Winter 2007/08): 53–81, for an analysis of how these riots resulted in further restrictions and efforts to prohibit Asian immigration into Canada.

15 For the specific language of the amendment, see https://pier21.ca/research/immigration-history/continuous-journey-regulation-1908.

16 See Brij Lal, 'East Indians in British Columbia, 1904–14: An historical study in growth and integration', 15, for a list of migrants admitted into Canada from 1904 to 1914. The significant years are 1906–07 at 2120 and 2620 in 1907–08.

17 Circular No. 12, Indian Agitation in America, 17 December 1912, IOR/L/PJ/12/1, 3.

18 C.J. Stevenson-Moore, Director of Criminal Intelligence, stated that the *Free Hindusthan* was 'an exact copy in size and get up of Shyamji Krishnavarma's *Indian Sociologist*, the chief anti-British revolutionary organ', Circular 5 of 1908, 'Note on the Anti-British Activity Among Natives of India in America', 5.

19 Ibid.

20 See the South Asian American Digital Archive (SAADA), https://www.saada.org/browse/source/the-free-hindusthan, for images of the first issue in April 1908, published in Vancouver, as well as the third issue in November–December 1908 from Seattle. All remaining issues appear in original form in IOR/L/PJ/6/1137, File 38710, including editions published in Seattle in July 1908 and the New York editions from November–December 1908, July–August 1908 and March–April 1910. The file also includes a signed copy of the first number sent to Hopkinson's informant, Swami Trigunatita, in San Francisco.

21 *Free Hindusthan*, April 1908, 1.

22 Ibid., November–December 1908, 1.

23 Ibid., 2.

24 In the fall of 1908, the British Empire had initiated a programme to transport and resettle British Indian labourers from British Columbia to British Honduras for work on sugar plantations and railroads. This proposal developed in the context

of heightening anti-Indian agitation in Canada as well as the notion that Indians would fare better in the environment of Honduras rather than Canada. Due to widespread opposition, the scheme failed to materialize but served as a marker of the perception of Indian migration to BC at the turn of the century.
25 Cited in Circular No. 12, Indian Agitation in America, 17 December 1912, IOR/L/PJ/12/1, 4.
26 Ibid.
27 Bryan was a US senator from Nebraska in the 1890s and US Secretary of State from 1913–1915. Sympathetic to the cause of Indian independence, after a tour of India in 1906 he wrote a condemnation of British colonialism in India titled *British Rule in India*. This was reproduced in the newspapers *India* on 20 July 1906, the *Bengalee* on 4 August 1906 and later published and circulated by the Yugantar Ashram of San Francisco.
28 IOR L/PJ/6/1137, File 320/1909, 'Confidential Memorandum on Matters Affecting the East Indian Community in British Columbia', by Colonel E.J. Swayne.
29 See Harald Fischer-Tine and Carolien Stolte, 'Imagining Asia in India: Nationalism and Internationalism (ca. 1905–1940)' *Comparative Studies in Society and History* 54, no. 1 (2012): 90–91.
30 For primary source accounts of this event, see Mohandas Gandhi, *Satyagraha in South Africa* (Ahmedabad: Navajivan Trust, 1950), 57–58 and Fatima Meer, ed., *The South African Gandhi: An Abstract of the Speeches and Writings of M.K. Gandhi, 1893–1914* (Durban: Madiba, 1995), Document 51, 232.
31 The historiography of Gandhi's life in South Africa is vast and recent critical work has focused on his racialism and embrace of the British Empire during his South African period. See Goolam Vahed and Ashwin Desai's *The South African Gandhi: Stretcher Bearer of Empire* (Stanford, CA: Stanford University Press, 2015), a response to Ramachandra Guha, Gandhi before India:
32 Das' handwritten mailing list of forty-three Indians in South Africa, as well as records of a shipment of copies of *Free Hindusthan* to South Africa were found by Canadian authorities in 1908. See Tapan Mukherjee, *Taraknath Das*, 15.
33 Bartolf, ed., 18.
34 Ibid., 25.
35 Ibid., 26.
36 Ibid., 50.
37 Ibid., 52.
38 Bartolf, ed., 25.
39 The 'Natal Act', was part of an inter-imperial set of discussions between settler colonies in Australia, Canada, South Africa and other regions in the 1890s, focused on how specifically to exclude Asiatics – in this instance, referring primarily to Indians – without naming race explicitly in the legislation. See Adam McKeown,

Melancholy Order: Asian Migration and the Globalization of Borders (New York: Columbia University Press, 2008), esp. his 'The "Natal Formula" and the Decline of the Imperial Subject, 1888–1913', 185–214; Jeremy Martens, 'A Transnational History of Immigration Restriction: Natal and New South Wales, 1896–97' *The Journal of Imperial and Commonwealth History* 34, no. 3 (2006): 323–344; and John Price, 'Canada, White Supremacy, and the Twinning of Empires' *International Journal* 68, no. 4 (December 2013): 628–638.

7

From British colonial subject to Mexican 'Naturalizado': Pandurang Khankhoje's life beyond the reach of imperial power (1924–1954)

Daniel Kent-Carrasco

In early 1924, K.L.F. Armitage, Deputy Commissioner at Wardha, received an application from one Sadashio Venkatesh Khankhoje, a petition writer from Palakhwadi village, requesting that a passport be issued to his son, Pandurang Khankhoje, who was stranded in Mexico. Sadashio claimed his son had left India in 1906 'for education in Japan and America'. The young Khankhoje, his father went on, had 'utilised this period in the best possible way and ha(d), by his own earnings, prosecuted his studies and become a Bachelor of Science in the University of California and a Master of Science in the University of Washington'. His 'special subject', the letter emphasized, was 'agriculture'. As a scientist, he had done 'important research work' and had 'learnt various industries' including 'canning of fruits, match, candle, soap, tin printing and box manufacture (*sic*)'. The applicant argued that, growing old and feeling increasingly frail, he was 'anxious to see his son back' and 'pray(ed) that a passport be kindly issued' so that he could make his way back from Mexico.[1] In May 1924, Sadashio's request was denied. Armitage clarified that only British consuls abroad could emit passports for subjects not present in India. He made it clear that Pandurang should not attempt to travel without a valid passport unless he wanted to court

---

I wish to express my gratitude to Ana Savitri Sawhney Khankhoje for her kind disposition and openness. A big thank you to Daniela Gleizer and Pablo Yankelevich who shared with me crucial archival data on Pandurang Khankhoje's stay in Mexico. Daniela's feedback and kind comments guided my understanding of the complex history of naturalization and migration policies in Mexico during the early twentieth century. Thanks to Mauricio Tenorio, who allowed me to use his email exchanges as revealing historical sources.

arrest.² The exiled agronomist would not return to his native Maharashtra until 1954. Sadashio died before ever seeing his son again.

Born in 1884 in Wardha, Maharasthra, Pandurang Khankhoje was forced to leave India in 1905 due to his involvement with anticolonial activities and subversive nationalist agitations. During the next half century, he lived an itinerant life marked by uprooting, learning and adaptation. Pandurang visited Colombo, Japan, Belgium and Soviet Russia and spent considerable time in the United States, Persia, Germany and Mexico. As part of his transcontinental trajectory, Pandurang Khankhoje's life linked with different ideological, political and scientific transformations taking place during the early decades of the twentieth century. As an anticolonial activist in North America, Europe and the Middle East, he played an important part in the short life of the *Ghadar* movement, was active in the radical and transnational milieu of early twentieth-century West Coast anarcho-syndicalism³ and participated in the transcontinental web of subversive anti-British activities promoted by the German Imperial Government during the 1910s. As a student in the United States, he was trained at a time of a profound transformation of the discipline of agricultural science that, several decades later, would lead to the emergence of the 'Green Revolution'. As a scientist in Mexico, he contributed to the consolidation of the scientific and educational establishment of the post-revolutionary state, especially through his work in the development of new varieties of maize and the creation of new schools of agricultural science. After returning to his native Maharashtra in 1954, he spent the last twelve years of his life as a misfit in the newly founded Republic of India.

This chapter focuses on the thirty years that Pandurang Khankhoje spent in Mexico (1924–1954) and traces his transit from subaltern British Indian subject and fugitive on the run to esteemed citizen of an independent Latin American country. After being a wage labourer, wanted fugitive and undercover agent across different corners of the world, in Mexico Khankhoje secured a satisfying and profitable job – first in government and later in the private sector – became a recognized scientist and obtained, for the first time in his life, legal rights of citizenship. He became a naturalized Mexican citizen in 1930 – one of the very few 'Hindustanis'⁴ to have been granted citizenship in Mexico during the first half of the twentieth century – married in 1936 and had two Mexican daughters. In the following pages, I will show that his assimilation in Mexico was made possible by Khankhoje's claim to two different kinds of legitimacy. On the one hand, his own revolutionary and anti-imperialist pedigree made him an acceptable foreigner at the time of gestation of a new brand of 'revolutionary nationalism' in Mexico, an ideology that crystallized the thrust and ideals of the Mexican Revolution (1910–1920). On the other, and much more crucially, his scientific training made him a valuable asset in the nationalist task of creating a new 'national agriculture' for post-revolutionary Mexico. With the aim of reconstructing the 'lived experience of connectedness' that marked Khankhoje's itinerant life,[5] this chapter will draw on diverse sources. These include documents located in the Pandurang Khankhoje Papers at the Jawaharlal Nehru Memorial Library, the archives of the Mexican Ministry of Foreign Affairs (*Secretaría de Relaciones Exteriores*) and the South Asian American Digital Archives (SAADA), as well as the recollections of Khankhoje's daughter, Ana Savitri Sawhney Khankhoje. As I will show in the next pages, in Mexico the markers of colonial difference that defined Khankhoje's early life as an imperial subject were eclipsed by his participation in the consolidation of a modernist project of nation-building and his ambiguous relationship with Mexican post-revolutionary *mestizo* identity. As a result of his engagement with these political and ideological trends, Khankhoje was able to escape the networks of control and surveillance forged by British colonialism across Asia, Africa and the Americas which marked the fate of the majority of South Asian migrants in the age of empire. At once an exception and an example of broader historical processes, Pandurang Khankhoje's life stands out as a fascinating anomaly in the history of early-twentieth century transcontinental migration.

Revolution and agriculture: A militant scientist in the US

Old Sadashio's claim that his son had left India 'for education in Japan and America' was only partially true. An equally important factor behind his son's departure were his links to the networks of anticolonial nationalism active in the early years of the twentieth century in Maharashtra. Pandurang, whose grandfather Venkatesh Bhijaki Khankhoje had been a fervent nationalist and member of the Indian National Congress since the early 1890s, had drifted towards anticolonial radicalism at an early age. In the opening years of the twentieth century, he became involved with the Nationalist Militant Party, headed by Bal Ganghadar Tilak.[6] According to his memoirs, as a young nationalist he had been 'obsessed' with the idea of an 'armed revolt' and had devised a plan to travel to Japan, where he imagined military training would be readily accessible. His interest in pursuing higher education abroad came in handy when he was preparing for his trip. In 1905, already under surveillance by British colonial authorities,

Pandurang appealed to the American consul in Bombay, before whom he 'extolled the virtues of the American system of education' and complained that as a result of the 'non-progressive education' procured in India young people like him were destined to remain slaves.[7] The American consul was apparently impressed by his appeal and agreed to grant the young Khankhoje a letter of recommendation that helped him make his way to Japan. Following a brief stay there, the young nationalist landed in San Francisco in late 1906, barely six months after the catastrophic earthquake that had devastated the port in April.

In North America, Khankhoje encountered a space of great possibilities and contradictions. During the opening decades of the twentieth century, the socioeconomic structures of large swathes of the North American West Coast were being transformed by profound economic changes and the expansion of novel brands of radical politics. The rapid expansion of a corporate and labour-intensive form of capitalism across the region following the gold rush and completion of the transcontinental railroad in 1869 attracted workers from across the world to the West Coast of North America. This gave rise to an international and multi-racial radical milieu in expanding urban areas like San Francisco, Los Angeles and Vancouver as well as in smaller cities like Sacramento, Stockton, Seattle and Yuba. The flow of people and ideas across the region fed the creation of a complex network of radical political groups and the growing exchange of publications, texts and political ideas among anti-imperialists, anarchists and socialists of diverse backgrounds. While these transformations led to increasing economic and racial tensions, they also propitiated the emergence of new forms of political engagement across language, cultural and ethnic divides.[8] The creation of these sites and networks of exchange was especially meaningful for those from colonial and non-Western regions who, perhaps for the first time, had the means to think of the struggle against the dominance of Western forms of economic and symbolical dominance as an interconnected and transnational enterprise.

Following his arrival in California, Khankhoje was quick to immerse himself in this complex radical milieu. He participated in the creation of the Indian Independence League in Astoria, Oregon, and was an active organizer of Indian workers and farmers across that state and much of Northern California.[9] Apart from his involvement with Indian students and workers, Khankhoje also developed ties of collaboration with activists of diverse national backgrounds. Among these, the large and active community of Mexican workers and activists was especially important. In his memoirs, Khankhoje remembers how, during his work in the fields, he 'was often taken for a Mexican' and how this identification led to a special 'affinity with them that would last a lifetime'.[10] Many of the Mexican workers that Khankhoje met during those years were members of the Partido Liberal Mexicano (PLM), an anarcho-syndicalist group with an important presence across California, Arizona and most of the northern states of Mexico.[11] The cadres of the PLM in the US were integrated by Mexican migrants who, although formally citizens of an independent country, had endured a long history of economic dispossession and, during the early years of the twentieth century, were increasingly vocal in their rebellion against new forms of economic imperialism headed by US private capital. The activism promoted by these Mexicans on both sides of the border brought them close to the International Workers of the World (IWW), and turned the PLM into an important symbolic point of reference for other non-white communities and leaders across the West Coast.[12] Shortly after arriving in the US, Khankhoje came to learn about the activities of the brothers Ricardo and Enrique Flores Magón, the main organizers of the PLM, who he came to identify as the 'great leaders' of the virtuous struggle being fought by the Mexican people 'against wealthy and oppressive landowners'.[13] The active participation of the Flores Magón brothers among different trade unions and anarchist collectives fed their reputation as important representatives of non-white radical sectors of the West Coast. Prominent members of the *Ghadar* party, including Lala Har Dayal and Taraknath Das expressed their admiration of the Flores Magón[14] brothers, while the latter acknowledged *Ghadar* as a group fighting for international 'social revolution'.[15]

For Khankhoje, as for many other labour activists of the region, revolution was linked to the promise and practice of agriculture. During his stay in the United States, Khankhoje, who had never been one of the 'salt-of-the-earth soldier-farmer-poets'[16] who were the force behind the *Ghadar* movement, strove to become not a farmer but an agricultural scientist. In 1908, less than two years after arriving in California, he enrolled in Berkeley University as a student of agriculture. In later years, he continued his studies at Oregon Agricultural College, Corvallis and obtained a Bachelor of Science degree from the State College of Washington in 1913.[17] Shortly after graduating in January 1914, he published the results of his scientific work on water use and plant breeding conducted at the experimental station at Pullman, Washington, in the *Journal of the American Society of Agriculture*.[18] With the production of this highly technical work, and almost certainly without being aware of it, Khankhoje was taking part in a different, and more far-reaching, revolution than that promoted by his *Ghadar* comrades. During the early decades of the twentieth century, a great effort was made to reconvert agriculture in the US according to scientific methods of rationalization and the tenets of economic efficiency. Following a period of agricultural depression in the 1890s, during the 1900s institutions like the State College of Washington and many others across the United States increasingly sought to develop a scientific and technical approach that could turn agriculture into a sound business. This included the adoption of new techniques of irrigation and reclamation of arid land, the increasing use of agricultural chemicals and, crucially, the development of new techniques of plant breeding following the principles of Mendelian genetics.[19] This transformation was fuelled by an impressive increase in the funds destined for agricultural research and the expansion of experimental work across the country.[20] Khankhoje's time as a student and activist in North America, then, coincided with a period of consolidation of a new scientific approach to agriculture, which would lay the ground for the expansion of agro-industry in the following decades.

Shortly after the publication of his first scientific article, Khankhoje enrolled in a doctorate programme at the University of Minnesota in early 1914. This institution – *alma mater* of Norman Borlaugh, the so-called father of the Green Revolution – had one of the most prestigious schools of agricultural science in the country at the time. However, the political turmoil unleashed by the eruption of war in Europe prevented the young migrant from obtaining a PhD degree. During 1914, anti-British activities in the United States including, notably, those of the recently founded *Ghadar* party, became an increasing cause of concern for the police, especially along the West Coast. This was part of a widespread enactment of repressive measures against radical groups across the country, which focused with particular virulence on immigrant parties and radical collectives.[21] This led to the attempt to deport Lala Har Dayal, who fled to Germany in April, and to the violence of the *Komagata Maru* incident in May, when hundreds of Punjabi migrants were denied permission to land in Vancouver and were subsequently returned to British India. On hearing of the arrival of the *Komagata Maru*, Khankhoje, who was already in Saint Paul, Minnesota, getting ready to begin his doctorate, decided to desist and fled east towards New York City from where he sailed to Europe in the summer of 1914. In his memoirs, his departure from the US is linked to the rise of repressive measures enacted against politically active immigrants following the start of the Great War.[22] However, in a letter written in 1953 to an old *Ghadar* comrade, Khankhoje describes his escape to Europe as part of a concerted plan to continue with the anti-British activities of the party in the Old World.[23]

In any case, Khankhoje arrived in Constantinople in September 1914. Through the contacts established between the members of *Ghadar* and the newly founded Indian Independence Committee of Berlin, the agricultural scientist joined the group led by German diplomat and spy Wilhelm Wassmuss. Following the start of the War in Europe, Wassmuss headed a series of 'exotic adventures among the tribes of Southern Persia' that aimed at weakening Russian and British positions in the region and to the north of Afghanistan.[24] Relieved at being one step closer to India, and 'very happy to be away from the Western World', during his time in Persia Khankhoje became close to Ameer 'Ashayer, the ruler of the southern Persian state of Fars. The latter was evidently impressed with the Indian traveller's scientific skills and decided to name him 'minister of education' and 'director of commerce and agriculture' of Fars. Incapable of returning to India, and unsure of his prospects in Europe, Khankhoje stayed in Persia for more than six years. In 1921, he left for Berlin, travelling with a Persian official document that identified him as the Ameer's business representative abroad.[25] Once in the German capital, he sought help from Virendranath Chattopadhyaya (*Chatto*) and managed to scratch a living as a door-to-door salesman.[26] According to his daughter, in later years Pandurang never discussed the details of his time in Germany; however, his family knew that he had faced starvation and that, following the end of the war and Germany's defeat, he had feared for his life.[27] In January 1924, following a series of disagreements with his Indian comrades in Berlin and sick of life in the city, Khankhoje sailed back to North America and landed in Mexico.[28]

Pandurang Khankhoje in Mexico: 1924–1954

There are no records of Pandurang Khankhoje's arrival in Mexico. Based on the fact that his father Sadashio had applied for a passport to help him travel from Mexico to India sometime in March or April 1924, it is safe to assume that Pandurang must have arrived in the country sometime in January or February and thereafter found a way of getting in touch with his family back in Wardha. I am unsure if father and son kept a correspondence during those months. However, and probably without knowing, Pandurang ended up following the advice of Deputy Commissioner Armitage and approached the British consul in Mexico City sometime in the summer of 1924. On 2 August, barely three months after Sadashio's request had been denied in India, Pandurang was issued a passport in Mexico which allowed him to travel across the country and other parts of the British Empire. The document, preserved in the archives of the Mexican Ministry of Foreign Affairs, lists Khankhoje as a British Indian subject: the registers for British 'protected' and 'person' are marked out. Along with his personal data, he is listed as a 'professor of agriculture'.[29]

Indeed, Khankhoje had started working as a teacher at the National School of Agriculture (NSA) in May 1924.[30] Originally founded in 1854, the NSA was undergoing a profound transformation at the time of his arrival. During the last months of 1923, the school had been moved from its original location in Mexico City to Texcoco, a small town thirty kilometres from the capital, where it occupied the reclaimed lands of the old *hacienda* of Chapingo. During the following decades, the NSA would play a central role in the consolidation of the ambitious plan of agricultural reform and modernization enacted by the post-revolutionary government across different regions of Mexico. Symbolically, its relocation to a reclaimed *hacienda* – the notorious symbol of the exploitative system of land tenure and economic model that the revolution was supposed to have vanquished – turned the school into an embodiment of the new regime's radical project of agrarian transformation, which joined the libertarian 'voice of protest' of groups like the Magonistas and the longing of the Zapatista peasants who had adopted the slogan of 'Land and Liberty' as their war cry.[31] At the same time, during the 1920s the NSA adopted the *motto* 'Teaching the exploitation of the land, not of men' and began acting as the core of a new scientific approach to agriculture in Mexico which addressed the needs and projects of a rapidly modernizing country and the grievances that had fuelled the Mexican Revolution of 1910.

According to his daughter, Khankhoje's presence at Chapingo was made possible by the good offices of Ramón P. Denegri, Minister of Agriculture of the Mexican government.[32] Denegri, who had met Khankhoje in California during his time as Mexican consul in San Francisco between 1913 and 1915 at the height of *Ghadar* activity, had been in charge of the relocation of the NSA to Chapingo and was head of the government's ambitious programme of land reform. As part of its new post-revolutionary phase, the school was put in charge of Marte R. Gómez, a close collaborator of Denegri. Gómez was a convinced modernist and fervent promoter of land reform. In his view, agrarian reform and scientific progress were the keys for prosperity and tranquillity in Mexico, as well as for international stability and peace.[33] Gómez turned the NSA at Chapingo into a hub of ideological and scientific enthusiasm. During his time as director, important artists like Diego Rivera and Tina Modotti were invited to contribute and document the work of the school. Between 1924 and 1927, Rivera completed the decoration of the famous Riveriana chapel of the hacienda and, during the latter part of the decade, Modotti photographed and documented the academic and research activities of the school. During his tenure, Gómez approved a grant of a few acres of land near the school for the creation of a new set of experimental fields and stations modelled on the workings of research institutions in the United States.[34]

From the beginning, Khankhoje became involved in the research conducted at these new experimental fields at Chapingo. There he conducted what were perhaps the first experiments of scientific crop improvement in Mexico. With full support from Gómez, Khankhoje applied the skills he had developed as a student of agricultural science in the United States to develop new maize 'seeds capable of resisting disease, frost and drought' and thriving in the fickle and unpredictable climate of the central Mexican plateau. The evident success of his experiments was greeted heartily by Waldo Soberón, who succeeded Gómez as director of the NSA in 1925. Excited by the work being conducted at the experimental fields, Soberón facilitated the grant of twenty-five acres of reclaimed agricultural land for the expansion of the research project led by the Indian scientist, which soon attracted the attention and participation of a large number of students and other scientists working at the school.[35] Beyond the fields of Chapingo, the experiments conducted by Khankhoje soon caught the attention of diverse communist and agrarian organizations. In December 1924, less than a year after his arrival in Mexico, Khankhoje participated in the Second Congress of the Agrarian Communities of Veracruz, headed by the agrarian leader and founder of the Peasant International (KRESTINTERN) Úrsulo Galván.[36] During the meeting, the work being done at Chapingo served as platform for the creation of a new set of Free Schools of Agriculture (*Escuelas Libres de Agricultura*) across the country. This new pedagogical project aimed to take agricultural education to the peasant classes, especially among adults, and provide practical and scientific knowledge that would contribute to agricultural production, rural cooperativism and the development of an anti-capitalist revolutionary pedagogy.[37] In light of his successful management of the experimental fields of Chapingo, Khankhoje was named director of these Free Schools. During the following years, Khankhoje, who had already proven his worth as a scientist, made his talent for administration clear as he presided over the expansion of these new Free Schools: in 1928 six campuses had been created in the rural regions surrounding Mexico City,[38] and by 1933 the project had been implemented in the neighbouring state of Veracruz, where five more schools were created.[39]

By early 1925, Khankhoje had good reason to stay in Mexico. The prospects of returning to India seemed dim and after leaving Berlin he had cut himself off completely from the network of Indian anticolonial activists in Europe and the United States. Mexico, on the other hand, offered him exciting professional opportunities and the chance to expand his scientific research and apply it for the sake of peasants and labourers. In the face of this promising scenario, Khankhoje began the process of applying for Mexican citizenship in July 1925.[40] Initially, the officials in charge of the procedure recognized that the 'Hindu national' complied with all the requirements posed by Mexican naturalization laws to begin the procedures and requested the intervention of two witnesses that could support the truthfulness of Khankhoje's statement regarding his life in the country.[41] One of the witnesses chosen by the agricultural scientist was none other than Enrique Flores Magón, brother of the deceased Ricardo and original founding member of the PLM.[42] Once again, Khankhoje's activist past in the United States came in handy in the process of his finding a place in Mexico. Due to a number of administrative issues, the process was delayed until early 1930 when it was certified before a Mexico City district judge that Khankhoje had fulfilled all the necessary requirements to become a naturalized Mexican citizen. However, he was then asked to produce evidence of 'having observed proper conduct' during his stay in the country as a foreigner.[43] In response to this final request, Khankhoje presented two letters of reference from people associated with his work at Chapingo. The first was signed by Waldo Soberón, director of the NSA since 1925. The engineer, who had known Khankhoje for half a decade, exalted the immigrant's 'industriousness and interest' in contributing to the development of 'national agriculture' in Mexico. Making reference to the scientist's work at the experimental fields of Chapingo, Soberón certified that the NSA was willing to keep Khankhoje as part of its faculty and research team.[44] The second letter was signed by engineer Juan A. González, a high-ranking officer at the Department of Agriculture and Livestock of the Mexican Government. Gonzalez's letter was enthusiastic and convincing. He celebrated and emphasized the importance of Khankhoje's success in the 'creation of new varieties of cereal unknown in the country up to (that) date' and his invaluable contribution to the consolidation of 'national agriculture' in the country. The official highlighted the fact that Khankhoje had not only published his important findings in recognized scientific journals in Mexico and the United States but that he was also devoted to 'imparting [his knowledge] personally at the Free Schools of Agriculture, which he had founded' for the service of the *campesino* population that had long been excluded from the benefits of science and modern education in Mexico.[45] In short, these letters and testimonies put forward by the witnesses made clear that Pandurang Khankhoje was not only legally fit to become a Mexican citizen, but that he was also a committed defendant of the revolutionary and modernizing project of the Mexican state. He was finally granted citizenship in June 1930.[46]

Khankhoje's naturalization was an anomaly that illustrated the contradictions and flexibility of immigration policies and *mestizo* nationalism in Mexico during the 1920s and 30s. During these decades, processes of naturalization in Mexico were highly arbitrary.[47] Different, and often contradictory, logics were applied simultaneously, while procedures often took years, if not decades, to complete. Unlike other countries in the Americas, during the nineteenth and early twentieth centuries Mexico was never a nation of immigrants. Despite a long-standing fantasy nurtured by nationalist elites since independence (1821) that imagined the settlement of modern and industrious Western European migrants as a solution to the backwardness and scarce population of the country, by the mid-1920s foreigners amounted to less than one per cent of the population.[48] However, the robust brand of nationalism that congealed following the end of the revolutionary conflict reified the perception that immigrants represented a threat to the entitlements of Mexican citizens. This led to the adoption of an official rhetoric based on the idea that certain 'races' and nationalities were unassimilable to the Mexican nation.[49] This conviction was heightened by the arrival of immigrants deterred by the increasingly restrictive migratory laws enacted in the United States during the opening decades of the century, especially those from outside Western Europe. The increasing rejection of 'Asians' sparked notorious incidents of anti-Chinese violence in places like Torreón and Hermosillo.[50] As in the United States, Chinese immigrants – and, by extension, most 'Asians' – were linked to the danger of sanitary risk and social disturbance, while other inassimilable populations were seen as carriers of criminal propensities and undesirable habits. From the early 1920s, among Mexican official circles the order was spread to limit the entry into the country of foreigners belonging to 'African', 'Australian', 'yellow' and 'Mongolic' 'races', as well as to those of Turkish, Afghan, Albanese, Abyssinian, Egyptian, Moroccan and other 'threatening' nationalities.[51]

This increasingly inhospitable official disposition towards immigrants mirrored the anxieties of the Mexican regime regarding its defence of *mestizaje* as the only true basis for a new brand of 'Revolutionary Nationalism'.[52] The idea that Mexican nationality stemmed from the union of pre-Hispanic and European, mostly Iberian, heritages lay at the heart of this conception of *mestizaje*. Thus, populations deemed to be unassimilable presented not only the potential for social and economic disturbance but also a threat to the essence of Mexican nationalism itself. In this scenario of increasing social and governmental racism, it has been noted that during the 1920s an increasing number of immigrants turned to the possibility of naturalization as a way of dealing with the threat posed by this excluding brand of nationalism. For many immigrants with family and business ties in Mexico and little chance of returning to their native lands, naturalization appeared as a pragmatic strategy of survival.[53] This was made possible by legislation approved in 1866, which remained active until 1932, according to which nationality should not be erected upon the 'feudal' links created by the 'accident' of birth, but by the free choice made by individuals.[54] Thus, during the early decades of the twentieth century, Mexico received more immigrants – and rejected more applications for naturalization – than at any other point of its independent history.[55]

The relative ease with which Pandurang Khankhoje was granted rights of naturalization draws a sharp contrast with this scenario of increasing xenophobia and nationalist racism. In his case, it is clear that the involvement on his behalf of figures of proven revolutionary pedigree and important public servants was a crucial factor in the granting of his Mexican citizenship. Moreover, unlike other immigrants from non-Western European origins who were linked to the spread of 'parasitic' socioeconomic activities,[56] Khankhoje, who had been trained in the United States and had proven his worth as a scientist in an esteemed teaching institution, was in the position to contribute decisively to the consolidation of a prosperous and modern 'national agriculture' in Mexico. At the same time, it is perhaps not too adventurous to suggest that the ambiguous position held by Indians in the racial categories of the time – defined by amorphous categories like 'Black', 'Asian' or 'White' – could have also contributed to his assimilation in Mexico. As we have seen, during his years as a student and agricultural worker in the US, Khankhoje had been surprised to confirm that he was often mistaken for a Mexican and was rarely grouped with other immigrants brought together under the label of 'Asians'. Towards the end of his life, Khankhoje was reportedly fond of saying that, after spending three decades in Mexico working along *campesinos*, he had become 'doubly an Indian',[57] making reference to the land of his birth and to one of the pillars of Mexican *mestizo* nationalism.

As a Mexican citizen, Khankhoje's career as a scientist thrived during the next two decades. In 1934, he presented his resignation at the NSA following ten years of service. He was thereafter named Director of the Genetics Section of the newly founded Biotechnical Institute, which formed part of the Ministry of Agriculture[58] and recruited as top scientific adviser for the government in the creation of the National Plan of Agricultural Action, a project that aimed at gathering information on agricultural activities across the country.[59] Khankhoje's ascendant trajectory among the official circles of post-revolutionary Mexico culminated in 1935, when he was named Head of the Office of Agricultural Promotion of the Ministry of Agriculture of the Lázaro Cárdenas administration.[60] After 1936, he began working for the private sector. In November he was hired by the Southern Pacific Railroad of Mexico, and as an employee of the company, during the following years he conducted experiments across a large swathe of territory in Northwest Mexico.[61] His work for the private sector took him to different corners of the country: in 1942 he was hired by the Standard Fruit Company to conduct research in Tabasco and Southern Veracruz,[62] and in 1946 he began working for Vick's Chemical Company.[63]

During his time in Mexico, Khankhoje blossomed professionally, financially and personally. In 1936 he married Jeanne Sindic, a woman of Belgian origins who had settled in Mexico during the early 1930s. In the following years, the couple had two daughters, Ana Savitri and Maya. With his earnings as an employee of the government and the private sector, Khankhoje was able to provide a comfortable life for his family and even invested in a failed mining enterprise during the late 1940s.[64] Beyond work and family life, Khankhoje kept in contact with old friends like Ramón P. Denegri throughout his stay in Mexico, and cultivated a cosmopolitan group of friends, including the exiled Italian anarchist Calogero Speziale, the communist artists Diego Rivera and Tina Modotti, and his own compatriot Heramba Lal Gupta.[65] At the turn of the 1950s in Mexico, old Khankhoje had not only obtained legal citizenship of an independent country, but he had also managed to live a privileged life well beyond the reach of the dangers and anxieties that had led him to leave India in 1906.

Epilogue: An old Mexican scientist in postcolonial India

Despite the fortune he enjoyed during his time in Mexico, the prospect of returning to India was always at the back of Khankhoje's mind. After the transfer of power in 1947, Khankhoje swiftly began to make travel plans. However, reports of the widespread violence that followed independence prevented him from making the trip with his family.[66] In 1951, Khankhoje received a 'commission from the Mexican government to establish cultural and diplomatic relations with India' and was finally able to travel to the new independent Republic.[67] He spent two years in the land of his birth as a Mexican citizen and returned to Mexico in early

1953. The old scientist was finally able to move back permanently to India in November 1954. He was seventy-one years old. Following the arrival of his wife and daughters in 1956, the family settled in Poona.[68]

Old Khankhoje soon grew disappointed by the situation in India. He was alarmed by the violence unleashed by Partition, and depressed by his inability to secure a job. Taking advantage of his status as an emissary of the Mexican government, Pandurang wrote to Jawaharlal Nehru personally and offered his services as a scientist. The Prime Minister wrote back stating that there was no possibility of obtaining a job in the newly founded government. The official letter was accompanied by a Rs. 100 note, which Khankhoje initially felt inclined to shred to pieces. However, he restrained from doing so, given his desperate economic situation. Unlike in his adopted country, there seemed to be no place for him in the new India. As time passed, he gradually lost touch with his friends and acquaintances in Mexico and became increasingly detached from the world around him. In his final years, the veteran scientist, whose health was beginning to falter, focused on re-learning Marathi and Sanskrit and hatched a plan to write a history of *Ghadar,* which never materialized.[69] In 1961, a friend of Khankhoje's wrote to the government of Maharashtra on his behalf pleading for help for the ageing scientist, whose eyesight was 'dimming' and health 'failing'.[70] He was eventually granted Indian citizenship and a monthly pension of Rs. 250 from the government, which sustained him during his final years. In 1965 he relocated to Nagpur. His daughters both married and founded new households: one in India and one in Mexico. His wife Jeanne, who was more than ten years younger than Pandurang, secured a job in Delhi in 1966. The old revolutionary scientist died in January 1967 in Nagpur, accompanied by a distant relative.[71]

Beyond the narrative richness of his fascinating transformations, the life of the itinerant scientist Pandurang Khankhoje presents the historian with important questions. On the one hand, his unknown story shows that, as Clare Anderson has pointed out, marginality and subalternity have historically often been contingent processes rather than fixed markers of identity.[72] During his life, Khankhoje played the role of anticolonial activist, postgraduate student, modernist scientist, businessman, family man and, ultimately, tinkered with the ideal of *sannyas* during his final years.[73] The disenchantment that followed his return to the newly independent Republic of India drew a sharp contrast with his life in Mexico, where his scientific accomplishments allowed him to engage in constructive political activities and lead a meaningful and comfortable life. Similar to many other subalterns moving through the networks created by colonialism and anticolonialism during the first half of the twentieth century, for Khankhoje liminality did not necessarily translate into powerlessness.[74]

However, as his return to the homeland made painfully clear, national belonging did not always translate into acceptance and fulfilment.

At the same time, Khankhoje's story shows that nationalism is not always accompanied by the benefits and rights of nationality. Khankhoje lived his life on the global stage of the first half of the twentieth century. His political, professional and family trajectories developed independently from national or regional allegiances and followed the capricious law of contingency. At the same time, his wanderings were marked by devotion to the cause of anticolonial Indian nationalism and the desire to return to India. Having done so at the end of his life, Khankhoje felt unappreciated and out of place in the country he had longed for as a young man fleeing across the world. Despite the formal and symbolic recognition of Indian citizenship that came at the end of his life, the only non-colonial form of official identity held by Khankhoje for most of his life was that of a Mexican naturalized citizen. Despite the political devotion formed as a radical young nationalist in Maharashtra, Khankhoje was, practically and experientially, a Mexican for most of his life. This uncomfortable blend helps to explain the very minor role played by him in Indian national historical accounts, limited to a handful of mentions of his participation in the *Ghadar* party, and his surprising absence from Mexican historiography, despite the relevance that his work had for the consolidation of a post-revolutionary 'national agriculture'. At the same time, while this absence from national historical rendering is understandable, Khankhoje has, until now, also been excluded from non-national narratives of the Indian radical diaspora of the early twentieth century. Unlike some of his comrades and contemporaries, like Lala Har Dayal, M.K. Gandhi, Aurobindo Ghose or Virendranath Chattopadhyaya, who moved among what Elleke Boehmer has called the multiple-centred network of interrelating margins that constituted the globalized formations of imperial power,[75] after settling in Mexico Khankhoje effectively subtracted himself from the global circuits of surveillance and anticolonial activism that joined India, Europe, South Africa, the Caribbean and North America. In other words, the circumstances that allowed him to live and thrive off the grid of these transcontinental networks of control and exchange also excluded him from accounts focused on the history of transnational lives lived under the constraints of empire. In this chapter, I have attempted to weave the various strands of material available on Pandurang Khankhoje's life to paint a picture that makes justice both to the colourful exception he embodied and the ways in which he participated in broader historical processes taking place beyond the dynamics of imperial and national trajectories during the early decades of the twentieth century.

Notes

1. Copy of Order from K.L.F. Armitage, Deputy Commissioner, Wardha, on the Application of Sadashio Venkatesh Khankhoje, Petition Writer, for issuing Passport, 29 May 1924, in Jawaharlal Nehru Memorial Museum and Library Archives, P.S. Khankhoje papers, Subject File 3, 14–15. (Hereafter PSK, SF)
2. Refusal by the Consul at Mexico of a passport to Mr. Pandurang Sadashiv Khankhoje to return to India, PSK, SF, 16.
3. According to Maia Ramnath, during 1913 and 1914, Khankhoje directed the inner circle of the Yugantar Ashram and headed the *Ghadar* committee 'focused on militant action', *Haj to Utopia. How the Ghadar Movement Charted Global Radicalism and Attempted to Overthrow the British Empire* (Berkeley and Los Angeles: University of California Press, 2011), 45.
4. During the 1930s, the Mexican government recognized a variety of 'undesirable races' which should be banned entry into the country in order to prevent racial degeneration. The list included, among others, individuals of 'African or Australian race', 'yellow or Mongolian race', and all those individuals belonging to the 'people of Hindustan', the 'Ceylon Islands', 'Beluchistán (*sic*)', Central Asia and Malaya, Persia, Afghanistan, Abyssinia, Palestine, Armenia and USSR nationals. See Circular Confidencial num. 157, México, 27 de abril de 1934, Archivo Histórico del Instituto Nacional de Migración, file 4-350-2-1933-54, cited in Daniela Gleizer, 'Los límites de la nación. Naturalización y exclusión en el México posrevolucionario', in *Nación y Alteridad. Mestizos, indígenas y extranjeros en el proceso de formación nacional*, ed. Daniela Gleizer y Paula López Caballero (México D.F.: UAM-Cuajimalpa, Ediciones Educación y Cultura, 2015), 128–129. Translation from Spanish by the author.
5. This expression is used by John-Paul A. Ghobrial to illustrate the potential of blending global history and biography for the sake of a conveying a more nuanced picture of the interconnectedness of the past. See 'The secret life of Elias of Babylon and the uses of global microhistory', *Past & Present* no. 222 (February 2014): 57.
6. Savitri Sawhney, *I Shall Never Ask for Pardon. A Memoir of Pandurang Khankhoje* (Delhi: Penguin Books, 2005), 7.
7. Ibid., 36.
8. See, for example Kenyon Zimmer, *Immigrants against the State. Yiddish and Italian Anarchism in America* (Chicago: University of Illinois Press, 2015) and Peter Cole, David Struthers and Kenyon Zimmer (eds.), *Wobblies of the World* (London: Pluto Press, 2018).
9. Ramnath, *Haj to Utopia*, 31–33. According to Maia Ramnath, Khankhoje's activism in the region laid the ground for the creation of the *Ghadar* party in late 1913.
10. Sawhney, *I Shall Never*, 63.

11 For more on the transnational workings of the PLM, William D. Raat, *Revoltosos: Mexico's rebels in the United States, 1903-1923* (College Station: Texas A&M University Press, 1981) and Claudio Lomnitz, *The return of comrade Ricardo Flores Magón* (New York: Zone Books, 2014).
12 For more on the impact of Mexican anarcho-syndicalist activity in the conformation of a non-white milieu of radical activism, see Christina Heatherton, 'The Color Line and the Class Struggle: The Mexican Revolution and Convergences of Radical Internationalism, 1910-1946' (PhD diss., University of Southern California, 2012) and Devra Anne Weber, 'Wobblies of the Partido Liberal Mexicano: Reenvisioning Internationalist and Transnational Movements through Mexican Lenses'. *Pacific Historical Review* 85, no. 2 (2016): 188-226.
13 Sawhney, *I Shall Never*, 72.
14 According to Emily C. Brown, Har Dayal declared himself to be an admirer of the Flores Magón brothers, and Taraknath Das, who met Ricardo during their shared imprisonment at Leavenworth prison, identified the Mexican anarchist as an important leader in the international struggle against oppression and injustice. Emily C. Brown, *Har Dayal. Hindu Revolutionary and Rationalist* (Tucson: University of Arizona Press, 1975), 67; Christina Heatherton, 'University of Radicalism: Ricardo Flores Magón and Leavenworth Penitentiary', *American Quarterly* 66, no. 3 (Fall 2014): 557-581.
15 On 18 April 1914, the front page of *Regeneración* printed a strong indictment of the unjust arrest of Har Dayal, who was described by the Magonistas as a 'great Hindustan philosopher and champion of Social Revolution'. 'Contra la deportación de Har Dayal' *Regeneracion*,18 April 1914, 1.
16 Ramnath, *From Haj to Utopia*, 4.
17 Letter of recommendation from E.O. Holland, President of the State College of Washington, to Pandurang Khankhoje, December 1924, PSK, SF 4, 8.
18 Pandurang Khankhoje, 'Some Factors which Influence the Water Requirements of Plants', *Journal of the American Society of Agronomy* 6, no. 1 (January-February 1914): 1-23.
19 John H. Perkins, *Geopolitics and the Green Revolution. Wheat, Genes, and the Cold War* (New York: Oxford University Press, 1997), 75-101.
20 Between 1906 and 1914, the number of agricultural experimental stations in the country rose from 950 to 1,853, and public funds allocated for agricultural experimentation rose from $2 to $5 million. See Alfred Charles Treu, *A History of Agricultural Experimentation and Research in the United States, 1607-1925*, Miscellaneous Publication no. 251 (Washington, D. C.: Government Printing Office, 1937), 171, cited in Perkins, *Geopolitics and the Green Revolution*, 84-85.
21 Zimmer, *Immigrants Against the State*, 136-165 and Erin Matthew Plowman, 'The British Intelligence Station in San Francisco during the First World War', *Journal of Intelligence History* 12, no. 4 (2013): 1-20.

22 Sawhney, *I Shall Never*, 123–134.
23 Letter from Pandurang Khankhoje to Bhagwan Singh Gyanee, 7 October 1953, South Asian American Digital Archive (SAADA), Bhagwan Singh Gyanee Materials, https://www.saada.org/item/20120723-824, consulted on 10 May 2018.
24 Thomas Hughes, 'The German Mission to Afghanistan, 1915–1916', *German Studies Review* 25, no. 3 (Oct. 2002): 455.
25 Documents signed by His Excellency, the Ameer of Ghashghai State, Fars-Persia, Ameer 'Ashayer, Ghashghai Aspas, 3 November 1921, PSK, SF 2, 9, 11.
26 Sawhney, *I Shall Never*, 215–220.
27 Interview with Savitri Ana Sawhney Khankhoje, conducted on 15 April 1919.
28 Sawhney, *I Shall Never*, 224–225
29 Passport no. 95/24, in Expediente de Pandurang Khankhoje, Archivo Histórico Genaro Estrada, Fondo de Cartas de Naturalización, Clasificación Decimal III/5212 (42)/134, Topográfica VIII(N)-242-6 (Hereafter EPK, AHGE).
30 Oficio número 91992 de la Oficialía Mayor, Departamento de Administración, Sección de Personal, 11 de mayo, 1924, JNMML, PSK, SF 4, 24.
31 Marte R. Gómez, *Historia de la Comisión Nacional Agraria* (México D.F.: Centro de Investigaciones Agrarias, Secretaría de Agricultura y Ganadería, 1975), 21–23.
32 Savitri Sawhney claims that Khankhoje and Denegri met in San Francisco during her father's 'early years in California', *I Shall Never*, 73.
33 Ing. Marte R. Gómez, *La Reforma Agraria de México. Su crisis durante el período 1928–1934* (México D.F.: Librería de Manuel Porrúa, S.A., 1964), 123.
34 Artemio Cruz León, Isabel Arline Duque P. and Marcelino Castro, 'La investigación agrícola al momento del traslado de la Escuela Nacional de Agricultura de San Jacinto, D.F., a Chapingo, Estado de México, a través de las publicaciones de Pandurang Khankhoje', *Revista de Geografía Agrícola* 54 (enero-junio 2015): 49.
35 Pandurang Khankhoje, 'Nuevas variedades del maíz', *Boletín de Investigación. Estación Experimental Agrícola, Escuela Nacional de Agricultura* 1 (1930): 5.
36 For more on the life of Úrsulo Galván, see Jaime Irving Reynoso, *El agrarismo radical en México en la década de 1920: Úrsulo Galván, Primo Tapia y José Guadalupe Rodríguez (una biografía política)* (México: Instituto Nacional de Estudios Históricos de las Revoluciones de México, 2009), 9–45.
37 Aremio Cruz León and Marcelino Ramírez-Castro, 'Escuelas Libres de Agricultura de México: proyecto de la Liga de Comunidades Agrarias y antecedentes de las Escuelas Campesinas', *Revista de Geografía Agrícola* 57 (Jul.–Dic. 2016), 145.
38 Sawhney, *I Shall Never*, 245.
39 Ing. Florencio Palomo Valencia, Director General del Ministerio de Agricultura y Fomento a Pandurang Khankhoje, 10 de Junio, 1933, PSK, SF 4, 40.
40 Oficio dirigido a 'C. José López Corté, Secretario General del H. Ayuntamiento de esta Capital', EPK, AHGE, 9.

41 José López Cortés, Secretario General de Relaciones Exteriores, al C. Secretario de Relaciones Exteriores, 24 de Julio de 1925, EPK, AHGE, 49. Throughout the official documents dealing with his naturalization, Khankhoje is variously identified as a 'Hindu' (*Indú* or *Hindú*) and a 'British Indian'.
42 Oficio firmado por P K y dirigido al C. Juez Tercrero de Distrito Supernumerario, Julio 21 de 1926, EPK, AHGE, 6–8.
43 Licenciado Horacio Terán al C. Juez Quinto de Distrito del Distrito Federal, 14 de febrero de 1930. EPK, AHGE, 31.
44 Ing. Waldo Soberón al C. Secretario de Relaciones Exteriores, 3 de marzo de 1930 EPK, AHGE, 37.
45 Ing. Juan A. González al C. Secretario de Relaciones Exteriores, 5 marzo de 1930, EPK, AHGE, 36.
46 Expediente de naturalización ordinaria, 1930, Pandurang Khankhoje, EPK, AHGE, 1–2.
47 Gleizer, 'Los límites de la nación', and Pablo Yankelevich, 'Mexicanos por naturalización en la primera mitad del siglo XX. Un acercamiento cuantitativo' *Historia Mexicana* LXIV, no 4 (2015): 1729–1805.
48 Pablo Yankelevich and Paola Chenillo Alazraki, 'La arquitectura de la política de inmigración en México', in Pablo Yankelevich (ed.). *Nación y Extranjería. La exclusión racial en las políticas migratorias de Argentina, Brasil, Cuba y México* (México: UNAM-ENAH, 2009), 177–221.
49 For more on the debates and conflicts that arose from the project of *mestizaje* and their relationship to nationalism and nationalism in Mexico, see Alan Knight, 'Racism, Revolution and *Indigenismo*: Mexico 1910–1940', in Richard Graham, Thomas E. Skidmore, Aline Helg and Alan Knights (eds.); *The Idea of Race in Latin America* (Austin: University of Texas Press, 1990), 71–114; Pablo Yankelevich, 'Mexico for the Mexicans: Immigration, National Sovereignty and the Promotion of Mestizaje', *The Americas* 68, no. 3 (January 2012): 405–436; and Claudio Lomnitz, 'Los orígenes de nuestra supuesta homogeneidad: breve arqueología de la unidad nacional en México', *Prisma, Revista de Historia Intelectual*, no. 14; Daniela Gleizer and Paula López Caballero (eds.). *Nación y Alteridad. Mestizos, indígenas y extranjeros en el proceso de formación nacional*.
50 For more on anti-Chinese racism in Mexico, see Jason Oliver Chang, *Chino: Anti-Chinese Racism in Mexico, 1880–1940* (Chicago: University of Illinois Press, 2017), and Ana Luz Ramírez Zavala, 'La justificación higiénico-sanitaria en la campaña anti-china, 1924–1932', *Letras Históricas*, no. 14 (Primavera-Verano 2016): 159–183.
51 See Circular Confidencial no. 157, México, 27 de abril de 1934, Archivo Histórico del Instituto Nacional de Migración, file 4-350-2-1933-54, cited in Gleizer, 'Los límites de la nación', 128–9.

52 Gleizer, 'Los límites de la nación'.
53 Yankelevich, 'Mexicanos por naturalización'.
54 Pablo Yankelevich, 'Naturalization and citizenship in Postrevolutionary Mexico', *Estudios de Historia Moderna y Contemporánea de México*, no. 28 (Julio-Diciembre 2014): 118.
55 Gleizer, 'Los límites de la nación', 127–8.
56 Yankelevich, 'Mexicanos por naturalización', 1760.
57 Sawhney, *I Shall Never*, 266
58 Oficio 45, Escuela Normal Veracruzana Enrique C. Rebsamen, 29 de Enero de 1934, PSK, SF 5, 30.
59 Oficicio 5–404, Secretaría de Agricultura y Foment, 29 de Myo de 1934, PSK, SF, 10–14 and Oficio 5–840, Secretaría de Agricultura y Foment, 22 de Junio de 1934, PSK, SF 5, 15–16.
60 Oficio número 03540 de la Tesorería de la Federación, 1 de Enero de 1935, PSK, SF 4, 24. Many historians identify the government of Lázaro Cárdenas, 1934–1940, as the culminating moment of agrarian reform in Mexico and the highpoint of the revolutionary thrust inaugurated in the 1910s. Cárdenas expanded the programme of land redistribution considerably and nationalized the oil industry in 1938. See, for example, Adolfo Gilly, *The Mexican Revolution* (New York: New Press, 2005).
61 Oficio 11-5-40151 de la Secretaría de Agricultura y Fomento, firmado por el director J. de J. Urquizo, 16 de Noviembre 1936, PSK, SF 4, 33–34.
62 Carta de Gral. J. Salvador S. Sánchez, Jefe del Estado Mayor, a Tte. Nicolás Andrade Corro, Comandante del Destacamento Militar, Santa Lucrecia, Ver. 23 de Noviembre de 1942, PSK, SF 4, 53.
63 Sawhney, *I Shall Never*, 267.
64 Ibid., 254–270.
65 Gupta had been a member of the *Ghadar* party and had worked in collaboration with German agents during the famous Hindu-German Conspiracy case of 1915–1917. He arrived in Mexico in the late 1910s and, according to her great niece Lila Das Gupta, died in Mexico City in 1951 – private email sent by Lila Das Gupta to Mauricio Tenorio-Trillo, November 2, 2018. I thank Mauricio for his kindness in sharing this information with me. In Mexico Gupta published a translation of Tagore's play *Chitra* in 1919 (*Chitra – Drama en un Acto*) (México, D.F.: La Helvetia, 1919), and later secured a job as language professor at the National University. For more on his stay in Mexico, see Mauricio Tenorio-Trillo, *I Speak of the City: Mexico City at the Turn of the Twentieth Century*, (Chicago: The University of Chicago Press, 2012), 252–253. And for more on his involvement in the Hindu-German Conspiracy case, see transcript of District Attorney Joseph Flemming's statement before a jury, undated, Jawaharlal Nehru Memorial Museum and Library, P. S. Khankhoje Papers, Subject Files 2, 2–11.

66 Interview with Savitri Ana Sawhney Khankhoje.
67 Letter from Pandurang Khankhoje to Bhagwan Singh Gyanee, 7 October 1953, SAADA, Bhagwan Singh Gyanee Materials, https://www.saada.org/item/20120723-824, consulted on 10 May 2018.
68 Sawhney, *I Shall Never*, 298.
69 Interview with Savitri Ana Sawhney Khankhoje.
70 From H.B. Singh to The Chief Secretary, General Administration Department, Government of Maharashtra, Sachivalaya, Bombay, 31 October 1961, PSK, SF 4, 1.
71 Sawhney, *I Shall Never*, 299–304.
72 Clare Anderson, *Subaltern Lives. Biographies of Colonialism in the Indian Ocean World, 1790–1920* (Cambridge: Cambridge University Press, 2012), 1–22.
73 *Sannyas:* refers to the fourth life stage defined by the Hindu doctrine of the ashramas. According to Sanskrit texts, in this stage men must renounce material desires and prejudices and devote themselves to asceticism.
74 Ibid., 22
75 Elleke Boehmer, *Empire, the National, and the Postcolonial, 1890–1920. Resistance in Interacion* (New York: Oxford University Press, 2002), 5–6.

A woman of peace and calm: The story of Senthamani Govender

Devarakshanam Betty Govinden

Introduction

When you meet Senthamani Govender, also known as Salatchi and affectionately known to us as Granny, you are immediately drawn to her. Granny, who celebrated her ninetieth birthday in 2013, is the epitome of strength and grace. She is composed and focused with a remarkable memory of her young days, which she recalls with spirit.

Granny is among the many ordinary women of indentured stock who were born in South Africa, and who struggled against odds to establish a life for themselves and their families in this country. Her life is a remarkable story of endurance and strength in the building of this country. We need to remember that so much of our history is also shaped by women and men whose names never get into the history books.

Listening to Granny's story, I realize that here is a woman who moved six times in her lifetime. She settled into and adapted to a new home, only to move, for one reason or another, to a new place of abode. Her relocations were as much due to personal circumstance as to the vicissitudes of fortune and government policy. In her life we see played out the wider general story of South Africa – land of both discrimination and opportunity. Her story shows that the personal and private is always entrammelled in the wider public domain. Indeed, her story – of settling down in a home, dismantling it or being separated from it, and establishing a new home, of constantly making new beginnings – is a perennial, universal one. Her story of loss and restoration echoes in the lives of countless human beings, especially those dispersed across continents, settling in a land of adoption. Yet it is in the particularities of each story, especially those of individual women such as Granny, that we appreciate the contradictions and pressures played out in a single life.

Granny was born on 29 November 1923 in Nonoti Park, on the North Coast in KwaZulu-Natal, and her birth was registered nine days later, on 8 December 1923. Records reveal that the day of the week on which she was born was a Thursday, already suggesting that as 'Thursday's child', 'she had far to go'.

Granny hails from indentured stock, her father arriving from India to work on the tea estates in the Natal Colony at the turn of the twentieth century. His name was Kandasami Sami Gounden (Indentured Number 92720). Originally from the village of Kolapaloor in the District of North Arcot in Madras, India, Kandasami arrived in Durban on the ship *Umlazi* XV11 in April 1902 at the age of twenty-five years. His employer was William R. Hindson, who owned Clifton Tea Estate, in Nonoti, in the Stanger area. This was one of the many places where sugar cane and tea labourers worked when they arrived from India. On Granny's birth certificate, her father's occupation is listed as 'labourer'. She recalls that he also worked as a chauffeur for a white farmer in Nonoti called Ignis. Her father would occasionally ride a horse given to him by his employer, and he would travel around the estate supervising the workers. The photograph in Figure 8.2 portrays a person of strong will and determination, living on

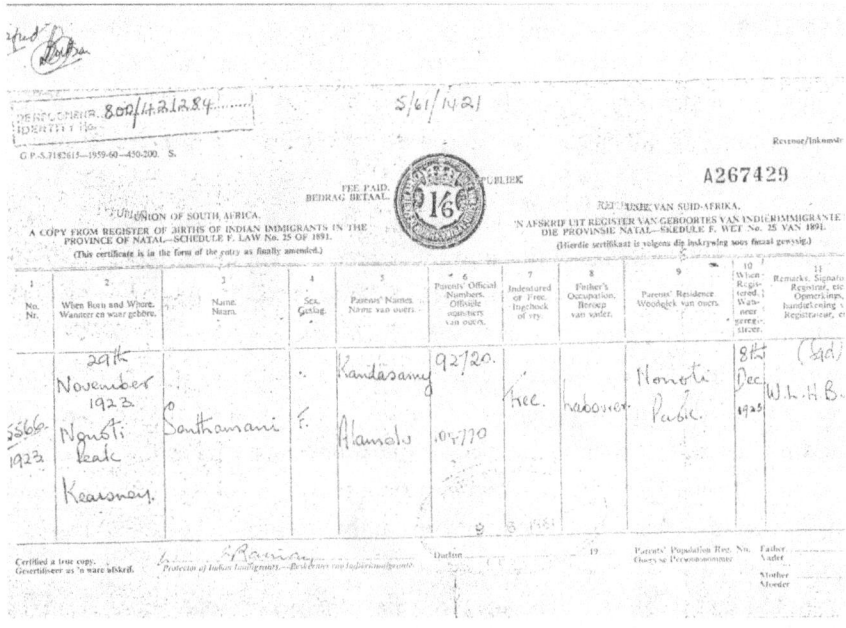

Figure 8.1 Birth certificate.

Figure 8.2 Kandasami Sami Gounden.

harsh soil, as the hardy cacti in the background would suggest. It also suggests strong individuality and contradicts the white, colonial practice of referring to all Indians derogatively and anonymously as 'Sammy' or 'Mary', according to gender. Granny points out that there were also sugar cane plantations on which Africans and Indians worked together, and there was much mutual tolerance and respect between the two groups of labourers.

The meeting and interaction of peoples from diverse backgrounds in the same colonial space is a feature of plantation history, even while a chasm existed between employer and employee. Meera Kosambi, drawing from Mary Louise Pratt and Indira Ghose, speaks of the 'notion of the "contact zone" – the social space where disparate cultures meet, clash and grapple with each other, often in highly asymmetrical relations of domination and subordination, like colonialism'.[1] This was true of the Hindson Estate as it was of similar estates elsewhere.

William Robert Hindson was born in Cumberland in 1852 and developed his skills as a 'tea-taster' from an early age. He came to South Africa in 1879, and amassed a considerable fortune through his work as an accountant and financial agent on the diamond mines in Kimberley. He purchased the Clifton Estate in the Kearsney District, a property of 350 acres. By 1892 the Estate had expanded to cover 4,000 acres and the commercial department was managed by Kenneth A. Brown. The brand of tea that was produced here was 'Natalinda', and even secured a gold medal in South Africa in 1905 – three years after Granny's father and a year after her mother arrived in Natal from India. The estate had advanced technology for its time, and was able to show an impressive turnover of tea. So phenomenal was the growth in general that in 1902 the tea industry applied for 19,000 coolies from the Immigration Department for the Colony, as coolie labour was deemed indispensable to its continued development and growth. It is important to note the contribution of Granny's parents, and so many others, to making this enterprise profitable.

What follows is a selection of photographs of the Clifton Tea Estate, taken from an early colonial compendium published at the turn of the twentieth century,[2] reflecting the estate during the time when Granny's father worked there.

Granny's mother, Alamelu Vythilingam (Indentured Number 104770), came to work on the same farm in 1904, two years later. Alamelu, who was twenty-two-years-old when she came from India, hailed from Tanjore, in the district of Nagapur, Madras. She travelled on the ship *Umlazi* XXII. She also went to work

Figure 8.3 General view, Clifton Tea Estate.

Figure 8.4 The factory with Indian barracks.

Figure 8.5 Indians picking tea leaves.

Figure 8.6 The factory – Clifton Tea Estate.

at Hindson Tea Estates, and it is clear that that is where she met met and later married Kandasami. Granny does not know if they were still indentured at this time, and whether they required permission to marry. By 1906, Granny's father and mother were among the 500 Indian workers on this highly successful tea estate, with four European supervisors.

Figure 8.7 Managing Director's house.

Who were Alamelu and Kandasami? Why did they leave India? What were they like? What was their long transoceanic voyage from India like? How did they feel about crossing the *kala pani*? What were their experiences on the tea estate in this outpost in Natal? Did they have families they left behind in India? What were their difficulties on the estate? Did they long for their homeland? What trauma of indentured exile did they experience? Did they want to go back to India? How did their sense of identity change with time? How did the memory of India and experience of the Colony coalesce? What were the specific things, real and imagined, that they brought in their gunny sacks? How different or similar were their experiences, compared to those of the other coolies? As *girmityas*, what coercion did they experience, what resistance did they display? How did they cope with some of the challenges of their new life given that a 'new vocabulary had to be learnt, an unfamiliar geography explored, a new terrain mastered, new pragmatic social relationships established'?[3] These and many more questions are not answered by the standardized, monochromatic 'Ship's List' that was completed for each immigrant, and which is our only link in many instances to that past. There is much in the past of Granny's parents that is a blank page. At a time when sheer survival preoccupied the immigrants, and when there was no value placed on one's life and story, or when one did not have the resources to record one's story, this is understandable. We need to remember the invisibilizing of histories of the colonized. Hershini Bhana Young points out, in her book, *Illegible Will – Coercive Spectacles of Labour in South Africa and the Diaspora*: 'In the plenitude of paper that is the archive, what is documented is less a trace where a black woman might be than the bureaucracy of imperial rule itself. In other words, the colonial archive does a fantastic job of documenting itself and its inability to recognize certain lives as relevant'.[4]

My style here, as in my account of 'My Grandmother', uses fragments of their stories to construct a story. It is similar to the style that Bahadur would use in composing the story of her grandmother in *Coolie Woman: The Odyssey of Indenture*.[5] As Bahadur notes about her process,

> where the voices of indentured women were absent, I used my own, as their descendant, to question the records as aggressively as I could … Whole sections of Coolie Woman unfold entirely in questions: mine, my great-grandmother's, the reader's, one relentlessly follows the next. These questions allow me to imagine interiorities withheld by the written record. They paint landscapes, advance the plot, convey a tone. They communicate my own attitude to the archive and its elisions and biases: I could never be neutral because I am, after all, a product of the history I've written.[6]

Granny was born into a world in 1923 when indentured labour had ended nine years before in South Africa, and three years before its demise in the rest of the British Empire. However, the colonial government in South Africa was set on a course of racial discrimination which would continue for the better part of the twentieth century. Gandhi had returned to India and began a 'non-cooperation movement' to oppose the South African government's policies. The resistance movement slowly gained momentum after the formation of the South Africa Native Council in 1914, later named the African National Congress. Indentured families like Granny's, who did not return to India, were slowly finding their footing in the Colony and were turning towards other forms of occupation.

Granny was the youngest in the family with two brothers and two sisters – Perumal, Soobramoney, Mariamma and Veeramma. She was raised with her siblings and has many wonderful memories of growing up in Nonoti Park, on the North Coast. The family was close-knit, and enjoyed a wonderful sense of community life among fellow labourers. They had a large, rambling farmhouse, made of wood and iron. She recalls a farmyard with an abundance of fruit and vegetables. This seems in clear contrast to the barracks-style houses that many labourers were consigned to on the plantations. Her descriptions suggest a carefree life, simple, but full of bounty; it belies the obvious difficulties that they would have also endured. Her father worked hard and was a great provider for the family. He was promoted to the rank of sirdar, and enjoyed a position of responsibility and privilege. It seemed quite common to elevate workers to the status of 'sirdar', so that they would exercise control over their compatriots.

As was customary at the time, the boys in the household were sent to school, but Granny did not receive any formal schooling. It seems that she became literate through contact with others. Granny, like so many other underprivileged women, was to learn much in the school of life through religion, absorbing a lively Hindu faith from her parents. She became fluent in Tamil and English and coped well with the changing demands of a life that would span the socio-historical spectrum of the twentieth century and early decades of the twenty-first century. Granny says that there was no time to read, nor was there available reading material when she was growing up. It was 'work, work, work, all the time'.

Sadly, her mother died when she was only eight months' old, and she has no memories of her. Why did her mother die, and at a relatively young age? Granny was told that her mother became ill from the time she (Granny) was born. Her father, Kandasami, remarried some four and a half years after her mother passed away and it was at this time that Granny went away from Nonoti to Durban. She lived with her step-grandmother, in a place called 'Popatlall's Yard', in Umgeni Road, Durban. She also remembers that her elder brother, Perumal, took great care of her as she was growing up. Granny continued to live with her stepmother's mother, who played a strong nurturing role in her life, up to the age of twelve.

After a while, the rest of her family, except her brother Perumal, also relocated to Magazine Barracks. When her father's employer in Nonoti died, he lost most of the privileges he had enjoyed on the farm and decided to move from Nonoti and seek new employment in the city. He became an overseer for a garden services company in Bulwer Park and, as he worked for the Durban Corporation, acquired a house in Magazine Barracks. Granny then moved to live with him and her stepmother.

When Granny was around six and a half years' old, her father and stepmother had a daughter who was named Parvathi. She remembers Parvathi well, and enjoyed a close relationship with her, up to the sad time of her early death in her fifties. Granny moved from Umgeni Road to Magazine Barracks in the mid-1930s, which marked a new beginning for her. The residential area known as Magazine Barracks was originally used to store magazine powder and the suburb was given to Durban Municipal employees from 1887. Like District Six, Cato Manor, Fietas, Soweto, Sophiatown and many other places, Magazine Barracks came to personify segregated living in the sociocultural imaginary, and occupies an important place in the iconography of memory in South Africa. Rather than erasing these spaces, we need to appreciate their place in the historical, political and cultural geography of South Africa.[7]

Granny was exposed to the vibrant community life in Magazine Barracks and she remembers that it was here that she entered puberty. Different from Nonoti, but nonetheless appealing in its own way, life in Magazine Barracks allowed her to enjoy a happy adolescence. She played with dolls and on the swings, enjoyed skipping and 'three tins', and remembers the community dances. The Diwali season was especially joyous and unforgettable as there was so much activity. Among the personalities who made an impression on her was Pushpa Murugan, the well-known writer and community worker from Magazine Barracks. Murugan's memoir, *Lotus Blooms on the Eastern Vlei*, is a description of life in Magazine Barracks, which also known as the Eastern Vlei. Sam Ramsamy and his family and 'Bull' Murugan, the linguist, were also prominent residents. The Magazine Barracks Temple was the centre of much community activity, and Granny also remembers 'Archary's Shop' in Somtseu Road, where she would go regularly to buy bread for the family. She recalls the police station next to the shop, as well as the school. It is common knowledge that Indian girls at this time were not encouraged to pursue formal schooling. Those who did were more the exception than the rule, and usually came from the elite and middle-class Indian families rather than from the working classes. Many educationalists and political figures, such as Dr Goonam, actively fought against the prejudice that kept Indian girls away from school.[8]

Family of Granny's husband

After her sixteenth birthday, Granny was introduced to Nallathambi Gounden, who lived in Westbrook, near Mt Edgecombe. Nallathambi seemed promising. At twenty-five years, he was already a sirdar working for the consortium, Natal Estates. In terms of their family histories, the couple had much in common. Muthu Gounden (Colonial Born Number 117370), Nallathambi's father, hailed from the village of Ponmarampatty in the District of Salem, in Tamilnadu, South India. He travelled from India on the SS *Pongola* in 1905, arriving in Durban two days before Christmas, on 23 December. He was accompanied by his brother Erusayi Velliah Gounden, and they were sent to work at the Umhloti Valley Central Sugar Mill. It seems that Nallathambi was born in 1914. Details of his background and that of his family before he met Granny are sparse.

A Woman of Peace and Calm

Senthamani and Nallathambi married at a temple in Westbrook around 1939, surrounded by a happy family of uncles, aunts, sisters and brothers and friends, as the photograph below shows. Her father, Kandasami, in his colonial-style hat, to the right in the photograph, was especially proud. The young bride looked demure, in a mauve cotton sari, and the bridegroom stood tall in a white cotton suit.

B.M.25

DEPARTMENT OF INTERNAL AFFAIRS
COPY OF SHIP'S LIST OF INDIAN IMMIGRANT

Serial Number	294
Colonial Number	117370
Date of Arrival	23:12:1905
Name of Ship	S.S. "PONGOLA"
Place of Registration	
Date of Registration	
Number in Register	
Name	MUTHU GOUNDEN
Father's Name	NADAYA GOUNDEN
Age	33 YEARS
Sex	MALE
Caste	VANNIA
District	SALEM
Thanna/Taluq	ATHUR
Village	PONMARAMPATTY
Height	5'6"
Bodily Marks	MOLE ON CHEST
Name of Next-of-Kin	FATHER
Relations Accompanied	ERUSAYI
Small Pox/Vaccinated	VACCINATED
Remarks	

Certified a true copy.

REGIONAL REPRESENTATIVE

DEPARTMENT OF INTERNAL AFFAIRS
REGIONAL REPRESENTATIVE
PRIVATE BAG/PRIVAATSAK X54
1985-04-18
DURBAN 4000
STREEKVERTEENWOORDIGER
DEPARTEMENT VAN
BINNELANDSE AANGELEENTHEDE

Figure 8.8 Information on Nallathambi's father.

Figure 8.9 Granny's wedding day.

Married life

The couple lived in Westbrook, where Asothiamma, her eldest child, was born. A second child, a boy, died in infancy. The family moved to Magazine Barracks, and it was here that her other children, Savithree, Vigie and Devan, were born. Nallathambi worked for the Durban Corporation, in Congella, earning a mere pittance. Both parents worked hard to consolidate their family and give their children a good start in life. Through their judicious endeavours, they were able to obtain a piece of land in Avoca while still in Westbrook.

Granny recalls a highlight of those years when she joined the large crowds to see the British royal family, King George VI and his wife Queen Elizabeth who, with their daughters, Elizabeth and Margaret, arrived in Durban in 1947. She can still picture the royal parade on the beachfront, and especially remembers the open car. This gathering was considered one of the largest of South African Indians, where 65,000 attended.[9] Granny also remembers the time of the 1949 Riots in Durban between Africans and Indians, although she did not experience any immediate or direct violence at Magazine Barracks.

The studio photograph in Figure 8.10 gives a perspective different from that of the couple on their wedding day. The husband and wife here look more self-assured and settled, surrounded by their well-groomed children. Unfortunately,

Figure 8.10 The family – Granny with husband and children, Asothie, Savy, Vigie and Devan.

Nallathambi died in May 1961 in an accident at work. He was only forty-seven years' old at the time when he was struck by a heavy iron, resulting in his tragic and untimely death. Granny points out that no proper compensation was received by the family, and she was paid a mere forty pounds.

With four teenage children to support and raise, Granny, at the age of thirty-seven, refused to succumb to penury, and left home for the first time to find work. At the time of her husband's death, the marriage plans for her eldest daughter, Asothie, were already being considered and she was determined to see them through. She found a job at Brighton Beach, where she worked as a cleaner and assistant at the swimming pool. She earned a pittance and it is surprising that she was able to raise her children single-handedly on this wage. She still ran the home and was gradually assisted by her daughters. There was also a period when she worked the afternoon to late evening shift at the swimming pool, coping with the use of public transport. She worked for over twenty-five years, up to her retirement at the age of sixty-two years. Many black women like Granny found unskilled work in the public sector such as cleaning, which was an extension of their domestic life, in order to earn a living.[10] These women thus operated in a restricted public space, unlike those of the professional classes. It is also necessary to appreciate that much of this women's work, both at home and in the workplace, was undervalued and underpaid.[11]

She saw her family gradually increase, and made provisions that both her daughters and son attend school. She achieved much in that she educated her children, inculcated in them the values of the Hindu faith, saw them married and setting up their own homes and families, and continued to support the growing families emotionally. The bashful bride of yesteryear gave way to provider and head of the family, and was hardly cast in the image of the reclusive, traditional, Hindu widow. Due to circumstances, Granny grew to play a pivotal role as mother and later, grandmother, assuming the role of benevolent matriarch with ease. She remains a crucial link in the family, connecting both past and present generations, and in the wider society, between the plantation economy of the early indentured labourers and the modern nation.

From Magazine Barracks, around 1964–65, Granny moved to Chatsworth. This relocation was due to Group Areas legislation, when thousands of Indians were forced to leave their homes in places like Magazine Barracks and Cato Manor. The Group Areas Act, promulgated in 1950, ensured that the different race groups lived separately, and much has been written to depict the trauma and loss caused by this internal uprooting. Although Granny missed Magazine Barracks greatly she slowly adjusted to her new home and its surroundings, and recalls the new community she then embraced in Chatsworth; among her neighbours was the David family who were Christians.

Granny's new home, *House 301, Road 242*, became the hub of much family activity. Although the practice of naming homes in this anonymous way became the signature of living in Chatsworth and many other black locations in apartheid South Africa, it is remarkable how the occupants resisted such depersonalization and imbued their lives and living with distinctiveness and individuality. Although Indian indentured labourers had been in the country for a hundred years at this time, they still did not enjoy the rights and privileges of a democratic society. After 1948 there were intentions to repatriate Indians to India, and it was only in 1961 that Indians were recognized as South Africans, although still not afforded full citizenry. The Tricameral Parliament introduced in the 1980s was an attempt, like the Bantustan policy, to divide and rule South Africans.

Alongside this political uncertainty, Granny experienced personal highlights in her life. She witnessed the marriages of her daughters and son, and watched with approval as her children set up their own homes and established their own nuclear families. She experienced a family tragedy again, when she sustained the loss of one of her daughters, Savy, some eight years ago. She took great pride in the arrival of her grandchildren, and occupied an honoured place in her extended family. Granny is remembered by the grandchildren for her generosity. She would regularly arrive on a Friday bearing gifts, which included cakes and sweets. Mags and Logan, her grandchildren, recall that they would eagerly run to meet her at the bus stop, to help her with her parcels.

Reflecting on segments of Granny's life – 'the war years'

It is important to remember that Granny, although she is still alive today, was born in the decade after the First World War, and spent much of her young life during 'the war years', up to the Second World War, trying to eke out a living. These decades were important in shaping South Africa as a whole, and had a direct bearing on Granny's life. In fact, the vicissitudes of the better part of the twentieth century, especially for all black groups, were to be endured and suffered, with respite being sought mainly in private and personal family life, as Granny's life demonstrates.

After indenture was abolished in 1917, the position of Indians in South Africa was ambiguous. The threat of repatriation to India remained until 1960. Gandhi had returned to India in 1915, leaving behind the important legacy of the Indian Congress, which had very active provincial formations. The year in which Granny was born – 1923 – saw the formation of the South African Indian Congress (SAIC), an amalgamation of the different Congress groupings.

The SAIC actively worked for the improvement of living conditions, the lifting of trade restrictions specially aimed at Indian economic activity and land acquisition for formerly indentured Indians who were settling in the Colony of Natal, and beyond; needless to say, the efforts of the SAIC were met with much opposition from the government of the time.

The Congress of SA Trade Unions (COSATU) formed in the mid-1980s, during the height of the struggle against apartheid. The reality, of course, is that little changed in the working lives of women like Granny. Granny married when she was sixteen years' old and, sadly, was widowed around the age of thirty-nine, forcing her to begin working outside the home. The irony is that South Africa's workers have continued to struggle for a better working deal even after 1994: the Marikana Massacre of 2012 remains a blot on the worker landscape of the country.

As pointed out already, from the turn of the twentieth century, many acts were aimed specifically at Indians to curtail business ventures, movement to other provinces, and land expropriation for the purpose of enforcing racial segregation – for example, the Slums Act: Demolition of Slums of 1934 and the Asiatic Land Tenure Amendment Act No 30 of 1936. Many of the worst apartheid laws were introduced in the 1950s, such as the Immorality Act of 1927 – amended in 1950 and again in 1957, then renamed as the Sexual Offences Act (1957) – and the Group Areas Act (1950) – amended in 1952, 1955, 1956 and 1957 – with the latter forcing Indians in particular away from the central city areas where many had previously operated their businesses. The Defiance Campaigns that emerged from passive resistance in the 1940s were aimed at what was dubbed the Ghetto Act, which restricted Indian land ownership and occupation in certain areas.

It is important to be sensitive to the intersectional dimensions of Granny's life, in terms of race as well as class and gender. From early on in the twentieth century, women were gradually coming to the fore to highlight gender discrimination and champion the cause of women's rights in different forms. The decades of the 1930s and 1940s, when Granny was growing up in a home of straitened circumstances saw the increasing politicization of women.

Women leaders from the Indian Congresses, such as Amina Cachalia, Fatima Meer and Ansuyah Singh, worked closely with leaders from the ANC Women's League during the Defiance Campaigns. It is not surprising that the Federation of South African Women (FEDSAW) inaugurated in 1954, provided a platform for women to draw attention to their daily struggles related to poverty, unemployment, passes and poor working conditions. These efforts – with key leaders such as Rahima Moosa, Josie Palmer, Cissy Gool, Helen Joseph, Lilian Ngoyi and Sophie Williams – culminated in the famous 1956 Women's March to Pretoria.[12]

Manilal Gandhi, the second son of Mohandas Gandhi remained in South Africa and played an important role in fighting for all oppressed groups in the decades that followed. He was an important presence and signatory when the Freedom Charter was launched in 1955. However, or alongside this, the lives of the oppressed groups on the ground were rather grim.

It is worth observing that Granny was forced into the public labour system, but remained an unskilled worker throughout her employable years. With increasing industrialization during these decades in South Africa, although dependent on an expanded labour force, the government exploited it at every turn, keeping workers impoverished and suppressed. The worldwide depression of the late 1920s exacerbated the poverty of all black groups, and women like Granny, who later joined the ranks of the unskilled labour market, were particularly affected.

One sees in Granny's life the perennial quest for house and home. We must remember that South Africa's racially segregated 'Group Areas' – a system whose remnants persist to this day – doggedly followed Granny for the better part of her life. She moved from Magazine Barracks, in the city centre, to Chatsworth, in the south of Durban, and then to Avoca, her present home, in the north of the city – all designated 'group areas' during the apartheid era. The experiences of apartheid with its uprooting and dislocation through the Group Areas Act, and forced removals, exacerbated a peripatetic, precarious condition, as exemplified in Granny's life. In a condition of rampant 'unhousedness' – the classic case must surely be Naipaul's *A House for Mr Biswas* – the question of ethics and justice in history might be foregrounded in any retrieval of personal stories, like those of Granny's.

Living under apartheid

Jacob Dlamini, in his autobiography on growing up in the South African township of Katlehong, *Native Nostalgia*, makes the important point that the dominance of the master narrative of struggle history in South Africa makes us forget the way ordinary people lived under apartheid. He encourages us to recall the richness and 'complexity of life among black South Africans, that not even colonialism and apartheid at their worst could destroy'.[13]

So many women, like Granny, effaced their own personal ambitions and aspirations and saw their mission as one of caring and providing for their families, spending their lives producing and nurturing future generations who would take their place as worthy citizens of this country. This is a thread that runs through the lives of black women in general in South Africa, and the stories of these women must also be celebrated. Feminists have engaged in much exploratory work to foreground the lives of women, whether well-known or obscure. Writing on the heroism of women, often undervalued in relation to men, Miriam Polster has rightly pointed out that 'women's quiet but profoundly courageous acts simply go unremarked, submerged in a subsidiary world of attachment and service'.[14]

In arguing this way, I am not condoning the structures and systems of oppression, and suggesting that if some people, like Granny, tried to shake off the victim image, then those who did/do not are somehow deficient. In *The Souls of Black Folk*, the African-American writer, Du Bois, criticized the spurious notion 'that oppressed groups are presented as problems rather than the systems that have oppressed them'. Fanon also criticized the tendency 'to hold those who suffer to be responsible for that suffering due to their own biological or cultural failings'.[15]

Granny lived in the Chatsworth home for a good fifteen years and then moved to Avoca around 1980. This was the property that Nallathambi had helped to secure years earlier. The Avoca home was developed by her son, Devan and herself. She resides there now, with her son and daughter-in-law, Indra. She says that she stills misses the community spirit of Chatsworth and finds that life in Avoca tends to be impersonal. Another highlight of her life was a trip she made to India and the Far East in 1985. She certainly enjoyed visiting the land of her parents, but observes that the Tamil she heard in Madras was quite different to the version she spoke in South Africa. She also felt indisputably that she belonged to South Africa rather than to India. At present, she has three surviving children, thirteen grandchildren and nineteen great-grandchildren. It is interesting to note that among her grandchildren are teachers, accountants, doctors and academics and other professionals. The majority reside in South Africa, while a few members of the family have emigrated overseas.

Figure 8.11 Granny at the centre of the family.

A Woman of Peace and Calm 219

Figure 8.12 Granny with Asothie, her daughter, Mags, her grand-daughter and Verushka and Rishane, her great-granddaughter and great-grandson.

Conclusion

Granny's story must be seen against the backdrop of broader historical changes. When Granny's father and mother arrived in South Africa in the early years of the twentieth century, the Indian indentured labourers had already been in South Africa for over forty years, having first arrived in 1860. Thanks to the hard work of the labourers, sugar and tea cultivation did much to improve the economy of the colony. Succeeding generations built on this legacy and helped to consolidate the life of the Colony. Women, as the example of Granny indicates, worked in both domestic and public domains, contributing to the stability of family life, the maintenance of civic life, and the perpetuation of religious and cultural traditions. Jon Soske, drawing from Partha Chatterjee, argues that 'nationalist ideology invested the home and family with a special function: to preserve the inner "spiritual" values of the nation, the cultural traditions that defined the separate identity of the colonized'.[16] This is especially true of diasporic and immigrant women and their descendants, and oppressed disenfranchised women in their own country, as we see with Jacob Dlamini's own mother raising her family in apartheid Katlehong, who felt the burden of maintaining stability in the 'inner sanctum' of the home in a foreign land.

It is also vitally important to consider how women's experiences of the physical spaces of houses and memories of home are linked to the development of the national imaginary.[17] Black women's experiences in South Africa in particular, given the apartheid history of internal movement, dislocation and relocation, as exemplified in some respects in Granny's life, need to be explored more closely.

The early labourers experienced discrimination and hostility; Gandhi, who was in the country at the time Granny's parents first arrived, started his Satyagraha Campaigns. The recorded history of this period shows many indignities to which Indian immigrants were subjected and the anti-Indian legislation that was promulgated. Granny's story must also be seen against the dominant historiography of the past century and even into the twenty-first century. The way people's lives are deemed history-making or newsworthy or not is controlled by a number of influences and assumptions. Political activism or educational and cultural accomplishments assured selected Indian women a revered, iconic place, and the 'little women' were erased. Class played an important role in this politics of recognition. Fame may also be enjoyed for 'achievements' such as winning beauty contests[18] or engaging in daring feats such as riding the 'wall of death'.[19]

Ironically, in the new democracy, there is a new silencing of people like Granny, who are cast in the role of liminal spectator. Yet the challenge is to resist hegemonic formations such as these and develop a subaltern historiography, where the lives of those relegated to the margins are explored. After all it was the unknown masses in the mass democratic movements in South Africa across the twentieth century who played anonymous, but pivotal or different roles in political struggles – alongside the Gandhis, Mandelas, Tambos, Kathradas and Sisulus. People like Granny are an important living and breathing archive that cannot be ignored. It is also necessary to explore how they script their lives; the way history, power and subalternity coalesce in their self-fashioning that makes them narrate their lives in particular ways.

During the rest of the twentieth century, South Africans of all race groups faced difficulties and challenges caused directly by apartheid legislation. Among these struggles was the fight for land and for homes, education and political rights. Granny tried hard to send both son and daughters to school, but regrets that she could not afford tertiary education for them. While the last century saw some of the most oppressive laws and practices in history, it also saw remarkable resistance. This resistance took the form of the formal opposition of the broad liberation front. It also saw the formation of strong community efforts for social upliftment and the sheer will and determination of countless ordinary individuals who struggled, survived and succeeded, in spite of apartheid. Granny did not participate in any political activism directly, but was aware of the many struggles being waged around her. Her story, like that of so many women, may be seen as a counter-narrative – or parallel narrative – of women's active participation in the liberation struggle in general and the passive resistance movements in particular. Yet, it is arguably no less valuable.

Indeed, Granny has been shaped by the forces of history as well as her own personal agency. Her story is a testimony of faith and belief in oneself, in one's dignity and intrinsic self-worth, in spite of systemic attempts to undermine this. When reading oppressed women's stories, postcolonial feminists have drawn attention to the multiple pressures on women's lives, and their resilience in overcoming adversity. At a time when women were 'doubly othered' – as woman and as colonized persons – we need to 'capture what is at stake in the practices of the self or agency in the contested margins of patriarchy, empire and nation'.[20] We must also not forget the existence of the hierarchies of caste, not to speak of class, that were inserted into South African Indian living. Indeed, Granny's story reveals the overriding compulsion to live life, not unaccommodated and bereft, but with beauty and truth, integrity and resilience. It is the story of so many women who have dedicated their lives to 'the making of a habitable world'.[21]

We need to appreciate that there are many faces of the Indian (or black) woman, across the historical span of the twentieth century, from indentured days to the present time. Many were not political or regarded as feminist; many were not professional women with formal training. Women of indentured stock, of the first generation, were largely labourers and combined manual work in the public space with their domestic duties. The second generation, such as Granny, lived very much in the footsteps of their mothers and grandmothers. Women like Granny straddled the traditional and the modern, and paved the way for the generations of women who took their place unambiguously in the public domain. It certainly does not help to develop a linear narrative of women's experiences and development; it is more helpful to consider the temporal and spatial differences.

Invariably, the political intersected with the personal, and their lives reflected this directly or indirectly. The tendency to speak of 'Indian identity' in monocultural – or even multicultural – terms, or any other identity for that matter, ignores the 'complexities in the cultural fabric that must be recognized if we are to approach the elusive nature of an identity that emerges in the margin, and understand the tension between public and private realities that undergirds women's lives'[22] at different times in history. Undoubtedly, for many women, especially our mothers and grandmothers, selfhood and subjectivity were shaped by and negotiated within an unquestioned patriarchal mould. Yet this does not deny the independence that was constantly struggled over and won.

Senthamani Govender joined the winding queues to cast her vote in 1994 in the first democratic elections in the land of her birth. She was seventy-one at the time, and now remarks that she has not missed voting on successive election days. At the age of ninety-seven, she remains a serene woman, thankful for a blessed life. Her name, which she noticed is pronounced 'Shanthamani' in India, means peace and calm. Her hope for the future is that there will be peace and calm, and that the country and the rest of the world will be free from fear.

Notes

1. Meera Kosambi, 'Introduction: Returning the American Gaze – Pandita Ramabai's "The People of the United States"', in *Pandita Ramabai's American Encounter: The Peoples of the United States (1889)*, trans. and ed. Meera Kosambi (Delhi: Permanent Black, 2003), 5.
2. *Twentieth Century Impressions of Natal: Its People, Commerce, Industries, and Resources* (Natal: Lloyd's Greater Britain Publishing Company), 1906.
3. Brij Lal, 'Girmit, History, Memory' in *Bittersweet: The Indo-Fijian Experience*, ed. Brij Lal (Canberra: Pandanus Books, 2004), 3–17.
4. Hershini Bhana Young, *Illegible Will – Coercive Spectacles of Labor in South Africa and The Diaspora* (Durham and London: Duke University Press, 2017), 183.
5. Gaiutra Bahadur, *Coolie Woman: The Odyssey of Indenture* (Johannesburg: Jacana Media, 2014).
6. Gaiutra Bahadur, 'How could I write about women whose existence is barely acknowledged'? *The Guardian*, 14 June 2016. Bahadur notes here that she was influenced by Christopher Barthelme's 'Concerning the Bodyguard', composed mainly through questions. He had heard Salman Rushdie read the short story.
7. Jacob Dlamini, *Native Nostalgia* (Johannesburg: Jacana Media, 2009), 163.
8. Kasavelu Goonam, *Coolie Doctor – An Autobiography* (Durban: Mabida Press, 1990).
9. Goolam Vahed, Ashwin Desai and Thembisa Waetjen, *Many Lives – 150 Years of Being Indian in South Africa* (Pietermaritzburg: Shuter and Shooter, 2010), 182.

10 In apartheid South Africa all races that were not Caucasian were referred to as 'non-whites'. In this chapter I refer collectively to all non-whites as 'blacks' to include African, Indian, Chinese and mixed race
11 Maheshvari Naidu, 'Glaring Invisibility – Dressing the Body of the Female Cleaner' *Anthropology Southern Africa* 32 nos. 3, 4 (2009): 128–138.
12 Devarakshanam Govinden, *Sister Outsiders – Representation of Identity and Difference in Selected Writings by South African Indian Women* (Pretoria: University of South Africa, 2008).
13 Dlamini, *Native Nostalgia*, 18–19.
14 Miriam F. Polster, *Eve's Daughters – The Forbidden Heroism of Women* (San Francisco: Jossey-Bass, 1992), 9.
15 Richard Pithouse, 'Shifting the Ground of Reason' in *Re-imagining the Social in South Africa – Critique, Theory and Post-Apartheid Society*, ed. Heather Jacklin and Peter Vale (Scottsville: University of KwaZulu-Natal Press, 2009), 141–176.
16 Jon Soske, 'Navigating Difference: Gender, Miscegenation and Indian Domestic Space in Twentieth-Century Durban' in *Eyes across the Water – Navigating the Indian Ocean*, eds. Pamila Gupta, Isabel Hofmeyr and Michael Pearson (Pretoria: Unisa Press, 2010), 197–219.
17 Antoinette Burton, *Dwelling in the Archive – Women Writing House, Home and History in Late Colonial India* (Oxford: Oxford University Press, 2003).
18 See Devi Rajab, *Women – South Africans of Indian Origin* (Johannesburg: Jacana, 2011).
19 See Riason Naidoo, *The Indian in Drum Magazine in the 1950's* (Cape Town: Bell-Roberts Publishing, 2008).
20 Susie Tharu and K. Lalita, 'Preface' in *Women Writing in India 600 B.C. to the Present, Vol. 1:600 B.C. to the Early 20th Century*, ed. Susie Tharu and K. Lalita (New York: Feminist Press, 1991), xvii.
21 Tharu, Susie and K. Lalita, 'Introduction', in *Women Writing in India*, 36.
22 Tharu, Susie and K. Lalita, 'Preface', in *Women Writing in India*, xix.

Epilogue: Ocean currents and wayward crossings

Renisa Mawani

In *Wayward Lives, Beautiful Experiments*, Saidiya Hartman explores the intimate lives created by Black women in turn-of-the-twentieth-century New York City and Philadelphia. Tracing their movements through streets and alleys, tenement housing, courtrooms and chorus lines, Hartman offers a glimpse into other worlds, where Black women actively made lives for themselves finding joy and pleasure at a historical moment in which Blackness continued to be pathologized and criminalized by state racism. Through close narration and counter-readings, Hartman invites readers into the alternative forms of intimacy, labour, and sociality that these women carved out, and the myriad laws and regulations they defied in the process. Waywardness, as Hartman formulates it, encompassed subversive acts as well as radical imaginaries. Take the example of Mattie Nelson. 'Mattie was desperate not to be a servant or drudge, but there was no ready blueprint for another life that she could follow besides the one she crafted, an inchoate plan and radical thought in deed were her resources'.[1] Through defiance, imagination and experimentation Mattie and her contemporaries recreated spaces in the city where they improvised different lives.

As the subtitle suggests – *Labour, Law and Wayward Lives* – this volume pays homage to Hartman's book. Whereas Hartman's focus is on Black women and the intimacies and kinship they crafted in the racially hostile environs of New York City and Philadelphia, the current volume traces labour, law and life in South Asian histories of migration. Hartman works on micro-scales, suturing biographical and historical detail to create a counter-narrative of the

---

Many thanks to Neilesh Bose for the invitation, Antoinette Burton for invaluable comments on an earlier draft, and Hardeep Dhillon for conversations that informed and shaped the title.

city. The contributors to this book, by contrast, write in broader scales and wider registers. Some contributors explore the journeys of Indian migrants – indentures, labourers, revolutionaries – others explore South Asian migration as global and comparative history. Read together, authors sketch the movements of South Asian men, and in some cases women, across imperial and national boundaries and over a critical 100-year period, from the 1860s to the 1960s, as the British Empire began its decline and as India struggled for and achieved formal independence. Indian migrants – including Taraknath Das and S.P. Khankoje – see Bose and Carrusco, this volume – were branded as radicals, challenging immigration regulations, allegedly plotting revolution and defying racial borders both within and beyond territories under British control.

In this epilogue, I reflect on how waywardness might invite new methods and approaches in South Asian migration, particularly as global and comparative history. 'Waywardness', as Hartman defines it 'is a practice of possibility at a time when all roads, except the ones created by smashing out, are foreclosed. It obeys no rules and abides no authorities. It is unrepentant. It traffics in occult visions of other worlds and dreams of a different kind of life'.[2] The politics of waywardness, as she describes it here, resonate with the journeys of Indian migrants. Men, and later women, departed on ships, crossed the *Kala Pani* and travelled to unknown places in search of new worlds and other futures. To be sure, these journeys demanded courage, determination and imagination, including different conceptions of home. Some Indian migration was coerced and forced, as the case of indentured labourer makes clear. But even those Indians that were considered 'free' were compelled to leave the subcontinent – in pursuit of education, employment and fortune – and in search of liveable lives. By the first decade of the twentieth century, and as they searched for other worlds, South Asian migrants confronted racially exclusionary laws and policies in territories under British control, most notably, though not exclusively, the white Dominions.[3]

Certainly, Indian migrants defied laws and created different futures other than the ones planned for them by the Indian colonial state. In Hartman's terms, they were indeed wayward. This is an insight that many have made, albeit drawing on different terms.[4] As I read it, the most promising aspects of placing *Wayward Lives* in conversation with histories of South Asian migration may be conceptual and methodological. In 'A Note on Method', which opens the book, Hartman offers some useful insights into her orientation and approach. Here, she clarifies that the rich and sensory accounts of Black urban life that she composes are not fictional. The 'cast of characters are real people', Hartman explains, their lives pieced together through a composite of photographs, police files, court records, newspapers and other state documents. Notwithstanding the inherent biases of official records, Hartman reads these in generative ways that present Black women as radical thinkers and wilful historical actors. The gaps and silences of official records and archives, she notes, are part of a much larger methodological problem: 'Every historian of the multitude, the dispossessed, the subaltern, and the enslaved is forced to grapple with the power and authority of the archive and the limits it sets on what can be known, whose perspective matters, and who is endowed with the gravity and authority of historical actor'.[5] Through waywardness, Hartman challenges us to think harder not only about sources but also our modes of reading and writing counter-histories of movement and subversion through critical imagination.

Recently, several scholars have pursued biographical writing, forgotten archives and innovative methods in South Asian histories of migration. Gaiutra Bahadur's *Coolie Woman: The Odyssey of Indenture* and Samia Khatun's *Australianama: The South Asian Odyssey in Australia* are two cases in point.[6] Focused on different places in the British Empire and on overlapping historical periods, Bahadur and Khatun draw on 'odyssey' – rather than 'wayward' – to track the ocean crossings and land-based movements of South Asian migrants. Despite their different objectives, styles and orientations, both break from the male dominated field of South Asian migration history and 'the masculinist assumptions that too often belies the field of Indian Ocean studies' to trace the intimacies of labour, law and life.[7] Bahadur's objectives are explicitly biographical. She enters the colonial archives in search of her great-grandmother, Sujaria, a high-caste Hindu who boarded the steamship *Clyde* in 1903 and gave birth to a son en route to the sugar plantations in British Guiana. Bahadur's pursuit for her great-grandmother introduces readers to a tumultuous world of gendered loss and violence. But by centering the lives of 'coolie women' she foregrounds their many acts of defiance, large and small. 'Sujaria had the most to lose by crossing the Indian Ocean', Bahadur writes. 'This was a forbidden passage, especially for a woman, especially for a Brahmin, and most especially for a Brahmin woman travelling without a male relative'.[8] The odyssey of indenture that she narrates through Sujaria's wayward crossing invites exciting ways to study histories of South Asian migration in global and comparative registers.

Khatun's *Australianama* also begins in a biographical key. In her quest for what appears to be a Bengali translation of a Quran in the nineteenth-century Australian interior, Khatun ends up charting a different course and with it a forgotten history. Drawing on non-English sources and oral accounts, she unearths the intertwined routes of South Asian and Indigenous labourers, traders and travellers along the Indian Ocean and into the Australian interior. Khatun skilfully weaves her family history of migration into the textures of her book. Her primary objective is to move away from conventional histories of Australia as a nation of British immigrants and more recently of multiculturalism, and instead to foreground a nation that emerged through entangled and intimate encounters between Indigenous peoples and Muslim traders and merchants. One of her 'most surprising discoveries was that the richest accounts of South Asians [in Australia] were in some of the Aboriginal languages spoken in Australian desert parts'.[9] Notwithstanding Khatun's interests in trains, camels and sand, the Indian Ocean features prominently. The mobilities and encounters that the ocean produced continue to exist in unexpected places. 'Today, in northern Australia', Khatun observes, '*rupiah* remains the word for "money" in Aboriginal languages spoken around Arnhem Land'.[10] These traces of South Asian travellers in Indigenous stories and languages highlight longer trade routes and encounters in Australia that have too often been eclipsed through violent myths of European discovery and settlement. These traces also remind us of the braided histories of mobility and dispossession that still need to be written.

In their respective works, Bahadur and Khatun draw different degrees of attention to the ship and the sea, and in so doing, open new points of convergence and comparison. Reading these texts together, we learn that Indian migrants, including women, travelled to lands that were already inhabited by Indigenous peoples. They were complicit in and also struggled against settler colonialism.[11] By tracing Sujaria's transoceanic passage aboard the *Clyde*, Bahadur situates the violence and coercion of Indian indenture alongside the horrors of the slave ship, speculating on their intersections and continuities. Indenture did not mark a clean break from slavery, she observes. 'Indenture vessels were, after all, crossing in the wake of slavers, with their well-documented horrors, from tragic mortality rates to the rape of women'.[12] For Khatun, the Indian Ocean enables other connections. It sits as 'an immense reservoir of knowledges' and a 'site of epistemic struggle' that extends further inland.[13] Tracking the stories, knowledges and texts that travelled with South Asian migrants, Khatun uncovers an Australia where the lives of Indigenous seafarers and labourers intersected, often intimately, with Muslim merchants and camel hands. For both Bahadur and Khatun, oceans and ocean crossings inform their rich historical accounts of South Asian migration and diaspora.

What would it mean to centre oceans and ocean currents in histories of South Asian migration? What kinds of global and comparative approaches could we pursue and develop by rethinking South Asian migration through oceanic registers? Reading Hartman with Bahadur and Khatun, I suggest here, opens innovative formulations of waywardness that might be pressed even further. Oceans, as I have argued elsewhere, are much more than sites and surfaces of travel. They offer dynamic methods of reading, writing and thinking along metaphorical and material registers. As vast, vigorous and ungovernable forces, oceans can redirect histories of Indian migration by drawing attention to the seaborne movement of ships, peoples and ideas, as well as the transnational – and global – forms of struggle they made possible.[14] Thinking with oceans opens connections between seemingly discrepant geographies and histories, inviting ways to analyse transatlantic slavery, Indigenous struggles against dispossession, Indian indenture and so-called 'free' migration within the same analytic frame.[15] The shifting intensities and instabilities produced by ocean currents already inhere within waywardness. For Hartman, wayward is 'related to the family of words: errant, fugitive, recalcitrant, anarchic, willful, reckless, troublesome, riotous, tumultuous, rebellious, and wild'.[16] These characteristics were routinely ascribed to Black women, Hartman reminds us, but they were also the properties of oceans, and those (un)authorized to cross them: Black sailors, lascars and non-European merchants. For many Indian migrants and travellers, oceans inspired global radical imaginaries of freedom from British imperial rule.[17] Thus, waywardness, as Hartman elucidates, is already oceanic. It 'articulates the paradox of cramped creation, the entanglement of escape and confinement, flight and captivity'. Waywardness, she continues, is 'to wander, to be unmoored, adrift, rambling, roving, cruising, strolling, and seeking'.[18] These words, with their aqueous resonances, hold promise and offer direction for charting South Asian migration as global and comparative history.

Notes

1. Saidiya Hartman, *Wayward Lives, Beautiful Experiments: Intimate Histories of Social Upheaval* (New York: W.W. Norton & Company, 2019), 60.
2. Hartman, *Wayward Lives*, 228.
3. See Marilyn Lake and Henry Reynolds, *Drawing the Global Colour Line: White Men's Countries and the International Challenge of Racial Equality* (Cambridge: Cambridge University Press, 2012).
4. See, for example, the case of *Ghadrs* and South Asian migrants associated with them. Kornel Chang, *Pacific Connections: The Making of the U.S. Canada*

Borderlands (Berkeley: University of California Press, 2012), especially chapter 4; Maia Ramnath, *From Haj to Utopia: How the Ghadr Movement Charted Global Radicalism and Attempted to Overthrow the British Empire* (Berkeley: University of California Press, 2011).
5 Hartman, *Wayward Lives*, xiii.
6 Gaiutra Bahadur, *Coolie Woman: The Odyssey of Indenture* (Chicago: University of Chicago Press, 2014); Samia Khatun, *Australianama: The South Asian Odyssey in Australia* (Oxford: Oxford University Press, 2018).
7 Khatun, *Australianama*, 25.
8 Bahadur, *Coolie Woman*, 21.
9 Khatun, *Australianama*, 3.
10 Ibid., 20.
11 Bahadur doesn't discuss Indigenous peoples in Guyana. On the politics of Indigeneity in Guyana see Shona Jackson, *Creole Indigeneity: Between Myth and Nation in the Caribbean* (Minneapolis: University of Minnesota Press, 2012). On Indigeneity and Indian migration see Renisa Mawani, *Across Oceans of Law: The Komagata Maru and Jurisdiction in the Time of Empire* (Durham: Duke University Press, 2018), especially chapter 4.
12 Bahadur, *Coolie Woman*, 50.
13 Khatun, *Australianama*, 21.
14 Some of these ideas are further developed in Renisa Mawani and Iza Hussin, 'The Travels of Law: Indian Ocean Itineraries' *Law and History Review* 32, no. 4 (2014): 733–747.
15 On 'oceans as method' see Mawani, *Across Oceans of Law* 8, 20–26.
16 Hartman, *Wayward Lives*, 227.
17 I make this argument with respect to Husain Rahim and Gurdit Singh. See Mawani, *Across Oceans of Law*, especially epilogue.
18 Hartman, *Wayward Lives*, 227.

Select bibliography

About, Ilsen, James Brown and Gayle Lonergan, eds. *Identification and Registration Practices in Transnational Perspective: People, Papers and Practices*. Basingstoke: Palgrave Macmillan, 2013.

Ahuja, Ravi. 'Mobility and Containment: The Voyages of South Asian Seamen, c. 1900–1960'. In *Coolies, Capital, and Colonialism: Studies in Indian Labour History*, edited by Rana Behal and Marcel van der Linden, 111–141. Cambridge: Cambridge University Press, 2006.

Aiyar, Sana. *Indians in Kenya: The Politics of Diaspora*. Cambridge, MA: Cambridge University Press, 2015.

Alexander, Clarie, Joya Chatterji and Annu Jalais. *The Bengal Diaspora: Rethinking Muslim Migration*. New York: Routledge, 2015.

Allen, Richard B. *European Slave Trading in the Indian Ocean, 1500–1850*. Athens, OH: Ohio University Press, 2014.

Allen, Richard B. 'Reconceptualizing the "New System of Slavery"'. *Man in India* 92, no. 2 (2012): 225–245.

Allen, Richard B. *Slaves, Freedmen, and Indentured Laborers in Colonial Mauritius*. Cambridge: Cambridge University Press, 1999.

Ali, Omar. *Malik Ambar: Power and Slavery across the Indian Ocean*. New York: Oxford University Press, 2016.

Alonso, Isabel Huajaca. 'M.N. Roy and the Mexican Revolution: How a Militant Indian Nationalist Became an International Communist'. *South Asia: Journal of South Asian Studies* 40, no. 3 (May 2017): 517–530.

Amrith, Sunil. 'Empires, Diasporas and Cultural Circulation'. In *Writing Imperial Histories*, edited by Andrew Thompson, 216–239. Manchester: Manchester University Press, 2013.

Amrith, Sunil. *Crossing the Bay of Bengal: The Furies of Nature and the Fortunes of Migrants*. Cambridge, MA: Harvard University Press, 2013.

Amrith, Sunil. *Migration and Diaspora in Modern Asia*. New York: Cambridge University Press, 2011.

Anderson, Clare. *Subaltern Lives: Biographies of Colonialism in the Indian Ocean World*. Cambridge: Cambridge University Press, 2012.

Anderson, Clare. 'Convicts and Coolies: Rethinking Indentured Labour in the Nineteenth Century'. *Slavery and Abolition: A Journal of Slave and Post-Slave Studies* 30, no. 1 (2009): 93–109.

Anderson, Clare. *Convicts in the Indian Ocean: Transportation from South Asia to Mauritius, 1815–53*. New York: St. Martin's, 2000.

Appadurai, Arjun. 'Globalization and the Rush to History'. *Global Perspectives* 1, no. 1 (2020): https://doi.org/10.1525/001c.11656.

Anderson, Michael. 'India, 1858 – 1930: The Illusion of Free Labour'. In *Masters, Servants and Magistrates in Britain and the Empire, 1562–1955*, edited by Douglas Hay and Paul Craven, 422–454. Chapel Hill and London: University of North Carolina Press, 2004.

Andrade, Tonio. 'A Chinese Farmer, Two African Boys, and a Warlord: Toward a Global Microhistory'. *Journal of World History* 21, no. 4 (December 2010): 573–591.

Andrews, C.F. and W.W. Pearson. *Report on indentured labour in Fiji: an independent enquiry*. Calcutta: Star Printing, 1916.

Arasaratnam, S. *Indians in Malaysia and Singapore*. London: Oxford University Press Institute for Race Relations, 1970.

Aurora, G.S. *The New Frontiersman: Indians in Great Britain*. Bombay: Popular Prakashan, 1976.

Bahadur, Gaiutra. *Coolie Woman: The Odyssey of Indenture*. Chicago: University of Chicago Press, 2013.

Bahadur, Gaiutra. 'Conjure Women and Coolie Women'. *Small Axe* 22, no. 2 (2018): 244–253.

Bahadur, Gaiutra. 'How could I write about women whose existence is barely acknowledged?' *The Guardian*, 14 June 2016. https://www.theguardian.com/books/2016/jun/14/gaiutra-bahadurindentured-female-labourers-coolie-woman.

Bald, Vivek. *Bengali Harlem and the Lost Histories of South Asian America*. Cambridge, MA: Harvard University Press, 2012.

Bald, Vivek, Miabi Chatterji, Sujani Reddy and Manu Vimalassery, eds. *The Sun Never Sets: South Asian Migrants in an Age of U.S. Power*. New York: NYU Press, 2013.

Balachandran, G. 'Atlantic Paradigms and Aberrant Histories'. *Atlantic Studies* 111, no. 1 (2014): 47–63.

Balachandran, G. *Globalizing Labour? Indian Seafarers and World Shipping, c. 1870–1945*. Delhi: Oxford University Press, 2012.

Balachandran G. and Sanjay Subrahmanyam. 'On the History of Globalization and India: Concepts, Measures, and Debates'. In *Globalizing India: Perspectives from Below*, edited by Jackie Assayag and C.J. Fuller, 17–46. London: Anthem Press, 2005.

Balibar, Étienne. 'The Borders of Europe'. In *Cosmopolitics: Thinking and Feeling Beyond the Nation*, edited by Pheng Cheah and Bruce Robbins, 216–232. Minneapolis: University of Minnesota Press, 1998.

Bandyopadhyay, Sekhar and Jane Buckingham, eds. *Indians and the Antipodes: Networks, Boundaries, and Circulation*. Delhi: Oxford University Press, 2018.

Banerjee, Sukanya. *Becoming Imperial Citizens: Indians in the Late-Victorian Empire*. Durham, NC: Duke University Press, 2010.

Bartolf, Christian, ed. *Letter to a Hindu: Taraknath Das, Leo Tolstoi, and Mahatma Gandhi*. Berlin: Gandhi Information Zentrum, 1997.

Basu, Helene, ed. *Journeys and Dwellings: Indian Ocean Themes in South Asia*. Hyderabad: Orient Longman, 2008.

Bates, Crispin. 'Some Thoughts on the Representation and Misrepresentation of the Colonial South Asian Labour Diaspora'. *South Asian Studies* 33, 1 (2017): 7–22.

Bates, Crispin. 'Coerced and Migrant Labourers in India'. *Edinburgh Papers in South Asian Studies* 13 (2000): 2–33.

Bates, Crispin and Marina Carter. 'Sirdars as Intermediaries in Nineteenth Century Indian Ocean Indentured Labour Migration'. *Modern Asian Studies* 51, no. 2 (2017): 462–484.

Bates, Crispin and Marina Carter. 'Enslaving Life, Enslaving Labels: A New Approach to the Colonial Indian Labor Diaspora'. In *New Routes for Diaspora Studies*, edited by Sukanya Banerjee, Aims McGuiness and Steven C. McKay, 67–94. Bloomington, IN: Indiana University Press, 2007.

Bayly, C.A. *The Birth of the Modern World, 1780–1914: Global Connections and Comparisons*. Oxford: Blackwell, 2004.

Bayly, C.A. *Remaking the Modern World, 1900–2015*. Oxford: Blackwell, 2019.

Beckert, Sven and Dominic Sachsenmeier. 'Introduction'. In *Global History, Globally: Research and Practice around the World*, edited by Sven Beckert and Dominic Sachsenmeier, 1–18. London: Bloomsbury, 2018.

Becoming Coolies: Rethinking the Origins of the Indian Ocean Labour Diaspora, 1772–1920. http://www.coolitude.shca.ed.ac.uk/about-project.

Behal, Rana P. *One Hundred Years of Servitude: Political Economy of Tea Plantations in Colonial Assam*. New Delhi: Tulika Books, 2014.

Bertz, Ned. *Diaspora and Nation in the Indian Ocean: Transnational Histories of Race and Urban Space in Tanzania*. Honolulu, HI: University of Hawaii Press, 2015.

Bhana, Surendra. *Setting Down Roots: Indian Migrants in South Africa, 1860–1911*. Johannesburg: Witwatersrand University Press, 1990.

Bhana Young, Hershini. *Illegible Will – Coercive Spectacles of Labor in South Africa and The Diaspora*. Durham, NC: Duke University Press, 2017.

Bhatia, Sunil. *American Karma: Race, Culture, and Identity in the Indian Diaspora*. New York: NYU Press, 2007.

Bhattacharya, Neeladri. *The Great Agrarian Conquest: The Colonial Reshaping of a Rural World*. Delhi: Permanent Black, 2018.

Bishara, Fahad. *A Sea of Debt: Law and Economic Life in the Western Indian Ocean, 1780–1950*. Cambridge: Cambridge University Press, 2017.

Boehmer, Elleke. *Indian Arrivals 1870–1915: Networks of British Empire*. Oxford: Oxford University Press, 2015.

Boehmer, Elleke. *Empire, the National, and the Postcolonial, 1890–1920. Resistance in Interaction*. New York: Oxford University Press, 2002.

Bose, Neilesh, ed. *Beyond Bollywood and Broadway: Plays from the South Asian Diaspora*. Bloomington, IN: Indiana University Press, 2009.

Bose, Sugata and Ayesha Jalal, eds. *Oceanic Islam: Muslim Universalism and European Imperialism*. London: Bloomsbury, 2020.

Bose, Sugata. *A Hundred Horizons: The Indian Ocean in an Age of Global Empire*. Cambridge, MA: Harvard University Press, 2006.

Breckenridge, Keith. *Biometric State: The Global Politics of Identification and Surveillance in South Africa, 1850 to the Present*. Cambridge: Cambridge University Press, 2014.

Breckenridge, Keith and Simon Szreter. *Registration and Recognition: Documenting the Person in World History*. Oxford: Oxford University Press, 2012.

Brettell Caroline B. and James F. Hollifield, eds. *Migration Theory: Talking Across Disciplines*. 3rd ed. New York: Routledge, 2015.

Brookes, Edgar Harry and Colin de B. Webb. *A History of Natal*. Pietermaritzburg: University of Natal Press, 1965.

Brown, Emily C. *Har Dayal: Hindu Revolutionary and Rationalist*. Tucson: University of Arizona Press, 1975.

Brown, Wendy. *States of Injury: Power and Freedom in Late Modernity*. Princeton: Princeton University Press, 1995.

Browne, Simone. 'Race and Surveillance'. In *Routledge Handbook of Surveillance Studies*, edited by Kirstie Ball, Kevin D. Haggerty and David Lyon, 72–80. New York: Routledge, 2012.

Buchigani, Norman, Doreen Marie Indra and Ram Srivastava. *Continuous Journey: A Social History of South Asians in Canada*. Toronto: McClelland and Stewart, 1985.

Burton, Antoinette. *Dwelling in the Archive – Women Writing House, Home and History in Late Colonial India*. Oxford: Oxford University Press, 2003.

Campbell, Gwyn, ed. *The Structure of Slavery in Indian Ocean Africa and Asia*. London: Frank Cass, 2003.

Campbell, Gwyn, ed. *Abolition and its Aftermath in Indian Ocean Asia and Africa*. New York: Routledge, 2005.

Caplan, Jane and John Torpey, eds. *Documenting Individual Identity: The Development of State Practices in the Modern World*. Princeton: Princeton University Press, 2001.

Carter, Marina. *Servants, Sirdars and Settlers: Indians in Mauritius, 1834–1874*. Delhi: Oxford University Press, 1995.

Carter, Marina. *Lakshmi's Legacy: The Testimonies of Indian Women in 19th Century Mauritius*. Stanley Hill: Edition de l'ocean Indien, 1994.

Carter, Marina and Khal Torabully. *Coolitude: An Anthology of the Indian Labour Diaspora*. London: Anthem, 2002.

Castles, Stephen, Hein De Haas and Mark J. Miller. *The Age of Migration: International Population Movements in Modern World*. 5th ed. New York: The Guilford Press, 2013.

Chakravarti, Ananya. 'Mapping "Gabriel": Space, Identity and Slavery in the Late Sixteenth-Century Indian Ocean'. *Past & Present* 243, no. 1 (May 2019): 5–34.

Chakravarti, N.R. *The Indian Minority in Burma*. London: Oxford University Press Institute for Race Relations, 1971.

Chanderbali, David. *Indian Indenture in the Straits Settlements*. Leeds: Peepal Tree Press, 2008.

Chatterjee, Indrani. 'Abolition by Denial: The South Asian Example'. In *Abolition and its Aftermath in Indian Ocean Africa and Asia*, edited by Gwyn Campbell, 150–168. New York: Routledge, 2005.

Chatterjee, Indrani. 'The Locked Box in Slavery and Social Death'. In *On Human Bondage: After Slavery and Social Death*, edited by John Bodel and Walter Scheidel, 151–166. Boston: Wiley-Blackwell, 2016.

Chatterji, Joya. 'On Being Stuck in Bengal: Immobility in the "Age of Migration"'. *Modern Asian Studies* 51, no. 2 (2017): 511–541.

Chatterji, Joya. 'Dispositions and Destinations: Refugee Agency and "Mobility Capital" in the Bengal Diaspora, 1947–2007'. *Comparative Studies in Society and History* 55, no. 2 (2013): 273–304.

Chatterji, Joya and David Washbrook, eds. *Routledge Handbook of the South Asian Diaspora*. New York: Routledge, 2013.

Chaudhuri, K. N. *Trade and Civilisation in the Indian Ocean: An Economic History from the Rise of Islam to 1750*. Cambridge: Cambridge University Press, 1985.

Chaudhuri, K. N. *Asia Before Europe: Economy and Civilisation of the Indian Ocean from the Rise of Islam to 1750*. Cambridge: Cambridge University Press, 1990.

Chakrabarty, Dipesh 'The Muddle of Modernity'. *American Historical Review* 116, no. 3 (June 2011): 663–675.

Chakrabarty, Dipesh *Rethinking Working Class History: Bengal 1890 to 1940*. Princeton, NJ: Princeton University Press, 1989.

Chakravarti, N.R. *The Indian Minority in Burma: The Rise and Decline of an Immigrant Community*. London: Oxford University Press, 1971.

Chakravorty, Sanjoy, Devesh Kapur, and Nirvikar Singh, *The Other One Percent: Indians in America*. New York: Oxford University Press, 2017.

Chang, Jason Oliver. *Chino: Anti-Chinese Racism in Mexico, 1880–1940*. Chicago: University of Illinois Press, 2017.

Chang, Kornel. *Pacific Connections: The Making of the U.S. Canada Borderlands*. Berkeley: University of California Press, 2012.

Clarence-Smith, William Gervase, ed. *The Economics of the Indian Ocean Slave Trade*. London and New York: Routledge, 1989.

Clarke, Colin, Ceri Peach, and Steven Vertovec, eds. *South Asians overseas: migration and ethnicity*. New York: Cambridge University Press, 1990.

Cole, Peter, David Struthers and Kenyon Zimmer, eds. *Wobblies of the world*. London: Pluto Press, 2018.

Coolitude Project. http://www.rajivmohabir.com/coolitude-project.

Cooper, Frederick. *Citizenship, Inequality and Difference: Historical Perspectives*. Princeton: Princeton University Press, 2018.

Corley, T.A.B. *A History of the Burmah Oil Company, 1886–1924*. London: Heinemann, 1983.

Cumpston, Ina. *Indians Overseas in British Territories, 1834–1854*. London: Dawsons of Pall Mall, 1969.

Curthoys, Ann and Marilyn Lake, eds. *Connected Worlds: History in Transnational Perspective*. Canberra: ANU E Press, 2005.

Das, Rajani Kanta Das. *Hindusthanee Workers on the Pacific Coast*. Berlin: DeGruyter, 1923.

Das, Ranendranath. *Taraknath Das—Ein Lebensbild des indischen Revolutionärs, Freiheitskämpfers und Gelehrten*. Berlin: Taraknath Das-Stiftung, 1996.

Dasgupta, Ashin. *Merchants of Maritime India, 1500–1800*. Aldershot: Ashgate, 1994.

Dasgupta, Uma. *The World of the Indian Ocean Merchant, 1500–1800: Collected Essays of Ashin Dasgupta*. Delhi: Oxford University Press, 2001.

Deacon, Desley, Penny Russell and Angela Woollacott, eds. *Transnational Lives: Biographies of Global Modernity, 1700–present*. Basingstoke: Palgrave Macmillan, 2010.

Desai, Ashwin and Goolam Vahed. *The South African Gandhi: Stretcher Bearer of Empire*. Stanford, CA: Stanford University Press, 2016.

Desai, Ashwin and Goolam Vahed. *Inside Indian Indenture. A South African Story 1860–1911*. Cape Town: HSRC Press, 2010.

Desai, Gaurav. *Commerce with the Universe: Africa, India, and the Afrasian Imagination*. New York: Columbia University Press, 2013.

Dhamoon, Rita, Davina Bhandar, Renisa Mawani and Satwinder Kaur Bains, eds. *Unmooring the Komagata Maru: Charting Colonial Trajectories*. Vancouver: UBC Press, 2019.

Dhupelia-Mesthrie, Uma. 'The Desirable and Undesirable in the Life of the Chief immigration Officer in Cape Town, Clarence Wilfred Cousins, 1905–1915'. *Itinerario* 42, no. 1 (2018): 50–66.

Dhupelia-Mesthrie, Uma. 'Betwixt the Oceans: The Chief Immigration Officer in Cape Town, Clarence Wilfred Cousins (1905–1915)'. *Journal of Southern African Studies* 42, no. 3 (2016): 463–481.

Dhupelia-Mesthrie, Uma. 'False Fathers and False Sons: Immigration Officials in Cape Town, Documents and Verifying Minor Sons from India in the First Half of the Twentieth Century'. *Kronos* 40 (2014): 99–132.

Dhupelia-Mesthrie, Uma. 'Split-Households: Indian Wives, Cape Town Husbands and Immigration Laws, 1900s to 1940s'. *South African Historical Journal* 66, no. 4 (2014): 635–655.

Dhupelia-Mesthrie, Uma. 'The Form, the Permit and the Photograph: An Archive of Mobility between South Africa and India'. *Journal of Asian and African Studies* 46, no. 6 (2011): 650–662.

Dhupelia-Mesthrie, Uma. 'The Passenger Indian as Worker: Indian Immigrants in Cape Town in the Early Twentieth Century'. *African Studies* 68, no. 1 (2009): 111–134.

Dhupelia-Mesthrie, Uma and Margaret Allen. 'Controlling Transnational Asian Mobilities: a Comparison of Documentary Systems in Australia and South Africa, 1890s to 1940s'. In *Making Surveillance States: Transnational Histories*, edited by Robert Heynen and Emily van der Meulen, 133–162. Toronto: University of Toronto Press, 2019.

Dlamini, Jacob. *Native Nostalgia*. Johannesburg: Jacana Media, 2009.

Dobbin, Christine. *Asian Entrepreneurial Minorities: Conjoint Communities in the Making of the World Economy, 1570–1940*. Abingdon: Routledge Curzon, 1996.

Falzon, Mark-Anthony. *Cosmopolitan Connections: The Sindhi Diaspora, 1860–2000*. Leiden: Brill, 2004.

Fisher, Michael. *Counterflows to Colonialism: Indian Travelers and Settlers in Britain, 1600–1857*. Delhi: Permanent Black, 2004.

Fischer-Tine, Harald. *Shyamji Krishnavarma: Sanskrit, Sociology, and Anti-Imperialism*. Delhi: Routledge, 2014.

Fischer-Tine, Harald and Carolien Stolte. 'Imagining Asia in India: Nationalism and Internationalism (ca. 1905–1940)'. *Comparative Studies in Society and History* 54, no. 1 (2012): 65–92.

Gabbacia, Donna and Dirk Hoerder, eds. *Connecting Seas and Connected Ocean Rims Indian, Atlantic, and Pacific Oceans and China Seas Migrations from the 1830s to the 1930s*. Leiden: Brill, 2011.

Gamsa, Mark. 'Biography and (Global) Microhistory'. *New Global Studies* 11, no. 3 (2017): 231–241.

Gandhi, Mohandas K. *Collected Works of Mahatma Gandhi*. 98 volumes. New Delhi: Publications Division, Government of India, 1999.

Gandhi, Mohandas K. *Satyagraha in South Africa*. Ahmedabad: Navajivan Publishing House, 1950.

Gardner, Andrew. *City of Strangers: Gulf Migration and the Indian Community in Bahrain*. Ithaca, NY: Cornell University Press, 2010.

Gardner, Katy. *Global Migrants, Local Lives: Travel and Transformation in Rural Bangladesh*. New York: Oxford University Press, 1995.

Ghobrial, John-Paul A. 'The Secret Life of Elias of Babylon and the Uses of Global Microhistory'. *Past & Present* 222, no. 1 (February 2014): 51–93.

Gilly, Adolfo. *The Mexican Revolution*. New York: New Press, 2005.

Gleizer, Daniela y Paula Lopez Caballero, eds. *Nación y Alteridad. Mestizos, indígenas y extranjeros en el proceso de formación nacional*. México D.F.: UAM-Cuajimalpa, 2015.

Goonam, Kasavelu. *Coolie Doctor – An Autobiography*. Durban: Mabida Press, 1990.

Gorman, Daniel. *Imperial Citizenship: Empire and the Question of Belonging*. Manchester: University of Manchester Press, 2006.

Govinden, Devarakshanam. *Sister Outsiders: Representation of Identity and Difference in Selected Writings by South African Indian Women*. Pretoria: University of South Africa, 2008.

Green, Nile. *Bombay Islam: The Religious Economy of the West Indian Ocean, 1840–1915*. Cambridge: Cambridge University Press, 2011.

Green, Nile. 'Migrant Sufis and Sacred Space in South Asian Islam'. *Contemporary South Asia* 12, no. 4 (2003): 493–509.

Green, Nile. 'Islam for the Indentured Indian: A Muslim Missionary in Colonial South Africa'. *Bulletin of the School of Oriental and African Studies, University of London* 71, no. 3 (2008): 529–553.

Guha, Ramachandra. *Gandhi before India*. Delhi: Penguin India, 2013.

Gupta, Charu. '"Innocent" Victims/"Guilty" Migrants: Hindi Public Sphere, Caste and Indentured Women in Colonial North India'. *Modern Asian Studies* 49, no. 5 (2015): 1345–1377.

Gupta, Charu. 'Saving 'Wronged' Bodies: Caste, Indentured Women and Hindi Print-Public Sphere in Colonial India'. *Proceedings of the Indian History Congress* 75 (2014): 716–722.

Gupta, Pamila, Isabel Hofmeyr and Michael Pearson, eds. *Eyes across the Water: Navigating the Indian Ocean*. Pretoria: Unisa Press, 2010.

Hartman, Saidiya. *Wayward Lives, Beautiful Experiments: Intimate Histories of Social Upheaval*. New York: W.W. Norton & Co., 2019.

Hartman, Saidiya. 'Venus in Two Acts'. *Small Axe* 12, no. 2 (2008): 1–14.

Harzig, Christiane and Dirk Hoerder, with Donna Gabbaccia. *What is Migration History?* Cambridge: Polity, 2009.

Hatcher, Brian. *Hinduism before Reform*. Cambridge, MA: Harvard University Press, 2020.

Heatherton, Christina. 'University of Radicalism: Ricardo Flores Magón and Leavenworth Penitentiary'. *American Quarterly* 66, no. 3 (Fall 2014): 557–581.

Hedge, Radha Sarma and Ajaya Kumar Sahoo, eds. *Routledge Handbook of the Indian Diaspora*. New York: Routledge, 2017.

Heidemann, Frank. *Kanganies in Sri Lanka and Malaysia: Tamil Recruiter-cum-Foreman as a Sociological Category in the Nineteenth and Twentieth Centuries*. Munich: Anacon, 1992.

Hoerder, Dirk. *Cultures in Contact: World Migrations in the Second Millennium*. Durham, NC: Duke University Press, 2002.

Hofmeyr, Isabel. 'The Black Atlantic Meets the Indian Ocean: Forging New Paradigms of Transnationalism for the Global South – Literary and Cultural Perspectives'. *Social Dynamics* 33 (2007): 3–32.

Hofmeyr, Isabel and Michelle Williams, eds. *South Africa and India: Shaping the Global South*. Johannesburg: Wits University Press, 2011.

Hussain, Purba. 'Protests at the Colonial Capital: Calcutta and the Global Debates on Indenture, 1836–42'. *South Asian Studies* 33, no. 1 (2017): 37–51.

Huttenback, Robert. *Racism and Empire: White Settlers and Colored Immigrants in the British Self-Governing Colonies 1830–1910*. Cornell: Cornell University Press, 1976.

Hundle, Anneeth Kaur. 'The Politics of (In)security: Reconstructing African-Asian Relations, Citizenship and Community in Post-Expulsion Uganda'. PhD diss., University of Michigan, 2013.

Hundle, Anneeth Kaur. 'Unsettling Citizenship: Race, Security and Afro-Asian Politics in Contemporary Uganda'. Unpublished conference paper, University of Victoria, 27 October 2017.

Hyslop, Jonathan. 'Oceanic Mobility and Settler-Colonial Power: Policing the Global Maritime Force in Durban Harbour c. 1890–1910'. *The Journal of Transport History* 36, no. 2 (2015): 248–267.

Jacob, Wilson Chacko. *For God or Empire: Sayyid Fadl and the Indian Ocean World*. Stanford, CA: Stanford University Press, 2019.

Jacobs, Margaret. 'Seeing Like a Settler Colonial State'. *Modern American History* 1, no. 2 (2018): 257–270.

Jackson, Shona. *Creole Indigeneity: Between Myth and Nation in the Caribbean*. Minneapolis: University of Minnesota Press, 2012.

Jaffer, Aaron. *Lascars and Indian Ocean Seafaring, 1780–1860: Shipboard Life, Unrest, and Mutiny*. Rochester: Boydell Press, 2015.

Jalal, Ayesha. *Self and Sovereignty: Individual and Community in South Asian Islam Since 1850*. New York: Routledge, 2000.

Jayal, Niraja. *Citizenship and its Discontents: An Indian History*. Cambridge, MA: Harvard University Press, 2013.

Johnston, Hugh. *The Voyage of the Komagata Maru: The Sikh Challenge to Canada's Colour Bar*. Vancouver, BC: UBC Press, 1989.

Kale, Madhavi. *Fragments of Empire: Capital, Slavery, and Indentured Labor in the British Caribbean*. Philadelphia: University of Pennsylvania Press, 2010.

Kauanui, J. Kehaulani. '"A Structure, Not an Event": Settler Colonialism and Enduring Indigeneity'. *Lateral: A Journal of the Cultural Studies Association* 5, no. 1 (2016): https://doi.org/10.25158/L5.1.7

Kelly, John D. *A Politics of Virtue: Hinduism, Sexuality, and Countercolonial Discourse in Fiji*. Chicago: University of Chicago Press, 1991.

Ker, James Campbell. *Political Trouble in India, 1907–17*. Calcutta: Superintendent Government Printing, 1917.

Kerr, Ian J. 'On the Move: Circulating Labour in Pre-Colonial, Colonial, and Post-Colonial India'. *International Review of Social History* 51 (2006): 85–109.

Khatun, Samia. *Australianama: The South Asian Odyssey in Australia*. London: Hurst, 2018.

Knight, Alan. 'Racism, Revolution and *Indigenismo*: Mexico 1910–1940'. In *The Idea of Race in Latin America*, edited by Richard Graham, Thomas E. Skidmore, Aline Helg and Alan Knights, 71–114. Austin: University of Texas Press, 1990.

Kumar, Ashutosh. *Coolies of the Empire: Indentured Indians in the Sugar Colonies, 1830–1920*. Delhi: Cambridge University Press, 2017.

Kumar, Ashutosh. 'Feeding the Girmitiya: Food and Drinks on the Indentured Ships to the Sugar Colonies'. *Gastronomica: The Journal of Critical Food Studies* 16, no. 1 (Spring 2016): 41–52.

Kumar, Ashutosh. 'Songs of Abolition: The Anti-Indenture Campaign in North Indian Public sphere'. In *Indian Diaspora. Socio-Cultural and Religious Worlds*, edited by P. Pratap Kumar, 38–51. Leiden: Brill, 2015.

Lahiri, Shompa. *Indian Mobilities in the West, 1900–1947: Gender, Performance, Embodiment*. New York: Palgrave Macmillan, 2010.

Laidlaw, Zoe and Alan Lester, eds. *Indigenous Communities and Settler Colonialism: Land Holding, Loss, and Survival in an Interconnected World*. Basingstoke: Palgrave Macmillan, 2015.

Lake, Marilyn and Henry Reynolds, *Drawing the Global Colour Line: White Men's Countries and the International Challenge of Racial Equality*. Cambridge: Cambridge University Press, 2008.

Lal, Brij V. *Intersections: History, Memory, Discipline*. Canberra: ANU E Press, 2012.

Lal, Brij V. *Chalo Jahaji: On a Journey through Indenture through Fiji*. Canberra: ANU E Press, 2012.

Lal, Brij V. *Girmityas: The Origins of the Fiji Indians*. Lautoka, Fiji: Fiji Institute for Applied Studies, 2004.

Lal, Brij V. 'Girmit, History, Memory'. In *Bittersweet: The Indo-Fijian Experience*, edited by Brij Lal, 3–17. Canberra: Pandanus Books, 2004.

Lal, Brij V. 'East Indians in British Columbia, 1904–14: A Historical Study in Growth and Integration'. MA Thesis, University of British Columbia, 1976.

Lawrence, Bonita and Enakshi Dua. 'Decolonizing Racism'. *Social Justice* 32, no. 4 (2005): 120–43.

León, Artemio Cruz, Isabel Arline Duque P., and Marcelino Castro. 'La Investigación Agrícola al Aomento del Traslado de la Escuela Nacional de Agricultura de San Jacinto, D.F., a Chapingo, Estado de México, a través de las Publicaciones de Pandurang Khankhoje'. *Revista de Geografía Agrícola* no. 54 (enero-junio 2015): 49–59.

Levi, Scott. *The Indian Merchant Diaspora in Central Asia and its Trade, 1550–1900*. Leiden: Brill, 2002.

Longva, Anh Nga. *Walls Built on Sand: Migration, Exclusion, and Society in Kuwait*. Boulder, CO: Westview Press, 1997.

Lowe, Lisa. *The Intimacies of the Four Continents*. Durham, NC: Duke University Press, 2015.

Lubbock, Basil. *Coolie Ships and Oil Sailors*. Glasgow: Brown, Son & Ferguson, 1935.

Lucassen, Jan and Sabyasachi Bhattacharya, eds. *Workers in the Informal Sector: Studies in Labour History 1800–2000*. New Delhi: Macmillan India/SEPHIS, 2005.

Ludden, David. 'Presidential Address: Maps in the Mind and the Mobility of Asia'. *The Journal of Asian Studies* 62, no. 4 (November 2003): 1057–1078.

Ludden, David. 'Cowry Country: Mobile Space and Imperial Territory'. In *Asia Inside Out: Itinerant People*, edited by Eric Tagliacozzo, Peter Perdue and Helen F. Siu, 75–100. Cambridge, MA: Harvard University Press, 2019.

Machado, Pedro. *Ocean of Trade: South Asian Merchants, Africa and the Indian Ocean, c. 1750–1850*. Cambridge: Cambridge University Press, 2014.

Maclean, Kama. *British India, White Australia: Overseas Indians, inter-colonial relations, and the empire*. Sydney: UNSW Press, 2020.

Mahase, Radica. '"Abolish Indenture" and the Indian Nationalist discourse in the Early Twentieth Century'. In *Historical Diversities. Societies, Politics and Cultures. Essays for V.N. Datta*, edited by Kundan Tuteja and Sunitha Pathania, 1–21. Delhi: Manohar, 2008.

Maira, Sunaina. *Desis in the House: Indian American Youth Culture in New York City*. Philadelphia: Temple University Press, 2002.

Major, Andrea. *Slavery, Abolitionism and Empire in India, 1772-1843*. Liverpool: Liverpool University Press, 2012.

Manning, Patrick with Tiffany Trimmer. *Migration in World History*. 2nd ed. New York: Routledge, 2013.

Mangru, Basdeo. *The Elusive El Dorado: Essays on the Indian Experience in Guyana*. Lanham, MD: University Press of America, 2005.

Mangru, Basdeo. *Indenture and Abolition: Sacrifice and Survival on the Guyanese Sugar Plantations*. Toronto: TSAR Publications, 1993.

Mangru, Basdeo. *Benevolent Neutrality: Indian Government Policy and Labour Migration to British Guiana, 1854-1884*. Hertford: Hansib, 1987.

Mangru, Basdeo, ed. *Kanpur to Kolkata: Labour Recruitment for the Sugar Colonies*. Hertford: Hansib, 2014.

Mangru, Basdeo, ed. *Colonial Emigration from the Bengal Presidency*. Hertford: Hansib, 2014.

Manjapra, Kris. 'Queer Diasporic Practice of a Muslim Traveler: Syed Mujtaba Ali's *Chacha Kahini*'. In *How to Write the Global History of Knowledge-Making: Interaction, Circulation, and the Transgression of Cultural Difference*, edited by Johannes Feichtinger, Anil Bhatti and Cornelia Hulmbauer, 151-166. New York: Springer, 2020.

Manjapra, Kris. 'Plantation Dispossessions: The Global Travel of Agricultural Racial Capitalism'. In *American Capitalism: New Histories*, edited by Sven Beckert and Christine Desan, 361-387. New York: Columbia University Press, 2018.

Markovitz, Claude. 'Afterword: Stray Thoughts of a Historian on "Indian" or "South Asian" "Diaspora (s)"'. In *Global Indian Diasporas: Exploring Trajectories of Migration and Theory*, edited by Gijsbert Oonk, 263-272. Amsterdam: Amsteradam University Press, 2007.

Markovitz, Claude. *The Global World of Indian Merchants, 1750-1947: Traders of Sind from Bukhara to Panama*. Cambridge: Cambridge University Press, 2000.

Markovitz, Claude, Jacques Pouchepadass and Sanjay Subrahmanyam, eds., *Society and Circulation: Mobile People and Itinerant Cultures in South Asia, 1750-1950*. London: Anthem, 2006.

Martens, Jeremy C. *Empire and Asian Migration: Sovereignty, Immigration Restriction and Protest in the British Settler Colonies, 1888-1907*. Crawley: UWA Publishing, 2018.

Martens, Jeremy C. 'A Transnational History of Immigration Restriction: Natal and New South Wales, 1896-97'. *The Journal of Imperial and Commonwealth History* 34, no. 3 (2006): 323-344.

Martin, Philip L, Susan F. Martin and Patrick Weil. *Managing Migration: The Promise of Cooperation*. Oxford: Lexington Books, 2006.

Mathew, Johan. *Margins of the Market: Trafficking and Capitalism across the Arabian Sea*. Berkeley: University of California Press, 2016.

Mawani, Renisa. *Across Oceans of Law: The Komagata Maru and Jurisdiction in the Time of Empire*. Durham, NC: Duke University Press, 2018.

Mawani, Renisa and Iza Hussin. 'The Travels of Law: Indian Ocean Itineraries'. *Law and History Review* 32, no. 4 (2014): 733–747.

McKeown, Adam. *Melancholy Order: Asian Migration and the Globalization of Borders*. New York: Columbia University Press, 2011.

McKeown, Adam. 'Periodizing Globalization'. *History Workshop Journal* 63, no. 1 (March 2007): 218–230.

McKeown, Adam. 'Global Migration, 1846–1940'. *Journal of World History* 15, no. 2 (June 2004): 155–189.

Meer, Fatima, ed. *The South African Gandhi: An Abstract of the Speeches and Writings of M.K. Gandhi, 1893–1914*. Durban: Madiba Press, 1995.

Menon, Dilip. 'Walking on Water: Globalization and History'. *Global Perspectives* 1, no. 1 (2020): https://doi.org/10.1525/gp.2020.12176.

Menon, Dilip. 'Not just indentured labourers: Why India needs to revisit its pre-1947 history of migration'. https://scroll.in/article/856271/not-just-indentured-labourers-why-we-should-revisit-the-history-of-migration-from-pre-1947-india, accessed 16 January 2018.

Metcalf, Thomas R. *Imperial Connections: India in the Indian Ocean Arena*. Berkeley: University of California Press, 2008.

Metcalf, Barbara D. and Thomas R. Metcalf. *A Concise History of Modern India*. Cambridge: Cambridge University Press, 2001.

Mezzadra, Sandro and Brett Nielson. *Border as Method, or, the Multiplication of Labor*. Durham, NC: Duke University Press, 2013.

Mishra, Amit. 'Global Histories of Migration (s)'. In *Global History, Globally: Research and Practice around the World*, edited by Sven Beckert and Dominic Sachsenmeier, 195–214. London: Bloomsbury, 2018.

Mishra, Amit. 'Sardars, Kanganies and Maistries: Intermediaries in the Indian Labour Diaspora during the Colonial Period'. In *The History of Labour Intermediation: Institutions and Finding Employment in the Nineteenth and Early Twentieth Centuries*, edited by Sigrid Wadauer, Thomas Buchner and Alexander Mejstrik, 368–387. New York: Berghahn Books, 2014.

Mishra, Amit. 'Indian Indentured Labourers in Mauritius: Reassessing the "New System of Slavery" *vs* Free Labour Debate'. *Studies in History* 25, no. 2 (2010): 229–251.

Mohammed-Arif, Amminah. *Salaam America: South Asian Muslims in New York*. London: Anthem, 2002.

Mohapatra, Prabhu. 'Eurocentrism, Forced Labour, and Global Migration: A Critical Assessment'. *International Review of Social History* 52, no. 1 (2007): 110–115.

Mohapatra, Prabhu. 'Assam and the West Indies, 1860–1920: Immobilising Plantation Labour'. In *Masters, Servants and Magistrates in Britain and the Empire, 1562–1955*, edited by Douglas Hay and Paul Craven, 455–480. Chapel Hill and London: University of North Carolina Press, 2004.

Mongia, Radhika. *Indian Migration and Empire: A Colonial Genealogy of the Modern State*. Durham, NC: Duke University, 2018.

Mongia, Radhika. 'Historicizing State Sovereignty: Inequality and the Form of Equivalence'. *Comparative Studies in Society and History* 49, no. 2 (2007): 399–403.

Mongia, Radhika. 'Gender and the Historiography of Gandhian Satyagraha in South Africa'. *Gender & History* 18, no. 1 (2006): 130–149.

Mongia, Radhika. 'Impartial Regimes of Truth'. *Cultural Studies* 18, no. 5 (2004): 749–768.

Mukherjee, Tapan. *Taraknath Das: Life and Letters of a Revolutionary in Exile*. Kolkata: National Council of Education, 1998.

Naidoo, Riason. *The Indian in Drum Magazine in the 1950s*. Cape Town: Bell-Roberts Publishing, 2008.

Naidu, Maheshvari. 'Glaring Invisibility – Dressing the Body of the Female Cleaner'. *Anthropology Southern Africa* 32, nos. 3, 4 (2009): 128–138.

Neame, L.E. *The Asiatic Danger in the Colonies*. London: George Routledge & Sons, 1907.

Ngai, Mae. *Impossible Subjects: Illegal Aliens and the Making of Modern America*. Princeton: Princeton University Press, 2004.

Oonk, Gijsbert. *Settled Strangers: Asian Business Elites in East Africa*. New Delhi: Sage, 2013.

Oonk, Gijsbert. *The Karimjee Jivanjee Family: Merchant Princes of East Africa, 1800–2000*. Amsterdam: Pallas Publications, 2009.

Oonk, Gijsbert. 'South Asians in East Africa (1880–1920) with a Particular Focus on Zanzibar: Toward a Historical Explanation of Economic Success of a Middlemen Minority'. *African and Asian Studies* 5, no. 1 (2006): 57–90.

Osterhammel, Jürgen. *The Transformation of the World: A Global History of the Nineteenth Century*. Princeton: Princeton University Press, 2015.

Pachai, Bridglal. *The International Aspects of the South African Indian Question, 1860–1971*. Cape Town: C. Struik, 1971.

Pandita Ramabai's American Encounter: The Peoples of the United States (1889). Translated and edited by Meera Kosambi. Delhi: Permanent Black, 2003.

Patwardhan, R.P. and D.V. Ambekar, eds. *Speeches and Writings of Gopal Krishna Gokhale*. Vol. 1: Economic. New Delhi: Asia Publishing House, 1962.

Pearson, Michael. *The Indian Ocean*. New York: Routledge, 2003.

Peebles, Patrick. *The Plantation Tamils in Sri Lanka*. London: Leicester University Press, 2001.

Perkins, John H. *Geopolitics and the Green Revolution. Wheat, Genes, and the Cold War*. New York: Oxford University Press, 1997.

Pithouse, Richard. 'Shifting the Ground of Reason'. In *Re-imagining the Social in South Africa: Critique, Theory and Post-Apartheid Society*, edited by Heather Jacklin and Peter Vale, 141–176. Scottsville: University of KwaZulu-Natal Press, 2009.

Plaatje, Sol T. *Native Life in South Africa*. Johannesburg: Ravan Press, 1995 [1916].

Plowman, Erin Matthew. 'The British Intelligence Station in San Francisco during the First World War'. *Journal of Intelligence History* 12, no. 1 (2013): 1–20.

Polak. H.S.L. 'South African Reminiscences'. *Indian Review* (October 1926): 621–630.

Polak. H.S.L. *The Indians of South Africa: Helots within the Empire and how they are treated*. Madras: G.A. Natesan & Co., 1909.

Poros, Maritsa. *Modern Migrations: Gujarati Indian Networks in New York and London*. Stanford, CA: Stanford University Press, 2010.

Prakash, Gyan. *Bonded Labor: Genealogies of Labor Servitude in Colonial India*. Cambridge: Cambridge University Press, 1990.

Prashad, Vijay. *The Karma of Brown Folk*. Minneapolis: University of Minnesota Press, 2001.

Price, John. *Orienting Canada: Race, Empire, and the Transpacific*. Vancouver, BC: UBC Press, 2011.

Price, John. 'Canada, White Supremacy, and the Twinning of Empires'. *International Journal* 68, no. 4 (December 2013): 628–638.

Price, John. '"Orienting" the Empire: Mackenzie King and the Aftermath of the 1907 Race Riots'. *BC Studies* 156 (Winter 2007/08): 53–81.

Raat, William D. *Revoltosos: Mexico's Rebels in the United States, 1903–1923*. College Station: Texas A&M University Press, 1981.

Rajab, Devi Moodley and Ranjith Kally. *Women: South Africans of Indian Origin*. Johannesburg: Jacana, 2011.

Rajan, S. Irudaya, ed. *Governance and Labour Migration: India Migration Report 2010*. Delhi: Routledge, 2010.

Raman, Parvathi. 'Being Indian the South African Way: The Development of Indian Identity in 1940s Durban'. In *Rethinking Settler Colonialism. History and Memory in Australia, Canada, Aotearoa New Zealand and South Africa*, edited by A.E. Coombes, 193–208. Manchester: Manchester University Press, 2006.

Ramasamy, P. 'Labour Control and Labour Resistance in the Plantations of Colonial Malaya'. *Journal of Peasant Studies* 19 (1992): 87–105.

Ramaswamy, Vijaya, ed. *Migrations in Medieval and Early Colonial India*. New York: Routledge, 2016.

Ramnath, Maia. *From Haj to Utopia: How the Ghadr Movement charted Global Radicalism and attempted to overthrow the British Empire*. Berkeley: University of California Press, 2011.

Ray, Karen A. 'The Abolition of Indentured Emigration and the Politics of Indian Nationalism, 1894–1917'. Ph.D. diss., Department of History, McGill University, 1980.

Reddy, Movindri. *Social Movements and the Indian Diaspora*. New York: Routledge, 2016.

Redclift, Victoria. *Statelessness and Citizenship: Camps and the Creation of Political Space*. New York: Routledge, 2013.

Revel, Jacques, ed. *Jeux d'Echelle: La Micro-Analyse a l'Experience*. Paris: Editions EHESS, 1996.

Saha, Panchanan. *Emigration of Indian Labour, 1834–1900*. Delhi: People's Publishing House, 1970.

Sanadhya, Totaram. *Bhootlen Ki Katha: Girmit Ke Anubhav*, edited by Brij V. Lal, Yogendra Yadav and Ashutosh Kumar. Delhi: Rajkamal Prakashan, 2012.

Sandhu, K.S. *Indians in Malaya: Immigration and Settlement, 1786–1957*. Cambridge: Cambridge University Press, 1969.

Sarkar, Sumit. *Modern India, 1885–1947*. Delhi: Macmillan, 1983.

Sarup, Leela Gujadhar. *Indentured Labour, Slavery to Salvation: Colonial Emigration Acts, 1837–1932*. Kolkata: Aldrich, 2004.

Sawhney, Savitri. *I Shall Never Ask for Pardon. A Memoir of Pandurang Khankhoje*. Delhi: Penguin Books, 2005.

Scott, James C. *Seeing Like a State: How Certain Schemes to Improve the Human Condition have Failed*. New Haven: Yale University Press, 1998.

Sekula, Alan. 'The Body and the Archive'. In *The Contest of Meaning: Critical Histories of Photography*, edited by Richard Bolton, 343–389. Cambridge: MIT Press, 1992.

Sen, Satadru. *Benoy Kumar Sarkar: Restoring the Nation to the World*. Delhi: Routledge, 2015.

Shah, Nayan. *Stranger Intimacy: Contesting Race, Sexuality, and the Law in the North American West*. Berkeley, CA: University of California Press, 2012.

Sharma, Nandita and Cynthia Wright. 'Decolonizing Resistance, Challenging Colonial States'. *Social Justice* 35, no. 3 (2008–09): 120–38.

Shankar, Shobana. 'A Tale of Two Gandhis: Complicating Ghana's Indian Entanglements'. In *Afro-South Asian in the Global African Diaspora*, edited by Omar Ali, Kenneth X. Robbins, Beheroze Schroff and Jazmin Graces, forthcoming.

Shankar, Prabha Ravi. *G.A. Natesan and National Awakening*. New Delhi: Bibliophile South Asia, 2015.

Sharma, Jayeeta. *Empire's Garden: Assam and the Making of India*. Durham, NC: Duke University Press, 2011.

Sharma, Lalbihari. *1916 I Even Regret Night: Holy Songs of Demerara*. Trans. Rajiv Mohabir. Los Angeles: Kaya Press, 2018.

Sheriff, Abdul and Enseng Ho, eds. *The Indian Ocean: Oceanic Connections and the Creation of New Societies*. New York: Oxford University Press, 2014.

Shukla, Sandhya. *India Abroad: Diasporic Cultures of Postwar America and England*. Princeton: Princeton University Press, 2007.

Singh, Gadadhar. *Thirteen Months in China*. Ed. and trans. Anand Yang, Kamal Sheel and Ranjana Sheel. New York: Oxford University Press, 2017.

Singha, Radhika. *The Coolie's Great War: Indian Labor in a Global Conflict, 1914–1921*. Delhi: Oxford University Press, 2020.

Singha, Radhika. 'Finding Labor from India for the War in Iraq: The Jail Porter and Labor Corps, 1916–1920'. *Comparative Studies in Society and History* 49, no. 2 (2007): 412–445.

Sinha-Kerkhoff, Kathinka, Ellen Bal and Alok Deo Singh. *Autobiography of an Indian Indentured Labourer: Munshi Rahman Khan (1874–1972)*. Delhi: Shipra Publications, 2005.

Sinha, Mrinalini. 'Premonitions of the Past'. *The Journal of Asian Studies* 74, no. 4 (November 2015): 821–841.

Sinha, Mrinalini. 'Totaram Sanadhya's *Fiji Mein Mere Ekkis Varsh*: A History of Empire and Nation in a Minor Key'. In *Ten Books That Shaped the British Empire*, edited by Antoinette Burton and Isabel Hofmeyr, 168–189. Durham, NC: Duke University Press, 2014.

Sivasundaram, Sujit. 'The Indian Ocean'. In *Oceanic Histories*, edited by David Armitage, Alison Bashford and Sujit Sivasundaram, 31–61. Cambridge: Cambridge University Press, 2017.

Sohi, Seema. *Echoes of Mutiny: Race, Surveillance, and Indian Anticolonialism in North America*. New York: Oxford University Press, 2014.

Soske, Jon. *Internal Frontiers: African Nationalism and the Indian Diaspora in Twentieth-Century South Africa*. Athens, OH: Ohio University Press, 2017.

Soske, Jon. 'Navigating Difference: Gender, Miscegenation and Indian Domestic Space in Twentieth-Century Durban'. In *Eyes across the Water – Navigating the Indian Ocean*, edited by Pamila Gupta, Isabel Hofmeyr and Michael Pearson, 197–219. Pretoria: Unisa Press, 2010.

Stanziani, Alessandro. *Sailors, Slaves, and Immigrants: Bondage in the Indian Ocean World, 1750–1914*. New York: Palgrave Macmillan, 2014.

Steinfeld, Robert J. *Coercion, Contract and Free Labor in the Nineteenth Century*. Albany: SUNY Press, 2001.

Sturman, Rachel. 'Indian Indentured Labor and the History of International Rights Regimes'. *American Historical Review* 119, no. 5 (December 2014): 1439–1465.

Subramanian, Lakshmi. *The Sovereign and the Pirate: Ordering Maritime Subjects in India's Western Littoral*. Delhi: Oxford University Press, 2016.

Subramanian, Lakshmi, ed. *Ports, Towns, and Cities: A Historical Tour of the Indian Littoral*. Mumbai: Marg Foundation, 2009.

Subrahmanyam, Sanjay. *Europe's India: Words, Peoples, Empires, 1500–1800*. Cambridge, MA: Harvard University Press, 2017.

Subrahmanyam, Sanjay. *Three Ways to be Alien: Travails and Encounters in the Early Modern World*. Waltham, MA: Brandeis University Press, 2011.

Subrahmanyam, Sanjay. 'Holding the World in Balance: The Connected Histories of the Iberian Overseas Empires 1500–1640'. *American Historical Review* 112 (2007): 1359–1385.

Subrahmanyam, Sanjay. 'Historicizing the Global or Labouring for Invention'. *History Workshop Journal* 64 (Autumn 2007): 329–334.

Subrahmanyam, Sanjay. *The Career and Legend of Vasco Da Gama*. Cambridge: Cambridge University Press, 1998.

Subrahmanyam, Sanjay. 'Hearing Voices: Vignettes of Early Modernity in South Asia, 1400–1750'. *Daedalus* 127, no. 3 (Summer 1998): 75–104.

Subrahmanyam, Sanjay. 'Connected Histories: Notes Towards a Reconfiguration of Early Modern Eurasia'. *Modern Asian Studies* 31, no. 3 (1997): 735–762.

Swan, Maureen. *Gandhi. The South African Experience*. Johannesburg: Ravan Press, 1985.

Swanson, Maynard. '"The Asiatic Menace": Creating Segregation in Durban, 1870–1900'. *The International Journal of African Historical Studies* 16, no. 3 (1983): 401–421.

Tagliacozzo, Eric, Peter Perdue, and Helen F. Siu, 'Introduction: Seekers, Sojourners, and Meaningful Worlds in Motion'. In *Asia Inside Out: Itinerant People*, edited by Eric Tagliacozzo, Peter Perdue, and Helen F. Siu, 1–28. Cambridge, MA: Harvard University Press, 2019.

Tayal, Maureen. 'Indian Indentured Labour in Natal, 1860–1911'. *Indian Economic and Social History Review* XIV, no. 4 (1977): 519–549.

Taylor, Barbara. 'Separations of the Soul: Solitude, Biography, History'. *American Historical Review* 114, no. 3 (June 2009): 640–651.

Tenorio-Trillo, Mauricio. *I speak of the city: Mexico City at the Turn of the Twentieth Century*. Chicago: The University of Chicago Press, 2012.

Tharu, Susie and K. Lalita, eds. *Women Writing in India 600 B.C. to the Present. Vol. 1: 600 B.C. to the Early 20th Century*. New York: Feminist Press, 1991.

Tinker, Hugh. *A New System of Slavery: The Export of Indian Labour Overseas*. London: Oxford University Press, 1974.

Treu, Alfred Charles. *A History of Agricultural Experimentation and Research in the United States, 1607–1925*. Washington, D.C.: Government Printing Office, 1937.

Tumbe, Chinmay. *India Moving: A History of Migration*. Delhi: Penguin, 2018.

Vahed, Goolam and Surendra Bhana. *Crossing Space and Time in the Indian Ocean: Early Indian Traders in Natal – A Biographical Study*. Pretoria: UNISA Press, 2015.

Vahed, Goolam, Ashwin Desai and Thembisa Waetjen. *Many Lives – 150 Years of Being Indian in South Africa*. Pietermaritzburg: Shuter and Shooter, 2010.

Varma, Nitin. *Coolies of Capitalism: Assam Tea and the Making of Coolie Labour*. Berlin: De Gruyter, 2017.

Veracini, Lorenzo. *Settler Colonialism: A Theoretical Overview*. Basingstoke: Palgrave Macmillan, 2010.

Veracini, Lorenzo. *The Settler Colonial Present*. Basingstoke: Palgrave Macmillan, 2015.

Verma, Radhey Shyam. 'Gopal Krishna Gokhale and his Contribution to Struggle of People of Indian Origin in South Africa'. *Proceedings of the Indian History Congress* 70 (2009): 860–868.

Visram, Rozina. *Ayahs, Lascars and Princes: Indians in Britain, 1600–1947*. London: Pluto Press, 1986.

Vitalis, Robert. *America's Kingdom: Mythmaking on the Saudi Oil Frontier*. New York: Verso, 2009.

Vora, Neha. *Impossible Citizens: Dubai's Indian Diaspora*. Durham, NC: Duke University Press, 2013.

Wang, Gungwu. *Home is Not Here*. Singapore: NUS Press, 2018.

Wang, Gungwu. *Don't Leave Home: Migration and the Chinese*. Singapore: Eastern Universities Press, 2003.

Wang, Gungwu. *The Chinese overseas: From Earthbound China to a Quest for Autonomy*. Cambridge, MA: Harvard University Press, 2000.

Wang, Gungwu, ed. *Global History and Migrations*. Boulder, CO: Westview Press, 1997.

Wolfe, Patrick. 'Settler Colonialism and the Elimination of the Native'. *Journal of Genocide Research* 8, no. 4 (December 2006): 387–409.

Wright, Andrea. '"The Immoral Traffic in Women": Regulating Indian Emigration to the Persian Gulf'. In *Borders and Mobility in South Asia and Beyond*, edited by Reece Jones and Md. Azmeary Ferdoush, 145–166. Amsterdam: Amsterdam University Press, 2018.

Yang, Anand. *Indian Penal Labor in Colonial Southeast Asia*. Berkeley, CA: University of California Press, 2020.

Yang, Anand. 'Indian Convict Workers in Southeast Asia in the Late Eighteenth and Early Nineteenth Centuries'. *Journal of World History* 14, no. 2 (2003): 179–208.

Yankelevich, Pablo. 'Naturalization and Citizenship in Post-revolutionary Mexico'. *Estudios de Historia Moderna y Contemporánea de México*, 28 (Julio-Diciembre 2014): 113–155.

Yankelevich, Pablo. 'Mexico for the Mexicans: Immigration, National Sovereignty and the Promotion of *Mestizaje*'. *The Americas* 68, no. 3 (January 2012): 405–436.

Zachariah, Benjamin. 'A Long Strange Trip: The Lives in Exile of Har Dayal'. *South Asian History and Culture* 4, no. 4 (2013): 574–592.

Zeleza, Paul Tiyambe. 'African Diasporas: Toward a Global History'. *African Studies Review* 53, no. 1 (April 2010): 1–19.

Index

abolition 7, 9, 14, 16–17, 27, 31–2,
54–5, 57–61, 67, 86, 88, 104–6, 109,
114–15, 117–18, 127–8, 130–2, 135,
138, 231, 234, 239, 241, 244
  abolitionism 132–3, 241
  abolitionist 118–20, 128, 133
Abu Dhabi 72–8, 83–4
Aden 70–1, 74, 82
African Americans 173
agency xiii, 1, 16, 86–7, 89, 221, 235
agriculture 19, 107, 118, 130, 132, 136,
144, 160, 179, 181, 183–8, 190,
193
All-India Muslim League 44, 49
annexation 38
anti-Indian
  agitation 146, 177
  legislation 38, 145, 147, 220
  rulings 146
  sentiment 2, 146
Arabic 13, 63, 66, 69, 72, 83
Arya Samaj 14, 57
assimilation 9, 19, 23, 174, 180, 190
  racial assimilation 7, 11
Awali 63, 66, 79

Bahrain 17, 63, 65–6, 72, 75, 79–84, 237
belonging xiv, 8, 119–20, 129, 140, 151–2,
189, 193–4, 237
Bengal 12–14, 22, 24, 27, 30–1, 42, 88, 108,
115, 117, 123–4, 131, 134–7, 160,
165, 170, 173, 231, 235, 241
Boer 39, 43, 142, 170
Bombay 28, 41–2, 44, 46, 49, 55–6, 71,
81–2, 119, 123, 137, 143, 160, 182,
199, 237
border controls 8
border regimes 7, 22
boundaries xii, 3–4, 17, 74, 116, 133, 139,
226, 232
Brahmo Samaj 14
Braudel, Fernand 11

Britain 7, 10, 25–6, 38, 41, 44, 65, 87, 89,
102, 108, 124, 127, 136, 141, 148–9,
222, 232, 237, 242, 247
British
  Caribbean 80, 239
  colony 2, 51, 146
  Columbia xiii, 29, 157, 159–62, 169,
  172, 174, 176, 177, 240
  Empire 10, 12, 26–7, 37, 39, 41, 43, 46,
  65, 67–8, 86, 114, 136, 141, 149,
  159, 163–5, 167–70, 172, 176–7,
  186, 194, 208, 226–7, 230, 232–3,
  244
  governance 43
  imperial government 57, 61
  Indian subjects 55, 114–15, 118, 121,
  126–7, 180, 186
  navy 65
  Raj 67, 80

Calcutta 42, 44, 46, 49, 53, 56–7, 62, 81,
90, 100–1, 104, 113, 117–20, 123,
134–6, 159, 161–2, 176, 232, 238–9
Canada xvi, 2, 7, 12, 18–19, 29, 41, 105,
146, 153, 157–9, 161–70, 174–8,
229, 234–5, 244
Canadian xv–xvi, 2, 63, 161–2, 165–6, 173,
176–7
Cape Colony 2–3, 48
Cape Town 2, 5, 42, 145, 169, 236
capital 7–8, 25, 30, 37, 70, 80, 134, 169,
183, 185–6, 196, 231, 235, 238–9
  mercantile 33
capitalism 7, 32, 80, 108, 136, 182, 241,
247
Caribbean 7, 10, 14, 16, 80, 85–6, 88, 127,
193, 230, 239
Cawnpore 55, 98
Ceylon 57, 88, 108, 115, 124–7, 194
Chinese 2–3, 23, 39, 139–40, 144, 148–50,
153, 167, 174, 189, 197, 223, 232,
235, 247–8

Chitnavis, Gangadhar Rao 54
Churchill, Winston 65
citizenship 7, 9, 14, 19–21, 33, 39, 127,
    140, 142–3, 152, 157, 165, 168, 174,
    180, 188–93, 198, 235, 238–9, 244,
    248
  imperial 43, 139, 141, 150–1, 170, 237
commercialization 11
consent xii, 19, 67–8, 79, 102–3, 113–14,
    117, 119–22, 128, 131–2
coolie 10, 16, 25–7, 32, 42, 51, 53–4, 85,
    87, 89–90, 100, 102, 105, 107–9,
    118–19, 128, 134–6, 204, 207–8,
    222, 227, 230–3, 237, 239–40, 247
Cooly Protection Society 57
colonial
  governance 64, 143
  India 7, 16, 19, 21, 29, 62, 66, 80, 86–7,
    89, 103, 105–8, 110, 113, 132, 157,
    160, 223, 233–4, 238–9, 244
  labour 64, 69, 89
  South Africa xiii, 31, 237
  South Asia 32–3, 114, 233
  subject xiii, 88, 116, 179
  subjugation 64
colonialism 15, 64, 78, 88, 136, 151, 192,
    199, 204, 217, 231, 237
  anti-colonialism 165, 168, 174
  British colonialism 25–7, 65, 177, 181
  settler colonialism 12, 18, 29–30, 150,
    153, 228, 239, 244, 247–8

Dadabhoy M.B. 53
Das Island 73, 75, 83
Das, Taraknath 2, 18, 157, 159–60, 163,
    175–7, 183, 195, 226, 232, 236, 243
descendant 19, 26, 208, 219
discrimination 42, 70, 107, 146, 148–9,
    169, 201, 208, 216, 220
Dubai 64, 66
Durban 4, 52, 140, 145–7, 153, 169–70,
    177, 202, 209–10, 212, 217, 222–3,
    238, 244, 246–7

East Africa 7, 26, 145, 152, 243
economic geography xii, xiv
education xii, 42, 68, 77, 159, 169, 172,
    179, 181–2, 185, 187, 188, 220, 226,
    243

Ellore 54
emancipation 37, 88, 106
empire xiii, xv, 3–4, 11, 13, 16–17, 22–3,
    25, 29–30, 44–5, 49, 52, 58–60,
    79–80, 85, 105, 107–9, 132–5, 137,
    143, 150–3, 162, 173, 175, 181, 193,
    199, 221, 237–42, 246
Eurocentrism 15, 107, 110, 242
expansion 7, 37, 133, 168, 182, 184, 187
extremist 43, 56, 160

family networks 11, 15
famine 67, 161, 163
Federation of Australia 1
Fiji 1, 4, 10, 14, 25–6, 37, 46, 56–7, 62,
    91, 93–6, 107–8, 123, 128, 130–1,
    137–8, 162, 164, 222, 232, 239–40,
    246
free movement xii
freedom 16–17, 64, 67–9, 72, 81, 85–6,
    88–9, 97, 102, 104–5, 109, 162–4,
    229, 234
frontier violence 12

Gandhi, Mohandas K. 17–18, 32, 37–42,
    44–6, 52, 58–61, 127–8, 130, 137–8,
    143, 145, 152, 157–8, 167–73, 175,
    177, 193, 208, 215, 220, 232, 236–7,
    242, 247
Gandhi, Manilal 216
gender xiv, 10, 21, 26, 68, 132–3, 137, 170,
    204, 216, 223, 239, 243, 246
  gendered xiii, 227
global colour line 4, 9, 23, 152, 167, 229,
    240
global history 2, 4
globalization xiv, 4, 7–9, 12, 15–20, 22, 24,
    31, 33, 59, 61, 105, 157, 173, 178,
    232, 242
Gokhale Gopal K. 16, 37, 38, 40–2, 46–8,
    51, 53–4, 56, 60, 62, 127–9, 137,
    243, 247
Government of India 42–3, 46–8, 50,
    53–4, 56–7, 114, 118–21, 125–6,
    130, 134, 136, 145–6
Guntur 54

Hartman, Saidiya xvii, 18, 225–7, 229–30,
    238

idea xii, xiii, xiv, 9, 66, 71, 78, 88, 100, 124, 129, 141, 144–7, 163–8, 171, 172, 174, 181, 182, 189, 229
identity xiv, 1, 3, 5, 17, 28, 33, 52, 129, 139–41, 145, 150, 153, 175, 181, 192–3, 207, 219, 221–3, 233–4, 237, 244
ideology xiv, 64, 88, 143, 172, 181, 219
   ideological 107, 141, 143, 150, 180–1, 186
immigration
   Anglo-Indian immigration 165
   1891 Immigration Act 144
   1902 Immigration Act 2
   1906 Immigration Act 2, 39
   1908 Immigration Act 161
   1897 Immigration Act 173
   1917 Immigration Act 166
   Immigration exclusions 2–4
Immigration Restriction Act 1, 144
Indian immigration 1–2, 48
immigrant xv, 1, 25, 86, 108, 142, 144, 150, 152, 161, 184, 188, 207, 219, 235
   immigrants xiii, 1, 5, 29, 118, 121, 133, 140–1, 144, 151–2, 158, 161, 166, 184, 189–90, 195, 207, 220, 228, 236, 238, 246
imperial
   British 10, 15, 37, 57, 61, 141, 173, 229
   citizenship 43, 59, 139, 141–2, 150–2, 170, 232, 237
   connections 242
   conquest 17
   context 18
   council 54
   expansion 7
   government 47, 142, 180
   governance 158
   histories 12, 29, 168, 231
   Legislative Council 41, 53–4, 57, 127
   labour 16, 63, 68
   networks 2
   policy 117, 168
   power 15, 179, 193
   rule 208, 229
   space 162
   subject 24, 141–3, 152, 178, 181
   surveillance 157
   territory 240

indenture xv, 1, 14–16, 18–20, 26, 43–5, 47–58, 60–2, 64, 67–9, 85–90, 96–7, 100–5, 107–10, 114, 124, 126, 128–30, 134–7, 208, 215, 222, 227, 230, 232, 238–41
   Indian 17, 37–8, 46, 59, 136, 228–9, 234, 236
indentured
   emigration 37, 43, 47, 49–50, 53, 56–7, 59–61, 100–1, 103, 105, 120, 126, 244
   contract 102–5
   Indians 25, 27, 31, 46, 48, 53, 102–5, 135, 215, 237, 239
   labour [labourers/workers] xiii, 1, 4, 7, 9–10, 14, 16, 18–20, 23, 25, 27, 31–3, 37, 45–8, 51–5, 57–8, 64, 67–8, 78, 80, 85–9, 86, 101–2, 105, 109, 113–30, 133–8, 141, 144, 146, 150, 169–70, 208, 214. 219, 226, 231–3, 239, 242, 245–7
   migration 37–9, 43–6, 86–8, 96–7, 100, 102, 104–5, 107, 120, 128
   ships 107–9, 239
   women xvii, 1, 57, 62, 129, 201, 206–8, 238
Indian National Congress 39–44, 46, 53, 143, 181
Indian
   British 44, 51, 55, 58, 63, 114–15, 118, 121, 126–7, 141–2, 144, 146, 150–1, 173, 176, 180, 186, 197
   Government 46–7, 49–51, 68–9, 71–2, 146, 148, 241
   in South Africa 37, 40–4, 46–9, 51–2, 170, 177, 215
   migrants 14, 25, 52, 69, 78, 137, 142, 146, 158, 162, 168–70, 172–3, 226, 228–9, 233
   nationalism 18, 57, 59, 105, 158, 161, 167, 170, 172, 193, 244
   nationalist 11, 20, 37, 40–3, 52, 58–9, 68, 104–5, 127, 131, 157, 159, 161, 167, 231, 240
   population 46, 48, 50–2, 58, 145
   South African 52, 55–6, 60, 140, 212, 216, 221, 223, 237, 243
   South African League 46, 55
indigenous 29–30, 38, 115, 229, 239

indigenous peoples 12, 25, 228, 230
information xii, 2, 3, 70, 71, 96, 128, 163, 191
international law xiv, 14
Islam 13–14, 27–8, 30–1, 100, 233, 235, 237, 239
Italy 20, 168

Jebel Dhanna 72–4, 76, 83
justice xiv, 49, 97, 106, 193, 217

khaliji 72–4, 76–8
Khankhoje, Pandurang 18, 179–99, 240, 245
Kunti 57, 127–8, 137
Kuwait 63, 65–6, 81, 240

labour
  contract 45, 64, 164
  free 7, 31, 64, 71, 108, 118, 123, 232, 242
  Indian 10, 25–6, 31, 38, 44, 47, 53, 57–8, 87, 117, 127, 134, 231, 234, 242, 244, 247
  recruitment 7, 10, 129, 135, 241
  shortage 37, 48, 68
  skilled xiii, 19, 80, 82, 130–1
  supply 38
  unskilled xiii, 19, 57, 66, 123, 125, 130–1, 213, 216–7
Lahore 46
Land Act of 1913 50, 61
land settlement 7
Latchimin 1, 4
law xii, xiii, xiv, 5, 7, 14, 15, 17–19, 22, 28–9, 38–42, 45, 47, 49–50, 68–9, 75, 77–8, 87–9, 96, 102, 104–9, 119, 123–5, 127, 130, 132–4, 139, 143, 146, 149, 152–3, 161, 165, 169–173, 175, 188–9, 193, 216, 220, 225–7, 230, 233, 236, 241–2, 245
legal
  activism 7
  system 9, 45
legislation 2, 38–9, 48, 50, 52, 85, 87–8, 103, 115, 119–21, 124–6, 131, 135, 140, 143–7, 149–51, 161, 166, 170, 173, 177, 190, 214, 220
liberalism 17, 64, 88–9
Lord Harcourt 51, 81

Luce, William 75–6, 83
Lucknow 1, 47, 98

Madras 41–2, 44, 47, 54–5, 60, 90, 117, 119, 160, 202, 204, 218
Mahomed, Dawud 51–2
Malaysia 20, 57, 106, 108, 232, 238
Malaviya, Madan Mohan 46, 53, 129–30, 138
maritime 24–5, 132, 236, 246
  expansion 7
  force 4, 238
  trade 11
Marwaris 56–7
Mauritius 26–7, 31, 38, 80, 92, 114, 117–25, 133, 135–6, 164, 231, 234, 242
merchant 11, 15, 21, 25–6, 127, 137, 148–9, 163, 228–9, 236, 240–1, 243
  class 38
Mexico xiii, 179–81, 185–98, 235, 239, 244, 247–8
middle class 44, 58
Middle East 7, 16, 24, 65, 72, 79–80, 82, 180
migrant
  labour 51, 64, 69
  labourers 80, 233
migration xiv, 1, 5, 9, 11, 13, 21–5, 29–31, 33, 37–9, 46, 52, 57–9, 61, 79, 81, 85–6, 88–9, 96–7, 102, 104–5, 107–10, 114–15, 120, 124, 126–7, 129, 131–2, 134–9, 145, 152–3, 157–8, 172, 177–9, 181, 225, 229–31, 233–5, 237–8, 240–2, 244, 247
  Bengali Muslim 12
  Colonial 64
  patterns 8, 14
  South Asian xvi, 4, 7–8, 10, 12, 14, 19–20, 27, 175, 226–9
missionary 31, 56, 113, 130, 237
mobility xv, 1–4, 7–9, 12, 21, 25, 31, 81, 97, 105, 120, 126–7, 130–1, 228, 231, 235–6, 238, 240, 248
moderate 41–3, 46, 127, 170
modern state xii, xiii, 3, 8, 9, 22, 58, 79, 107, 134, 153, 242
modern world system 8, 158
modernist 181, 186, 192
modernity 21, 23, 81, 175, 234–6, 246
modernization 8, 23, 31, 186

modernizing 186, 189
Montagu, Edwin 55
Moor, F.R. 47, 50
Mother India 20–1

Nagpur 42, 53, 192
Natal 1–3, 24, 37–40, 42–4, 46–53, 56–61, 93, 121, 127–8, 137, 140, 143–5, 147, 151, 169, 172, 178, 202, 204, 207, 210, 215, 222, 234, 241, 247
    Natal Act 173, 177
Natal Indian Congress 38, 40, 51–2, 56, 170
nation xii, 8, 16, 33, 68, 77, 78, 129, 164, 189, 214, 219, 221, 228, 245, 246
    nation state xii, xiv, 8, 9, 11, 17, 19, 20, 22, 81, 89, 131, 143, 173
national security 64, 72, 77
nationalism xii, 12, 18, 20, 57, 66, 157, 158, 161, 168, 170, 172, 173, 174, 181, 189, 190, 193
    methodological nationalism xii, xiv
nationalist 11, 15, 18, 20, 37, 40–4, 52–3, 56–9, 68, 104–5, 127–8, 131, 137, 157, 159–62, 164, 167, 170, 173–4, 180–2, 189–90, 193, 219, 231, 240
nationality 39, 63, 66, 70–1, 129, 142, 152, 189–90, 193
neoliberal 64, 69, 79
New Delhi 69, 71, 82
New South Wales 1, 143, 178, 241

oil
    company 63–7, 70–4, 76–80, 83, 235
    Middle Eastern 64
    production 63–6, 72, 76, 79
    reserves 63, 65, 79
Oman 63, 65, 76
Orange Free State 38, 40, 47–8

Pacific coast 20, 159–61, 165, 174–5, 235
pan-Arab movements 65, 73–4, 76–8
Persian Gulf xiii, xv, 17, 79, 81–2, 167, 248
plantation 14, 16, 31–2, 67, 86, 96, 106, 108, 118, 130, 204, 214, 241–3
    'global plantation complex' 16, 31
    plantation complex 14, 16, 31–2
political
    activism 220–1
    activist xiii, 14, 157

politics 5, 7, 11, 18–19, 21, 26–7, 33, 43–4, 46, 59, 63–4, 72, 74, 79, 105, 131, 150–1, 157, 159–60, 167–70, 172–3, 182, 220, 226, 230–1, 234, 238–40, 244
post-colonial 12, 20, 110, 239
postmodern xiii
power xiv–xv, 4, 11, 13, 15, 21, 28, 32, 43, 49–50, 65, 79–80, 89, 101, 106, 118, 122, 129, 148, 158, 163–4, 167, 191, 193, 220, 227, 231–2, 234, 238
    bargaining 85–7, 89
    colonial 4, 108, 238
    foreign 114, 116
    territorial 114
protectionism xii
Protector of Emigrants 67–9, 71, 121
Punjab 42, 160–1, 165
    Punjabi 184

Qatar 63, 72, 77, 82, 84

race 6, 21, 28–9, 33, 41, 45, 52, 106, 136, 140, 150, 170, 174–7, 194, 197, 214, 216, 220, 223, 232–4, 238–9, 244–6
racialized
    divisions 64
    hierarchies 64, 72
    labour hierarchies 69–70, 78
    opposition 172
regulation xiii–xv, 16, 20, 87, 89, 102, 115, 119–20, 123–6, 130–1, 135, 176
religion 8, 11, 13, 31, 66, 87, 115, 123, 129–30, 158, 162, 164, 166, 171, 174–5, 209
remigration 1
resistance xiii, 4, 29, 39–40, 43–5, 56, 106, 127–8, 162, 171–2, 199, 207–8, 216, 221, 233, 244–5
revolution 159–60, 162–3, 170, 180–1, 183–4, 186, 195, 197–8, 226, 231, 237, 239, 243
Robertson, Benjamin 50

Sanderson Committee 50
Satyagraha 39–40, 58, 137, 177, 220, 237, 243
Saudi Arabia 63, 65, 78, 82, 84, 247
segregation 70, 127, 146–7, 153, 216, 247
self-government 38–9, 52

settler 136, 141
  European 37, 141–2, 147, 169
  white 1, 38–9, 42, 44, 139, 141–7, 150–2, 172–3, 238
sexuality 10, 26, 28–9, 57, 175, 239, 245
science 18, 27, 188
  agricultural science 180, 184, 187
  pseudo-science 171–2
Sheikh Shakhbut 74–5
Singapore 7, 20, 23, 106, 108, 232
slave xiii, 4, 16, 19, 32, 45, 54, 106, 114, 228, 231
  trade 113, 115, 117, 119, 132, 134, 235
  Trade Act 64, 67
  trafficking 17, 114–21, 133
slavery 10–11, 16–17, 25, 27, 32–3, 37, 45, 54–5, 64, 67–8, 80, 85–8, 105–6, 115, 117–18, 120, 128, 132–3, 135, 143, 163–4, 171–2, 175, 228, 231, 234–5, 239, 241–2, 245, 247
  anti 86–7, 104, 133
  Abolition Act 67, 117
  long-distance 11
  trans-Atlantic 7, 9, 14, 31, 229
South Africa xvi, 2–5, 7, 12, 14, 17–20, 28, 31, 37–53, 58–61, 127–8, 137, 139–53, 157, 162–3, 167–72, 177, 193, 201, 204, 208, 210, 214–20, 222–3, 233–4, 236–8, 243–4, 246–7
South African Republic 39, 142, 169
South Asia xv, xvi, 8, 11, 13–14, 16–17, 20–1, 23, 26–7, 29–31, 64, 72, 81, 114, 116, 118, 132, 173–4, 231, 241, 246, 248
South Asian 174
  diaspora 28, 32–3, 152, 228, 233–5, 241, 243, 245
  exceptionalism 14–15, 31
  Islam 31, 237, 239
  labour 32–3, 64, 72, 78–9, 88, 170, 228, 233
  merchants 25, 240
  Muslims 28, 242
Southeast Asia xv, 10, 16, 23–5, 27, 88, 96, 133, 248
statist xii
state formation 8, 11–12
Subrahmanyam, Sanjay 9, 11, 19, 23–4, 26, 32, 174, 232, 241, 246

sugar 219
  cane 169, 202, 204
  colonies 4, 10, 16, 25, 27, 85–6, 89, 104–5, 107–9, 135, 239
  estate 119
  plantation 38, 86, 164, 169, 176, 204, 227, 241
  planter 58
  production 38
Standard Oil of California 63, 65
strike 63–4, 66, 70–8, 83, 141
surveillance xv, 5–6, 11, 28, 157–8, 166, 175, 181, 193, 234, 236, 246
  racializing 3–4
  systems 4, 7
Sydney 1, 29, 240

taxes 38, 50, 161, 171
Thackersey, Vithaldas Damodar 49
trade 11, 25–7, 38–9, 64, 88–9, 118–20, 146, 228, 235, 240
  unions 77, 183, 215
transnational xiii–xiv, 2, 5–6, 51, 88, 144, 175, 178, 180, 182, 193, 195, 229, 231, 233, 235–6, 241
trans-regional xiii, 12, 14, 33, 158–9, 161
Transvaal 38–41, 44–5, 47–8, 51, 53, 127, 141, 146, 151, 164
tyranny 43, 162, 171–2

United States xvi, 3, 18–19, 28, 30, 79, 87, 89, 106, 144, 152, 157–60, 162, 164–9, 173–7, 179–81, 183–4, 187–90, 194–5, 222, 232, 235, 242–7
Uttar Pradesh 57

Viceroy Minto 43, 49, 117, 164
victims 19, 48, 55, 57, 62, 129, 138, 163, 238
violence 12, 73–4, 86, 160, 169–72, 184, 189, 191–2, 212, 227–8

West Indies 1, 4, 108, 242
white settler 38, 42, 44, 141, 144–7
white settler colony 1, 39, 44, 139, 142–4, 172–3, 150–1
working conditions 38, 63–4, 67–71, 86, 216

xenophobia xii, 190

www.ingramcontent.com/pod-product-compliance
Lightning Source LLC
Chambersburg PA
CBHW072132290426
44111CB00012B/1859